A HUNDRED YEARS OF CIVIL ENGINEERING AT SOUTH KENSINGTON

1. The Central Institution. Architect's drawing by A. Waterhouse, 1881
(reproduced by permission of Imperial Collage Archives)

A HUNDRED YEARS OF CIVIL ENGINEERING AT SOUTH KENSINGTON

The Origins and History of the Department of Civil Engineering of Imperial College 1884–1984

compiled and edited by

Joyce Brown, MA

Civil Engineering Department
Imperial College
LONDON
1985

ISBN 0-85287-150-3

Printed by Butler & Tanner Ltd, Frome and London

Contents

Illustrations

Photographs

Tables

Figures

Foreword

This book tells the story of the gradual transformation over a century of a modest civil engineering department into one of the leading centres of research and advanced instruction in its field to-day. This achievement was brought about by the selfless efforts of many people and this history is dedicated to all of them. The recent years have not been easy for universities, but our problems are placed in perspective when one recalls the much greater difficulties that were overcome by our predecessors.

The greatest natural resources of this country are the talents of its people and these skills must be fostered by educational facilities of the highest order. In the emerging post-industrial society the full utilisation of advanced technology will be a necessary prerequisite for this island's prosperity.

The past century has been characterised by a broadening of knowledge relevant to civil engineering. Could Unwin have visualised the widening of the subject to include modern scientific methods to tackle problems of pollution, the development of sophisticated stochastic models for hydrological systems, the complexity of decision-making with respect to transportation and urban planning, the exploitation of finite element techniques in structural analysis and geomechanics, and could he have prophesied the power and availability of modern computational devices? The rate of change is accelerating and who can presently visualise the impact that will be made by the Fifth Generation of Computation and its Knowledge Information Processing Systems and who can visualise the new construction materials that will become available to us in the next decades?

I am very grateful to Joyce Brown and to all who have helped her in recording the achievements of the past century. I am confident that, given adequate support of the government and of our industry, this Department will continue to train young men and women to meet the challenges faced by civil engineering in a changing world and also to take a lead in revealing new knowledge through its research.

JOHN MUNRO
South Kensington
July 1984

Acknowledgements

The idea that we should write our history in our centenary year came from Professor J. Munro, the current Head of Department. The book was envisaged as a corporate effort by staff of the Department, both past and present, in writing certain parts of the book, or supplying information or providing technical expertise. My function has been to co-ordinate their efforts and to update, expand and largely rewrite, in the first six chapters, an earlier history written for internal use of the College in 1965 by B.G. Manton, a member of staff of the Department from 1920–62. Manton's story ends in 1956, and in order to supply the details of our post-war development (since 1945), the history of each Section of the Department has been related in Chapter 7 by members of present and former staff associated with it.

The main source materials used were the College *Calendars*, the *Dean's Annual Reports to the City and Guilds Institute*, *Engineering Board Minutes*, *Board of Study Minutes*, *Triennial Research Reports*, and biographical material from a range of sources, such as the memoirs of the Royal Society, and the Institution of Civil Engineers. Much of this material is held in the Imperial College Archives and I am grateful to the College Archivist, Mrs J. Pingree, for her assistance. Mr. C. Springgay kindly made student records freely available to us.

Sectional histories in Chapter 7 were written by the following:

Structures	E.H. Brown, P.J. Dowling, J.E. Harding
Hydraulics	J.D. Hardwick
Surveying	B. Chiat
Highway Engineering & Transport	D.A.M. Gilbert
Concrete Technology	J.C. de C. Henderson
Soil Mechanics & Engineering Seismology	P.R. Vaughan
Public Health Engineering	F.E. Bruce, E.M. Shaw
Hydrology	E.M. Shaw
Timber Engineering	L.G. Booth

Systems and Mechanics	D. Lloyd Smith
Environmental Studies	M.W. Baldwin

The history of the Library in Chapter 8 was written by Mrs M. Carter. I am indebted for help with the history of technical services to J.E. Neale and R.W. Loveday, and for notes on the modern secretary's life to Mrs S. Wright. Chapter 9 on distinguished alumni was written by T.A. Wyatt. Information about the new building was contributed by R.J. Ashby, on post-war undergraduate courses by R.J. Ashby and F.H. Potter, on the Marine Technology Centre by A.B. Vincent, and on computing facilities by C.J. Burgoyne. The information in Chapter 4 on the value of salaries was kindly supplied by Professor Z.A. Silbertson of the Department of Humanities.

The Appendices involved much labour in the records and thanks are due to Miss E.M. Shaw for assistance with Appendix A (staff lists) and for compiling Appendix C (DIC lists), to Mrs K. Crooks for Appendix B (research degree titles), and to L.G. Booth for assistance with Appendix D (ACGI lists). These lists will inevitably contain some errors, for which we apologise, but we have done our best to record accurately the details of former staff, as well as the names of the 8,000 or more students who have received an award at undergraduate, postgraduate or research level during the last 100 years.

Several colleagues commented helpfully on the manuscript and here I may mention J. Munro, A.W. Skempton, Miss E.M. Shaw, J.E. Neale and A.C. Cassell.

The technical aspects of the production of the book required assistance from a number of staff. Most of the unacknowledged photographs were taken by Miss J. Gurr; R. Packer produced prints of these and of the remaining photographs, which were taken by himself or A. Chipling. The graphic material for Figs. 1–5 was prepared by Miss E.M. Shaw and for Fig. 6 and 7 by J.C. de C. Henderson. It was traced by Mrs A. Langford, while the arduous task of typing the final manuscript was undertaken by Miss A. Hikel. Useful advice and help with the production of the book was given by M.W. Baldwin, and by P. Mattocks of Butler & Tanner Ltd. The book cover design is by Ellis Horwood Ltd., publishers. I am grateful to Miss J.D. Troy for preparing the index.

The last to be mentioned is not the least, and here I acknowledge the enormous support given by L.G. Booth, whose good-humoured endurance in the task of editing proved invaluable, and whose support throughout the project has been inestimable.

Without the co-operation of so many people, this book would not have been written, and I thank everyone who has helped in any way.

JOYCE BROWN
Imperial College, London
July 1984

~ 1 ~

Origins

The origins of the teaching of Civil Engineering at South Kensington go back one hundred years to the establishment of a new college in Exhibition Road on a site now occupied by the Department of Mechanical Engineering at Imperial College. The foundation of the Central Institution of the City and Guilds of London Institute and the appointment in 1884 of a professor to teach Civil and Mechanical Engineering is where our story begins.

The establishment of a specialist technical college has to be seen against the background of technical training in the nineteenth century. Craft training of all kinds had traditionally been in the hands of the guild companies through their apprenticeship system and the tight control they exerted in earlier times over standards of excellence and admission to the freedom. As cities grew in size, the control of the guild companies was superseded by other forms of training and apprenticeship. The skills, however, required by advances in technology in the nineteenth century could no longer be supplied by such rule-of-thumb methods; it was becoming increasingly necessary for workers to understand the scientific principles which lay behind the machines and materials they were handling. In a period when secondary, or even elementary, education of any kind was a luxury, it is not surprising how few educational institutions existed which could offer technical training.

The most prolific in the first half of the nineteenth century were the Mechanics' Institutes, attended in the main by artisans in the evenings. Their popularity was such that it is estimated that by 1850 there were 610 in England and Wales with a membership of more than half a million. Indeed, a situation was arising in which shortage of teachers was proving a stumbling-block to further expansion. There was, however, a dearth of educational establishments capable of providing such teachers. Technical colleges developed only slowly during the century, and in 1856 there were only four universities in England (Oxford, Cambridge, Durham and London) and four in Scotland (St Andrews, Glasgow, Aberdeen and Edinburgh).

Engineering did not fare better than other technical studies and was taught at only a limited number of places. Notably, there were Engineering courses at Glasgow University (made famous by Professor W. J. M. Rankine), at Owens College, Manchester, at University College, London, and at King's College, London. In 1871, lack of professionally trained civil engineers led to the foundation of the Royal Indian Engineering College at Cooper's Hill, Egham, to train men for service in the Public Works Department in India. Engineering degrees could be taken by internal and external candidates in various universities from the following dates: Trinity College, Dublin (BAI 1872), Edinburgh (1873), Glasgow (1873), and Manchester (Victoria University) (1882). The Cambridge Mechanical Sciences Tripos was not established until 1894 and in Oxford Engineering Science was not taught as a complete course until 1909. The professional bodies, the Institution of Civil Engineers and the Institution of Mechanical Engineers, founded in 1818 and 1847 respectively, as yet played no part in the development of engineering education.

Throughout the century, however, there was a growing need for technical and engineering skills as Britain advanced into the industrial age, with its revolution in manufacturing processes and transportation, and its need for new technologies to deal with the huge urban problems of water supply, sewage disposal, electrical and gas transmission, road and rail transport and so on. New engineering materials, such as cast and wrought iron, had to be understood, and complex structures on a massive scale, carrying hitherto undreamt of loads, had to be designed and built.

Signs that technical education was receiving attention appeared with the foundation of the Royal College of Chemistry in 1845, the School of Mines in 1851 and a new government Department of Science and Art in 1853. The latter offered 'payment by results' to teachers forming classes, many of which were eagerly organised by the Mechanics' Institutes. The fault of these early courses seems to have been that they were entirely theoretical and did not offer any practical training for those who would later work in manual trades requiring workshop skills.

A further attack on the problem of technical education was made after the 1867 Paris Exhibition, when there was some evidence that Britain, having led the world into the industrial age, was being rapidly overtaken by foreign competitors. Envious eyes were cast across the Channel at the Continental technical institutions which were springing up in France and Germany and at the new Polytechnics at Zürich and Delft. A Parliamentary Select Committee discussed the deficiency of science teachers in 1868 and a Royal Commission on Technical Instruction sat from 1870–1875.

Eventually, the Guild Companies of London became involved when it was suggested to them, by Gladstone among others, that they might help in the promotion of technical education in some way, now that their original control over craft training had been eroded. The well-endowed Guild Companies had started thinking along these lines, since they already supported schools and charities in London and the provinces. Initially, they agreed to provide money for scholarships and bursaries at provincial universities, but in November 1877 the new City and Guilds of London Institute was inaugurated, formed from the Corporation of London and sixteen Guild Companies. In 1879, the Institute took over the system of examinations in technical subjects which had been begun by the Society of Arts in 1873, and thus saw itself as the guardian of standards of technical knowledge through the issue of its own certificates—a system which continues to the present time, the 'City & Guilds' certificate still being an authoritative technical qualification.

Educational work began almost immediately with the establishment of evening classes in 1878 in a school in Cowper Street in Finsbury, its pupils either young persons who wished to have some basic training at sixteen, or men and women already at work who wished to improve their knowledge and skills. The building of the Finsbury Technical College followed, providing an education intermediate between school and places of higher learning; the Institute also established the South London School of Technical Art and supported Chairs at King's College and University College.

The Institute intended from the start to establish a Central Institution for its educational activities. This was to be an advanced technical college, with its emphasis on providing a scientific training directly applicable to various manufacturing industries. It hoped to be comparable with the technical institutions on the Continent. Its students would be fully trained to become technical teachers; mechanical, civil, electrical and sanitary engineers; architects, builders and decorative artists; and principals, superintendents, and managers of manufacturing works.

In 1881, a site for the new college was leased from the Commissioners of the 1851 Exhibition, who owned much of the land in the South Kensington area, and the architect, Alfred Waterhouse, was commissioned. Waterhouse was also the architect of the Natural History Museum (1881) in Cromwell Road. The handsome five-storey red brick building he built on Exhibition Road was decorated with terra cotta coats of arms and the arms of sixteen principal manufacturing towns. It cost £100,000 to build and £20,000 to equip, and lasted until 1962, when it was demolished to make way for the new buildings designed as part of the expansion of Imperial College. All that remains of the building is the clock and bells from the clock turret. The bells have been rehung at the back of the modern Department of Mechanical Engineering building, which stands on the site of the old Waterhouse building, and the clock, restored in 1972, is displayed in a large glass-sided show-case in the entrance hall there.

The Central Institution

The new building was opened on 25 June 1884. It had four Departments: 'Chemical,' 'Physical', 'Mechanics and Mathematics', and 'Engineering', each under a professor. All four professors were to become distinguished in their fields and Fellows of the Royal Society:

H. E. Armstrong, PhD, FRS	Professor of Chemistry
O. Henrici, PhD, FRS	Professor of Mechanics and Mathematics
W. E. Ayrton, FRS	Professor of Physics
W. C. Unwin, BSc, FRS	Professor of Engineering

The College was organised internally by a Board of Studies of the professors with a Dean appointed from among them as Chairman, an Organising Director, and a chief clerk to be Secretary to the Board.

The course of interest to us is the Engineering course, which had the objective of giving a 'practical scientific training' and

> ... instruction ... adapted to those who have already spent some time in the office of a civil engineer or in engineering works, as well as those who desire to obtain in the College a sound theoretical knowledge of the principles of science applicable to their future career, and an insight into the practice and manipulative work in which they will be subsequently engaged. (*Scheme for the Organisation of the Central Institution*, 1884)

The appointed professor was to lecture on 'the strength of constructive materials; the construction of docks, roads, bridges and roofs; machine designing; hydraulic and other machinery; steam engines, gas engines &c.' He was also to teach levelling, surveying and laboratory work and he was to have an assistant to teach marine drawing, a workshop instructor and one or two laboratory demonstrators, as well as men to look after the engines and machines.

Courses in the College were to last three years, at the end of which a Diploma and Associateship of the Institute would be awarded to those who completed the course and passed the examinations. This award is still made, although nowadays it goes hand-in-hand with the award of the BSc (Eng). In the early days it did not, as the College was not part of the University of London and separate examinations had to be taken for each qualification. Fellowship of the Institute was to be awarded to those who had been in practice for at least five years and had contributed original and valuable research work or had advanced industry in some way. Former students and staff of the Department who received the Fellowship of the Institute are listed in Appendix D.

~ 2 ~

The combined course in Civil & Mechanical Engineering, 1884–1913

The scene was now set for a course in Engineering to begin and it is in this course which combined Civil Engineering and Mechanical Engineering subjects that we find the origins of the teaching of Civil Engineering at South Kensington. The separation of Civil from Mechanical Engineering did not come until 1913. During this first period, the Department was ruled in succession by Professor W. C. Unwin from 1884 to 1904 and Professor W. E. Dalby from 1904 to 1913. In 1913, a Department of Mechanical Engineering continued under Professor Dalby, and a separate Department of Civil Engineering was formed.

Professor W. C. Unwin, 1884–1904

The appointment of William Cawthorne Unwin (1838–1933) as

2. The first two Heads of Department: Professor W. C. Unwin, (1884–1904) and Professor W. E. Dalby (1904–13)

our first Head of Department was a particularly fortunate one for the Department, since he brought to his task experience in both civil and mechanical engineering. This, combined with his experience as a teacher, which had allowed him to formulate some clear educational objectives, made him probably the best man for the job at the time.

Unwin was born in Coggeshall in Essex and was the oldest son of William Jordan Unwin, a Congregational minister, a man also interested in education, who later became principal of the Congregational theological college at Homerton. Unwin attended the City of London School, and then spent a year at New College, St. John's Wood, a theological college where the breadth of its curriculum allowed him to study science. At the age of eighteen an excellent place was found for him with the distinguished engineer, William Fairbairn, of Manchester. Fairbairn had done much work on the strength of materials, a key subject in this period when widespread use of materials such as wrought iron was becoming established for large engineering structures. He had, for example, been involved in 1849 in carrying out tests for Robert Stephenson on the wrought iron plates for the box girder of the famous Britannia Bridge. Unwin was taken on in 1856 as an assistant and stayed with him for six years, doing much of the experimental work and helping Fairbairn to write reports. Their researches on materials included impact, vibratory, and long-continued cyclical change of load tests on iron; work which allowed them to deduce many of the fundamental facts of fatigue theory. They also carried out experiments on the properties of steam, the collapse of boiler flues, and comparative testing of Fay and Newall continuous brakes used on trains. An account of this period is given in E. G. Walker's *The Life and Work of William Cawthorne Unwin* (1938). Unwin for the rest of his life cherished this association with Fairbairn, to whom he referred fondly as 'my old chief'. During this period he took his BSc from London University in 1861 by studying in the evenings.

With this propitious start to his training as an engineer, Unwin went on to gain experience as a works manager, first at Williamson and Bros. in Kendal, where some of the work involved the design of turbines and waterwheels. The interest aroused in him in hydraulic problems was to be given an authoritative form later in his *Treatise on Hydraulics* (published in 1907, based on an article in 1881 in *Encyclopedia Britannica*), an important contribution to this subject. In 1864, Unwin returned to Fairbairn and became manager of the Fairbairn Engineering Works in Manchester.

Unwin was, however, evidently attracted to teaching and he gave his first lectures on Engineering to Royal Engineers at Chatham in 1864–65, and lectured again between 1868 and 1871. In the same period he was Instructor in Marine Engineering at the Royal School of Naval Architecture and Marine Engineering at South Kensington (a school which was to be the forerunner of the Royal Naval College at Greenwich). Finally, in 1872, Unwin obtained a permanent teaching appointment as Professor of Hydraulics and Mechanical Engineering at the newly established Royal Indian Engineering College at Cooper's Hill, Egham. Unwin was there for twelve years prior to his appointment to the Central Institution. This link of the Central Institution with Cooper's Hill through Unwin is of some interest, in view of the high reputation of Cooper's Hill in its short history from 1871–1906.

Unwin thus brought to the setting up of a new course in Engineering particularly relevant experience in both Civil and Mechanical Engineering subjects. He was appointed in 1884 and received his first four students in February 1885. He had one assistant to teach Mechanical Drawing and a 'principal mechanic'. It was necessary to devise a suitable course, and, interestingly, what emerged in the first few years under Unwin was to remain the basic course until 1913.

Entrants to the course were usually sixteen or seventeen years old and had to pass an entrance examination in Mathematics and Mechanics, Mechanical Drawing, Physics, Chemistry, and French or German. The instruction in each year took the form of lectures, drawing-office classes, engineering laboratory courses and workshop courses. All first year students to the College had a common course devoted to Mathematics, Physics, Chemistry and Engineering in roughly equal proportions. In the second year, Mathematics, Physics and Chemistry continued, but more hours were devoted to Engineering subjects, and in the third year students spent two-thirds of their time on Engineeering, and the rest on a little Mathematics and one day a week on Physics or Chemistry. Table 1 shows the distribution of time between subjects and Table 2 the Engineering subjects studied. There was much emphasis on the use of workshop tools, and for this period a surprisingly high emphasis on laboratory work. Because of Unwin's own interest in and knowledge of the strength of materials, there was an emphasis on the strength and properties of materials, but the steam engine also received its share of attention.

		Maths.	*Physics*	*Chemistry*	*Engineering*
1st year	All students	9	7	7	7
2nd year	Engineering students	8	$5\frac{1}{2}$	$3\frac{1}{2}$	13
3rd year	Engineering students	4	one day per week in another Dept.		rest of time

Table 1: *Distribution of time, Engineering Department, 1889-90* (hours per week)

Unwin's book on *The Testing of Materials* was published in 1888, and went into three editions. His book on *Elements of Machine Design*, published in 1877, passed through innumerable editions, reprints and translation into French and German. The latter was recommended for first year; in second year, the books were J. H. Cotterill's *Applied Mechanics* (1884) and *Short Logarithmic Tables*; in third year, J. H. Cotterill's *Steam Engine considered as a Thermodynamic Machine* (1878), and W. J. M. Rankine's *Manual of Civil Engineering* (1862).

Surveying played a more prominent part in the course after the appointment of an instructor of Surveying in 1889, and included fieldwork. The annual Surveying camp came to occupy an important place in the Department's life. In 1899, an Estimating Course was added, in which students learned to estimate earth cuttings and embankments; quantities of brickwork and masonry; the weight of iron in bridges, and so on. From 1902, two hours a week were devoted to a course in Workshop Book-keeping and Accounts. Other textbooks were added to the list: J. A. Ewing's *The Steam Engine and other Heat Engines* (1894); T. Baker and F. E. Dixon's *Rudimentary Treatise on Land and Engineering Surveying* (1898); F. C. Lea's *Hydraulics for Engineers and Engineering Students* (1908); R. E. Middleton and O. Chadwick's *Treatise on Surveying* (1899-1902); W. E. Dalby's *The Balancing of Engines* (1902) and his *Valves and Valve Gear Mechanisms* (1906)—these last four books by members of the staff.

The laboratory and workshops were well equipped. Unwin in a *Report of the Board of Studies on the equipment of the Central Institution with Apparatus and Tools*, 1889, stated that the Engi-

	Lectures	*Drawing-office*	*Workshop*
1st year	Properties of materials Machine design	Use of drawing instruments Projection, colouring, shading Arrangement and proportion of elementary parts of machines Arrangement of brickwork and masonry	Woodworking Chipping, filing, and forging
2nd year	Mechanism Application of dynamics to some practical problems Strength of materials Hydraulics	Design of machines and some simple structures	Use of machine tools
3rd year	Strength and stability of structures Cases of combined stress and the more advanced parts of the theory of the strength of materials Theory of the steam engine and valve gears Water supply Girder bridge construction	Designing of machinery and structures	Use of machine tools Practical investigations of the properties of materials Steam engine

Table 2: *Syllabus of instruction in Engineering subjects, 1887*

neering Laboratory was 'in many respects very well furnished, and has served as a model in arranging the laboratories at Leeds and Manchester'. He believed that 'measurements of the elastic strains in materials have already been carried out in the Central Institution to an accuracy not before approached in this country'. Unwin was, however, anxious to have more apparatus for experiments on friction, improved experiments on hydraulics and the experimental boiler, and, in addition to the existing 100-ton Wicksteed testing-machine, he also wanted an American Emery testing-machine, which at £800 was twice the cost of any other, but justified by Unwin as 'it would serve as an advertisement of the laboratory that we had the most delicate testing machine in the country'. The Emery machine had been invented by A. H. Emery of New York in 1879 and was a 800,000 lb (357-ton) machine but sensitive enough to show on its strain gauge a load of 1 lb applied to break a horse's hair.

A description of the Engineering laboratory in *Engineering*, 16 November 1888, describes the Wicksteed testing-machine, and mentions a complete cement-testing plant by Kuhlman and Faija, apparatus devised by Unwin for torsion and bending experiments, micrometers of various kinds, an experimental engine, a calibrated water tank of 512 cu ft capacity and two or three smaller tanks fitted with orifices of different shapes and sizes for experiments on coefficients of discharge and velocity. In addition, there was 'one of Professor Reynolds' arrangements for illustrating the method in which liquids flow through tubes, depending on whether the velocity exceeds or falls below a certain critical velocity'.

Unwin did not obtain the Emery machine, but the 1911–12 syllabus describes a 100-ton testing-machine by Buckton of Leeds, a 30-ton testing-machine by Riehlé Bros., a 60-ton Amsler-Laffon press, measuring equipment, extensometers, boilers, steam engines, gas engines, petrol motor engines and steam turbines.

The establishment grew very slowly from the original staff of three: Unwin; an instructor in Mechanical Drawing and Engineering Design (A. Sharp, 1885–98) and a workshop superintendent (H. Gillett, 1885–1920). An instructor in Surveying was taken on in 1889 (R. E. Middleton, 1889–97); in 1898 an instructor in Engineering Design and Applied Mechanics (F. C. Lea, 1898–1911), and in 1899 an assistant professor (A. G. Ashcroft, 1899–1911). By the end of Unwin's reign in 1904, there were six members of academic staff and three technical staff. After 1905 the titles of the posts changed slightly and the establishment showed a professor,

3. Unwin's 100-ton testing-machine with H. M. Martin, one of Unwin's first four students, holding the control lever

an assistant professor, three lecturers, two instructors and a junior lecturer, while the workshop staff had grown to a superintendent, two workshop instructors and an assistant.

Not much is known of these early members of staff. Middleton's book with Sir Osbert Chadwick, already mentioned, went into several editions, the sixth in 1955. Ashcroft, who had been Principal of Woolwich Polytechnic, taught Surveying until his sudden death in December 1911. F. C. Lea (1871–1952), awarded the DSc in the session 1910–1911, left in 1911, and in 1913 took the Chair of Civil Engineering at Birmingham when its holder, S. M. Dixon, accepted the Chair of Civil Engineering at the City and Guilds College. Lea later became Professor of Engineering at Sheffield University, and was awarded the OBE for his work on aeroplane engines. W. Hewson, who taught Surveying from 1898, had been an instructor in Machine Drawing at the Municipal Technical School, Birmingham. He was a gentle lovable man, deeply religious, and popular with students and colleagues. He was also interested in astronomy and the application of astronomy to geodetic surveying. Manton tells a story of Hewson and students plotting a line for an imaginary railway across Hyde Park, and enjoying the sensation of horror created in an inquisitive old man when, in answer to his enquiry, he was told they were 'prospecting for a railway'!

Student numbers grew fairly quickly. The College had been designed to house 200 students, with an intake of 70 a year. By 1889, there were 48 in the first year, and the total attending all four departments was 95. In addition to these, there were 30 departmental students attached to individual departments on a part-time basis. The College also provided short special courses, summer technical courses and elementary teachers' courses. Special courses included, for example, in 1888–89 'Mr Banister Fletcher's Course on Architecture', 'Mr Faznacht's Architectural Class' and 'Mr Harvey's Masonry Class', and in 1889–90 Professor Marshall Ward's eight lectures on 'the structure and character of various kinds of Timber, illustrated by very beautiful photographs of microscopic preparation of Timber'.

The numbers of students attending for Engineering are shown in the gradual increase in numbers from some half-dozen in the first few years to 30 in third year in 1899 (23 ACGI diplomas awarded), rising to 47 in third year in 1904 (36 ACGI diplomas awarded). (Fig. 1.)

The students were carefully supervised. Classes were from 10.00

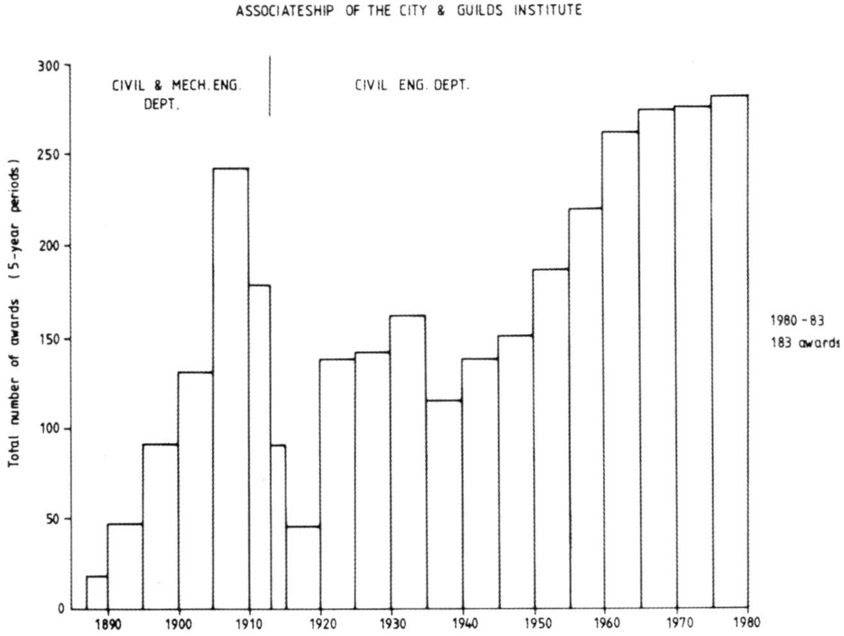

Figure 1

till 5.00 and students had to submit a written explanation for lateness to the Dean. They were not allowed to smoke except in the basement corridor during the lunch-hour. They were urged to be careful with ink. Despite this there is some evidence that they were quite lively and inclined to 'rags' in the classroom. Unwin himself had no problem with discipline. He allowed an impressive silence to fall if anyone misbehaved. He carried out much of the teaching personally and was admired for his clear expositions. Above average in height, he is described as having 'an active bearing ... linked with an old-world refinement and orderliness, precision of behaviour and a reserve and modesty that amounted, on occasions, almost to shyness'. A bachelor, he took a constant and lively interest in both current and former students. He had a little Skye terrier which accompanied him around the building and which the students took some delight in teasing when they saw it lying outside the Professor's room.

Unwin himself was extremely busy, partly with College duties (he was Dean from 1885–96, and again from 1902–04) and partly as a consultant. There were few important engineering works in progress on which he was not consulted—the Forth Bridge (Unwin was a personal friend of Sir Benjamin Baker, the designer), the Manchester Ship Canal, the Periyar power scheme in Madras, the Aswan dam, water-supply for the Coolgardie goldfields, the water-supply of Birmingham, the Derwent Valley waterworks, the Central London Railway, the Mersey Tunnel, the London electricity supply and so on. A notable contribution was the report he prepared in April 1891 for a Commission appointed to advise on the development of the Niagara Falls for power.

Other research fields to which he made a contribution were works on establishing the principles of power transmission by compressed air, principles and formulae for determining flow in gas mains, the stability of dams for storage, and the testing of the diesel internal combustion engine.

Unwin also sat on innumerable committees, both during his time at the College and afterwards in retirement right up to his 90th year. In 1895, he was Chairman of a Home Office Committee on the safety of cylinders for compressed gases; in 1896, he was appointed to a Committee of the Board of Trade on the loss of strength of steel rails under prolonged use. He was Secretary of a British Association Committee on the calibration of instruments and was also on the Main Committee of the Engineering Standards Committee (British Standards Institution), for whom he carried out experimental work involved in the standardisation of rolled steel sections.

Along with this, he had a huge output of written papers on a wide range of subjects, including new areas such as the petroleum engine, the testing of cement mortars, the transmission of power and so on.

His distinction in so many aspects of engineering brought him many honours: FRS (1886), President of the Institution of Civil Engineers (1911–12), President of the Institution of Mechanical Engineers (1915–17), and President of the Engineering Section of the British Association (1892–93). He was awarded medals and prizes for individual papers and was the first recipient of the Kelvin Medal in 1921 presented by the three leading Engineering Institutions for outstanding eminence in engineering.

Recognition by the University

During this period, a number of organisational changes took place. In 1893, the name of the College changed to Central Technical College; and in 1900 on the reorganisation of the University of London, it was included as a School of the University in the newly created Faculty of Engineering. It is interesting to note Unwin's comment in the discussions about the latter proposal: 'It is the function of an Engineering School to teach students to do things as well as to know things', an argument for credit being given for work in laboratories and drawing-offices as well as examinations. This principle has continued to be acknowledged in our examination system today. Unwin was appointed a professor of the University of London, and was also the first representative of the Faculty of Engineering to serve on the Senate.

Inclusion as a School of the University of London meant that students could take the BSc (Eng) examination as internal students. Then, as now, the examination involved three years' study. Students entering for the degree were required to have passed matriculation and the Intermediate BSc examination of London University. The latter was first taken by students of the College in 1902 when the subjects taken were Mathematics; Applied Mathematics; Electricity and Magnetism; Engineering Drawing; Heat, Sound and Optics; and Chemistry. The subjects studied in final year are shown in Table 3. The first BSc (Eng) degrees were awarded to students of the College in 1904, when six students graduated; W. S. Strachan has the privilege of being the first student of the College to gain BSc (Eng) in Civil and Mechanical Engineering with first class honours.

	Subjects	*Requirement for Pass Degree**	*Examinations*
Group A	Theory of machines Theory of structures & structural design Strength & elasticity of materials Electrical technology	only 3 subjects	1 × 3 hours paper and coursework in each subject
Group B	Hydraulics Surveying Theory of heat engines Design of electrical machinery and apparatus	at least 2 subjects from whole group B	2 × 3 hours paper and coursework in each subject
	Generation, transmission and distribution of electrical energy Mathematics Advanced theory of machines		2 × 3 hours paper in each subject

* Requirements for Honours: 3 subjects from Group A and at least 3 from group B, and standard reached must be higher than for Pass degree.

Table 3: *Subjects for BSc (Eng), final year, 1902*

Unwin's achievement

Unwin retired in 1904. His main achievement had been to establish a course which successfully achieved its objectives of bridging the gap between the study of abstract science and the knowledge a practising engineer required. Many of his students reached senior engineering posts, as described in Chapter 9. The course he established lasted for twenty years and was admired worldwide, bringing to the Central Institution a distinction which made it worthy of university status and eventual incorporation into a College of the University. Unwin's own stature and distinction as an engineer also did much to enhance the standing of the Central Institution's Engineering Department.

Of the man himself, several vignettes remain. His biographer in 1938, E. G. Walker, requested Unwin's early students to send him memoirs. The dog is often mentioned. 'If it were following its master down Exhibition Road, the dog's head was considered to be that part of its body which went foremost ...' wrote G. J. Gibbs (1886–88). Another student, A. C. Cookson (1886–88) wrote, 'If I could sketch I might send two pictures—first, Unwin in the well of the 100-ton testing machine, with his little dog sitting and looking down at him, and barking furiously because some of us used to scuffle with our feet knowing that the dog would kick up a row if we did so; secondly, Unwin at lecture time, after discoursing on adiabatic curves, etc., pushing up his glasses and surveying us with that quizzical look with one eyebrow up and the other down, as much to say, "Now, you blighters, how much do you understand?"' A story told by H. A. Humphrey (1885–87), one of Unwin's first four students, is of an accident to a compound condensing steam engine which had been designed by Unwin. A contractor's man trying to lift a heavy drain cover rolled it from one square edge to the next and it came too near the engine. 'I called out to stop the man, but it was too late. The movement of the drain cover brought it directly under the crank pin of the engine and there was a tremendous crash. The engine was pulled up in a fraction of a revolution and Unwin turned to see the momentum of the flywheel lift the crankshaft, smash both main bearings and strain the whole engine. I saw Unwin's eyes blaze and a look of horror was on his face; his lips twitched and I expected some angry and forcible language from him. Instead, he walked away from the engine for half a dozen paces, paused, took out his tobacco pouch, filled and lit his pipe, then walked to the farthest extent of the laboratory, followed by his shaggy-haired terrier. He sat on a bench and patted his dog. A few minutes later he went to his private room. Not a single word had been said.' Humphrey also told the story of how he had been offered a promising post in the Public Works Department in Egypt 'at £500 per year, a good salary for a student straight from College'. Unwin advised him to decline it, saying, 'I would sooner see you take a job without pay somewhere where you can gain wide experience and get the corners rubbed off; you are too good a student to go to Egypt where the outlook is limited.' Humphrey took his advice and soon found himself working in overalls, without pay, in a large works in Manchester. But, he writes, 'I owe a great debt of gratitude to Unwin for that sound advice'.

Professor W. E. Dalby, 1904–13

Unwin's place was taken by Professor William Ernest Dalby (1862–1936). Dalby, less involved in civil engineering than Unwin had been, was nevertheless a first rate mechanical engineer and maintained the course that Unwin had set up until the subjects were divided in 1913. His career continued thereafter in the Department of Mechanical Engineering until his retirement in 1931.

Born in London, Dalby's childhood had been overshadowed by the premature death of his father, which left his mother to bring up three sons in straitened circumstances. Consequently, at the age of fourteen he began an apprenticeship as a railway engineer at the Stratford works of the Great Eastern Railway. In the evenings he studied and at twenty won a scholarship at the Science Schools of South Kensington, and the greater distinction of a Whitworth Scholarship. His apprenticeship over, he entered the Crewe Works of the London and North Western Railway, where he seemed set on becoming a very able railway engineer. He also in this period studied and obtained his BSc from London University. In 1891, however, he received an invitation from Professor J. A. (later Sir Alfred) Ewing to assist him at Cambridge in setting up the Engineering Department there, and this work was rewarded by the conferment of an Honorary MA in 1894 and his admisssion as a Member of Trinity College.

His academic career developed and in 1896 he accepted the post of Professor of Mechanical Engineering and Applied Mechanics at Finsbury Technical College. There he was able to indulge his interest in research into reciprocating engines and he produced papers whose ideas were later enshrined in his book *The Balancing of Engines*, published in 1902 and destined to become a classic. It gave Dalby an international reputation in this field. His appointment to the Central Technical College, an institution well equipped for experimental work on machines, was very much to Dalby's taste, and the distinction he was gaining as a mechanical engineer made him a worthy successor to Unwin.

The course remained the same under Dalby as under Unwin with a mixture of Civil and Mechanical Engineering subjects. Students were still expected to possess and acquire skills in the use of a large range of carpentry and workshop tools. The laboratory apparatus was constantly receiving additions, much of it reflecting Dalby's own interest in engines.

Dalby's own research continued to be on the technology of steam and he published a 760-page book, *Steam Power*, in 1915. His attention was also turned to the problems posed by the coming of the motor car and he carried out research with Professor H. L. Callendar (1863–1930) of the Department of Physics in the Royal College of Science on the problems of temperature measurement of the internal combustion engine, publishing a paper on this subject in 1907. Later in his career he became more interested in materials, particularly the mechanical properties of steel, especially steel rails; he published *Strength and Structure of Steel and Other Metals* in 1928. Dalby also carried out work on stress, applying tensile, compressive, torsional and impact stresses to the material and studying the effects of stress reversal. He devised new methods of measuring and recording, with great accuracy, the deformations produced in test specimens and confirmed the accepted theories of elasticity, plasticity and 'space-lattice' structure of the metal. He was appointed to the Bridge Stress Committee of the Institution of Civil Engineers and in a noteworthy lecture to the Institution in 1929 exhibited some ingenious models which demonstrated very clearly that the impact effects produced by locomotives on the track were due to the dynamic action of the balance weights placed in the driving wheels. Dalby was, indeed, a very able designer of experimental apparatus and often used models in his teaching. His autographic stress-strain recorder is described in the *Proceedings of the Institution of Civil Engineers* in 1912.

The numbers attending the Engineering course continued to grow steadily as did the total number of students attending the College. From the handful of students in the first years, the numbers grew to 140 out of a total of 409 in the College in the last year of Unwin's headship. By 1914, in the peak year of the joint subjects Department, the Engineering students totalled 278 out of the City and Guilds College total of 532; 90 of them were in the third year. These large numbers after the turn of the century exerted great pressure on the space available, and made the acquisition of additional rooms and laboratories a matter of some concern.

The number of staff also increased (Fig. 2). After the incorporation of the College in Imperial College in 1907, the staff was rearranged and new posts created in 1910. At the time the Departments separated in 1913, the staff comprised the professor (Dalby), three assistant professors (W. Hewson, A. J. Margetson and A. Cruikshank), three lecturers (E. F. D. Witchell, R. F. McKay and E. Chappell), four instructors (H. Whittaker, G. C. Wells, J. V. Howard and K. Newton), one junior lecturer and laboratory assistant (W. H. Day) and two draughtsmen to assist with advanced courses—of which more will be said shortly. With the exception of one of the draughtsmen and Wells (who left in 1913), all these members of staff remained with Dalby in the Department of Mechanical Engineering and Motive Power. Mar-

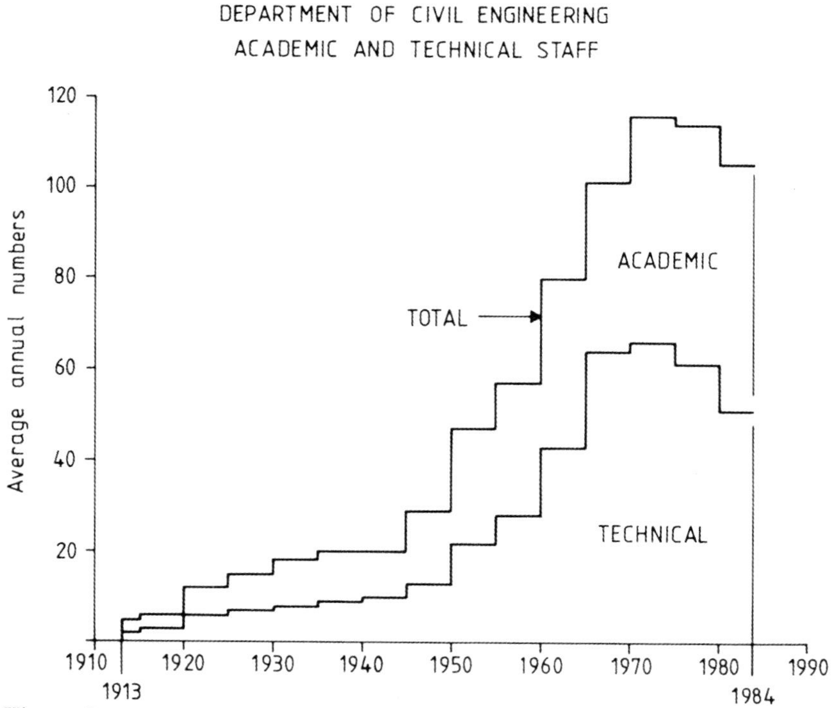

Figure 2

getson left in 1914 to become Professor of Civil and Mechanical Engineering at Finsbury Technical College. Witchell (C & M 1898–1901) returned to the College as a teacher of Engineering Drawing and Applied Mechanics in 1905. He remained in the Department of Mechanical Engineering, where he became a professor in 1931 and was there until his retirement in 1946. He was probably the first City and Guilds student to reach the rank of professor in his own College.

Incorporation with Imperial College, 1907

Alongside the Central Technical College there existed in South Kensington the Royal College of Science and the Royal School of Mines, institutions which had also evolved from simpler beginnings. By the turn of the century their separateness from one another was producing some anomalies. There was, for example, duplication in the fact that Physics and Mathematics were taught in both the Central Technical College and in the Royal College of Science. Electrical Engineering, necessary to the education of mining engineers, was taught in the Central Technical College but not in the School of Mines. The full quota of 200 students had been reached in the Central Institution by 1892–93, and there was a shortage of space for further development and expansion in all three colleges. At the same time anxiety was again being felt that the colleges were not reaching the standards of the *Technische Hochschulen* and the idea for the creation of a great technical university began slowly to evolve. Its principal advocate was R. B. Haldane (later Viscount). One effect of his interest was the setting up of the Mowatt Committee, which reported in 1905 and recommended the amalgamation and reinforcement of the existing colleges. The new Imperial College was to be

> an institution ... where the highest specialised instruction should be given, and where the fullest equipment for the most advanced training and research should be provided in various branches of science, especially in its applications to industry ...

The Report also commented on the inadequacy of the accommodation and recommended that 'the provision to be made for the future should include not only a fully developed School of Mining and Metallurgy and Departments for the principal branches of Engineering, but also for other special subjects'.

The upshot of this recommendation was the decision to erect a new building for the Royal School of Mines on Prince Consort

4. The Goldsmiths' Extension (*photograph of a painting by R. T. Cowern, 1962*)

Road and to join the Central Institution building to it by an L-shaped extension, one arm on Exhibition Road north of the Central Institution and one arm on Prince Consort Road abutting the Royal School of Mines building. As, in the end, most of the money to pay for the engineering extension was donated by the Goldsmiths' Company, it became known as the Goldsmiths' Extension. It now forms part of the domain of the Royal School of Mines.

The architect was Sir Aston Webb, RA, architect of, *inter alia*, the Victoria & Albert Museum and the east façade of Buckingham Palace. The Extension was built between 1911 and 1914, but twelve years were to elapse before the engineers got the full use of it.

In 1907 during the discussion on the future of Imperial College, a Special Committee was appointed by the Governing Body under Sir John Wolfe-Barry, best known to us as the engineer of Tower Bridge, to review the work of the Engineering departments. Its Report in 1908 recommended the expansion of activities to include postgraduate work in various branches of engineering—civil, mechanical, electrical, aeronautical—and the creation of six separate engineering departments in Motive Power Engineering, Structural Engineering, Hydraulic Engineering, Electrical Engineering, Telegraphy and Telephony, and Surveying.

One result of the creation of Imperial College was that the City and Guilds (Engineering) College, as the Central Technical College was now to be known, gave up its departments of Mathematics, Physics and Chemistry and became a purely Engineering college. The City and Guilds of London Institute was very reluctant to lose control over its college, with the result that in 1910 a Delegacy, composed of representatives of Imperial College, the Institute and the Goldsmiths' Company was created to manage the City and Guilds College. Although the Delegacy has been in suspension for the last fifteen years, there is still a separate Engineering Board dealing with the affairs of the City and Guilds College. Professor Unwin, in retirement, represented Imperial College on the Delegacy from 1911 to 1926.

The commitment of Imperial College to advanced study had an almost immediate effect, with the decision to award its own Diplomas (DIC) for two years' study in advanced science and technology. This in practice meant the completion of third and fourth year courses in the same subject. Dalby immediately began a postgraduate course in Railway Engineering in 1908 and the first DICs in Civil and Mechanical Engineering were awarded in this subject in 1909. This course was very near to the heart of Professor Dalby and was open to holders of the ACGI diploma or an engineering degree. It was a full-time course lasting the whole session and made use of outside lecturers as well as Dalby himself. The need for additional workshop space and in particular a laboratory to house apparatus for this course, including a wind tunnel, led to the extension of the workshops into three large bays, roughly 64 to 70 ft long and 32 ft wide on vacant ground behind the building. Apart from a break between 1916 and 1921 caused by the First World War, the Railway Engineering Course lasted successfully until 1932.

It has sometimes been suggested that the joint course in Civil and Mechanical Engineering was dominated by the teaching of Mechanical Engineering. This is not true. The interest in the properties and behaviour of materials received as much attention under Dalby as under Unwin. It is also a fact that the first postgraduate course in civil engineering began under Dalby. This was an advanced course in Structural Engineering, first run in 1910–11, and leading to the award of the first three DICs in Structural Engineering in 1912. The course covered topics such as water supply, the design of retaining walls and masonry skew bridges, and incorporated experimental work on the behaviour of metals near yield point. Dalby gave some of the lectures, and later three former students assisted: M. G. Weekes (C & M 1894–96) on water supply, Oscar Faber (C & M 1903–06) on 'ferro-concrete', and Ralph Freeman (C & M 1897–1900) on 'steel structures'. This course was taken over by the Department of Civil Engineering in 1913. Meanwhile organisational changes were about to be made.

In 1913, as the Extension was nearing completion and as a first step towards carrying out the 1907 recommendations, a Special Committee of the Delegacy under Sir John Wolfe-Barry recommended the division of the Civil and Mechanical Department into three: Mechanical and Motive Power; Civil Engineering; and Surveying. In practice, two departments were created. Dalby remained as Head of the Department of Mechanical Engineering and Motive Power, and Civil Engineering and Surveying were combined under Professor S. M. Dixon, appointed to the new chair.

Dalby's contribution

Dalby was to continue to be actively engaged in the affairs of the Department and of the College. He was Dean from 1906 until his retirement in 1931 and Dean of the Faculty of Civil and Mechanical Engineering of the University from 1908–12. He was an able and devoted administrator and active over a number of years in persuading the university to award the BSc degree on the ACGI diploma examinations, thus obviating the need for the students to take two separate sets of examination papers. This concession took effect for the first time in 1926. Elected FRS in 1913, Dalby also received academic honours from the Institution of Civil Engineers: the George Stephenson Gold Medal (1906), the Crampton Prize (1911), and the Howard Quinquennial Medal (1927). He was a member of Council in 1925 and a Vice-President in 1933. He was also Vice-President of the Institution of Mechanical Engineers, and honorary Vice-President of the Institution of Naval Architects.

On his retirement the Engineering Board recorded a minute in July 1931 which stated 'He (Dalby) has exercised a great influence in the development of the College and in establishing it in its present position with the University of London. The prestige of the College in the Engineering world is largely due to his skilled guidance and enthusiasm, and the Board desire to express their high appreciation of these great services to the College and to engineering education'. There is no doubt that the City and Guilds

College was successful within the University, gaining, for example, between 1903 and 1913, 235 internal degrees out of 520 conferred.

In personality, Dalby seems to have been austere, devoid of humour, stern and very frightening. His *Dean's Annual Report* sometimes commented on the students' behaviour—their admirable discipline, keenness, diligence and so on—no doubt seen at its best when he was around. An example of their excellent behaviour is cited in his *Report* of 1911–12 when he describes with approval the students' keenness when subjected to a vigorous programme at their Surveying camp at Farnham at Easter, working from 7.00 am until 5.00 pm each day for a fortnight in conditions like those which would exist in actual practice. Edwin Glaister, however, who was on his staff in the Department of Mechanical Engineering, brings out a warmer side of Dalby when he describes his contact with him in the laboratory: 'It was when assisting the Professor in some kind of experimental work that one saw him as a human being, full of an almost boyish enthusiasm, and appreciated the essential kindliness which the brusqueness of his more usual manner obscured'. His war effort must also not go unnoted, where he flung himself with enthusiasm into the task in hand, as described later.

~ 3 ~

The new department begins

Professor S.M. Dixon, 1913–33

Nothing could be a greater contrast to Dalby's personality, it appears, than that of the newly appointed Professor of Civil Engineering. Dixon is described as a volatile Irishman with a sparkling wit, sometimes exasperating, but incapable of a mean action and respected and loved by his staff and students.

Born in Dublin, Stephen Mitchel Dixon (1866–1940) took his degree at Trinity College, Dublin, where two of his brothers in later years occupied professorial chairs. He studied Physics and Civil Engineering and obtained the degrees of MA and BAI. After research work at Trinity College, he proceeded to acquire practical training in civil engineering on railway works in England.

In 1892, he turned to academic life and although only twenty-six was appointed to the newly established Chair of Civil Engineering in the University of New Brunswick at Fredericton, where he was responsible for the financing, building and equipping of the new school. Ten years later, he was invited to Dalhousie University, Halifax, Nova Scotia, to perform the same function. During his stay in Canada he was engaged as a consultant on railway and other engineering projects in addition to his academic duties.

He returned to England in 1905 and was the first occupant of the Chair of Civil Engineering at the University of Birmingham. Eight years later, he was invited for the fourth time to organise a new Department of Civil Engineering—this time at the City and Guilds College.

The Goldsmiths' Extension

Dixon's first task on appointment was to undertake the equipping of the new laboratories in the Goldsmiths' Extension preparatory to running a separate course in Civil Engineering from 1914. He was given four members of staff to assist him: J. Purser as Assistant Professor, a graduate of Dublin University, who had been a lecturer in Dixon's Department in Birmingham from 1907–13; J. Tullis as junior assistant, a graduate in Civil Engineering of Aberdeen University in 1912; W.R. Deuchar, a drawing-office

5. The first two Heads of the new Department: Professor S. M. Dixon (1913–33) and Professor A. J. S. Pippard (1933–56) (*Photograph of Professor Pippard by Elliot and Fry, reproduced by permission of Bassano Studios*)

assistant for advanced courses, who transferred from the joint subjects Department; and T. Bryce, a draughtsman.

Progress on the completion of the Goldsmiths' Extension was disrupted partly by a strike for several months at the beginning of 1914 and then by the outbreak of war. The new building was to provide additional classrooms and offices on three floors and space to house new laboratories. These were situated in the angle between the two limbs of the 'L' at the rear of the building in an extensive glass-roofed structure. This part of the building housed four large bays 113 ft long and 37–41 ft wide. Two of these bays became Mechanical Engineering Laboratories and the remaining two Structures Laboratories. In addition, a large Hydraulics Laboratory was to be housed in the basement under the north wing of the main building. Equipment for it, to the value of £5,200, was provided by Charles Hawksley in memory of his father, Thomas Hawksley, both father and son having been well-known engineers specialising in hydraulic problems. A commemorative plaque acknowledged this gift.

The new laboratories

Dalby, aided by the advice of Professor Unwin and Professor E.G. Coker (of Finsbury Technical College), played a large part in planning and equipping the new Hydraulics Laboratory, which by any standards was a magnificent one for its period. It was 166ft long and 48 ft wide with a height from floor to ceiling of 33 ft. It had a gallery on three sides of the building 19 ft above the floor and a small mezzanine gallery of 9 ft above floor level on the west side. It was supplied with water from two large tanks holding

6. The Hawksley Hydraulics Laboratory in the 1930s (*photograph from the City and Guilds College Jubilee Album*, 1935)

8,000 and 8,500 gallons placed in a rectangular shaft running from the top to the bottom of the building in the north-east corner. When full, they were at heights of 72 ft and 42 ft above the basement. Two sumps were provided below the level of the basement floor and water could be raised from them by electrically-driven centrifugal pumps to the storage tanks. This arrangement created a closed circuit and water could be passed through any piece of apparatus in any part of the laboratory by an elaborate system of pipes. An Escher Wyss pump and turbine set was also installed during 1914–15, and the laboratory was then ready for handing over to the Department of Civil Engineering.

Dalby was also involved in the design of the Structures Laboratory, which had a strongly constructed floor and was fitted with a travelling crane capable of lifting 5 tons. The offices and stores at one end of the laboratory had a strong concrete roof, which later formed the floor of a well-equipped machine shop. Testing-machines of various capacities were installed: 100-ton Buckton horizontal testing-machine, 30-ton Buckton vertical testing-machine, 10-ton Buckton spring testing-machine and two 10,000 lb Buckton vertical testing-machines. Concrete slab-testing apparatus was also installed, the gift of the Institution of Civil Engineers. It was able to test slabs measuring $7\frac{1}{2}$ by 15 ft.

The Department in war-time, the First World War

The stage was now set for the course in Civil Engineering to begin in 1914. The proposed course envisaged a common course for all Engineering first year students, and a course common to all second year Engineering students with three hours a week devoted to either Civil, Mechanical or Electrical Engineering. In third year, apart from four hours on Mathematics, the rest of the time would be spent on Civil Engineering. The disposition of time and subjects is shown in Table 4. A postgraduate course envisaged the selection of subjects by students from courses in Structural Engineering, Hydraulic Engineering, and Surveying and Geology (Fig. 3).

The course for second years therefore began in 1914 with 36 students in the year, but the outbreak of war in August 1914 very shortly affected both staff and student numbers. Of the 36 students in second year, 26 joined up during the session 1914–15. Ralph Freeman, lecturing to the four students taking the postgraduate course, invited them to join his firm, Sir Douglas Fox and Partners, on work for an explosives factory, and three out of the four departed with him, leaving Dixon to supervise the remaining student. Dixon was seconded to the Ministry of Munitions from July 1915 until 1916; in 1917 he accepted a commission in the Royal Engineers as Railway Transport Officer behind the British lines in France. Purser and Tullis were called up on active service, as also were members of staff in the Department of Mechanical Engineering. Attempts to keep the Civil Engineering course going gradually petered out, and at the beginning of the 1916–17 session

	Hours per wk	Location
1st YEAR: COMMON COURSE		
Mechanics & Maths	11	C & G
Eng. Drawing and Workshop	6	C & G
Physics (first ½ session)	13	RCS
Chemistry (second ½ session)	13	RCS
	30	
2nd YEAR		
Strength of Materials, Mechanism, Machine Drawing, Design and the Steam engines	11	C & G
Electrical technology	5	C & G
Mechanics & Maths	8	C & G
Chemistry	3	RCS
Optional subjects (CE, ME or EE) (CE, in practice, meant Surveying)	3	CE Dept.
	30	
3rd YEAR: COURSE 3B in CIVIL ENGINEERING		
Hydraulics	5	CE Dept.
Field Engineering & Foundations	4	CE Dept.
Structures	8	CE Dept.
Hydraulic Eng. *or* Roads and Materials	3	CE Dept.
Mathematics	4	RCS
Geology	6	RCS
	30	

Table 4: *Distribution of time and subjects, Civil Engineering, 1914*

it was decided to suspend the course and revert for the duration of the war to the old Civil and Mechanical Engineering course.

Meanwhile, the Army Pay Department took over two floors in the Extension and the Admiralty commandeered the laboratories for experimental work with Dalby appointed as a consultant to them. Here research was carried out for the Board of Inventions and Research, the Admiralty, and the War Office, among others,

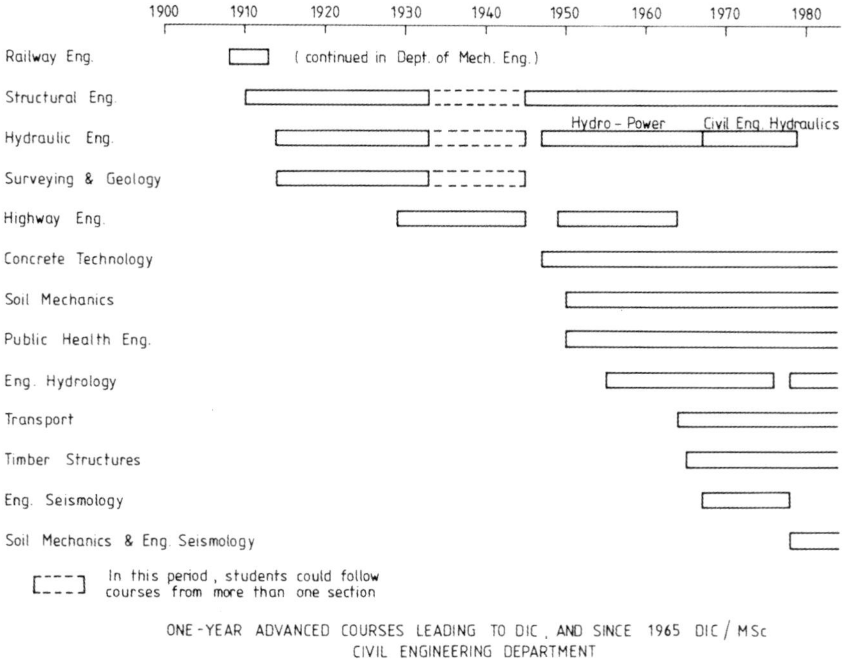

Figure 3

on new condensing plant for warships, the strength of wood struts used in aircraft building and the strength of Ingles bridge members for a type of bridge erected on the spot during the war. Dalby also plunged vigorously into the production of munitions in the workshops of the Mechanical and Electrical Engineering Departments. The workshops ran for 60 hours a week including the vacations and Dalby reported proudly in his annual *Dean's Report* that none of the staff or student volunteers involved had had more than one week's holiday during the summer. Between June 1915 and August 1917, over 9,300 items were made—gauges, fuses, models, instruments and parts of machines—all executed on contracts with the Admiralty, War Office, Royal Aircraft Factory, Ministry of Munitions and so on, to the value of £22,044, earned for the College. Of particular value was the manufacture of hardened screw precision gauges to very fine tolerances. Dalby spent the summer of 1915 trying to find suitable steel for them and to arrange the quickest system of production. He supplied seventy different types of precision screw gauges and made 5,460 in total.

Many staff and students were involved in the services as the following table shows.

Service with the Forces—City & Guilds College, 1914–18 (*Delegacy Report*, 1918–19)

	Officers	*Men*	*Totals*
Service:			
Past students	867	150	
Present students	290	133	
Staff	21	23	1,484
Casualties:			
Killed or died of wounds	173	29	202
Wounded			244
Decorations and distinctions			601

The names of the dead were commemorated in a plaque in the College.

~ 4 ~

Between the Wars, 1919–1939

Post-war recovery

The end of the war in November 1918 signalled a return to normality. The staff on active service returned early in 1919, and as a preparation for the resumption of the Civil Engineering course, Dixon gave a special second year course in Civil Engineering in the second half-session, so that 25 students could be admitted to the Civil Engineering third year in October 1919. The Admiralty vacated the Hydraulics Laboratory in July 1919, but it was found that the floor had been damaged and it was 1922 before compensation was agreed and repairs carried out. It took until October 1920 to induce the Admiralty to depart completely from the building.

Purser and Tullis returned from service, and additional staff were appointed. M.K. Rice-Oxley (C & M 1900–03), who had been a lecturer in the School of Engineering in Giza and had also served in the Sudan Public Works Department, was appointed to lecture in Surveying; he became Assistant Professor in 1921, Reader in 1931 and was to remain on the staff until 1942. A.F. Wickenden, a man with architectural experience, was appointed as draughtsman and drawing-office assistant in place of Deuchar; he became a lecturer in 1920 and had general charge of postgraduate students. In the same year, B.G. Manton was appointed demonstrator when Tullis left. A London graduate, Manton had been an engineer with the Port of London Authority. He has left an affectionate account of his first meeting with Dixon when he was an undergraduate at University College and Dixon used to come down from Birmingham to give some lectures. 'He would frequently take tea with us in the College refectory before his lecture,' Manton wrote, 'and would delight us with his witty conversation'. Eight years later the acquaintance was renewed when Manton was appointed to the staff; he could only 'regard Professor Dixon's action in giving him the post as a stroke of great good fortune, leading, as it did, to a connection with the College lasting for over forty years'. Manton eventually became a reader and remained on the staff until his retirement in 1962.

A blow to the efficiency of the College in the next few years came in the form of increasing financial difficulties because of the rise in the cost of living and materials. The Dean reported in 1919–20 that it was difficult to fill junior appointments, and by 1922–23 he recorded that the College would be unable to use the Extension unless it received more money to cover the cost of the rates and the maintenance of the laboratory equipment. The College was exceeding its budget by several thousand pounds. Students' fees were raised from £36 to £60 per annum in 1920. The Meston Committee, set up at the request of the Treasury in 1921, advised only a slightly increased grant, and threatened to stop the grant if the College did not stay within its budget! Consequently, departments had to accept a reduction in the budget for 1923–24. The only way this constraint could be met was by reducing the salaries of professors and some grades of laboratory and administrative staff, continuing staff vacancies, postponing developments and keeping down departmental expenses. Some of this has a distinctly contemporary ring! Dixon's salary was reduced from £1,500 to £1,350 per annum and certain technical staff had to take a reduction of 10% on their earnings. Dixon's salary was restored to £1,425 in 1925, but it was 1930 before it reached £1,500 again. Fortunately for the College, assistance of £3,000 per annum for five years beginning in 1922 was given by the Clothworkers' Company and helped to keep the College going in this bad financial period, but the Finsbury College had to close to release funds for the Institute's other activities, with effect from 1926. The College's financial position improved in 1925 when an appeal to the Treasury brought additional funding. This made it possible finally to put into use the whole of the Goldsmiths' Extension, which was officially opened in October 1926.

It is perhaps of some interest now to see the annual cost of running the Department in this period. The statement for 1926–27 reads as follows:

Professor Dixon	£1,425
Asst. Prof. J. Purser	648
Asst. Prof. M.K. Rice-Oxley	600
Lecturer, W.V. Shearer	360
Demonstrator, B.G. Manton	300
Demonstrator, E.F. Gibbs	250
Asst. Demonstrator, F.G.H. Blyth	200
Draughtsman, T. Bryce	400
Tracer, Miss H. Doezy	156

Lab. and Workshop Assistants:	
G.G. Pirie	248
W.A. Bryan	248
Lab. Attendant:	
A.S. Amos	211
Departmental Labourers:	
H.G. Fisher	208
E. Sinfield	195
E.J. Howe	200
Laboratory boys:	
4 at £39 p.a. each	156
Hydraulic Engineering Special Lecturers	120
Structural Engineering Special Lecturers	300
Materials	1,200
Survey Camp	120
	£7,545

Whereas Professor Dixon's salary is equivalent to about £25,000 today (i.e. well above the current average received by a professor), all his staff earned considerably less than today's equivalents. The two assistant professors would be about half-way down the current lecturer scale, and Shearer would just about make the bottom rung. Thus, although comparisons with current salaries are imprecise, the differentials between professors and other staff have narrowed considerably since Dixon's day.

Despite the financial problems of the immediate post-war years, the Department soon settled into a pattern of life which was to continue until the appointment of a new head of department in 1933.

The undergraduate course resumed much as it had been envisaged in 1914. (Table 4). Civil Engineering students in second year spent their optional three hours on Surveying. Only in third year did students specialise in Civil Engineering subjects, with the core subjects of Hydraulics, Structures and Geology receiving most of the time. The examination marks for each year (500 for the first year, 1,000 for second year and 1,500 for third year) were aggregated for the award of honours or a pass. Entrants were still required to pass an entrance examination or to gain matriculation from London University, but it was possible to enter directly into second year if Intermediate or Higher School Certificate examinations had been taken, the equivalent in standard of first year examinations. To allow for the fact that some students might omit first year, the system was modified in 1926, and no marks were carried forward from the first year. Another problem relating to course length was that degree regulations up to 1940 required matriculation and three years' internal registration. Thus those who had qualified in two years' study could be awarded the ACGI diploma but not the degree until another year had passed. A result of this was that such students often took a DIC or began work for a research degree—one reason for the long history of post-graduate work in the Department.

The numbers attending grew steadily from 23 in the third year in 1920 to between 35 and 47 in the period up to the outbreak of World War II (Fig. 1). Records show that they were not all successful in obtaining degrees. In 1925, for example, of the 35 students who sat the final examination, only 14 graduated (2 with first class, 5 with second class, and 7 with a pass); a further 9 qualified for ACGI only, 6 received 'certificates of attendance' and 6 'failed totally'.

Field courses

An important and much enjoyed feature was participation in the various field courses. The organisation of the Surveying field course which had been established in Unwin's time was taken over by the Civil Engineering Department for second year students of both Civil and Mechanical Engineering. After the interruption of the war, the camps began again in 1920. The camp lasted three weeks in some location such as Blenheim or Ibsley in Hampshire and involved the setting out of a line for a railway, tacheometric and photographic surveys, and field astronomy. Dixon himself had carried out research on the use of the camera in surveying, and he enjoyed work with the photo-theodolite. Several members of staff attended, with Dixon himself, attired in dungarees, revelling in what he described as 'pioneer conditions'. He would walk for miles along the surveys and enjoyed the mid-day picnic lunches of sandwiches with tea brewed over a wood fire. Manton recalls how on one occasion the students forgot both milk and sugar, with the nearest supply several miles away, but 'the Professor's displeasure was very soon forgotten and we consumed black, unsweetened tea to the accompaniment of his customary fusillade of witty Irish quips'.

Accommodation was in tents, and there was also a photographic dark-room tent, an office tent and two large tents in which meals were served. The field kitchen of two stoves in a small tent was manned by two members of the workshop staff, usually assisted by two laboratory boys.

Dixon had always recognised the importance of an understanding of geology to the civil engineer and this study formed part of the third year course. Indeed, a petition still exists which was presented in 1921 by forty-eight third year students to the Governing Body asking that Geology should be recognised as an examination subject in the BSc (Eng) degree; seven hours a week out of a total of thirty were devoted to this subject, which, as they put it, 'is admittedly essential to the civil engineer'. Their plea was actively supported by Dixon, who had already put if forward without success. The concession was eventually granted in 1925.

From 1925 there were also geological field trips in the Easter vacation arranged for third year Civil Engineering students and led by staff of the Geology Department. Areas such as Dartmoor, the Malvern Hills and the Pennines were visited. Among the members of staff of the Geology Department associated with the trips were A. Brammall and F.G.H. Blyth. Blyth had been a student in the Civil Engineering Department from 1921–24 and later a demonstrator from 1926 until he transferred to the Geology Department in 1931. His name is well known in association with his classic book *A Geology for Engineers* (1943; sixth edition, 1974).

Gauging the Severn

Dixon's particular enthusiasm, however, centred round the gauging of the River Severn. The idea for the work was prompted by the Second Interim Report of the Water Power Resources Committee of the Board of Trade in 1920. In this the Committee commented on the lack of existing sources of information on the flow of rivers in Britain. Dixon's investigation was undertaken to find the best method of gauging river flow and to accumulate information with regard to variations in discharge and their relation to the rainfall. From 1921–23, the Department of Scientific and Industrial Research took on the funding of the 'methods' part of the research. The Severn was chosen because it was near London and was a large river free from artificial controls and river-traffic. Dixon's task was to accumulate and analyse readings of the river's discharge. Measurements were taken, partly by hand-held meters and partly by means of gauges installed at different positions. One of these was read daily from March 1921 until 1936 by boys from a local school at Bewdley. Dixon took many readings himself and Manton describes how batches of students would leave Paddington for Bewdley on an afternoon train, spend the next day in carrying out different methods of flow measurement and then return to London the same evening. Both staff and students stayed at 'The George', a fine old coaching inn where, for some time, the bedrooms continued to be lit by candles and beer was brewed on the premises. The periodical gaugings of the river were supplemented by readings from a permanent recorder. The installation of this involved the drawing up of an agreement between the Delegacy and Birmingham Corporation whereby the Professor was allowed to install his equipment on payment of a rental of 5s per annum (the equivalent of 25 new pence).

Manton also tells the story of how on one chilly spring day, while making an adjustment to the current meter, Dixon fell overboard and had to be hauled back into the punt by the students, but he writes, 'It says much for his fortitude and stamina that he refused to return to the hotel for a change of clothing and continued his work for the rest of the day . . .'.

This work on the Severn reached its culmination in a paper by Dixon, M.A. Hogan and G. Fitzgibbon (the latter two research assistants who had helped him) entitled 'The flow of the River Severn, 1921–36', published in the *Proceedings of the Institution of Civil Engineers* in 1937, for which the authors received a Telford Premium. In 1936, the Catchment Board, observing the usefulness of such records, undertook to continue the readings at Bewdley.

Another of Dixon's hydrological interests was expressed in work he did from 1914 to measure as accurately as possible the volume of overflow over the Caban dam in a reservoir in the Birmingham Water Works. Dixon and F.W. Macaulay of Birmingham Corporation Water Department were appointed by the Water Committee of the City of Birmingham, who were anxious to know the accuracy of the yield of the Elan gathering-ground. Work was delayed by the war but began again in 1919.

Research under Dixon

Within College, in the Hydraulics Laboratory, various researches, were in train. From 1922 Dixon undertook research on Standard Tests for Water Turbines at the request of a Joint Committee of the Institution of Civil Engineers and the Institution of

Mechanical Engineers. New plant included apparatus for measuring discharges through apertures of various sizes and under different heads, a Francis turbine and a Pelton wheel mounted over a concrete channel, and another Francis turbine discharging over a weir. The first PhD awarded in the Department was for a thesis in 1927 by M. Amin on the flow of water in canals fitted with Venturi flumes. In the next few years research on movable crest weirs, flow through orifices, and standing waves, shows the way in which some of the fundamental aspects of hydrodynamics were being examined.

Another of Dixon's research interests was the work he did from 1924 for the Safety in Mines Research Board on the strength of wire ropes and the support of workings in mining. This research involved the installation of special plant and the appointment of three research assistants.

One of these, M.A. Hogan, after several years' work, received his DSc in the 1928–29 session for his thesis on 'The support of underground workings in coal mines'. Dixon had repeatedly urged that the Structures Laboratory should be equipped with a testing-machine having a capacity of 300 tons or more, and this ambition was achieved through this work on safety in mines. In order to test the efficiency of various underground supports in mines, an appliance was designed to deal with structures 10 ft high, 8 ft long and 8 ft wide; it had a loading capacity of 400 tons. The apparatus was designed by J. Whittaker, a research assistant, and constructed by workshop staff. A vertical wire-rope tester was also installed, in which loads up to 100 tons could be applied to specimens up to 30 ft long.

The Structures Laboratory also contained a 100-ton Riehlé testing-machine, adaptable for tensile, compressive and bending tests. It was large enough to take 8 ft high columns or 16 ft span beams. Dixon was an enthusiastic advocate of full-scale testing and he designed equipment to test the strength of brick or concrete arches of 20 ft span, constructed in situ and supported at their springings by massive brick piers. These structures could be loaded up to 120 tons by hydraulic jacks. The first PhD awarded in Structures was for a thesis in 1928 by L.G. Brazier on the flexure of thin cylindrical shells.

The basement beneath the Structures Laboratory was devoted to concrete testing and contained a concrete mixer, machines for crushing test cubes, various machines for testing road materials by attrition and abrasion, and a concrete slab-tester. Arrangements for curing concrete were provided in a separate laboratory on the second floor, under the direction of Assistant Professor Rice-Oxley. Under Dixon some basic research was carried out by postgraduates on the nature of concrete. The first MSc degree in this subject was awarded to A. Dean in 1923 for research on Portland cement. Four more MScs in 1926 and 1927 were on cinder concrete, aerated concrete and the microstructure of Portland cement.

From 1919 tests were carried out on timber specimens for a Committee of the Institution of Civil Engineers on the Deterioration of Structures exposed to Sea Action; this involved treating them with various chemicals such as arsenic compounds and creosote. The results of this work were presented to the Institution in 1930.

Postgraduate courses became an established feature of the Department. These could be taken in either Structures or Hydraulics or in a mixture of the two. The Special Lecturers who had worked for the College pre-war returned. Ralph Freeman continued to lecture on steel bridges, Oscar Faber on reinforced concrete, M.G. Weekes on public works (surveying, management, etc) and from 1921, Harald Lundgren, chief turbine designer of Boving & Co., on hydraulic machinery. Freeman and Faber had by now established their reputation as design engineers, and Weekes was an engineering inspector attached to the Ministry of Works. It was also possible to take a course in Hydro-Electric Engineering, spending part of the course time in the Department of Electrical Engineering. The numbers attending postgraduate courses ranged in this period between 12 and about 20 annually.

The Maybury Chair of Highway Engineering, 1929

From 1929 it was also possible to take a postgraduate course in Highway Engineering. This followed the establishment of a new chair in 1929, the Maybury Chair of Highway Engineering, sponsored jointly by the Paviors' Company and the Institution of Municipal and County Engineers, who guaranteed £1,500 per annum for five years. The Maybury Chair was named in honour of Sir Henry Maybury, Director-General of Roads in the newly formed Ministry of Transport. As Brigadier-General in the war he had been responsible for road construction and repair carried out by the Royal Engineers in France. The chair was a part-time appointment and the first holder was R.G.H. Clements (1880–1953). Educated in Edinburgh at Heriot-Watt College, where he was a medallist, he worked for some years in the Ordnance Survey Office and in the Public Works Department in Edinburgh. When war broke out he was working as Deputy Borough Surveyor of Brighton, but served with the Royal Engineers in Europe from 1916–1919, attaining the rank of major. He was responsible for about 3,000 bridges administered by the Army of the Rhine, and was awarded the MC. After the war he was Divisional Roads Engineer for the Ministry of Transport and later in private practice as a consultant in highway and town planning matters. He appeared as a technical witness, from time to time before House of Commons Committees, and was engaged very frequently at Public Enquiries.

On his appointment as Maybury Professor, Clements entered into academic work with great enthusiasm and obvious pleasure, and although Highway Engineering was primarily a postgraduate course, he lectured on roads to third year undergraduates and usually appeared for a few days at the survey camp. He was tireless in helping students, both by elucidating difficulties in their work and by assisting them in obtaining suitable posts on leaving. He served on many committees of the Road Research Board, Ministry of Transport, British Standards Institution and so on. He retired from academic life in 1939 and received the Fellowship of Imperial College in 1952.

Clements' style was breezy and genial, and Manton writes that this did not always harmonise with Dixon's satirical Irish humour. Manton, who eventually became a lecturer in Clements' Section, had the awkward task of acting as a conciliator.

A separate Highway Engineering Laboratory was created in what had previously been the cement-testing laboratory on the second floor. Here over the years postgraduate work was carried out on bitumen, tar, concrete and other road materials, the behaviour of bituminous joints, and so on. The postgraduate course encompassed the study of highway design, surveying, materials, strength of bridges, geology and chemistry.

Some of Clements' special knowledge was incorporated in a new postgraduate course in Building Science, which ran from 1933–35. This course was carried out in collaboration with the Building Research Station, which supplied some of the teachers. Its syllabus included the study of building requirements (heating, lighting, ventilation, etc.), the materials of construction and methods of design and construction.

Dixon's staff

The staff remained very small with an establishment of seven teaching staff in 1920 and ten men and boys in the workshop. Twelve years later there were only ten teaching staff and eleven in the workshop. Of the original staff, Purser stayed until 1933, teaching Hydraulics. Manton became a lecturer and assisted Clements. Wickenden left in 1926 to become Professor of Architecture at Cairo University. His place was taken by W.V. Shearer, a graduate of Glasgow University, who had been Principal of the Department of Mechanical Engineering at Giza. He collaborated with Rice-Oxley, who was still on the staff, to produce *Astronomy for Surveyors* in 1929. E.F. Gibbs, a student in the Department from 1922–25, was appointed in 1925 to teach Hydraulics; he took his MSc in 1933 and his PhD in 1937, when he left to take up a lectureship at Bristol University and went on to become Assistant Dean to the Faculty of Engineering there. Another junior place was filled in 1926 by F.G.H. Blyth, already mentioned in connection with the Geology course.

The relations between Dixon and Dalby appear to have been rather strained, perhaps because of their very different temperaments. Friction arose, often over trivial matters such as keys, and almost a year after his appointment Dixon complained that he still had no key to the front door to the City and Guilds building and had to wait on the front doorstep for the caretaker to let him in if he returned to the College out of hours. The question of keys cropped up again after the war, and Dixon gave great offence by taking unilateral action and changing the locks on the communicating doors between the Civil Engineering Department and the Royal School of Mines—as a protection against thieves, he said, but was there some kind of revenge motive?

Dalby was Dean from 1904 until his retirement in 1931—it is not clear now how he retained the office for so long since it was by then held for only two years—but Dixon was able to enjoy this office only briefly from 1931–33 before his retirement.

On retiring, Dixon settled eventually in France with his second wife, who was French. He died in Nice in 1940 at the age of seventy-three. Despite the disruption of the war, his achievement had been to develop, in a marvellously complete way for their period, the two large laboratories of the Department. Under him research was begun into the basic properties of cement and concrete, and experimental hydrodynamics, with work also on the strength of concrete arches and welded joints in steel members.

Between 1923 and 1933, 24 MSc degrees were awarded and 2 PhD degrees. The scene was set for the active development of engineering research which followed in the years up to 1939. Through the vibrancy of his own personality, Dixon welded together a small but united team, who clearly enjoyed their work and their happy annual field trips with him and the students. His work for the Safety in Mines Research Board was important and competently executed, and brought him the award of the OBE in 1937.

Tributes to Dixon after his death included that of Purser, who had been on his staff at Birmingham, moved with him to London, and worked with him until 1933. He wrote in *The Central*, 'In obtaining a start in life for his students his success is unparalleled ... Then there was his kindness to all those who worked for him, his continual interest in their welfare, and his efforts to improve their material position ... All who worked with him, colleague, student or workshop hand, loved him and would have done anything for him just as he was willing to give of his best for them ... He was very ingenuous and would never believe ill of anyone without clear proof, in which case his denunciation of the culprit used to be very forceful ... When he wanted a thing done he always did it himself if possible.' In the same issue, H.J.B. (later Sir Harold) Harding, a former student (1917–18, 1918–22), speaks of the 'freshness about the work of the Civil Department which was very cheering though at that time we knew we had not reached that cold and ruthless efficiency which we met in the old building where, over a period of years, everything had been cut and (thoroughly) dried ...' (under Dalby), and he gives us a good idea of why students were fond of Dixon: 'Here was a man, at the top of his profession ... who did not seem unduly obsessed with mathematical matters, so there was still hope for us. In fact "Dikko's" lectures on conjugate stress gave one the idea of a necessary evil to be got over before dealing with really interesting matters ... His eyes would twinkle and his mouth twitch as he came out with statements just nicely twisted round to give a humorous or unexpected touch which made things pleasant to listen to and easier to remember. He put the whole disgusting business of the Ellipse of Stress in its proper place and perspective by this memorable statement: "This is regarded as very important, Dj' see. It is not really important at arl, Dj'see, but still it *is* very important".' Not the orthodox treatment of this subject, but a point seems to have been made.

A change of leadership: Professor A.J. Sutton Pippard

Professor Dixon's place was taken in 1933 by an engineer who had already established a name for himself in aeronautical research and had published some forty papers in this and related fields prior to his appointment. He had also held two other university chairs in Civil Engineering.

Born in 1891, Alfred John Sutton Pippard was the son of a building contractor in Yeovil. After a general education at Yeovil School and a year's apprenticeship with a local firm of engineers and architects, he entered the Merchant Venturers' College, Bristol (which became part of the University of Bristol in 1909), and graduated from it in 1911 with first class honours in Civil Engineering. His father having died, money was very short, but he was able to obtain one of the newly instituted Industrial Bursaries of the Commissioners for the 1851 Exhibition and became an articled assistant with A.P.I. Cotterell, MICE, of Bristol. His practical training completed, he became engineering assistant to the Pontypridd and Rhondda Joint Water Board. When war broke out, and he failed to obtain a commission in the Royal Engineers because of poor eyesight, he entered his name on a list being compiled by the Institution of Civil Engineers whose object was to help their members obtain positions where they could be most useful to the war effort. As a result, his name was passed to the Air Department, Admiralty, and he was appointed a technical adviser in the Structures Section under its leader, Harris Booth. Later the Section was transferred to the Ministry of Munitions. The Section's work was concerned with the stress analysis of aeroplane frames to ensure the safety of aircraft in flight. The Section was also responsible for developing new methods of analysis and their dissemination among the firms working for the Admiralty. One of the members of the Structures team was Miss Letitia Chitty, who was to become a lifelong friend and associate of Pippard. Soon after the war ended, Pippard and J.L. Pritchard (second-in-command in the Section) published *Aeroplane Structures* (1919), a book which became a standard work for many years and was published in a revised edition as late as 1935. A year later, in 1920, Pippard received his DSc degree from Bristol University.

After the war Pippard became a Director of Ogilvie and Partners, who acted as consultants for a number of aircraft manufacturers and transport companies. In this period he was on a number of committees concerned with aeronautical research and development, including that which investigated the R.38 airship disaster. Between 1919 and 1922 he enjoyed his work as visiting lecturer in the Department of Aeronautics at Imperial College, and with some satisfaction, since he loved teaching, was able in 1922 to secure the Chair of Engineering at University College, Cardiff. The department dealt with Civil, Mechanical and Electrical Engineering, had a very small staff, did not engage in much research, and prepared students to pass degree standard only. In 1928, Pippard was invited by his old university, Bristol, to succeed his former head of department, Professor R.M. Ferrier, in the Chair of Civil Engineering. In this period at Bristol he was also checking airworthiness for the Air Ministry of their two new airships, the R.100 and R.101. When the latter crashed in October 1930, the Public Enquiry found that the failure was in no way due to faults in structural or aerodynamic design, but the episode, in which several of his friends died, was a severe blow to Pippard, and marked the end of his direct involvement in aircraft structures, although he did later carry out research for the Aeronautical Research Council. Indeed, Skempton, in his memoir for the Royal Society, believes that Pippard was 'never devoted to aircraft as such, but rather to the structural problems they presented and the intellectual challenge of designing complex frameworks with minimum weight, but adequate factors of safety'. When the Chair of Civil Engineering at Imperial College became vacant, he was pleased to accept the headship of a larger department where research and specialities were already developing. The post would also allow Pippard closer links with the Institution of Civil Engineers.

In the first years after his appointment, Pippard appointed new staff to replace those who had left. C.M. White came in Purser's place in 1933 to be Reader in Hydraulics. After graduation from University College, Nottingham, and war service, White had been a lecturer at King's College, London from 1927–33. In the same year as White, S.C. Redshaw, from University College, Cardiff, was appointed as a demonstrator and taught Structures. He was awarded his PhD in 1936 for research on the strength of curved plates, then left to join the staff of the Building Research Station at Garston; he subsequently became Professor of Civil Engineering at Birmingham University. In 1934, two further members of staff were appointed: S.R. Sparkes and Miss L. Chitty. Sparkes was a graduate of Bristol University and had spent a year with Dorman Long; he came as a demonstrator to teach Structures; he became

Professor of Engineering Structures in 1958, and remained on the staff till his retirement in 1973. Miss Chitty had been a Mathematics student at Newnham College, Cambridge, when the interruption of the war brought her to the Air Ministry, where she met Pippard, as already mentioned. After the war, she returned to Cambridge and changed her course to Engineering, graduating in 1921 with first class honours in the Mechanical Sciences Tripos, the first woman to gain a first in this examination. She continued to work in the Air Ministry, under R.V. Southwell (later Sir Richard, and Rector of Imperial College 1942–48). Appointed as a research assistant in 1934, she worked closely with Pippard, using her mathematical ability to complement his work. She became a lecturer in 1943 and remained on the staff till her retirement in 1962.

Staff surviving from the Dixon era were Clements and Manton, both engaged in Highway Engineering; Rice-Oxley, Shearer and Chilton in the Surveying Section; and Gibbs in Hydraulics (until 1937).

In 1936 W.T. Marshall, a student of the Department from 1926–29, was appointed assistant lecturer, and was mainly con-

7. Staff group 1935 (*Back row, left to right*): R. G. Hayward, H. Semon, H. G. Fisher, A. S. Amos, W. A. Bryan, H. R. Thomas, T. Bryce, E. J. Howe, G. G. Pirie, E. Sinfield, J. Watt, V. G. Coad, J. Mitchell. (*Front row, left to right*): Miss L. Chitty, W. G. Wren, S. R. Sparkes, S. C. Redshaw, B. G. Manton, Asst. Prof. C. M.. White, Prof. R. G. H. Clements, Prof. A. J. S. Pippard, Asst. Prof. M. K. Rice-Oxley, W. V. Shearer, E. F. Gibbs, O. H. Chilton, F. J. R. Smith, Miss M. Wingate

cerned with structural design and concrete. He subsequently became Regius Professor of Civil Engineering at Glasgow University. A year later, A. Stephenson was appointed assistant lecturer in Surveying. Stephenson was a graduate of Cambridge, having taken the Geographical Tripos in 1930. He had been a demonstrator in the Department of Geography at Cambridge in 1931–32 and a lecturer in 1933–34. Interspersed with this was experience as Chief Surveyor with the Polar Expeditions of 1930–31 and 1934–37, on both of which occasions he was awarded the Polar Medal. He was also Meteorological Observer with the 2nd International Polar Year Expedition to the Great Slave Lake, North West Territories, in 1932–33. A.H. Yates, a research assistant in the Aerodynamics Department of the Royal Aircraft Establishment, was appointed to succeed Gibbs in Hydraulics.

As this account of staffing implies, the Department was becoming increasingly sectionalised into specialities: Structures, Hydraulics, Highway Engineering, and Surveying.

Pippard's first action as head of department was to set up a Small Model Structures Laboratory, so that students could learn 'modern methods of mechanical stress analysis which have become so important in the field of structural engineering' (*Dean's Report*, 1935–36). He was able to do this through a donation of £2,000 from the Clothworkers' Company given in 1935 to commemorate the 50th year Jubilee of the City and Guilds College. Apparatus added to the laboratory included some erected or made by workshop staff—a 10-ton Buckton testing-machine and apparatus to study fluid mechanics.

Pippard also took immediate action to have Structures and Hydraulics taught in the second year as well as Surveying, the only civil engineering subject previously taken by students opting for Civil Engineering. The addition of two or three hours a week in

	Lectures per week
Surveying	4
Engineering Construction	5
Hydraulics	2
Structures	2
Field Astronomy	1 (for 2 terms)
Quantities and Specifications	1 (for 2 terms)

Table 5: *Syllabus for third year students, 1934–35*

these subjects no doubt gave a better basis for the work of the third year. The third year lecture programme is shown in Table 5.

Pippard had as an undergraduate been introduced to the work of Castigliano on strain-energy methods of stress analysis and of Karl Pearson on masonry dams, and the influence of these brought a distinctly more 'modern' look to bear on the teaching of Structures.

The old postgraduate course in Structures was abandoned and students could select whole or partial courses among a range of subjects:

Advanced Theory of Structures
Advanced Theory of Hydraulics
Steel Construction
Reinforced Concrete Construction
Engineering Practice
Geology (taken in the Geology Department)
Timber (taken in the Botany Department)
Hydro-Electric plant (taken in the Electrical Engineering Department)
Surveying
Highway Engineering

The numbers attending in this pre-war period ranged between 21 and 26 per annum. Skempton, in his memoir of Pippard, says 'the lectures in structures and hydraulics were probably the most advanced and the most demanding of any being given in the country'.

Research under Pippard

Pippard was a keen research worker, constantly in the laboratory. With Miss Chitty he investigated topics such as stress distribution in disk wheels, a continuation of research on the loading of wheels begun at Cardiff, since, as he wrote, the wheel is 'one of the commonest units employed in engineering construction'. The same year, 1936, they published a paper in the *Proceedings of the Royal Society* on an experimental method for the solution of plane stress problems. With E. Tranter and Chitty, Pippard investigated stress in arches of the voussoir type, a subject which interested him since he believed the behaviour of this very common type of arch was not properly understood. He was to carry out work on it for a number of years. Committee work in

8. Tests on the voussoir arch, 1938

this period included membership of the newly constituted Research Committee of the Institution of Civil Engineers, and of the Sub-Committee of the Building Research Station on Wind Pressure Experiments. In 1935, he was appointed consultant to the Department of Scientific and Industrial Research to collaborate with the Ministry of Transport on the strength of existing bridges. One piece of research related to this was his work with J.P.A. de Waele in 1937 on the inter-connection of bridge girders. Pippard was also on the Accident Sub-Committee and the Structures Sub-Committee of the Aeronautical Research Council and one of the subjects investigated in this connection was an analysis, made with Sparkes, of rings used as stiffeners in aeroplane fuselage construction. Another, with Chitty, was on the effect of stiffened holes in a continuous sheet, an attack on the problem of monocoque aeroplane fuselage having holes for pilots' cockpits, and so on.

Pippard also produced in this period, in collaboration with J.F. Baker (subsequently Lord Baker of Windrush), his well-known book *The Analysis of Engineering Structures* (1936), now in its fourth edition. Baker had worked with him at Cardiff on research for the Aeronautical Research Council and became a life-long friend, succeeding Pippard at Bristol in 1933.

White with equal enthusiasm was improving the equipment in the Hydraulics Laboratory and supervising research on fluid motion and the effect of roughness; laminar and cavitating flow; and the design of fish ladders, the latter work undertaken for the Research Committee of the Institution of Civil Engineers. In 1936, this same committee asked him to investigate the forces due to wave action and in 1937 Major R.A. Bagnold was appointed as his assistant. The next few years were to see the emergence of some classic papers by Bagnold on the formation of sand dunes in the Libyan desert. Skempton writes of this period: 'Pippard and White almost lived in the laboratories, directing and carrying out research work and inspiring a love of scientific enquiry in the minds of those students willing and able to respond'. Skempton was in fact one of those students himself, taking a postgraduate course in 1935–36.

Work on road materials continued under Clements, assisted by Manton. In 1936, Clements was researching bituminous expansion jointing for reservoir walls (work undertaken for the Institution of Civil Engineers), and the use of rubber in highways, on behalf of the Rubber Growers' Association.

In 1936 and 1937 alone, 11 research degrees were awarded, and for the whole period 1934–39 there were 11 PhD and 27 MSc degrees.

The department seemed well set for a continuing and rapid expansion of its research activities. The declaration of war with Germany in 1939, however, and the consequent disruption for six years delayed for a decade the development so fruitfully established in Pippard's first years.

~ 5 ~

The Second World War, and post-war recovery, 1939–56

The Department in the Second World War

On the outbreak of war some of the members of staff departed on war service. Pippard had already in April 1939 been invited to join the Civil Defence Research Committee and on the commencement of hostilities he joined the Research and Experiments section at Princes Risborough. He and his family lived in Haddenham for the duration of the war, but from October 1940 he travelled to College four days a week to resume his teaching duties. Student numbers were less severely affected than in the first war as Engineering and Science students were allowed to complete their education before being called up. One curiosity of this concession was that the government refused to grant state bursaries to Civil Engineering students unless they took a course in Mechanical Engineering on heat engines instead of Geology. In practice, they seem to have done both, with no formal credit for the Geology. Undergraduate courses continued much as usual during the war, including the annual Surveying camp for second years. In 1942, the College was asked to admit Polish students whose engineering education had been interrupted by the war. Several of these took Civil Engineering and went on to have distinguished engineering careers. Postgraduate courses ceased altogether during the war.

In Pippard's absence from 1939–40, Rice-Oxley was in charge of the Department, but increasing ill-health obliged him to resign in 1942, three years before the statutory date for retirement. Chilton left in 1939 to become a Reader in Surveying at Oxford. Professor Clements was appointed Deputy Chief Engineer in the Ministry of Home Security and was engaged in the construction of deep shelters and in providing camouflage for the large reservoirs between Sheffield and Manchester. He reached retiring age before the end of the war and thus did not resume his appointment as Maybury Professor.

Sparkes was appointed an inspector in the Passive Air Defence Department of the Ministry of Supply and later became Research and Development Officer. He was largely concerned with the protection of vital plant at important factories and with the extensive war-time building carried out for the Ministry. He visited India at the request of the government as Structural Precautions Adviser and returned to the Supply Ministry as Senior Technical Officer. He was recalled to the College to resume his duties as lecturer in 1944.

Stephenson served with the RAF as chief instructor in the Allied Air Photo Interpretation Unit, for which work he was awarded the OBE. It led after the war to an invaluable contact with the major air survey companies.

Bagnold, a research assistant in 1937–38 and still closely associated with White's work, served as major in the Royal Corps of Signals and was mentioned in dispatches.

Research during the war

The facilities available in the civil engineering laboratories for testing and research were utilised by several government departments.

Pippard extended the work he had done pre-war on the voussoir arch by undertaking research for the Structural Engineering Committee of the Scientific Advisory Council of the Ministry of Supply on the carrying capacity of existing masonry and brickwork arch bridges. His research enabled him to compile tables for easy reference so that military personnel could assess safe loads, according to the span, thickness of arch ring, and depth of fill at crown. He and Miss Chitty went on to study the effect of propping a masonry arch as a temporary strengthening measure where bridges were too weak to carry military loads. Their investigation concluded that propping would serve no useful purpose and might introduce serious risk unless carefully controlled; alternative strengthening arrangements would be better. They also did further work on the voussoir arch to investigate the effects of repeated loads.

Pippard and Miss Chitty also carried out work for the Director of Scientific Research of the Admiralty to supplement research into the behaviour of submarine hulls subjected to underwater explosions. The work involved an experimental study of the behaviour of cylindrical shells when loaded beyond the plastic range by forces acting on a small area of the surface and under certain specified conditions of support. While waiting for the manufacture of test specimens, Pippard found small household milk and coffee tins and steel drums normally used for storing cement to be quite adequate for the tests. The main finding was that the stiffness of the end plates had a marked effect on the type of distortion. Work was also done by Pippard and Chitty on stresses in extensible suspension cables and the problems presented by cable bracing. Formulas were developed to allow the elastic stretch of the cable to be taken into account. Other structures work involved tests of pulley blocks for barrage balloons.

Research was undertaken in 1943 by White and Y.K. Gayed, a temporary lecturer, on model earth banks in the hope of discovering the rapidity with which a breached earth dam would release flood water. Model dams were constructed in glass-sided containers and subjected to the erosive action of flowing water so that the modes of failure could be studied. In some of these tests the collapse of the dam was filmed by cine-camera and each phase in the process examined by projecting the film on a large screen. This work had a bearing on the possible breach of the banks of reservoirs through bombing.

White also carried out work on the Mulberry Harbours, floating structures used in the Normandy landings. He also continued his own research on the influence of transported solids on rivers, on fish passes and on other fundamental problems of hydrodynamics.

The Highways Engineering Laboratory was constantly employed in carrying out tests on tarmacadam and asphalt used for airfield runways, and on cement-stabilised soil for the rapid construction of farm roads where new areas of land were being put into cultivation by the government to augment food supplies. An investigation into a rapid method of road construction by grouting with a mixture of cement and sand was carried out during a later part of the war period when damaged highways formed a hindrance to military movements.

Other war-time research included work on fog dispersal on airfields by air currents set up by flame heaters.

The possible evacuation of the City and Guilds College to Edinburgh was discussed, but decided against and the Department remained in London throughout the war. No direct damage was caused to the main building or to the Goldsmiths' Extension, but in September 1940 a high-explosive bomb 'of heavy calibre' dropped through the skylight of the boilerhouse in the Mechanical Engineering Department. Three members of workshop staff, including John Watt, a member of our staff, stayed there, with some courage, to prevent the flooding of the building if the bomb exploded, which fortunately did not happen. Another high-explosive bomb fell in the middle of Exhibition Road, causing a large crater and dislocating water-mains and other services, but it did no damage to the Waterhouse building. Other buildings in the area suffered—the east end of the Natural History Museum received a direct hit and the Bibliothèque Française at the corner of Prince Consort Road and Queen's Gate was completely demolished. A third year student was killed when his digs in Elvaston Place received a direct hit.

The basement beneath the Structures Laboratory was used as an air-raid shelter for staff and students. The students, with irrepressible high spirits, greeted the abrupt termination of a lecture with glee and occupied their time in the shelter by employing the buckets of water and stirrup pumps with which the basement was liberally provided as offensive weapons.

Security precautions at one stage of the war reached absurd heights. No-one was allowed to enter the College without carrying a gas-mask and showing the door-keeper an identity card. Manton recalls how he arrived one morning at the entrance to the Waterhouse building without these two essential items. 'The commissionaire at the door,' he writes, 'was an ex-naval petty officer who had seen him arrive every day during term-time for at least twenty years, but the ingrained discipline of the Royal Navy was not to be lightly discarded and orders must be obeyed. Permission to enter was firmly refused and no arguments had the slightest effect. A freely accessible entrance to the Structures laboratory in the College backyard, however, was found to be unguarded and unlocked, and here, it must be confessed, an illegal entry was successfully made.'

Manton also recalled an examiners' meeting with flying bombs passing overhead. Professor C.L. Fortescue of the Electrical Engineering Department was in the chair, and, after opening the proceedings, announced with his characteristic dignity that should imminent danger occur those present should take cover as quickly as possible beneath the table. Fortunately this did not prove necessary.

It is not known exactly how many staff and students, past and present, of the City and Guilds College were on active service, but a large number were, and 115 are known to have died.

Post-war development, 1945–56

Immediately after the war, courses resumed as before. First priority for admission was given to ex-servicemen and scholarship holders. On the first year course in 1946–47, of the 62 admitted, only 1 was a school-leaver; 58 were ex-service students and 3 were ex-industry. The second year course that year contained 26 students, 25 of them ex-service and 1 ex-industry.

Up to this time degree examinations were taken in two stages, Part I at the end of second year and Part II at the end of third. War-time conditions shortened all undergraduate courses to two years for suitably qualified candidates. In 1946 new regulations added a third year course to Parts I and II, but the old regulations remained in force for ex-service personnel until 1951. Entrants after 1946 had the General Certificate of Education at Advanced Level or equivalent qualifications and it was therefore possible for students to take Part I at the end of first year instead of second. The first year course was completely common for all Engineering students; for this reason, Structures and Surveying were dropped from it. The new Part III had no written examinations and the Department had considerable freedom to devise courses and make changes. The situation is summarised as follows:

Old regulations (1913–1940)	*Marks*		*New regulations (post–1946)*	*Marks*	
	Exams.	*Coursework*		*Exams.*	*Coursework*
Intermediate	—	—			
2nd year, Pt I	600	400	1st year, Pt I	600	400
3rd year, Pt II	960	640	2nd year, Pt II	960	640
			3rd year, Pt III	—	1400
TOTAL	2600			4000	

The common first year course operated in the Engineering Departments from 1946 until 1965. The subjects studied are shown in Table 6.

Of the pre-war staff those still there in 1945 were Pippard, Sparkes, White, Chitty, Manton and Stephenson. It was therefore imperative to take on more staff, in particular to increase the number of senior staff. Pippard was also keen to encourage the development of special interests and to establish new areas of research.

In the established Sections of Structures, Hydraulics and Sur-

	ASSESSMENT BY EXAMINATION	
PART I (1000 marks)	Mathematics (2) Applied Mechanics (2) Applied Heat Engineering Drawing Applied Electricity	
PART II (1600 marks)	Mathematics Strength of Materials Theory of Structures Fluid Mechanics & Hydraulic Engineering Surveying Geology Civil Engineering I Civil Engineering II	
PART III (1400 marks)	*ASSESSMENT BY PROJECTS AND COURSEWORK*	
	Compulsory subjects: Theory of Structures Engineering Construction Properties of Engineering Materials	
	Options: Fluid Mechanics Soil Mechanics Concrete Technology	 Air Surveying Highway Engineering Mathematics Steelwork Design

Graduates classified as First or Second Class Honours or Pass

Table 6. *Degree subjects under the new regulations, 1947–1948*

veying, he took on more staff, but the Chair of Highway Engineering remained vacant. In the Hydraulics Section, a new university Chair of Fluid Mechanics and Hydraulic Engineering was established in 1945 and deservedly conferred on White in recognition of his important work on friction in closed circuits, sediment transport and scour. In 1946 the English Electric Company provided generous financial support for a postgraduate course in Hydro-Power, and this ran for several years with the assistance of two Special Lecturers, Dr C. Jaeger and J.M. Gray, both distinguished engineers in this field.

In 1947, the College had the opportunity to acquire a new Life Sciences Field Station at Silwood Park near Ascot. This replaced a smaller field station at Slough which had been in use since 1928. At Silwood Park, an estate of 240 acres was available, primarily for the use of Life Sciences staff and students, but also accessible to other groups in the College for practical work. The Surveying camp for second year students was held there for the first time in 1947.

Up to the 1939–45 war, building in structural steelwork dominated the construction industry in this country for the main framework in buildings. Subjects such as the theory of structures were taught largely in terms of steelwork. However, in the 1930s some architects and a few engineers, particularly those who had settled from the Continent, specialised in the structural use of reinforced concrete in the new architecture. The use of reinforced concrete for a complete building required a modification and development of design methods both in theory and construction.

The war period saw an immense increase in the use of reinforced concrete for every conceivable form of structure, both here and on the Continent, where the use of pre-stressed concrete also began.

Thus when in the 1943–44 session, an offer was made to the

9. A. L. L. Baker, Professor of Concrete Technology, 1945–73

10. F. E. Bruce, Head of Public Health Engineering Section, 1949–77

College by the Cement Makers' Federation to establish for ten years in the first instance a Chair of Concrete Technology, Pippard was eager to accept on behalf of the Department. Provision of bursaries of £200 p.a. each was made by eleven building and civil engineering contractors. The first holder of the chair in 1945 was A.L.L. Baker, a graduate of Manchester University who had had several years' experience as an engineer. He had been an assistant engineer on the Mersey Tunnel, and had spent several years abroad in Nigeria and Johannesburg. His book *Raft Foundations* had been published in 1937. His first postgraduate course was given in 1946–47.

Soil Mechanics developed much later than most other branches of engineering science. Terzaghi's principle of effective stress, which unifies the modern subject, was not elucidated until 1923, and only began to be applied to practical engineering in the 1930s, mainly in the United States. The first development of engineering significance in Britain was the founding of a laboratory at the Building Research Station in 1933. The subject was taught at undergraduate level in only one or two universities; Glasgow and Sheffield had courses from 1939.

Pippard was well aware of the importance of the new subject. He had played a major part in inviting Terzaghi to give the James Forrest Lecture at the Institution of Civil Engineers in 1939, which greatly increased interest in Britain. The Second World War then constrained further development, but in 1945 Pippard invited A.W. Skempton to give undergraduate classes as a visiting lecturer. Skempton had graduated from the Department in 1935 and taken an MSc in Concrete in 1936. In 1936 he had joined the small pioneering group at the Building Research Station and by 1946 he was already an established figure in the subject. Skempton joined the staff permanently in 1946, with the purpose of starting the first university Soil Mechanics School in Britain. He became Reader in 1947, and in 1955 he was appointed to the first chair in this country in this subject. The first postgraduate course was given in 1950–51.

The establishment of a Public Health Engineering Section resulted from an initiative of the International Health Division of the Rockefeller Foundation, which was anxious to extend teaching in this field to countries throughout the world. Long experience of Sanitary Engineering in American universities had shown that a thorough grasp of this interdisciplinary study could best be obtained by qualified engineers taking specialised postgraduate courses, preferably after a few years' practical experience. Although British engineers were pioneers in the development of the techniques of water supply and waste disposal, universities in Britain had, in the main, limited their teaching to short general courses at undergraduate level. Such courses did not give an adequate understanding of the chemical and biological processes involved, and by the 1940s large numbers of overseas students were being attracted to the American universities to study Sanitary Engineering.

Following a visit by Professor Gordon Fair of Harvard University to London, the Rockefeller Foundation afforded finance for three years to enable a postgraduate course to be set up jointly by Imperial College and the London School of Hygiene and Tropical Medicine.

To organise the proposed course, Pippard sounded out some of his former students, and the offer was taken up by F.E. Bruce, a graduate of the Department in 1936 with experience in municipal engineering and war service in the Royal Engineers. With a Rockefeller Foundation Fellowship he followed the Master's degree course in Sanitary Engineering at Harvard under Professor Fair during 1948–49, and on returning to the College in September 1949 was appointed Rockefeller Fellow in Public Health Engineering.

The Rockefeller Foundation provided finance for three years to pay the salaries of Bruce and of a part-time tutor, Dr R.F. Guymer, at the London School of Hygiene. The Foundation also gave funds for the purchase of laboratory equipment and books. Laboratory accommodation was made available in one small bay partitioned off from the City and Guilds Library on the top floor of the Goldsmiths' Extension. The equipment installed was sufficient for simple chemical analysis and some experiments on water treatment processes. Later, in the summer of 1951, an additional bay of the Library was made available, and a properly equipped chemical bench was installed. The postgraduate course began with 8 students in the session 1950–51.

Also under Pippard's administration came the establishment of a special study area in Hydrology. This followed the appointment of P.O. Wolf in 1949 as a lecturer in the Hydraulics Section. Wolf had had considerable experience in land drainage and coastal defence works, flood relief schemes and large hydro-electric projects. He had been for two years the Chief Designer to the Consulting Chief Engineer of the Scottish Hydro-Electric Board. About this time, the scope of the subject was being defined by the newly published textbooks produced by American civil engineers, but it was the Dobbie and Wolf studies of the Lynmouth Flood, in August 1952, which gave an impetus to the study of Hydrology in the United Kingdom. The post-war development of the emerging nations of the Commonwealth and the growth of water demand in the home country required a better evaluation of water resources. Wolf's appointment and hydrological expertise led to the initiation of both undergraduate and advanced training in the subject within the Department. A one-year full-time postgraduate course of instruction in Engineering Hydrology was offered for the first time in October 1955.

Pippard's research

Pippard's own work shows him still involved in experimental work and analysis. Some of the same topics recurred: the voussoir arch, for example, but he was also involved in important work with Sparkes and J.C. Chapman (a research assistant appointed in 1948) on the flexure of rectangular box girders of thin steel plating. This was the start of an important period of experimental work on the strength of ships' hulls for the British Ship Research Association.

Pippard also collaborated with Z.S. Makowski, a lecturer appointed in 1951, on analysis of braced domes, structures which posed a challenge to the structural engineer because of the difficulty of analysing them by conventional methods. The Dome of Discovery built for the Festival of Britain in 1951 was an example of such a structure. A model of it, 10 ft in diameter, was constructed in the laboratory and subjected to experimental stress analysis.

Of particular value was the work by Pippard in this period employing model dams. Pippard, in collaboration with Chitty, D. Allen and R.T. Severn, undertook mathematical and experimental analyses of the Dokan Dam, a large concrete arch dam in Iraq. The Dokan Dam was the first of its kind to be subjected to a rigorous analysis using the method of 'relaxation' devised by R.V. Southwell and the work was undertaken in collaboration with the Relaxation Group of the Department of Mathematics. It led to an interest in computational methods, which has continued ever since, and also marked the start of a new epoch in arch dam research, given focus in 1958 by the formation of the Arch Dams Committee of the Institution of Civil Engineers.

In April 1951 Pippard was appointed Chairman of the Thames Survey Committee set up by the Ministry of Local Government to report on the pollution of the tidal Thames. The scientific investigations of the hydraulics and chemistry of a stretch of water nearly 70 miles in length, which receives both domestic and industrial effluent from many sources, took many years. It was 1964 before the final report was made, containing recommendations to improve the river radically, a process that has gone on since with marked success.

Pippard's last years in the chair were happy ones and he received many honours. He was elected FRS in 1954 and was Pro-Rector of Imperial College in 1955–56. He had been on the Council of the Institution of Civil Engineers since 1944 and became President in 1958–59; he received the James Alfred Ewing Gold Medal in 1964, the highest award the Institution of Civil Engineers can give in recognition of research. At the age of seventy-five, he was awarded honorary degrees at Bristol and Birmingham Universities. The last meeting he attended at the Institution on 21 October 1969 was on the occasion of the presentation to Miss Chitty, his lifelong collaborator, of the Telford Gold Medal. This acknowledgement of her work gave him great pleasure. He died a fortnight later, aged seventy-eight.

'Letty'

Miss Chitty ('Letty') was a familiar figure in the Department for almost fifty years and it would be wrong not to leave some memoir of her. The work she did with Southwell and later Pippard on analysis of aircraft structures was very unusual for a woman in that period and her election as a Fellow of the Royal Aeronautical Society also very distinctive. Her own modesty and shyness, as well as the conditioning of the period in which she lived, made her content to remain in the background, glad to be of use but seeking no acknowledgement for herself. Her intense concentration often made her absent-minded and unaware of the passing of time, and she alone (maybe) would have been able to find anything in the piles of papers which covered every surface in her room. When she retired, Professor Pippard was invited to present the Department's gift to her—a self-winding wristwatch—which he observed to her affectionately she would find very useful. Her air of abstraction, however, could be instantly dispelled by anyone asking for help and those who did so found in her a kind and generous person eager to be of assistance, particularly if it would advance the cause of knowledge. She was a compulsive attender of evening lectures, interested in a wide variety of subjects ranging over the arts and sciences. She spoke several languages fluently and was also a skilled field botanist. Her little book, *An Alphabet of Flowers*, contains holiday reminiscences and beautifully painted flower studies. Retirement made no difference to her and she continued to attend College daily until she was over eighty. She died in 1982, aged eighty-five, generously bequeathing to the Department over £5,000, with which the Chitty Reading Room, an extension of the Departmental Library, is to be developed

'Pip'

Pippard ('Pip') was held in affectionate regard by his colleagues. A business-like and efficient administrator, he was nevertheless a warm and approachable man, interested in the details of other people's work and their problems. He set a high standard and was intolerant of slackness, but full of encouragement for those who wished to learn. His wit in the class-room and ability as a teacher were admired by students. As his obituary notice in the Proceedings of the Institution of Civil Engineers says, 'He had the supreme art of making it all sound simple, masking the amount of hard slog that prefaced his apparently effortless delivery'. Skempton in his memoir of him for the Royal Society draws attention to Pippard's last major publication on 'Elastic theory and engineering structures' given to the Institution in 1961, and writes, 'In this he shows total mastery of the art of lucid exposition in the subject to which he had contributed so much and by the teaching of which he greatly enhanced the intellectual content of university engineering education'. He left behind a department which had become during his headship the leading postgraduate school of civil engineering in the country, with the pattern for its future development clearly established.

A former student recalls the attention Pippard gave to his lectures which were carefully prepared and presented, his blackboards a model of neatness and clarity. On one occasion, after apologising to a class for the fact that he had had a cold the week before which might have affected his performance, he insisted on giving the whole lecture again. On another occasion a student phrased a question in such a way as to imply that the professor might be wrong. When Pippard began to argue the point, the student showed signs of surrender, but was urged by Pippard to stand his ground. He believed that if a person thought he was right, he should not be intimidated by the superior rank of others.

~ 6 ~

Expansion and specialisation, 1957–1983

Professor A. W. Skempton, 1957–76

Pippard was succeeded in 1957 by Alec Westley Skempton who had, as seen earlier, been invited by Pippard in 1946 to establish a new Section in Soil Mechanics, and in 1955 been appointed to the new Chair of Soil Mechanics. Two years later he was appointed to the headship of the Department. The increasing volume of administrative work led to the creation at the same date of the post of Assistant Director, and R. J. Ashby, Reader in Civil Engineering, was appointed to it, a post he held until 1977, when he retired. Skempton was to retain the headship until 1976, a period of rapid expansion and development, associated with the move to our new, and present, building in 1963.

The new building

An important date in the history of the College was 29 January 1953 when the government announced in the House of Commons its intention to provide a major expansion of Imperial College. Since the end of the war, students numbers had increased rapidly from 1100 to 1650, creating pressure on space and inhibiting the development of some branches of research. The College thus had the opportunity to produce a unified long-term proposal for expansion, which was called the Jubilee Plan.

Among the schemes for producing additional accommodation in the Department, a proposal at that time from Pippard as Dean was that an additional floor could be built without too much disturbance on the top of the Goldsmiths' Extension. The structural details suggested by Sparkes were accepted and carried out in the long vacation of 1953. Sparkes was subsequently seconded from the Department to take charge of the College Planning Office from 1953, and to become Director of Building Works from 1955–58.

The Jubilee Plan envisaged separate buildings for each Department with nearly all the premises on the central site being acquired for re-development in a phased programme that would involve the minimum disruption of academic work.

11. The new building, 1963 (*photograph by J. Jarvis & Sons, plc*)

A vacant strip of land and the demolition of two large lecture theatres with drawing offices above enabled a start to be made on the central section of the new Mechanical Engineering Building immediately behind the old Waterhouse building. Simultaneously the northern wing of the Imperial Institute and the miscellaneous outbuildings of the Office of Works were demolished to provide the sites for the Civil Engineering and Electrical Engineering buildings.

The architects for the Jubilee Scheme, Norman and Dawbarn, took a basic decision to work to a rectangular grid of 5 ft 6 in modules and as far as possible to unify floor levels throughout the central site. The façades of the School of Mines and the Goldsmiths' Extension and the structure of these buildings were to be retained, which meant that the Civil Engineering Department was undisturbed pending the completion of the new building.

The College gave each department a fairly free hand to make its own proposals within the restrictions on size which were mutually agreed. Greville Rhodes of Norman and Dawbarn had many meetings with Skempton and Ashby to formulate the requirements of the Department. One such requirement was for a

12. Professor White welcomes H.R.H. The Duke of Edinburgh to the new Hydraulics Laboratory, 12 July 1962 (*From left to right:* F. W. G. Annas, M. J. Davies, Sir Patrick Linstead, Sir Roger Makins, Mr Orr (detective), Prof. O. A. Saunders, the Duke, R. J. Ashby, Prof. A. W. Skempton, Prof. C. M. White, student usher)

limitation to not more than six levels to reduce lift waiting time. Another proposal was for the Hydraulics, Structures and Concrete Laboratories to be on the lower floors and the Soil Mechanics and Public Health Laboratories on the upper.

The Universities Grants Committee initially allowed 150 sq ft for a lecturer's room, 225 sq ft for a reader and 300 sq ft for a professor. An easier way to express this was to count the number of windows as a measure of one's status: four for a professor, three for a reader and two for lecturers and secretaries! Most restrictive was the allowance of 3.5 sq ft per student for lecture theatres inclusive of gangways, and so on. This meant that no arrangement of lecture theatres could cope with variations of class sizes and it was always recognised that drawing-offices would need to be used for lectures. The department was fortunate in that the UGC was looking to the College for guidance in setting norms for drawing-offices and laboratories. A drawing-office norm of 35 sq ft per student was accepted and no restrictions were placed on laboratories within the overall limit for the building as a whole. The only curtailment that was imposed on the final plans was a cut of 10% in the excavation for the tanks below the Hydraulics Laboratory.

The UGC allocated funds for the complete equipping and furnishing of the new building and very little of the old laboratory equipment was transferred from the Goldsmiths' building.

An L-shaped building of 44 ft width of leg was adopted to enclose a rectangular area for the large laboratories. At level 0, a large rectangular area was to be reserved for heating services, the larger laboratories, stores for materials delivered via hoppers at street level and minimum circulation areas. At level 1, an entrance hall for lifts, staircase and porter's desk. At level 2, lecture theatres mainly for undergraduates with circulation space and facilities to enable public lectures to be given and small exhibitions be arranged. At level 3, two undergraduate drawing-offices each for 60 places, staff rooms and postgraduate offices associated with Hydraulics and Concrete. At level 4, the Library and staff common room, staff and postgraduate offices for Structures. At level 5, Public Health and Soils Laboratories with 15 ft headroom, administration and staff rooms, and postgraduate offices. At level 6, offices and laboratories for Building Science, Transport and Surveying. To these requirements were added a goods lift at the east end and a concentration of passenger lifts, toilets on each floor, fire escape routes and service shafts at the angle of the L.

In essence these requirements were fully met in the building when completed, built by J. Jarvis & Sons, plc. Some extra benefits emerged as the detailed planning of the laboratories proceeded. The leg of the building facing directly on to Imperial Institute Road would link with Mechanical Engineering over a roadway serving the delivery area. The other leg would link with Electrical Engineering and by means of its northern staircase would provide a fire escape route. At level 2, windows from the area outside the two smaller lecture theatres would give a view into the upper part of the Structures Laboratory.

When the general shape of the building had been outlined, the Sections commenced formulation of specific requirements. The Department had succeeeded in obtaining approval for the provision and equipment of workshops sufficiently sophisticated to handle the manufacture of large models and other items for research projects.

Room 101, now a drawing-office, was originally intended for a model structures laboratory with a grid pattern of floor anchorages and socket outlets. Very heavy (and costly) floors were required for the major laboratories—Structures, Concrete and Hydraulics.

The long corridors were originally broken up by small waiting areas which had access to a balcony. Unfortunately such areas are early casualties when pressure for additional room becomes too great.

A few errors of judgement both architectural and technical were revealed when the new building was occupied. A visitor tried to walk through the large glass panels in the entrance hall. Repetition of the accident was avoided by the purchase of a reel of gold-coloured Sellotape! Mosaic has proved unsatisfactory as an external finish, and the sunshine record in Imperial Institute Road has not justified the provision of a 'brille-soleil' along the front of the building instead of a canopy against the rain.

One last item may be forgotten if unrecorded. At one time the estimates included £4,000 for a piece of statuary by the main

13. The visit of H.R.H. the Princess Margaret and Lord Snowdon, 8 October 1963 (*From left to right:* Professor A. W. Skempton, Professor S. R. Sparkes, Her Royal Highness, Lord Snowdon, Sir Owen Saunders, Sir Patrick Linstead)

entrance. It never materialised, but we have there instead a test prototype of a cast steel tubular node for an offshore jacket structure. This is on loan from the British Steel Corporation—not exactly the artistic work envisaged, but perhaps an apt symbol of the nature of the activity conducted within.

The entrance hall itself has been embellished by the photographs of bridges commissioned from Eric de Maré, mounted to occupy an entire wall in the vestibule. Throughout the rest of the building there are other enlarged photographs by de Maré of engineering works, strategically placed on staircases and landings.

Our move into the new building in April 1963 is still remembered by some of the present staff. It went reasonably well if you consider what could have gone wrong. Some academic staff never recovered from the disturbance of the strata of papers and books in their rooms in the old building, but the move provided an admirable opportunity to leave unanswered, for ever, certain academic correspondence in the pending tray!

Departmental developments

The structure of the Department into specialised Sections continued under Skempton. The established ones continued to expand as funds became available for additional staff. In 1958, a Chair of Engineering Structures was created and Sparkes was the obvious choice. 'Sammy' had by then served in every grade from demonstrator upwards. His service during the war and his important role in the planning of the College's expansion have been mentioned.

In 1962 Manton retired and the opportunity presented itself to rationalise the postgraduate course in Highway Engineering. The soil-testing element of it could be incorporated into the work of the Soil Mechanics Section and the traffic design work just beginning to be undertaken in the late 1950s could be taken over and expanded in a new Transport Section. A new Chair of Transport was created and conferred on C. D. (later Sir Colin) Buchanan in 1963. A graduate of the College, Buchanan had spent several years in the Ministry of Transport pre-war and the war years in the Royal Engineers, with mention in dispatches. From 1946 till 1961 he was in the Ministry of Town and Country Planning, and from 1961 till 1963 was Urban Planning Adviser in the Ministry of Transport. His celebrated report, *Traffic in Towns*, was published just at the time that he took up his appointment at Imperial College.

14. A. W. Bishop, Professor of Soil Mechanics, 1965–80

15. J. R. D. Francis, Professor of Hydraulics, 1966–79

In 1965, A. W. Bishop was appointed to fill the Chair of Soil Mechanics which had been vacant since Skempton's promotion as Head of Department in 1957, when he became Professor of Civil Engineering. A Cambridge graduate, Bishop had been in engineering practice with the Metropolitan Water Board. His interest in soil mechanics subsequently brought him to Imperial College to work on the stress analysis of embankment dams under Southwell. He was appointed to the Soil Mechanics Section of the Department in 1946 and became Reader in 1957.

In 1966 White retired from the Chair of Fluid Mechanics and Hydraulic Engineering which he had held since 1946. Under him much fundamental research had been carried out, as the number of research degrees in fluid mechanics testifies. He had developed the potential of the Hydraulics Laboratory in the Goldsmiths' Extension and had played a large role in the design of the Hydraulics Laboratory in the new building. His achievement had been the particular insight he showed in trying to bridge the gap between theory and engineering practice. His successor was J. R. D. Francis, who had been in his team from 1946 to 1961. Francis's background included experience in the Miscellaneous

Weapons Development of the Admiralty during the war, and this no doubt contributed to his special interest in waves. After a period of five years in the Chair of Municipal Engineering at the University of Manchester, he returned to College to succeed White.

Skempton was anxious to promote a high standard of teaching and research and to foster and reward excellence. During his tenure of office, a number of conferred titles were awarded in different fields, and these are listed in Appendix A. The title of Professor of Structural Analysis was conferred on E. H. Brown in 1971 in recognition of his contributions to structural mechanics over a period of many years after his appointment to the staff in 1948. He later had the distinction of serving as Dean from 1979–82. In 1973, the title of Professor of Engineering Seismology was conferred on Ambraseys in acknowledgement of his international reputation as a seismologist. The title of Reader had been introduced in the College in 1930 and eventually replaced that of Assistant Professor, although the title of Assistant Professor and Reader were held simultaneously at first. Fourteen readerships were awarded under Skempton.

Apart from the growth in the number of senior staff there was a rapid overall expansion of the Department as part of government policy for Imperial College. The establishment inherited by Skempton in 1957 comprised 4 professors, 3 readers, 16 lecturers, and 26 members of support staff, technical and secretarial, a total in all of 49.

By October 1963, when the first session in the new building opened, there were 5 professors, 10 readers, 2 senior lecturers, 2 research fellows, 19 lecturers, 2 assistant lecturers, 39 technicians and 11 library and secretarial staff—a total overall of 90—almost a doubling in six years.

Three new Sections developed as a result of special interests and expertise in existing members of staff. These were in Timber Structures and Technology, Engineering Seismology, and Systems and Mechanics. All came into being in response to particular needs in the profession.

L. G. Booth, a lecturer in the Structures Section since 1963, was an Oxford graduate who had taken his PhD degree in the Concrete Technology Section of the Department in 1954. His later experience included work for the Timber Development Association in their newly established laboratories. Booth's interest in timber engineering and its importance in many overseas countries gave a relevance to the development of a special course, which was given at postgraduate level for the first time in 1965–66.

An Engineering Seismology Section was established by N. N. Ambraseys in 1967. Ambraseys was a graduate of the National Technical University of Athens and had taken his PhD degree in the Soil Mechanics Section in 1959 on the seismic stability of dams. His research on seismic problems led to his founding and becoming the first Chairman of the British National Committee for Earthquake Engineering at the Institution of Civil Engineers in 1965, and this, combined with his appointment shortly afterwards as one of the six directors of the International Association of Earthquake Engineering, brought his work and the importance of the subject to the fore. A postgraduate course was first given in 1967–68.

A few years later, in 1971, J. Munro, a senior lecturer in the Concrete Technology Section, formed the Civil Engineering Systems and Mechanics Section. Munro, a graduate of Glasgow University, had had practical experience with Ove Arup and Partners before attending a postgraduate course in Concrete Structures in the Department, followed by a period of research on cylindrical shells. Appointed to the staff in 1957, his interests had gradually focussed on Systems Engineering, concerned with civil engineering decision-making. When in 1971, at the end of the first year common course, the responsibility for teaching Mechanics to first year students devolved on the Department, and at the same time the Computer Centre gave up its role of teaching Computing to our students, the time was ripe for the development of a new Section which could meet the requirements of these two course elements. Munro's interest in Systems and the application of Systems to the teaching of Structural Mechanics placed him in an admirable position to take on the leadership of the new Civil Engineering Systems and Mechanics Section.

In 1971 Stephenson retired from the Surveying Section, which he had organised since 1946. He was made a reader in 1947. He was involved for a number of years as Admissions Tutor, became Senior Tutor to the City and Guilds College from 1958–61, and Senior Warden from 1961–71. The latter appointment was associated with the period of expansion and was not repeated after 1971. It involved considerable committee work as indicated by the posts Stephenson held: Chairman of the following committees—Refectory, Athletics, Car Parking, Exploration Board—and Secretary of the Athletic Ground Committee. It was during this period that the new halls of residence were being designed and built and as Chairman of the Wardens' Committee, Stephenson had to devote considerable time and thought to administrative policies.

In his place, B. Chiat joined the staff as a senior lecturer in 1972. Originally from South Africa, where he had been a land surveyor both in private practice and with a local authority, Chiat taught at University College, London before his appointment to the Department.

Geology continued to be taught by the Geology Department in the Royal School of Mines. The field trip at Easter was established by this era as part of the second year course, with much enjoyed geological fieldwork in the Lake District, Yorkshire and similar locations, led by members of the Geology Department staff, under the direction for many years of Blyth, previously mentioned, until 1964, and later J. L. Knill.

In 1972 Buchanan retired from the Chair of Transport. His nine years in the Section had established a new approach to transportation engineering, one novel in its emphasis on consideration of environmental impact. Among honours bestowed on him, he became CBE in 1964 and a knight in 1972.

In 1973 two events brought about an interruption in the even tenor of the Department's life, affecting two of the principal sec-

16. Sir Colin Buchanan, Professor of Transport, 1963–72

17. Sir Alan Harris, Professor of Concrete Structures and Technology, 1973–81

tions, Structures and Concrete. Increasing blindness, against which he fought resolutely and with characteristic cheerfulness, induced Sparkes to resign prematurely from the Chair of Engineering Structures. His long service in the Department and fifteen-year tenure of the chair had consolidated and extended the work begun under Pippard. An important achievement was his realisation that meaningful results could be obtained only through experimental work on a sufficiently large scale to reproduce constructional imperfections in the members being tested. In the Structures Laboratory, which he himself had planned, he introduced extensive facilities for testing and developed skills in his team of technicians which are probably unrivalled anywhere in the world. The large-scale testing now possible owes everything to his foresight and administrative skills. His role in the early day of the College has been noted. He was Dean from 1964–67 and was a very active President of the Rugby Football Club. The death of this ebullient and vital personality on 9 February 1976 was felt with deep sadness in the Department.

The vacant chair was taken by Professor B. G. Neal, a member of the Imperial College staff from 1961, but based in the Department of Mechanical Engineering where he held the title of Professor of Applied Science (with special reference to Engineering). Bernard George Neal took his degree in Cambridge, and after the interruption of the war, in which he was an Experimental Officer with the Admiralty, he returned to Cambridge and took his PhD degree in 1948. He remained in Cambridge on the teaching staff until 1954 and was elected a Fellow of Trinity Hall. From there he accepted the newly established Chair of Civil Engineering at University College, Swansea, and was there until his appointment to Imperial College. One of his main tasks was the organisation of the first year common course until 1971 when it ceased. He was also Dean from 1964–67. In his special field of structural engineering, he had already in 1956 published *The Plastic Methods of Structural Analysis*, a book which has become a classic and been translated into several languages, including Russian. He also published *Structural Theorems and their Applications* in 1964.

Simultaneously with Sparkes' retirement, Baker retired from the Chair of Concrete Technology. His twenty-eight years in the chair had covered the post-war period of large-scale building in reinforced and prestressed concrete, and under his direction a specialist team had been assembled. The Section had become renowned worldwide and attracted a large number of postgraduate students to it. Baker had published a number of important books during his years in the chair: *Reinforced Concrete* (1949); *The Ultimate Load Theory Applied to the Design of Reinforced and Pre-stressed Concrete Frames* (1956); *The Inelastic Space Frame* (1967); *Limit State Design of Reinforced Concrete* (1970). He was made an Honorary ACGI and received an Hon DTech from Bradford University in 1971.

Baker's place was taken by A. J. Harris, a practising consulting engineer. A London graduate, Harris had fought in the Royal Engineers during the war and been involved, for example, in the design of the Mulberry Harbours; he was awarded the Croix de Guerre in 1945 for his war service. He then spent three years with Eugène Freyssinet in Paris studying prestressing, and this interest led to his becoming a Director of the Prestressed Concrete Com-

	UNIVERSITY EXAMINATIONS
PART I	Mathematics (2)
(800 marks)	Applied Mechanics (2)
	Applied Heat
	Engineering Drawing
	Applied Electricity
PART II	Mathematics
(1600 marks)	Strength of Materials
	Theory of Structures
	Fluid Mechanics & Hydraulic Engineering
	Surveying
	Geology
	Civil Engineering I
	Civil Engineering II
PART III	*COURSEWORK EXAMINATIONS*
(2400 marks)	Engineering Economics (LSE)
	Engineering Construction
	Geology
	Concrete
	Timber
	Metallurgy
	Air Surveying

Second Class Honours divided
Coursework examinations introduced into the Third Year

Table 7 *Examinable subjects, BSc (Eng), 1957–58*

pany from 1949–55. He then formed his own private practice and was later joined by his brother, J. D. Harris, and R. J. M. Sutherland—the original directors of the firm of Harris and Sutherland.

Undergraduate courses continued in the pattern set down in the new regulations of 1946, but some important innovations occurred. In 1957–58 the marks for Part III were awarded for examinations as well as coursework, and second class honours was divided into upper and lower classes for the first time. The examinable subjects in 1957–58 are summarised in Table 7. The common course for Engineering students continued with only a few minor changes in 1965, but from October 1971 first year students were housed in the Department instead of in the Department of Mechanical Engineering. There was therefore an opportunity to create a first year course for Part I more specifically suited to Civil Engineering students. Some of the subjects were the same as before, but with a stronger Civil Engineering bias (Table 8). A course on Civil Engineering Materials was introduced, and the teaching of Applied Mechanics was reformed. Whereas before, one part of the course had been taught in the Department of Mechanical Engineering and the other by Civil Engineering staff, both were now taught in the Civil Engineering Department. A new course in Engineering Mechanics given by the staff of the newly formed Systems and Mechanics Section replaced the part originally taken in the Department of Mechanical Engineering; the other part continued to be taught in the Department but under the description Structural Mechanics. Some teaching of Thermodynamics continued and was given as part of the Fluid Mechanics course. A further novelty was the introduction of a course entitled Engineering and the Environment, although this subject did not form part of Part I examinations until the 1977–78 session. Its purpose is to introduce students to the idea that the engineer does not work in isolation from his environment or the impact he has on it. A new Section, entitled Environmental Studies, was created under T. A. Wyatt, a lecturer in Structures (subsequently a reader).

Between 1978 and 1984 second year students were also able to choose an optional course from a range offered by an interdepartmental group, the Department of Associated Studies (now Department of Humanities), selecting from Literature, History, French, Music, Economics, Philosophy, History of Engineering, and so on.

From 1964–65, the MSc degree was awarded on one-year examined courses and the old MSc (Eng) given for research disappeared

	UNIVERSITY EXAMINATIONS
PART I	Civil Engineering Materials
(800 marks)	Electricity
	Engineering Mechanics
	Mathematics
	Fluid Mechanics & Thermodynamics (2)
	Structural Mechanics
PART II	Geology
(1600 marks)	Hydraulics
	Mathematics (2)
	Soil Mechanics
	Strength of Materials & Theory of Vibrations
	Surveying
	Theory of Structures
PART III	*COURSEWORK EXAMINATIONS*
(2400 marks)	*Compulsory*
	Engineering Economy
	Engineering Materials
	Soil Mechanics
	Theory of Structures or Hydraulics
	Transport
	One of the following pairs of subjects:
	Engineering Hydrology & Public Health Engineering
	Advanced Engineering Geology & Rock Mechanics
	Mechanics & Systems Engineering
	Metallurgy & Timber Structures and Technology

Common First Year Course abolished

Table 8. *Examinable subjects, BSc (Eng), 1971–72*

and was replaced by the degree of MPhil for two years' research. The postgraduate courses available throughout the history of the Department are shown in Fig. 3.

It seems best to review the development of postgraduate courses and research in the period after 1945 to the present time as a unified account and this follows in the next chapter.

'Skem'

In 1976 Skempton ('Skem') resigned from the headship of the Department to devote himself without distraction to a research career which had gone on unabated from his appointment to the College. His contribution to the science of Soil Mechanics is outlined in the next chapter and he has received many public acknowledgements of his distinction as a scholar and engineer—FRS in 1961, the James Alfred Ewing Medal of the Institution of Civil Engineers in 1968, election to the Fellowship of Engineering in 1976, and honorary degrees from Durham (1968), Aston (1980) and Chalmers University, Sweden (1982). Two awards in 1981 gave him particular pleasure—the Karl Terzaghi Award of the American Society of Civil Engineers and a Gold Medal of the Institution of Structural Engineers. He was a member of Council of the Institution of Civil Engineers from 1949–54 and Vice-President from 1974–76. His contributions to Engineering Geology were recognised in the award of the Lyell Medal of the Geological Society in 1972.

From quite early in his career Skempton developed a particular interest in the history of engineering and has added immensely to the corpus of knowledge in what was a fairly neglected field, ranging in his research over topics such as the history of iron-framed buildings, harbour works, drainage schemes, dock works and river navigations. Much of his research has centred on the work and engineers of the eighteenth and early nineteenth centuries, and with Charles Hadfield he wrote *William Jessop, Engineer* in 1979, and edited *John Smeaton, FRS* in 1981. An important addition to the bibliography of the subject in his *Early Printed Reports and Maps (1665–1850) in the Library of the Institution of Civil Engineers* (1977). Over the years he has given a lecture course on the history of civil engineering—never exactly the same from one year to the next, for each year brings new discoveries into the story. Many former students remember these lectures and ask if they still go on, which they continue to do. An honour conferred on Skempton in this respect, and one he valued highly, was his election as President of the Newcomen Society for the Study of the History of Engineering and Technology from 1977–79. He received the Dickinson Medal of the Newcomen Society in 1974 for his contributions to the history of engineering. He was also gratified by his election as President of the Smeatonian Society in 1981, securing him a place in a chain of civil engineers stretching back to the Society's foundation in 1771.

Under Skempton there is no doubt that the Department gained further renown. His headship coincided with the many years of planning and discussion which brought the Department from its first home into a new building. His high standing as an engineer attracted many staff to wish to work under him and during his period of office Sections became highly specialised. The complete freedom given by him to members of staff to develop their individual areas of study, the respect shown to those whose special knowledge was different from his own, combined with an infectious enthusiasm for new discoveries—these are among his gifts to the Department. A more tangible gift was the presentation of his own collection of books and papers on Soil Mechanics to the Library of the Department, where they are housed separately as the Skempton Collection. This gift was accompanied by another bibliographic treasure, *A Bibliographical Catalogue of the Collection of Works on Soil Mechanics (1764-1950)*.

Skempton's ability to reduce any problem rapidly to its essentials make him a good teacher, while his gift of rendering complex engineering ideas comprehensible and his obvious absorption in his subject have endeared him to lay and technical audiences alike. His wide-ranging interests encompass art and music; he became a competent flautist and for many years played in a small group which took part annually in the Dorking festival under the direction of Ralph Vaughan Williams. He retired in 1981 with the title of Emeritus Professor and is still on the staff as a Senior Research Fellow. His most recent honour was his election to the Fellowship of Imperial College, and in June this year the Section produced a small volume of his selected papers on soil mechanics (published by Thomas Telford Ltd.), in honour of his seventieth birthday. This book encapsulates his contributions to his subject. Perhaps it should be called 'The Essential Skempton'.

Professor B. G. Neal, Head of Department, 1976-82

The position of head of department was filled in 1976 by Neal, who, as seen earlier, had been appointed Professor of Engineering Structures in succession to Sparkes. By this stage, the office of head of department had become a limited term appointment not to exceed ten years. Neal held it for six years until his retirement from the College.

Coincident with the start of Neal's headship, Ashby gave up the post of Assistant Director in 1977 when he retired. He had been

18. The most recent Heads of Department: Professor A.W. Skempton (1957–76), Professor B.G. Neal (1976–82) and Professor J. Munro (1982 to present)

on the staff of the Structures Section since 1946, was appointed Reader in 1953 and was joint author with A.M. Chilver of *Problems in Engineering Structures* in 1948. His work as Assistant Director involved him for many years in the efficient day-to-day running of the Department. He also served on College Committees concerned with the training, appointment and promotion of technical staff. He gave very good service to the University of London through his twenty-five years as Chairman of the Examining Board in connection with external examinations for the BSc (Eng), including the period of transition when London External Degrees were making way for those of the Council for National Academic Awards. In 1977, he was appointed Secretary of the Delhi Committee, a group set up to promote links between Imperial College and the Indian Institute of Technology at Delhi. His place as Assistant Director was taken by P. Minton, a senior lecturer in Hydraulics.

One of Neal's first acts was to set up working-parties to review the undergraduate course. This activity produced several changes, mainly affecting third year subjects. Electricity was finally dropped from the first year course and Thermodynamics reduced to one or two lectures. An innovation was the introduction in first year of mini-projects containing a 'design' element to give students some idea of the 'feel' of the subject—literally, in fact, since they had previously been denied the pleasure of making concrete until their third year! Another novelty was the creation of a course for first year students on Presentation of Information, bringing together into one unit the teaching of writing, drawing and public speaking skills. The course began in 1977 with the Drawing under the supervision of J. C. de C. Henderson, a reader in the Concrete Section, who had a background of training as an architect, and Sketching in the care of members of staff of the Royal College of Art. These last, led originally by B. Myers and Miss C. Fenn, had been giving instruction in Sketching for several years prior to this date. The course on writing and speaking began under Miss J. M. Brown, an Arts graduate, who was also given the task by Neal of co-ordinating the teaching of communication skills in the undergraduate course. The first complete year of the new course under Neal was given in 1979–80, and the examinable subjects are summarised in Table 9.

During Neal's tenure of office four titles were conferred and there were changes of head of section in all the major Sections. The title of Professor of Engineering Geomorphology was conferred in 1977 on J. N. Hutchinson, in acknowledgement of his research in the engineering and geomorphological aspects of mass movements on slopes and the engineering geology of the Quaternary. Advances in the understanding of the behaviour of plated structures by P. J. Dowling brought him the title of Professor of Steel Structures in 1979, while a year later the contributions of J. Munro in three distinct research fields, namely shell structures, frame structures and civil engineering systems, led to the conferment of the title of Professor of Civil Engineering Systems.

In 1977 Bruce retired from his position as Head of the Public Health Engineering Section. An able administrator, he had successfully fulfilled the intentions of the Rockefeller Foundation, when they helped to establish the Section, of making the study of Public Health Engineering one of serious concern in this country. His course supplied many excellently trained engineers for service in this country and abroad, and this is perhaps the achievement which gave Bruce the greatest pleasure. He was elected President of the Institution of Public Health Engineers in 1963 in recognition of his standing in this subject. The Section's work had in-

PART I (1000 marks)	Structures (2) Fluid Mechanics & Thermodynamics Civil Engineering Materials Mathematics (2) Engineering and the Environment	
PART II (1600 marks)	Mathematics (2) Mechanics of Materials Soil Mechanics Geology Structures Fluid Mechanics	
PART III (2200 marks)	Mechanics Structures Soil Mechanics Systems Economics Materials Advanced Engineering Geology	
	2 options from the following subjects:	
	Civil Engineering measurements	Rock Mechanics
	Engineering Hydrology	Systems Engineering
	Engineering Seismology	Timber Engineering
	Fluid dynamics	Transportation Engineering
	Hydraulics of Structures	Highway Engineering
	Public Health Engineering	Associated Studies

First complete year of new course

Table 9. *Examinable subjects, BSc(Eng), 1979–80*

cluded work on water quality and because of the increasing involvement of hydrologists with this aspect as well as with resources, it now seemed logical to Neal to link the Hydrology staff with those in the Public Health Engineering Section. The new Section, Public Health and Water Resource Engineering, was set up under R. Perry, who had been a lecturer in the Section since 1970. A graduate of Birmingham University in Chemistry with post-doctoral experience in Chemical Engineering, Perry had specialised in advanced analytical techniques and could thus bring to bear skills now needed in the field of Public Health Engineering where the problems relating to pollutants have become very complex. Perry was created Reader in Public Health Engineering in 1977 and in 1981 was awarded the conferred title of Professor of Public Health and Water Technology.

In 1979, the sudden death of Francis left a vacancy in the Chair of Hydraulics. Forthright in style, he was a good organiser and teacher and enthusiastic exponent of whatever subject he had in hand. His abilities as a communicator are seen in his book *A Textbook of Fluid Mechanics for Engineering Students* (1958), which has gone into a number of editions. He was Staff Orator of the College for three years and also a Governor for four years. He served on several of the major committees of the Institution of Civil Engineers—those on Education, Examinations and the Professional Interview. His wide knowledge of engineering education led to his nomination by the College as their representative on the European Society for Engineering Education and in the year of his death he was President-elect.

A period of financial stringency, in which no vacancies could be filled, led to the chair remaining vacant for four years. In the interim, M. J. Kenn, a senior lecturer, was Acting Head of Section. Eventually, in 1982, permission to fill the chair was given and P. Holmes was appointed, with effect from May 1983. Holmes, a graduate of University College, Swansea, had spent two years at the US Navy Civil Engineering Research Laboratories, California, before his appointment as lecturer at Liverpool University in 1965. Nine years later he became the first Professor of Maritime Civil Engineering there, and in 1979 Head of Department. His research interests and reputation in offshore and coastal engineering were obviously of interest to Neal, as will appear later.

In 1980 Bishop resigned as head of the Soil Mechanics Section because of ill-health. A brilliant experimentalist, Bishop was an inspired designer of apparatus. There are few Soil Mechanics laboratories in the UK and overseas which do not contain equipment based on designs developed under Bishop. He was involved in the design of many large or novel earth and rockfill dams, and was appointed by the Institution of Civil Engineers to serve on the *ad hoc* Committee on Reservoir Safety, whose recommendations led to the introduction of new legislation. He led the team of technical advisers at the Aberfan Tribunal and was involved in the advice given to the Institution of Civil Engineers on subsequent legislation and regulations. He served the College as Dean from 1970–73.

Bishop's place was taken by J. B. Burland. After graduating from the University of Witwatersrand, Burland spent two years with Ove Arup in London before taking his PhD at Cambridge. From 1966 he was at the Building Research Station where in 1972 he became Head of the Geotechnics Division. While there, he gained extensive field experience and had been involved in schemes such as the design of the M40 cutting through the Chilterns and the underground car-park at the Houses of Parliament.

Meanwhile, a change was also necessary in the Concrete Section with the retirement of Harris from the Chair in 1981. His eight years in the Department had proved a stimulating time for both staff and students by virtue of his lively and witty style. His contributions as an engineer were acknowledged in the knighthood conferred on him in 1980. His most recent honour is the award in 1984 of the Gold Medal of the Institution of Structural Engineering.

Harris's place was taken by J. W. Dougill. Dougill had been in the Department as a postgraduate student and later as a research assistant from 1961–64, when he had accepted a post at King's College, London, as a lecturer. His career there brought him a readership and then the Chair of Engineering Science.

At the same time, P. J. Dowling was appointed to succeed Neal, who resigned from the position of head of Section in 1981 in preparation for his retirement a year later. Dowling, a graduate of University College, Dublin, had taken his PhD degree in the Department in 1965. After three years with the British Constructional Steelwork Association, he returned to College as a Research Fellow where he was closely involved for several years in research on box girder bridges. His appointment to the established British Steel Corporation Readership in Structural Steelwork in 1974 was followed, as seen earlier, by the conferment on him five years later of the title of Professor in the same field. In 1983 he was elected to the Fellowship of Engineering, the youngest person ever to receive this award.

An opportunity to widen the interests of the Department occurred under Neal's headship. In 1975 the Engineering Board of the Science Research Council (SRC) invited applications from universities to participate in research on the design and maintenance of fixed and floating offshore structures. Neal was quick to recognise the opportunity this presented and he was actively involved in the setting up of the SRC (later Science and Engineering Research Council (SERC)) London Centre for Marine Technology jointly at Imperial College and University College—the largest of six research centres set up at UK universities. Neal was Chairman of the Centre Co-ordinating Committee for five years from 1976–81, during which time the Centre was awarded nearly £3 million by the SERC through its Marine Technology Directorate. In addition, under the 'additional SRC funds in 1978/79 in support of the construction industy' scheme, the Centre was awarded a considerable contribution for building adaptations. The sum of £73,400 was spent in the Department in constructing the conference room and offices for the Marine Technology Centre on level 6 and the new mezzanine floor in the Concrete Laboratory. Neal's efforts in this direction in bringing to the forefront the relevant expertise which existed within the Department are among his outstanding achievements during his term of office.

Neal retired from the College in 1982. His headship coincided with a period of financial stringency resulting from government policies towards university education. The reduction in the current grant in the last few years required very careful house keeping to avoid staff redundancies. Here his administrative skills and ability to find funding from unexpected sources guided the Department into smoother waters. His distinction as an engineer was acknowledged in his election to the Fellowship of Engineering in 1980.

Modest and slightly shy in style, many students and members of the Department did not realise that Neal was a distinguished sportsman who had been a Cambridge Tennis Blue and Captain of the Cambridge Tennis Team. He was subsequently a member of the All England Lawn Tennis and Croquet Club and was All England Croquet Champion for several years, as well as Captain of the England Croquet Test Team on various occasions. He was recently elected to the Committee of the All England Club.

The detached style of Neal's leadership inspired respect and confidence, while much pleasure was derived from the lightness of touch and wit he displayed as a public speaker on formal occasions. One such was his recent visit to the Department on the occasion of the hanging of a portrait of him painted by Richard Foster, R.P., an artist who had also painted Skempton's portrait in 1981.

Professor J. Munro, appointed Head of Department, 1982

Neal was succeeded in 1982 by Munro, who, as described earlier, had established a new Section of Civil Engineering Systems and Mechanics in 1971. His success in this direction had led to a readership in the subject in 1974, and the conferment of the title of Professor of Civil Engineering Systems in 1980.

In 1983 Minton retired from the College and from the post of Assistant Director in which he had shown himself to be an able administrator. His tactful, patient and pleasant style was appreciated by the Department. Appointed as a lecturer in 1956, he became a senior lecturer in 1967. He was a gifted teacher, popular with students and known to many through his wardenship of Garden Hall from 1957–67 and of Linstead Hall from 1968–73. The position of Assistant Director was filled by B. Chiat, a senior lecturer in Surveying.

Several changes have been made to the undergraduate course and brought into operation in the current section (1983–84). The main alteration has been to remove the teaching of Hydraulics from first year and place it in second year, to allow Hydraulics to be taught consecutively in the second and third years. To accommodate this, Geology has been moved from second year to first year. The Humanities courses have been dropped in second year and added to the list of optional subjects in third year. One intention of these changes has been to ease the load in first and second years, but a main purpose has been to pave the way for the introduction of a four-year course, possibly in 1985. Such a course would allow more time for in-depth study of special branches of engineering chosen as options.

One of Munro's first acts as Head has been to improve radically the computing facilities of the Department. In recent years, advances in micro-electronics have encouraged a move away from large mainframe computers towards small microcomputers which are cheap enough to be made available in large numbers in drawing-offices. These are particularly useful in civil engineering which, being a relatively long established discipline, has many solution techniques which involve modest amounts of computation, but are tedious to perform by hand; such tasks are ideally undertaken by microcomputers. A microcomputer laboratory has been established in the Department for use in the first and second year courses. The Department is also involved, with the other City & Guilds College Departments, in planning a central facility which can run commercial Computer Aided Design (CAD) packages for third year and postgraduate students. To support research work, a number of powerful machines have also been installed. For example, in the Soil Mechanics Section there is a Prime mini-computer, and there are a considerable number of 16-bit micro-computers spread through other Sections.

The benefit of these new machines will be fully realised when the Departmental computers and peripherals are linked to the local Campus Network. This will enable us to put micro-computers or terminals wherever they are needed to advance teaching, laboratory work and theoretical research. A number of word processors have also been installed as a back-up to the use of computers.

The start of Munro's headship has thus shown him to be eager to equip the Department to take full advantage of modern technology. He has also exhibited concern about the details of every aspect of the Department's work, drawing upon apparently inexhaustible reserves of energy and enthusiasm. We look forward to a productive period under his leadership.

~ 7 ~

The history of the Sections since 1945

As described in earlier chapters, the tendency of the Department has been to increasing specialisation, and from 1945 onwards distinct Sections have emerged. Different events have imposed a different pattern on each Section's growth; new buildings, new sources of funding, new Sectional heads and the response of individuals in the whole period to new problems intrinsic to the subject. It seems best, therefore, to allow the events of the last forty years, the period of such rapid change and development, to be told by the Sections themselves, and, as far as possible, in the sequence in which they were established. The postgraduate courses available in this period are shown in Fig. 3, the numbers of DIC awards in Fig. 4 and the number of research degree awards in Fig. 5.

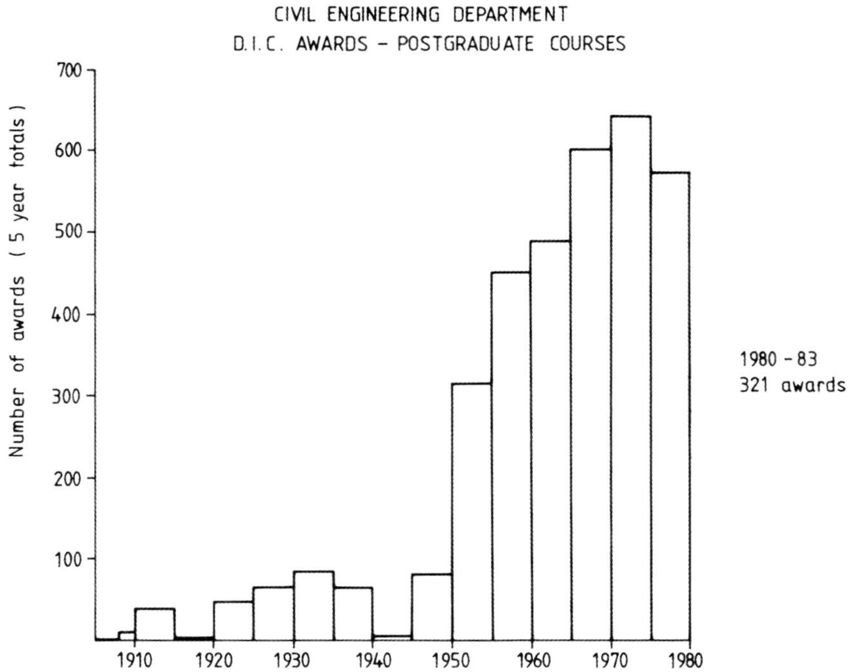

Figure 4

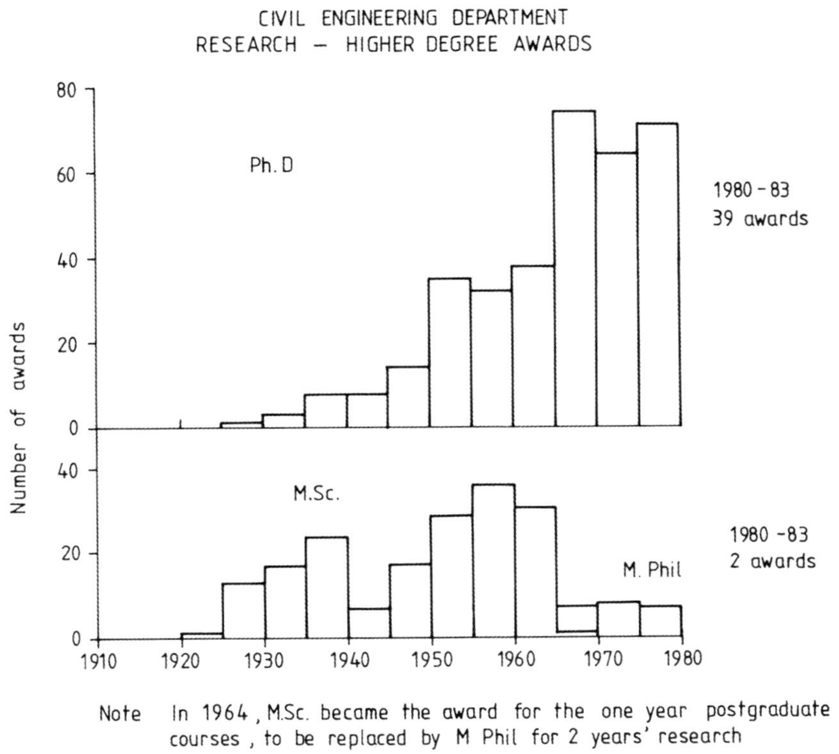

Figure 5

Structures

The development of the undergraduate course

Structural engineering, it has been said, is the art of moulding materials we do not really understand into shapes we cannot really analyse, so as to withstand forces we cannot really assess, in such a way that the public does not really suspect. In the early days of the teaching of Structural Engineering at Imperial College, as elsewhere, the treatment of the subject as an *art* was much more apparent than it is today. Not only have great strides in the scientific understanding of structures been taken since those days: there has been a revolution amongst engineers in the *expectation* of understanding, and slowly (and how reluctantly!) an acceptance of the relevance and utility of mathematics in achieving the scientific art necessary for the design of, say, the Post Office Tower or the Humber Bridge.

The event which more than any other set the scene for the growth of a scientific treatment of Structures in the Department was the appointment in 1933 of A.J.S. Pippard to the Chair of Civil Engineering.

In his activities at the Air Department, Admiralty, Pippard had encountered R.V. Southwell (who was to be Rector of Imperial College just after the Second World War). Southwell was an applied mathematician, who tackled problems of stress analysis with a rigour inherited from the legendary A.E.H. Love; to him the behaviour of solids was an aspect of natural philosophy, and he *expected* to be able to relate structural performance to basic laboratory observation. Pippard's respect and affection for Southwell emerged frequently in his conversation and there is no doubt that Southwell was one of the great influences on his own activities. The other main influence was Andrews' 1919 translation of Castigliano's Treatise *Théorie de l'équilibre des systèmes et ses applications*, in which three theorems of strain energy were shown to enable the expression of equilibrium, compliance and compatibility in convenient terms for structural analysis. Pippard devoted much of his life's energy to popularizing the theorems and demonstrating their applicability to elastic structures, and in particular to statically indeterminate elastic structures.

If we scrutinise the final year Theory of Structures examination paper for 1933, we find but one statically indeterminate problem: a propped cantilever under a uniformly distributed load. By 1936 Pippard's interests have wrought a change: there are now four statically indeterminate structures to solve and a question on the displacements of a space frame.

The other topics commonly examined in this period were reinforced concrete beams, the Euler and Perry theories of columns, influence lines, stiffened suspension cables and voussoir arches. And two of the ten questions were always devoted to the Rankine and Coulomb theories of earth pressure; until Soil Mechanics appeared as a separate undergraduate examination, the tradition held that what coverage there was of the subject fell under the Structures umbrella, a practice which continued until 1954.

In those days a considerable area of what would now be called central Theory of Structures was shared with the Mechanical Engineering Department under the misnomer Strength of Materials. This was mainly concerned with the behaviour of structural elements and the basics of continuum mechanics. Principal stresses and strains, beam bending theory, including shear stress distribution, the torsion of shafts, helical springs, and thick tubes under internal pressure all counted as Strength of Materials, and were taught largely by the Mechanical Engineering Department.

Imperial College does not appear to have fully joined in the pre-war vogue for graphical methods. However, the students encountered Maxwell diagrams for trusses, Mohr's circle, Williot displacement diagrams, Howard's circle for struts, and graphical integration for beam displacements; but several of these had gone by the time Pippard was followed by S.R. Sparkes as head of Section. The emphasis on strain energy theorems gave way to a wider syllabus which, for the first time, included limit analysis theorems and other aspects of plasticity at the instigation of E.H. Brown, who had returned from a year and a half of study at Brown University in the USA. His influence was also to be seen in the appreciation of virtual work, in its modern form, as the basic theorem for giving mathematical expression to the physical principles of equilibrium and compatibility, as well as for calculating displacements, influence lines, collapse loads, and other structural responses to load. The advent of the digital computer led to the systematic formulation of analysis in matrix terms. An introduction to various more advanced topics, especially to do with plate behaviour, was added to the undergraduate course by several of the lecturers involved in teaching the postgraduates.

Undergraduate instruction in Design was for many years wholly a third-year matter. The minor project in steel design (a week's full-time work) followed a course of ten or twelve lectures, which were concerned with conceiving structures to carry load rather than with detailing. When the curriculum was reorganised under Neal, Design was introduced into the second year and even in a small way into the first. In the third year the minor project was no longer taken and the subject for the first time came under the umbrella of written examinations. The second year lectures culminated in a one day mini-design project of a simple building or bridge. These were now to be followed by a further ten or twelve given in the third year. Those final year students with a special interest in structural design could opt to take a major design project ranging from the conceptual design and detailing of a power station to the invention of a movable canopy covering the Centre Court at Wimbledon. What Pippard would have made of all this it is difficult to know, but the present system does reflect the enthusiasm of many members of staff for an undergraduate course with more professional content, and there can be little doubt that the newly formed Engineering Council will look with satisfaction on the direction in which the Imperial College undergraduate course has evolved.

The development of postgraduate teaching and research

Staff, 1946–1963

Teaching at postgraduate level has long been a major commitment of the Structures Section staff and major changes have occurred in the content and indeed scope of the one-year course nurtured within the Section before the Second World War. As the shape of the course owes so much to the staff members and their background and research interests it seems appropriate to recall those engineers, some gone but others happily still with the Section, who laid the foundations for the highly successful and sought after MSc course in Structural Steel Design which the College offers today.

R.J. Ashby and Sparkes were two central figures in the immediate post-war years under the direction of Pippard. Sparkes was to play an important role in the development of the Structures Section. Ashby, a research assistant to Pippard in 1937–38, returned as a lecturer in 1945, and was eventually to become Assistant Director of the Department, as already described. Sparkes, after his involvement in the College Planning Office as Director of Building Works, was appointed to the newly established Chair of Engineering Structures in 1958 on Pippard's retirement. Miss Chitty continued to work in the Section although she retired formally only a few years after Pippard. Her interest in numerical methods, applied in particular to arch dams, occupied her for many years and kept her in more or less constant attendance in the Department.

E.H. Brown and J.C. Chapman, appointed shortly after Ashby's return (as lecturer and research assistant respectively), together with Z.S. Makowski, A.C. Cassell, A.R. Flint and A.R. Gent, appointed as lecturers in the fifties, completed the team which, under the leadership of Sparkes, was to shape the Structures Section over the twenty-year period following the Second World War. During that time there was a major growth in the postgraduate teaching and research activities of the Structures staff. The new DIC course in Engineering Structures was introduced in 1958 and the planning of the new departmental building was completed. The period culminated in the move to the new building with its splendid Structures Laboratories in 1963. Their unique facilities have profoundly influenced the subsequent activities of the Section and the Department owes a great debt to Professor Sparkes and his colleagues for the foresight they displayed in planning them.

Chapman, who assisted Sparkes during the planning was to play a major role in establishing many lines of research within the Section which are pursued to this day. He was particularly interested in industrially related research and carried it out with distinction. He was also prominent in the running and equipping of the Structures Laboratories. Chapman left the College in 1971 to become Director of the Constructional Steel Research and Development Organisation, CONSTRADO. Chapman's contemporary colleague, Brown, had quickly established a reputation for dedication to teaching and an interest in theoretical research, both of which are as much in evidence today as they were over thirty years ago.

Mac, as Makowski was affectionately known to his students, developed the interest in space structures with which his name is now inseparably linked, whilst at the College. At least one of his old students amongst the current staff recalls the pleasures and pains of calculating the deflections of space frame roofs by solving six or sometimes more simultaneous equations on hand calculating machines. The pleasure came on producing the right answer, after a seemingly endless struggle with the calculating machine, the pain on discovering that because of an error the calculation had to be repeated by twirling the handle of the calculator over a further two days. Unfortunately, Mac departed and subsequently became Head of the Civil Engineering Department at the new University of Surrey, just before electrically operated calculating machines, and soon afterwards the electronic computer, came to relieve arms aching from the pursuit of knowledge.

It was Cassell's interest in numerical methods which brought him into early contact with the computer. His close collaboration with Visiting Professor J.R.H. Otter in the development and application of dynamic relaxation is well known within research circles, as is his later work on the finite element method. Flint's main interest was in design and he became the anchor man for the teaching of structural steel design on the postgraduate DIC course in Engineering Structures. He was appointed to the newly established Readership in Structural Steelwork in 1958. This post, together with several bursaries linked to the DIC course, was sponsored by the steel manufacturers and fabricators and provided a direct link with the steel industry, which still continues. Flint left the College in 1972 to dedicate his full time to running the consultancy practice he had started some years earlier; an example of the two-way traffic between industry and academic life which has been so important in the Section. Gent concentrated on the torsional behaviour of columns restrained by other members of a steel building frame.

1963–1984

A second generation of staff, appointed in the sixties and seventies after the new building was opened, have now largely succeeded the post-war team. During the sixties T.A. Wyatt, P.J. Clark and R.E. Hobbs, all of whom had completed their undergraduate training at the College, joined the staff, as did L.G. Booth, A.K. Basu and P.J. Dowling, who had all done their postgraduate studies in the Department.

Booth and Wyatt brought new expertise in timber structures and aerodynamics respectively into the Section. Together with F.H. Potter, Booth formed the Timber Structures group in 1965, which functioned for some years as part of the Structures Section, but eventually detached itself to form a separate Section. Wyatt had worked on the Severn bridge before returning to the College and was to share in the prestigious MacRobert Award in 1970 for his contribution to that project.

Clark, with a family background in the steel fabricating industry and personal experience of design and fabrication, was well suited to helping Flint with the teaching of steel design. Dowling's training in research and design on steel bridges helped to greatly strengthen the Section's activity in steel plated structures and he soon established a talented research group in that field.

After completing his PhD, Basu taught Structural Analysis for five years from 1964. He left to become Associate Professor, and eventually Professor, of Civil Engineering at the Indian Institute of Technology, New Delhi. The College has had a close association with the Institute since his foundation, which is maintained through the Delhi Committee. Sparkes, a member of the committee from 1965 to 1971, was awarded an honorary DSc of IIT, New Delhi to mark his outstanding personal contribution to its welfare. Hobbs eventually took over the Structural Analysis teaching after Basu's departure.

B.G. Neal, the distinguished plastician, succeeded Sparkes as

Professor of Engineering Structures and head of the Structures Section in 1973. The switch from the leadership of Sparkes to that of Neal was a smooth one, greatly facilitated by the warm generous nature of the former and the tactfully efficient approach of the latter.

In 1972 Neal had participated in the appointment of G.W. Owens, a graduate of Bristol University, who took over the lecturing on steel design after Clark's departure. J.W. Bunce, appointed in 1973, worked on theoretical studies of frame behaviour and couple stresses for three years before returning to the earthier fields of offshore fabrication. Soon after his own appointment Neal made further appointments in Structures by bringing onto the staff two talented young researchers, M.J. Baker, a pioneer in the application of reliability theory to civil engineering structural safety, and J.E. Harding, who had been working with the plated structures team. In 1978, he appointed G.W. Hunt, who had built up a strong reputation for his work on elastic stability whilst at University College, to a lectureship.

In 1976 the Section learned with great regret of the passing of Emeritus Professor Sparkes, who had struggled so bravely against his failing sight and then against cancer.

Neal's leadership, which was cool but firm in style, spanned a period where small but significant changes were needed in the administrative, teaching and research activities of the Section, all of which he effected in a most efficient manner and with the minimum of fuss. One of his contributions to the Section was to put it on a very efficient working basis by identifying and mobilising the academic and organizational skills of his staff. The financial affairs of the Section, the largest in the Department, were put on a sound basis. Secondly, his initiative in forming the London Centre for Marine Technology, during a period when the country faced the energy crisis, helped redirect the Section's research efforts to the solution of a national problem. His action ensured that funds were available to support the Section's research activities when alternative funding was very scarce. Indeed, at one stage almost every member of the Section was engaged on research funded through the Centre. This same initiative ensured the survival of the pool of highly skilled technicians who staff the Structures Laboratories. A third contribution was his implementation of a change in direction for the postgraduate course from Engineering Structures to Structural Steel Design in 1975, which more clearly matched the demand from industry for a supply of top quality steel designers with a sound postgraduate training.

In 1981 Dowling, who had already been appointed in 1979 to the newly established British Steel Corporation Chair of Steel Structures, succeeded Neal as head of Section. In 1984 the Section consisted of two professors, two readers, two senior lecturers, four lecturers, a visiting professor and an honorary senior lecturer, together with a research, technician and secretarial staff totalling altogether some 50 people, almost twice as many as constituted the whole Civil Engineering Department staff before the Second World War.

Research, 1945–63

Just as the opening of the new Civil Engineering building had a profound effect on the constitution of the staff, so too did it both directly, through the commissioning of the new Structures Laboratories, and indirectly through the introduction of new blood, greatly influence the breadth of research undertaken within the Section. It is of interest, therefore, to review briefly research pre-1963 and post-1963.

Examination of the old research reports of this period shows that many of the topics studied then are the subjects of 'new' areas of research of the last few years. Methods and understanding have improved, but some of the old problems, albeit now requiring a more sophisticated level of understanding, remain to this day. During the period from 1946–51, for instance, a study was made of the behaviour under bending and torsion of thin-walled box girders. A sequel to the work occurred in the 1970s when a major programme of box girder tests was undertaken, following several major bridge disasters.

Research in the Structures Section has always reflected an interest in fundamental behaviour as well as in design-related problems. In the latter context a combination of long-term research projects and shorter term industrial work has produced a research output which has affected structural design through the production of design codes, numerous papers in learned engineering journals, and research reports. Three major areas of research interest during this period can be readily identified. These were arch dams, ship structures and composite construction. The Section's contribution to the understanding of the behaviour of arch dams and their interaction with their valley foundations is well known through the writings of Sparkes and his colleagues. Major dams in Africa, Spain and the United Kingdom were modelled analytically and experimentally and the results confirmed by the satisfactory behaviour in practice of these majestic structures.

The application of finite difference techniques to idealised two-dimensional problems such as stress diffusion between a ship's hull and superstructure was a forerunner to the early and rapid adoption of numerical solution techniques for other problems researched within the Section. In those early days Southwell's relaxation techniques were frequently used. Indeed, it is amusing to recall a visit of the mother of one of the current staff to her student son's flat in the early 1960s where she was distressed to see a text labelled *Relaxation Methods* displayed prominently on his bookshelf. Her immediate concern, which manifested itself in the form of advice to 'take things easy and have a break', was quickly dissipated when she saw the sub-title referred to approximate methods for the solution of differential equations!

The introduction and use of 'electronic' computers in the late 1950s greatly extended the application of numerical techniques, so that by the end of the period in question three-dimensional analyses of arch dams were being undertaken on the Mercury and, later on, the Atlas computers.

Composite concrete and steel structures were being studied by a group led by Chapman in the late 1950s. A.O. Adekola, now Vice-Chancellor of the Federal University of Technology, Bauchi, Nigeria, was one of his early students and produced an outstanding piece of work on composite beams. The research of this group was to lay the foundations of the first British code on composite beams for bridges, CP 117 Part 2, produced some fifteen years later.

Other topics which were researched at that time were space frames, an interest stimulated by the structures envisaged for the Festival of Britain, and elastic stability problems of brittle columns, thin metal plates, and planar frames. Gent's interest in inelastic behaviour of steel frames, developed during this period, was to reap rich rewards in the understanding of such behaviour some years later.

Large-scale structural testing, currently being encouraged by the Science and Engineering Research Council as a priority area for research, has long been a speciality of the Structures Section. For example, in 1952, during construction of the Bessemer Laboratory, jack loads were applied to the frame and the resulting stresses monitored. It was concluded that the addition of concrete in the form of beam and column casing and floor slabs reduced stresses by 50%, a concept that is still not used to full advantage to this day. A similar study by Cassell during the construction of the Mechanical Engineering building some five years later showed how complex and unpredictable the behaviour of a real structure can be.

Research, 1963-84

Many of the principal lines of research pursued in the old building were to flourish and develop in some unexpected ways with the introduction of new facilities and staff, following the move to the new building. The Structures Laboratories in the new building provided facilities for experimental research which were greatly in advance of any existing facilities at the time of the opening of the new building in 1963. The main laboratories, with 8,000 sq. ft. of floor area and a reinforced slab with a grid of anchorage holes, provide a facility capable of resisting loads of the order of 1,000 tons and at the same time isolate impacts from the remainder of the building. Hardware is of no use, however, without technical expertise and willing co-operation. The skilled team of technicians, led since 1948 by Jack Neale, has contributed much to the enormous reputation the laboratories now have throughout the structural engineering world. Jack's unique blend of skill, enthusiasm and humour has fixed him indelibly in the minds of generations

19. Jack Neale and Roy Loveday with the imperfection measuring frame for offshore cylindrical tests, 1984

of research workers who have passed through the laboratories over the past thirty-five years. His two senior colleagues, Bob Philpott and George Scopes, will also be recalled as key men who helped many a greenhorn research student through his time in the laboratories.

The enlarged facilities and increased number of staff led to such an expansion of research topics in the last twenty years that any short resumé is almost impossible. Interest continued, however, in plated structure behaviour, in dams, and in composite construction. Dowling, one of Chapman's team, fostered, with some brilliance, the research on plated structures, whilst extending the application from ships to bridges. In recent years Harding joined his group and the plated structures interest now encompasses the behaviour of shells.

Perhaps the largest research impetus came in the late 1960s and early 1970s when, following a major bridge disaster, a multitude of quarter-scale box girder tests (some 80 in number) were undertaken in connection with the government enquiry into the behaviour of box girder bridges led by Sir Alec Merrison, Vice-Chancellor of Bristol University. Flint was a key member of that committee. This exciting period produced many talented research workers and stretched the endurance and capabilities of staff and technicians to the limit.

Although priority was given to producing experimental data which could be used to explain the strength of welded box girders, and in particular the effects of initial geometric distortions and residual stresses caused by the fabrication process, a major initiative was the analytical study of nonlinear inelastic buckling behaviour of such plated structures. All of the expertise which had

20. Test on a box girder beam, 1971

been accumulated in studying elastic buckling behaviour of stiffened plating by computer-based numerical techniques was mobilised and extended to tackle the inelastic buckling behaviour of such plates and assemblages. The total behaviour up to and beyond collapse of complex irregularly stiffened portions of boxes, consisting of the box walls and internal diaphragms, could be predicted theoretically by 1979. The validity of these computer studies was verified by tests. In retrospect, it can be claimed that the progress in understanding achieved during the seventies was nothing short of spectacular.

Significant strides in the fundamental understanding of elastic stability have been taken by Hunt and Brown during this same period. Hunt and his former colleague, J.M.T. Thompson of Uni-

21. Tests on a two-span beam of composite construction, 1970

versity College, have written two important text books describing their work.

Work on composite construction flourished in the first decade after the new laboratories were opened. Investigations ranged from the fatigue strength of continuous composite steel and concrete beams under fluctuating load to the ultimate strength of composite plates. Indeed there has traditionally been an overlap between the personnel working on composite construction and plated structures within the Section. This started with Pippard, was encouraged by Sparkes through Chapman, and is maintained by Dowling to this day.

The move to offshore applications encouraged by Neal has directed the plates team to look at shells as used in offshore rig construction, applying and extending the powerful numerical tools which they have developed to analyse the behaviour up to collapse of plated structures. Similarly the enthusiasm for composite studies has led a group to look at the behaviour of grouted tubular connections. This work, which has been undertaken in conjunction with industry, has benefited from the large-scale testing tradition, the numerical computer-based expertise and cross-fertilisation from fundamental work on material strength being carried out in the Concrete Section.

Invaluable support for the application of numerical methods has been provided by the research carried out by Cassell and Hobbs in that area. As converts to the technique of dynamic relaxation introduced by Visiting Professor Otter, these two members of staff have themselves made significant contributions in the field and helped popularise it within the Section for use in conjunction with the method of finite differences to solve non-linear problems.

Work by Wyatt on wind-induced vibrations in guyed masts and other suspended structures has attracted much attention from academics and practitioners alike. More recently the interest in dynamic behaviour has been extended to offshore structures, where both wave and wind induced effects are of importance. Currently the Section's interest in dynamics has been extended further to include earthquake effects on structures. In fact, the recently installed Departmental shake-table facility is manned and managed by Structures staff.

Studies on steel frame behaviour by Gent are now widely known and recently Owens has begun related studies in the field of composite construction.

In a very different area, but one which embraces all interests, Baker and a team of researchers have developed and applied the theory of reliability to the field of safety in structural engineering. Its application to the evaluation of safety factors for codes with limit state format has resulted in a major change in Codes of Practice. The interests of more traditional steelwork research have been maintained by Owens with his research on behaviour and design of connections. The mammoth task of modelling a bifurcated highway interchange (a 30 ft laboratory model) occupied much of Owens' time prior to his joining the permanent staff in 1973.

Lines of research introduced in recent years include the fatigue behaviour of wire ropes and cables and the buckling of pipelines. There is now a flourishing research team looking at several aspects of the behaviour of cables and cable structures from the interwire behaviour at the micro level to the calculation of fluctuating cable forces in suspended structures at the macro level.

If Pippard were to walk through the laboratory today, he would see work on wire ropes, steel pipes, composite joints, connections, and on shells. Nothing much would seem to have changed, and yet how they have changed, changed utterly.

22. Construction of the formwork for the structural model of the Verwoerd Dam, 1966

Industrial work

The scope of industrial work undertaken within the Section is perhaps even more varied than the research. Although projects such as the box girder programme have a direct link with practical design, the Section also has a tradition of involvement with the modelling and testing of particular structures.

Many such projects spring to mind. The study of arch dams has involved the use of several models, one of the largest being the model of the Verwoerd Dam on the Orange River. Around the same time, the 1960s, tests were performed on one of the models of the Commercial Union Assurance Building in London, the Almondsbury Interchange, the Grosvenor Bridge, amongst other structures.

More recently the testing of representative sections of the Ronan Point structure followed the sudden collapse of a new form of building system, and El Atazar dam in Spain and the Lower Yarra bridge were also the subject of research. The Section was

23. Model of a Thames Barrier gate arriving for testing, 1973

also involved in investigations on the failure of the Sea Gem drilling rig.

Perhaps the most notable industrial participation of all came in 1973–74 with the testing of a 1/6th scale model of a Thames Barrier rising sector gate and gate arm. This project brought together several of the academic and research staff of the Section under the leadership of Dowling. Harding and Owens survived to tell the tale and attend, in 1984, the opening ceremony of one of Britain's major civil engineering structures built during this century.

The activity in the North Sea over the past decade has brought with it a need for large-scale industrial testing under demanding conditions of timing and costing which the Engineering Structures Laboratories have been able to meet. The new generation tension leg platform positioned in the Hutton Field in July of 1984 is an excellent example of a major industrial project which utilised very fully the facilities of the Section. Its columns were checked against buckling using the analytical tools developed as part of the plated structures research, the reliability expertise was used to organise the quality assurance techniques adopted in the inspection of the hull, the cross load bearing arms at the connection between the hull and tethers were tested in the laboratory and the riser joints were tested for fatigue under a complicated spectrum of loading using the most up-to-date testing facilities recently installed in the laboratory.

There can be little doubt that the Structures Section not only has but can be seen to have fulfilled the College's Royal Charter 'to give the highest specialised instruction, and to provide the fullest equipment for the most advanced training and research ...', especially in its application to industry.

Hydraulics

The post-war years saw two periods of vigorous activity in Civil Engineering Hydraulics. The first was based in the Hawksley Hydraulic Laboratory under the direction of Professor C.M. White. The second period, 1966–1983, commenced with the appointment of J.R.D. Francis to the Chair and an expansion of the facilities in a new laboratory.

The period 1946–1966
C.M. White and staff

The new university Chair of Fluid Mechanics and Hydraulic Engineering was, as seen earlier, conferred on C.M. White in 1945. White saw a widening gap between the foundations of hydrodynamics on the one hand, and, on the other, the engineering problems of increasingly ambitious and complex hydraulic structures. He sought to fill that gap with design data from a wide range of experimental studies to which he was able to give careful and thoughtful interpretation. His stimulating and perceptive approach to the subject was a source of inspiration to both his colleagues and some forty research students who came under his supervision.

In 1946, J.R.D. Francis and S.P. Hutton joined White on the staff of the Hydraulics Section. Francis's experience in the Miscellaneous Weapons Development Department of the Admiralty during the war gave him a sailor's interest in the influence of wind on waves. He was on the staff until 1961. Hutton had an aeronautical background which he brought to bear on studies of hydraulic machinery. A postgraduate course in Hydro-Power, River Structures and Fluid Mechanics was inaugurated in 1946, for which the College secured the part-time services of C. Jaeger and J.M. Gray through the generous support of the English Electric Company Ltd.

An authority on open channel flow and water hammer, Jaeger had been a distinguished professor of the Federal Institute of Technology at Zurich and was currently a Consulting Engineer with English Electric. Gray had wide experience in the field of hydraulic machinery.

In 1949, Hutton became Head of the Fluids Section of the National Engineering Laboratory and was succeeded by P.O. Wolf who, as seen earlier, went on to develop in 1955 a postgraduate course in Engineering Hydrology. The sectional strength was increased to four with the appointment of D.A. Clarke (1948–51) who was followed by D.H. Kent. After three years, Kent joined his family's instrumentation firm, eventually to direct its operations in New Zealand. M.J. Kenn joined the staff for one year, 1954–55, after working with the Metropolitan Water Board. He returned in 1962, having had experience in the interval of research and teaching at the University of Toronto and King's College, London. P. Minton, an Aeronautical Engineering graduate of the College, was appointed in 1956 after service in the navy where he had taught at the Royal Naval College, Greenwich. In 1961, J.D. Hardwick joined the staff with a background of postgraduate research into flow-induced vibration. One of White's doctoral students, M.B. Khalil, had a lectureship for the year 1963–64 and on his return on an academic post in Egypt he was succeeded by D.E. Wright, a graduate of the Department and also one of White's former doctoral students. The staff was increased to six with the appointment of B. MacMahon who had industrial experience both in Britain and France.

Development of the Laboratory

The original emphasis on closed conduit flow and flow-metering in the Hawksley Hydraulic Laboratory gradually gave way to studies of open channel flows, sediment transport and waves. The study of hydraulic machines continued and to the original Escher Wyss pump and turbine set had been added smaller and more easily tested units at gallery level. The open, craned spaces of the main and mezzanine floors had proved to be highly suitable for civil engineering models which required large plan areas but relatively shallow depths of flow. The longest open channel, originally intended for towing, latterly became useful as a wave tank with a paddle at one end and energy absorbers at the other.

Activities of the Hydraulics Section

The three activities of research, model investigations for industrial projects and teaching were always closely linked.

Research

The most important areas of fundamental research reflected White's interest in sediment transport in rivers and canals. Correlations were made between the hydraulic characteristics of streams and the movement of grains, ripples and shoals of bed material. New techniques using light particles of sediment and resins to fix bed-forms were developed. Studies were conducted into the influence on sediment transport of temporal variations of flow due to tidal and turbulent effects. In studies of secondary motions it was found that a change in the velocity distribution of the flow entering a series of five bends had as significant an influence on sediment movement in the fifth bend as in the first. Local scour and deposition patterns were observed near simulated outfalls and obstructions such as bridge piers and spurs. At one stage a model of a reach of the Thames was constructed as a guide to the practical interpretation of the results from less complex models.

Research was carried out on waves by Francis, who developed a wind tunnel blowing air over a trough which could be filled with liquids of differing properties. The apparatus demonstrated the rise of mean liquid level in the direction of the wind due to the shear forces at the interface. Data were assembled for the design of sea defences and ships from measurements of wave-impact forces. It was found that a one-metre high wave could generate an impact pressure equivalent to that of a static column of water 100 m high. Following the disastrous 1953 North Sea Floods, a 50-mile stretch of the coast south of the Humber was surveyed and photographed in an assessment of damage by waves.

Models of machines using water or air were studied from the standpoint of improving the performance of pumps and turbines. Cavitating conditions, which sometimes lead to damage in full-scale machines and Civil Engineering structures, were predicted from pressure measurements on small-scale models.

24. Model of proposed dam and floodgates at Owen Falls, Uganda, *c.* 1950

Industrial work

Important links with industry were forged through laboratory studies of a wide range of design and operating problems. Model investigations in connection with Scottish Hydro-Power development were carried out for dams at Pitlochry and Clunie and for the Mulardoch-Fasnakyle-Affric scheme. Designs for various types of spillway were assessed and often greatly improved in the course of model studies. These included investigations for the Owen Falls Scheme in Uganda, the Dokan Dam in Iraq and the Atiamuri Scheme in New Zealand.

Several models of the Queen Mary Reservoir near Staines and a proposed reservoir near Walton were constructed in an attempt to achieve a satisfactory circulation of the impounded water through the mixing action of the jets supplying the reservoirs. Thermal effects were modelled in a study of the cooling water intake and outfall for a proposed thermal power station at Castle Donnington on the River Trent. The final investigation before the laboratory was dismantled was concerned with the stability in waves of a novel design of marine platform.

Teaching

Lecturers in the Hydraulics Section taught elementary Fluid Mechanics to all classes of the first year common course. Civil Engineering students in the second year attended lectures by White and his colleagues and were introduced to set laboratory practicals. Towards the end of the period, all students in the third year attended a short course in Hydraulics and had the option of further studies which included a small research project in the laboratory.

From 1946, a one-year postgraduate course offered lectures on analysis and design for Hydro-Power Engineering. The cornerstones of the course were Jaeger, White and Gray with additional support from the Hydrology and Soil Mechanics Sections and the Electrical Engineering Department. An important element of the course was a tour of Scotland at Christmas and the Continent at Easter to visit hydro-power installations. Students undertook a series of design studies and over the nineteen years in which the course was given, more than 150 DICs were awarded to candidates from Britain and overseas.

The period 1966–1983

J.R.D. Francis and staff

On the retirement of White, Francis returned to College from Manchester to take up the Chair. He had many interests in common with White, and his successful book, *A Textbook of Fluid Mechanics*, showed the benefit of their earlier years of collaboration. As a teacher Francis had infectious enthusiasm and a boundless interest in new techniques. His sudden death in 1979 was a sad blow to the Section.

In 1966, the staff comprised Francis, senior lecturers Kenn and Minton and lecturers Wright, MacMahon and Hardwick. That year the strength of the Section was increased to seven on the appointment of A. Scott-Moncrieff who had consulting engineering experience in Canada. In 1973, a distinguished graduate of the College, P. Ackers, was appointed special lecturer and later Visiting Professor. He had been the Assistant Director of the Hydraulics Research Station at Wallingford and was currently a consultant for Binnie and Partners.

In 1969, Wright resigned to take up a post with the Construction Industry Research and Information Association. He was replaced in 1970 by C.R. Head, who had been working on hydraulic structures for a water authority. In 1974, he resigned to take up a special posting with the Overseas Economic Development Corporation and later joined a firm of consultants.

On the death of Francis, Kenn served as Acting Head of Section for the period 1979–83, at the end of which he retired to devote more time to a small consulting partnership. Minton, a dedicated teacher and latterly Assistant Director of the Department, retired at the same time to take up a temporary posting with the Australian National Maritime College in Tasmania.

The vacant chair was eventually filled in 1983 by P. Holmes, formerly Professor of Maritime Engineering at the University of Liverpool. Later in the year the strength of the Section was increased to five with the appointment of K. Anastasiou, who had a background of research experience in the techniques of mathematical modelling.

The new Hydraulics Laboratory

The new laboratory which became available in 1963 incorporated many design features of its predecessor. The scheme envisaged a main floor (area 750 m^2) at subground level, overlooked on two sides by a gallery (200 m^2), 5.3 m above. A new feature was a high platform (88 m^2) at one end of the laboratory and 8.4 m above the main floor, which was designed for studies of cavitation. Five axial flow pumps by Sulzer, discharging 0.14 m ^{3}/s each, were sited at intervals along the 70 m length of the main floor and could pump water from a sump to low, medium or high head tanks, respectively 11 m, 15 m and 24 m above the main floor. A 250 mm diameter ringmain supplied all areas of the laboratory and could be fed by any of the three supply tanks. A pair of measuring tanks was sited beneath a testing bay on the gallery. The raft foundation of the laboratory took the form of a series of cells, some of which were interconnected to form the sump and some were subdivided to form measuring tanks, which were emptied by submersible pumps. A calorifer and a water purification system were incorporated in the water supply. A special basin was designed for Civil Engineering models (67 m^2) and another housed an artificial catchment for hydrological studies (73 m^2). A 33 m^3 tank with glass windows was designed for experiments requiring a large volume of quiescent water. A wave and towing channel 2.7 m wide, 1.6 m deep and 60 m long ran the length of the north wall. A turntable 7.5 m in diameter reproduced Coriolis accelerations for models of reservoirs. Numerous flow channels and smaller pieces of equipment were dispersed throughout the laboratory with a concentration of teaching apparatus in the gallery area.

Research

Studies of the stability and movement of sediment were continued in three areas. In the first, Francis demonstrated that the shape of single particles was critically important to their saltation from both smooth and rough beds. In a second area, P.A. Mantz, a research fellow, correlated the transport rate of cohesionless sediments with the stream power intensity of the flow. A third area of activity was concerned with the movement of bed material by jets and waves and in the vicinity of bridge piers and river bends.

Laboratory and field studies were carried out under the supervision of Wright to provide design information on friction losses for steady flow through partly-lined tunnels in rock. Minton showed that the varying friction losses for an oscillating flow in a smooth pipe could be six to eight times greater than that for a

25. Sand erosion at the bed of a channel caused by a constriction such as a bridge pier, *c.* 1970

steady flow of the same mean velocity. The first laboratory investigation of the flow-induced vibration of circular cylinders in a direction *parallel* to an oncoming stream was directed by Hardwick. He also studied mechanisms of flow-induced vibration for hydraulic gates. Wave-induced resonances in harbours, wave diffraction near breakwaters and edge-waves on beaches were investigated in physical and theoretical model studies by MacMahon. He conducted research into the second order effects which cause the scattering of waves by isolated structures.

Apparatus demonstrating cavitation and cavitation damage near free shear layers was developed by Kenn. The cause of extensive damage in tunnels at the Tarbela Dam in Pakistan was successfully diagnosed as attack by cavitating eddies. Kenn explored the scaling laws which relate the model and prototype behaviour of air-entraining siphons and investigated the behaviour of air bubbles in accelerating flows of water. Air-entrainment on model and prototype spillways was studied by Scott-Moncrieff. He directed investigations into the efficient design of stepped spillways and examined problems of guiding high-velocity flows at the toes of spillways.

The influence of the earth's rotation was reproduced in studies of mixing in reservoirs and a new photogrammetric technique was developed to deduce the pattern of flow in a model reservoir using tethered floats.

Industrial work

In one of many collaborations with consultants a new model-making technique using a vacuum-forming process was used for a scale-model of a complicated manifold for a hydro-power scheme in Malawi. Models provided a guide to the performance of spillways and energy dissipators for the Wimbleball and Meldon Dams in the UK, the Planicie Banderita Scheme in Argentina and the Gargar Dam in Algeria. A simplified model was devised for a control structure in the Cerros Colorados Scheme, also in Argentina, with the aims of confirming assumptions about water-levels and identifying possible economies in the design of the stilling basin. Energy reduction and wave suppression were enhanced for a canal-head structure controlling irrigation water from the Roseires Dam in Sudan. For the same scheme the design of an inverted siphon was greatly improved with the aid of a model.

Investigations were made into the most appropriate shape and operating procedures for the rising sector gates of the Thames Barrier Scheme. The feasibility of installing the gates from a pontoon subsiding on the falling tide was investigated using a scale model. Vibration studies were made on models of three types of gate for a proposed flood protection scheme on the River Scheldt

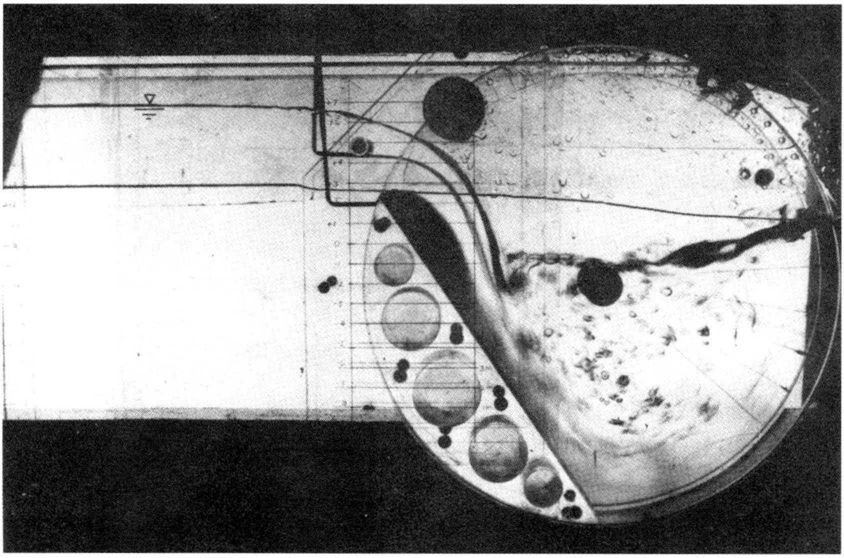

26. Hydraulic model of a rising sector gate for the Thames Barrier, 1974

near Antwerp. Problems of gate-vibration at the El Chocon Scheme in Argentina and dam vibration at Bolargue in Spain were each diagnosed and economically resolved.

Work on projects for the UK was generally concerned with flood protection. Models were made of new flood relief structures on the River Wey in Surrey and at the River Wyre in Lancashire. A proposed new weir was designed for Ennerdale Water in Cumbria and recommendations were made for increasing the capacity of a spillway for the Upper Slade Reservoir in Devon.

Two theoretical studies of offshore engineering problems were undertaken. The stability of a proposed oil storage tank was predicted and an estimate was made of the wave resistance of an oil production platform while being towed into position. A physical model was constructed to demonstrate the response to waves of an articulated landing stage in the River Mersey.

Teaching

With encouragement by Francis, new designs of teaching apparatus were evolved, some of which could be wheeled into lecture rooms. In this period the time allotted for Hydraulics at the second and third year level was gradually decreased owing to demand by other Sections and by 1979–80 the Hydraulics teaching available in the third year was limited to two options and the possibility of choosing a major project in the subject. In response to these imposed changes, the Section attempted to improve the quality of the teaching in the shorter time available.

A one-year postgraduate course leading to an MSc in Civil Engineering Hydraulics was first offered in the 1968–69 session. The course flourished for eleven years and attracted a total of nearly eighty full-time students.

Surveying

Surveying as a subject was initially very important in the Department. In the period of the joint course in Civil and Mechanical Engineering, it was studied in the second year and Dalby enthusiastically promoted the idea of the two- or three-week Surveying camp at Easter. When Dixon was appointed in 1913, his title was Professor of Civil Engineering and Surveying, and the title of the Department was Civil Engineering and Surveying until 1947. The Surveying camps continued under him and the Civil Engineering content of the course for second years was made up exclusively of Surveying—three hours a week. Under Pippard, it occupied three hours a week in second year and four hours a week in third year, as well as the annual camp. In the last ten years, however, Surveying has had to give way to the demands of new subjects and the expansion of the established ones. Nevertheless, an engineer's training is not complete without knowledge of how to use surveying instruments and of the more advanced techniques available. Indeed, in the first years of an engineer's working life the need for surveying expertise may well predominate over other special knowledge. Although the number of hours spent on Surveying has been substantially reduced, currently twenty-five hours per year are spent on Surveying in second year, and the annual Surveying camp at Silwood in the summer vacation is still a feature of the first year course. Surveying can be taken as an optional subject in third year and it also forms part of the optional Highways Engineering course.

Field Astronomy taught in Dixon's era has now disappeared completely from the time-table. Photogrammetry, once taught to all, has been reduced to featuring as part of the third year optional course, although for several years the Section collaborated with the Department of Photogrammetry and Surveying at University College London to provide a course on an intercollegiate basis. As a result, close ties between the two departments have been maintained.

In the post-World War II period the Section was led by A. Stephenson, a distinguished surveyor, who had undertaken a number of mapping expeditions, for example in British Grahamland and the Falkland dependencies. He became a reader in 1947. From 1946, he was assisted by H. Ainsworth, a Cambridge graduate, who had extensive surveying experience involving air photography. He had worked in South America and just prior to his appointment to the Section he had been engaged on river surveys in Surrey.

Surveying practice was carried out in Hyde Park and Kensington Gardens in the early days, while the camps were held at some distance from London in different locations. The acquisition of Silwood Park by the College in 1947 was a great asset to the work of the Section. This large 240-acre estate with two manor houses and areas of grassland, marshland, woods, agricultural land and a lake made an ideal site for the annual camps. These lovely grounds have given much pleasure over the years to Surveying classes and staff. The first task of the Civil Engineering students on their Surveying field course in 1947 was to compile a 1:1250 plan of the site, with every substantial tree plotted. The map was drawn by Ainsworth and to this day it remains in regular use in updated form.

Conditions at Silwood were at first very primitive. Sleeping quarters were in battered Nissen huts and students were issued with palliasses and straw. When these huts were eventually abandoned in 1974 in favour of slightly less spartan ones more centrally located, they were taken over and used for chickens needed in

27. A group of staff in the hut at Silwood, 1970 (*From left to right:* P.J.E. Sullivan, H. Ainsworth, C.R. Head, A. Stephenson, R. Brannan)

research! The staff did rather better than the students, as the Department contributed towards the construction of a hut on which it had first call to house its staff during field courses. The Dixon tradition of involving as many staff members to assist as possible has continued, and over the years many have given their services in this way.

The Section continued to give optional one-week field courses in the Easter and summer vacation for students of the Department of Mechanical Engineering in continuation of a long tradition begun under Dalby. Although popular, the course had to cease after 1982 because of financial pressures.

For a period in the 1950s each autumn a Surveying course was held for Geology graduates from various universities who had been appointed to the Overseas Geological Survey. Other occasional courses involved Overseas Fisheries Officers concerned with the building of fish ponds and courses in Field Astronomy for surveyors appointed to the Falkland Islands Dependencies Survey.

Stephenson retired in 1971 after a service of thirty-four years in the Department, during which time he had given much service both to his subject and to the College. In retirement, he maintained links with the Expedition Committees of the Royal Geographical Society and the Young Explorers' Trust and in connection with these activities he and one other member of the Watkins 1930–31 Expedition to Greenland were invited in 1982 to join the British Schools Exploration Society's 50th anniversary expedition to East Greenland. On this visit a memorial cross was erected in memory of Gino Watkins, who was drowned in 1932.

Like Stephenson, another Old Centralian, E.W.K. Walton (1936–39) had participated in Antarctic exploration and he was emulated by his son Jonathan (1969–72), who went on to lead the Surveying Party which formed part of a major expedition to the Karakoram in 1982 to mark the Royal Geographical Society's 150th anniversary.

A blow to the Section came with the sudden death of Ainsworth in July 1972 on his way home on the last day of the students' field course at Silwood. His love for Silwood was expressed through the terms of his will whereby his ashes were scattered there. His place was taken by S.K. Sharma from a major air survey company, prior to which he was a mathematical adviser to the Survey of India.

Stephenson was succeeded by B. Chiat, whose practical and academic experience has been described earlier.

The research interests of the Section are in two main areas. One involves computer applications to surveying, in which more effective ways of processing surveying and photogrammetric data are sought. The other study area involves the use of short range photogrammetry in projects such as the measurement of gravel particles in relation to the efficiency of filter beds, and the study of current generation in a circular reservoir, using a model and photographs. The Section has also acted in a service capacity to other Sections in resolving measurement problems which have arisen in projects being tackled, for example, by the Soil Mechanics, Public Health Engineering and Hydraulics Sections.

Highway Engineering and Transport

Highway Engineering

The second chair established in the Department was, as seen earlier, in Highway Engineering with R.G.H. Clements as its first occupant. After Clements' retirement in 1945, the chair was not filled, but teaching and research continued under the direction of B.G. Manton, by this time Reader in Highway Engineering. At first, student numbers were relatively low and mainly from overseas, but in 1955 the Rees Jeffries Trustees offered to establish two or more bursaries every session for postgraduate Highway Engineering students. This generous offer, together with the start of the motorway building programme in Great Britain, created an upsurge in interest in home students for Highway Engineering, and postgraduate numbers began to rise. Manton observed that there were far more applications for admission to the post-graduate course than could be accepted. Postgraduate teaching covered the topics of geometric design, highway construction and material and traffic engineering studies. Students were also able to attend relevant parts of the postgraduate courses in Soil Mechanics and Concrete Technology, and a link was established with the London School of Economics, with some students attending lectures in Transport Economics.

During this period two distinct lines of research were pursued. First, the study of highway materials, and secondly, the relationship between highway design and traffic characteristics. The study of materials was concerned initially with devising effective stability tests for asphalt and other road materials, and latterly, because of the influx of postgraduate students from developing countries, with experimental work on low-cost methods of road construction. Traffic engineering research included studies of roundabout capacity, saturation flows at traffic signals and accident causation.

Transport

The move of the Department into the new building in 1963, the coincident retirement of Manton, and the appointment of Colin Buchanan to a new Chair of Transport heralded significant changes in the teaching of transport-related subjects at the College. The new post was created in response to the changing perceptions of the nature of traffic and transport problems. The appointment was made at the culmination of the work of a study group, set up by the Minister of Transport and led by Buchanan, to study the long-term problems of traffic in urban areas. The report *Traffic in Towns*, published in November 1963, had an immediate impact on professional thinking and practice.

In addition to Buchanan, the College appointed four other members of the 'Traffic in Towns' team: D.H. Crompton and Mrs A. MacEwen as research fellows and G.P. Crow and P.J. Hills as lecturers (the latter had been an undergraduate in the Department). Further research appointments were soon made. The new Transport Section represented a wide range of disciplines. Buchanan himself was a qualified engineer, town planner and architect, and his staff included engineers, architects, town planners and economists. The first full postgraduate intake was in October 1964. The course reflected much of the basic thinking of the 'Traffic in Towns' team; it adopted a multi-disciplinary approach to transportation planning and engineering in the context of land-use planning and a wider socio-economic framework. Mature students were attracted from practice at home and overseas. The lecture courses, project work and individual studies were all designed to give students a thorough understanding of the problems associated with movement and transportation in highly urbanised societies, and a comprehensive application of the many inter-related means of resolving them. During the next decade the ideas which had emerged in *Traffic in Towns* were tried and tested and further developed in many practical studies. The Nuffield Foundation gave a generous grant towards research into transportation survey methods, alternative movement systems and the whole question of environmental standards in relation to traffic. C.H. Oglesby, a Visiting Professor from Stanford University, laid the early foundations for a course of lectures in Transport Economics. In the early part of this period students shared courses with postgraduate students at the London School of Economics and the Architectural Association and courses in transport modelling were held at the University of London Computer Centre.

In this somewhat exhilarating atmosphere of rapid change, a major research programme was initiated to develop techniques for predicting and evaluating the impact of traffic on the environment. The most important of these early studies was an investigation of the relationships between traffic characteristics, layout of streets and buildings, environmental conditions, and subjective responses to those conditions. The main aim of the study was to develop practical techniques for determining the amounts of traffic that would be acceptable in different streets. The study of actual con-

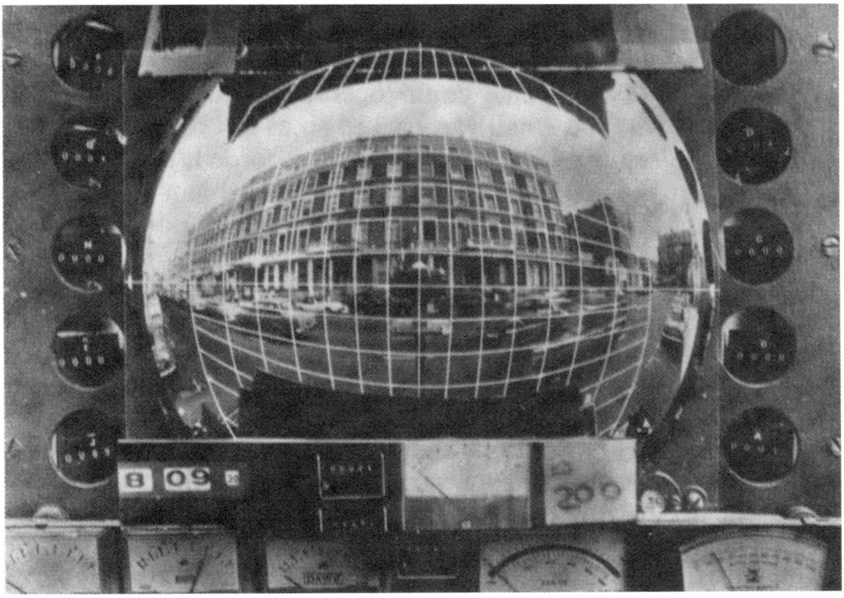

28. A single frame recording made by the Traffic and Environment Analyser, 1968

ditions in streets involved the survey and analysis of a large number of factors, some of which had to be considered concurrently. For this purpose a mobile unit—the Traffic and Environment Analyser (TEA)—was developed by the Section. The unit has three basic groups of measuring instruments to determine:

(i) traffic characteristics: volume, speed, composition and traffic flow distribution;
(ii) objective levels of sound, low frequency sound, vibration, diesel smoke and carbon monoxide concentration, delay to pedestrians, and visual obstruction caused by parked and moving vehicles;
(iii) subjective responses to actual conditions (continuous or component ratings at specific times and locations).

These three groups of instruments were linked by means of statistical analysers and counters which partially analysed the data (including the frequency distributions) as the survey proceeded. All the readings were recorded on time lapse film at pre-selected time intervals. A convex mirror having a horizontal viewing angle in excess of 190° was built into the unit to enable a study to be made of particular vehicle types, or particular flow conditions, and their impact on the environment. The considerable width of the visual angle meant that the number of frames per hour could be minimised. Two people could operate the unit on location, usually from within a small van parked so as not to interfere with traffic. If subjective responses were being recorded, up to five observers might be needed. The TEA unit was used in a wide variety of towns and traffic conditions, including London, Edinburgh and Canterbury.

The unit was programmable in a variety of ways to give the kind of information required for any particular study: for example, levels of noise associated with particular vehicle types could be examined, or prevailing conditions could be assessed over long periods in summary form only. For certain kinds of study, the use of recording film was dispensed with. The unit could be programmed either to record the proportion of time that up to five pre-selected environmental levels (sound, etc) is exceeded, or to show the extent to which such excesses occurred concurrently, or to take pictures of the vehicles and associated environmental levels only if pre-defined conditions were exceeded.

The successful completion of the studies with this unit was followed by a series of research projects sponsored by the Department of Environment. In these, prediction equations for individual environmental factors such as noise, noise pollution levels, carbon monoxide concentration, and pedestrian delay were developed. The research projects were supplemented by consultancy studies, whose purpose was to apply the techniques of prediction and evaluation of the impacts of traffic on the environment. Studies were made at Greenwich and Blackheath, North East London, Kings Lynn, Edinburgh, Bath, Chiswick, Wood Green, Tyneside, Sheffield/Rotherham, and at Bergamo in Italy. The methods developed in these studies are still widely used in transportation planning practice today.

In 1967, MacEwen resigned to concentrate on private practice, and Crompton and Crow were both promoted to senior lecturer. D.A. Briggs, a geographer, was appointed as lecturer. Buchanan, in addition to his duties as Professor of Transport and senior partner of a thriving transport and land use planning consultancy, was heavily involved in other professional and public duties. In 1963, he was President of the (Royal) Town Planning Institute in its golden jubilee year, and was awarded the Gold Medal of the Institute in 1969. From 1968 to 1971, he was a member of the

Commission of Inquiry on the Third London Airport (the Roskill Commission). He received the CBE in 1964 and was knighted in 1972.

On reaching normal retiring age, Buchanan resigned and for the next three years became the first Director of the School of Advanced Urban Studies at the University of Bristol (1973-75). Buchanan returned to Imperial College in 1975 as Visiting Professor of Transport for a period of six years until 1980. Hills resigned in 1972 to take up a position as Assistant Director of Research at the Institute of Transport Studies, University of Leeds, and subsequently as Professor of Transport Engineering at the University of Newcastle. Briggs resigned in 1973 to take up an appointment as Professor of Transportation Engineering at the Federal University of Rio de Janeiro. In 1973, D.A.M. Gilbert, previously a research assistant, and A. Tzedakis, an economist with the Ministry of Transport, were appointed as lecturers.

Following Sir Colin Buchanan's resignation in 1972, Crow became Head of Section and Director of the Postgraduate Course, and Crompton continued to act as Director of Research. The high level of research activity was maintained under Crompton's supervision, with funding from the Department of Environment, the Transport and Road Research Laboratory, the Post Office and the Nuffield Foundation. The studies included the further development of noise prediction and pedestrian delay models; a major study of pedestrians' exposure to risk in housing areas throughout the regions of England and Wales; a study, commissioned by the Long Range Studies Division of the Post Office, into likely future changes in transport and the built environment and the implication for telecommunications; a study, supported by the Nuffield Foundation, of transport policies in Greater London; and two studies for the Department of Environment of the relationship between environmental capacities (i.e. the environmentally acceptable flows) of an existing street system, and the design and evaluation of traffic management schemes.

During the 1960s and 1970s, developments took place in other aspects of the Section's teaching activities. The third year course in Highway Engineering as previously taught by Manton was replaced by one covering both Highway and Traffic Engineering (later to be called Transportation Engineering). All final year students undertook a minor project in Transportation and a significant number each year undertook a major project. During the changes to the undergraduate timetable in 1979, the undergraduate Transport course was replaced by two courses of similar length—Highway Engineering and Transportation Engineering—but sadly, due to the demands of other subjects, these courses were no longer compulsory. The Section took over responsibility for the Civil Engineering Economics course, and staff also made significant contributions to the first year Engineering and the Environment course. The Section also played an important role in the establishment of the Centre for Environmental Technology, an interdepartmental group, and staff teach regularly on its core and option courses.

Following this period of consolidation of research and teaching, Crompton retired in 1981, having directed a considerable number of major research projects which had drawn together research staff from a range of disciplines—engineers, planners, architects, economists, behavioural and environmental psychologists, physicists and mathematicians. A new intercollegiate course in Transport was initiated in the autumn of 1981, conjointly with staff of the Transport Studies Group at University College, the links between the two groups having grown over the previous two to three years. With the combined resources, more students have been taken on, and the curriculum has been broadened to include greater emphasis on traffic management and transport operations. It has also been possible to introduce a much greater number of options, including one dealing with the transport problems of developing countries. P. Rice had joined the Transport Section from University College as an SRC Research Fellow in 1978. T.M. Ridley, Managing Director (Railways), from London Transport was appointed Visiting Professor in Transport in 1981.

Meanwhile, traffic and transportation problems almost everywhere are seemingly as intractable as ever. It is clear that in both research and teaching terms there is still much to be done. New lines of research are continually emerging, in particular the need to develop more appropriate and comprehensive techniques for assessing the need for new transport infrastuctures. But of course there is nothing new under the sun, for an emerging area of interest is the provision of low cost roads in developing countries, which is where Manton came in!

Concrete Technology

A.L.L. Baker was appointed in 1945 to be the first Professor of Concrete Technology, a post which he filled until 1973. The appointment was supported by funds from the Cement Makers' Federation and later by the Cement and Concrete Association together with help from various countractors and consultants. Later on the UGC itself assured the main funds for the development and running of the Concrete course and its laboratory.

At no time has the Concrete Section operated on purely academic lines without having a firm commitment to the fundamental needs of industry and of consultants. The result has always been a keen demand from home and abroad for places on the post-graduate course. It must also be said that the object was not merely to train useful assistants for engineering firms, but to provide for a far wider field. The hope that many students would be qualified to occupy senior positions in due course has been justified.

The general philosophy of the course throughout is well described by Sir Henry Wotton in his slim volume *The Elements of Architecture* in which he says 'The end is to build well. Well building hath three conditions, Commoditie, Firmeness and Delight. Now for the attaining of these intentions we may consider the whole subject under two heads, the Seate and the Worke'.

That this was written in 1624 at the beginning of the English Renaissance of building and construction of all kinds is perhaps not surprising and it is pleasant to note its present day applicability to the building of modern engineering structures.

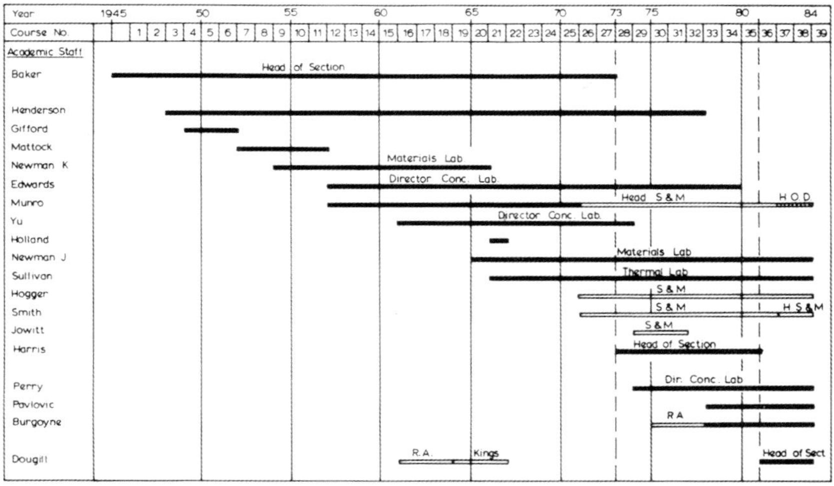

PRINCIPAL ACADEMIC STAFF LECTURING ON CONCRETE COURSE
Solid line indicates member of Concrete Section

Figure 6

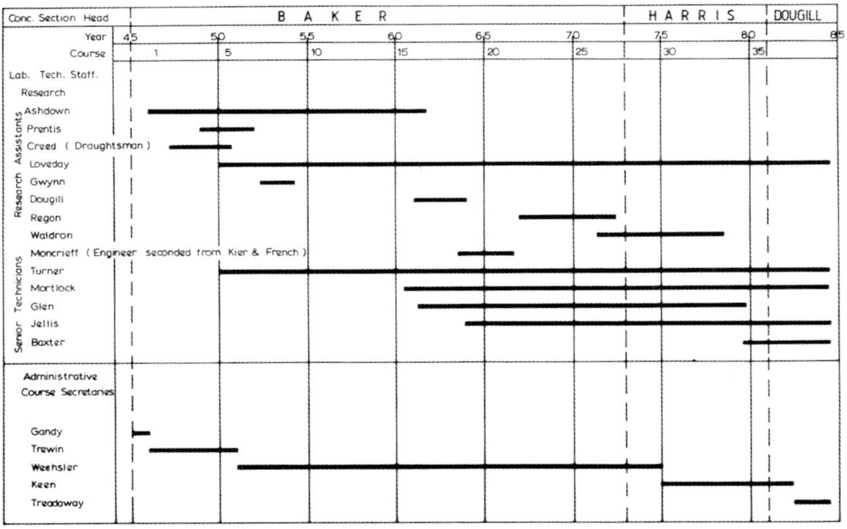

LABORATORY AND ADMINISTRATIVE STAFF SERVICE CONCRETE SECTION

Figure 7

For convenience, the description of the work of the Concrete Section is divided roughly into three periods headed by Professors Baker, Harris and Dougill respectively. Figures 6 and 7 the years of activity of the academic, technical and administrative staff.

Professor A.L.L. Baker, 1945–73

During the early part of this period the Concrete Laboratory was located in the basement of the Goldsmiths' Extension. The headroom (6 ft $8\frac{1}{2}$ in) was very restricting, but when compared with the Structures facility above, the Concrete Laboratory had the advantages of a solid floor and a relatively stable thermal environment. Baker gave his 'Tuesday' lecture throughout this period and covered a broad range of analytical and design methods of particular relevance to structural concrete. He introduced his students to the so-called δ_{ik} method as used by European structural engineers. He also touched on the analysis and design of shell structures which were beginning to be utilised by British engineers for large-span roof structures. Baker drew from his extensive industrial experience to motivate the students in design projects and was always careful to emphasise aesthetic considerations and the importance of good detailing. The research work with which Baker's name is principally associated is the attempt to develop a plastic theory of reinforced and prestressed concrete structures. The Baker method was notable for its treatment of problems of limited ductility.

Initially Baker taught unaided, but the foundations of a Sectional structure were laid by the arrival of, first, J.C. de C. Henderson, and then F.W. Gifford. Henderson originally trained as an architect, but had been employed by Ove Arup before serving in the Army. On his demobilisation Henderson attended the second Concrete postgraduate course and in 1948 joined the teaching staff and developed a pioneering course on matrix methods of structural analysis. Later he developed a further course on the elastic theory and analysis of shell structures, in which the principal feature was the application of matrix methods to problems of cylindrical shells. In both these courses Henderson benefitted from a close association with R.S. Jenkins, a graduate of this College and a partner of Ove Arup. Gifford developed the study of prestressed concrete—a relatively new field of university teaching. After three years' work in the Section he left to pursue a career in industry. He was replaced by A.H. Mattock, who took advantage of the earlier introduction of Jenkins' flexibility method to combine that method with the work of Guyon in designing prestressed indeterminate structures. A strong technical staff had been recruited and two members, R.W. Loveday and J.R. Turner, who joined the Section in 1950 are still in the Department. Loveday has recently (1984) been appointed Departmental Superintendent.

Baker had now developed his first team and the Concrete Section was well established. The postgraduate course was extremely successful and attracted large numbers of students each year, reaching a maximum of 54 students in the mid-50s. Baker recognised the need for greater expertise in the materials side of his subject and K. Newman was recruited first to help in the laboratory and later to lecture on Concrete Materials. Mattock left to pursue his career at the Portland Cement Association Laboratories in the USA and later became a Professor at the University of Washington in Seattle. A.D. Edwards and J. Munro joined the staff in 1957 and the second phase of the Section had begun. Edwards had had practical experience principally with Scott, Wilson and Partners after service in the Navy. He attended the postgraduate course in 1956–57 and took over the teaching of prestressed concrete in 1957. Munro's practical experience after army service was principally gained with Ove Arup and Partners before attending the postgraduate course in 1955–56 and working in 1956–57 on a research project in shells. He initially taught the course on shells and later expanded into other areas of structural mechanics. Newman had had practical site experience with McAlpine and the new team covered a wide range of relevant expertise. Henderson was promoted to senior lecturer and later reader and became recognised second-in-command of the Section. The postgraduate course broadened considerably and the formal structure of the course which largely persists to this day was created during this period. The dreaded examinations were introduced and mandatory and optional courses were identified. Baker was somewhat reluctant to see the informality of the early course disappear, but later recognised that the easy transition to recognition as an MSc course had been facilitated by these organisational changes. The design project continued to play an important rôle and Baker took a keen personal interest in this aspect of the course.

With Henderson and Munro concentrating on Structural Mechanics, Edwards on Prestressed Concrete and Newman on Materials, Baker felt that the practical design of reinforced concrete structures needed some additional coverage and C.W. Yu was recruited in 1961. Yu had been one of Baker's doctoral students and had subsequently worked at Ove Arup and Partners and at the Portland Cement Association laboratories in the USA.

After the Easter vacation of 1963 the Civil Engineering Department moved into the new building as has been described elsewhere. The new Concrete Laboratory was an immense improvement on the very restricted facilities of the old laboratory. The Section anticipated a great growth in experimental research and this was soon realised. The new laboratories were designed by the architects, Norman and Dawbarn, with Ove Arup and Partners as consulting engineers and in close co-operation with all the members of the Section staff. The laboratory had two main essentially separate sections—concrete material production in one and structural testing in the other. Many parts had to be thought out in great detail, such as the strong floor, the vibration testing facility, heating and ventilation control, and lighting. The overhead crane equipment and general local workshop all necessarily formed features of the design. The layout of the laboratory is the same to day with only minor changes after twenty years. This clearly reflects considerable credit on all those responsible for its planning. The most recent change has been the provision of the high level supervision offices against the west wall. This has been done with considerable skill and has helped in the control of the day-to-day running of the laboratory.

K. Newman left in 1966 to become Director of the British Ready-Mixed Concrete Association and was replaced by his namesake J.B. Newman. J.W. Dougill was one of Baker's research assistants in the early 1960s and worked on thermal effects in concrete and this work was continued by P.J.E. Sullivan, who joined the academic staff in 1967 and contributed to the teaching of material properties.

The important impact that computers have made in all aspects of engineering was anticipated by the first computer programming course in the Civil Engineering Department given by Munro and Edwards long before the College or University possessed any electronic computers! The course used the facilities of the early Ferranti computer installed at the then Northampton College of Engineering (now part of the City University).

In 1971, Skempton as Head of Department, asked Munro to be responsible for the teaching of Mechanics and Computing across the whole Department, with the resulting formation of the Systems and Mechanics Section under Munro. The history of that Section is given later in this chapter, but it should be noted that the new Section continued to supply service teaching to the Concrete postgraduate course.

Professor Baker retired in 1973, thus ending a very significant period in the life of the Section and indeed of the Department. He had started in 1945 with virtually no facilities and he left behind a flourishing postgraduate course, one of the best-equipped concrete research laboratories in the world and had recruited a distinguished team of colleagues. Henderson has now retired as Emeritus Reader. Gifford became a Director of a firm of Concrete Manufacturers, Mattock is a Professor of Civil Engineering in the University of Washington, K. Newman is Director-General of the British Ready-Mixed Concrete Association, Edwards is a Professor of Civil Engineering at Heriot-Watt University, Yu is a partner in Harris and Sutherland, the eminent Consulting Engineers, and Munro became Professor of Civil Engineering Systems and subsequently Head of Department.

Professor Sir Alan Harris, 1973–81

The second occupant of the Concrete Chair, like his predecessor, came from industry. Alan Harris had been a pioneer in the development of prestressing and had founded an eminent firm of consulting engineers. Harris naturally first concentrated his attention on the design projects and replaced the single major project with a series of smaller design projects to be tackled at regular intervals with each problem illustrating a new design theme. Harris's lectures covered two main fields, the first being the Philosophy of Structural Design and the second Design Aspects of Concrete Structures. These lectures were naturally allied to both current and past consulting work and covered very many practical ideas. Harris also coupled the course activities to various outside bodies, in particular the Cement and Concrete Association and l'École des Ponts et Chaussées in Paris. Students attended a one-week course on Concrete Structures given by the Cement and Concrete Association at Wexham Springs in the Easter vacation. This was both practical and theoretical and proved to be very successful. The French association provided an exchange system for a few of their students to attend our MSc course while some of our MSc students went on to do further work at the Ponts et Chaussées.

Through Harris's connection with the Royal Engineers, arrangements were made for the postgraduate students to attend a day of demonstration at Chatham each year, seeing heavy civil engineering and military equipment in use. During his headship Harris brought the students into close contact with the major aims of structural design such as function, safety and economy which may be taken as the modern terms for Wotton's famous statement referred to earlier.

In October 1980 a part-time student course was arranged to mesh with the MSc course of the full-time students, but taking an extra year to complete. During this period three new members of the teaching staff were recruited. S.H. Perry arrived in 1974 to replace Yu, and in 1978 M. Pavlovic and C.J. Burgoyne joined the Section. Pavlovic taught courses previously given by Henderson who retired in that year, whilst Burgoyne eventually taught some of the courses given by Edwards when he left in 1980.

Harris retired in 1981 and his reign left both a philosophical and practical outlook for the staff and students to consider. Henderson had also left his impression on the course—one of scholarly work and of dedication to the Section.

Professor J.W. Dougill, 1981—present

The third occupant of the chair is the first to come from an essentially academic background. Dougill had been a postgraduate student and later a research assistant in the Section, but in 1964 had gone to King's College, London, as a lecturer. During his time at King's he had risen to Reader then Professor of Engineering Science.

Dougill has maintained the general form of the course with the addition of a series of lectures given by himself on his specialist subject—the Mechanics of Materials—strongly linked to concrete and rock-like materials.

Research

In spite of the restricted conditions of the old laboratory, much experimental work was done there during the 17 years from 1946 in which it was operational. This brief account is subdivided into a number of periods covering the years 1946–84.

(1) *The period 1946–51*

At first the test measurements were mostly limited to mechanical methods, although electrical strain gauges were tried. Various practical difficulties appeared when applying the electrical gauges to concrete as compared to structural steelwork. After a number of years, with the help of the Structures Section, these gauges were markedly improved and could be used with confidence. At this time the application of the plastic hinge theory to concrete structures became a focus of attention.

It was decided to experiment with many small lengths of beams using a specially designed bending simulation machine. Though many tests were carried out in this way, it was not found easy to use. However, this method was employed until 1957, by which time it had outlasted its usefulness.

Improved methods in the production of higher strength concrete were needed because of the rapid increase in the importance of prestressed concrete. Considerable time was given to all the detailed aspects of this problem.

A large scale model circular cylindrical shell roof had to be built in the Structures Laboratory because of lack of room in the basement. It was tested to failure by being loaded with many layers of sandbags, but the actual distribution of load was rather imprecise. These were 'long' shells and the results for the elastic range confirmed the usefulness of the beam theory for this type. A plastic

29a. Tests on a model shell rook *c.* 1950: loading

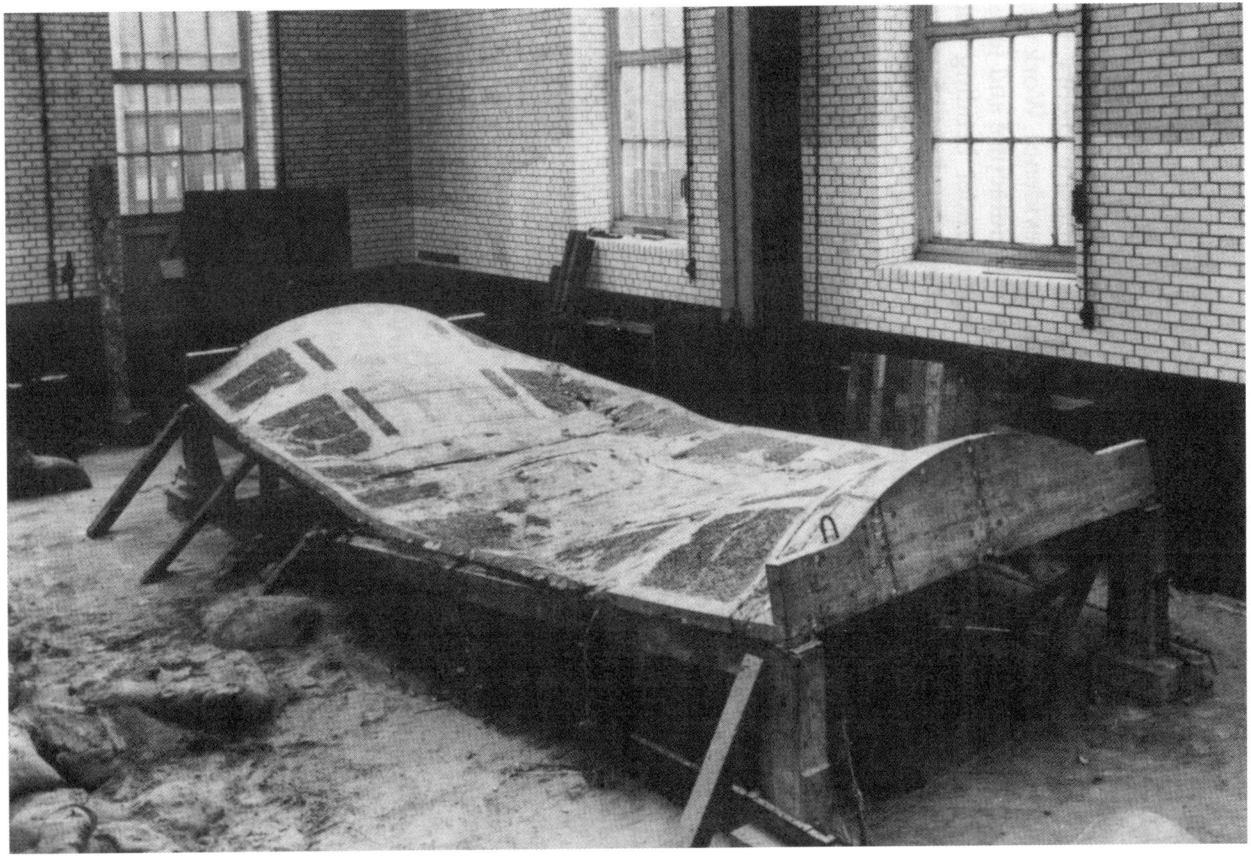

29b. Model shell roof after collapse

failure theory was also developed and compared with the collapse load.

(2) *The period 1952–55*

A short cylindrical shell was tested to failure confirming the advantages of the DKJ equation and an ultimate theory was attempted for comparison with the experimental evidence. Work was continued on the prestressed concrete beam manufacture and tests. The study of the failure conditions of beams under bending and short lengths of elements under compression was developed further.

On the concrete production side, the problems of mix design and vibration continued unabated. Particular attention was paid to experimental methods of mix design in the field.

(3) *The period 1955–58*

Investigations were started into the use of pretensioned units, which are post-tensioned to give continuity. This required special jacks to be fitted into a minimum working space which could apply loads of up to 20 tons.

The problem of the ultimate shear strength of concrete became one of international interest and the College was selected to investigate the effects of various parameters such as shear span, section shape and prestressing force.

Two short shells (one being a north light) were tested with an improved loading frame. The results showed a close agreement with elastic DKJ theory up to working load and a gradual divergence to the behaviour predicted by ultimate load theory.

(4) *The period 1958–61*

The main research covered the following topics: frames, shear, glass fibre as a reinforcing medium, relaxation of prestressing strand, doubly-curved shells, especially the hyperbolic paraboloid, mechanisms of concrete failure, and the properties of concrete.

Perhaps pride of place should go to the warnings given on the use of high alumina cement concrete, though this work was mainly directed to tropical conditions. Further work in this field at that time would have highlighted its importance and helped to avoid some of the troubles that followed in industrial and commercial practice.

(5) *The period 1961–64*

The move to the new laboratory occurred in this period and progress continued in the research described in (4) above. Soon after setting up in the new laboratory, experiments started on a large series of beam tests, which was coordinated by the European Concrete Committee with that of other European laboratories. Baker was a serving member of this committee. The United Kingdom Atomic Energy Authority contracted the Department to

30. Model of the concrete pressure vessel for a nuclear reactor, *c.* 1965

carry out tests on a spherical prestressed pressure vessel under conditions of elevated temperatures and high pressures. At the same time experiments were being conducted on concrete specimens at high temperatures to study the effects of the differing thermal properties of the mortar and aggregate.

Special machines were designed and constructed for subjecting a concrete specimen to genuine uniform compression, uniform tension and biaxial compression. The machines have proved successful in performance. All this work was included under the main scheme for the study of the mechanism of failure of concrete.

Special studies and experiments were made on prestressed continuous beams and three-span continuous box girders subject to HA loading. The results contributed to the economical design of such beams. A computer programme was introduced for this design method.

On the shell research side, progress was made on linear and non-linear theories and the elastic stability of shells. Stability tests were performed on cylindrical shells in the old laboratory. These were amongst the last tests ever done in that basement of trials and tribulations.

(6) *The period 1964–70*

Analysis of frames and shell structures. Efficient cycle systems were obtained for frames and the vectorial method of structural analysis was further developed, particularly in relation to the collapse of elastic-plastic skeletal frames. Problems associated with limited ductility, non-proportional loading, plastic hinge unloading and strain softening were studied. Some work was reported on probablistic structural analysis. For shells, numerical analyses were performed on a variety of static and dynamic problems and applied to special cases such as the design of cooling towers.

Shear in reinforced concrete members. More than 100 rectangular and T-beam elements were tested, and the many parameters associated with their strengths analysed. The final phase of the shear experiments was being completed by the end of this period and the results of 300 tests from this laboratory and others analysed to provide design proposals.

Model pressure vessel for nuclear reactors. The tests on the 1/11.5 scale model as previously described were completed by 1967. These experiments were under the supervision of M.L.A. Moncrieff, seconded from Kier and French. This work made a distinguished beginning for the specialised facilities of the new laboratory.

Prestressed concrete structures. Eight simply supported box beams were tested to destruction and their characteristics compared with those obtained from finite element analysis. Fatigue tests were carried out on post-tensioned concrete I-beams. Detailed work was done on fatigue characteristics of prestressing strand and on the problems of bond deterioration.

Criteria of failure of concrete and concrete material research. The new testing apparatus included an ultra high pressure triaxial pressure cell of 20.000 p.s.i. capacity and a special loading machine capable of applying 20 tons f. designed for use with the triaxial cell to exert a vertical pressure of up to 100,000 p.s.i. on concrete specimens. A research programme was started on failure criteria of concrete under multiaxial stress. Its object was to provide information of direct use to structural engineers. In the microscopic investigation, local interparticle matrix stresses were measured by combined photoelastic and strain gauge techniques.

Flat slab construction. Tests on a 20ft × 20 ft four-panel slab supported by nine columns under the action of various loadings were begun and completed. The work has resulted in the forming of a design method for these structures under the combined action of vertical and horizontal loads.

The fact that so many experiments could be carried out in the new laboratory in this period shows the great advantages resulting from the space available and from the care and forethought in the early planning.

(7) *The period 1970–77*

Structural analysis. The flexibility method as used in skeletal structures was extended to more general cases making use of cycle bases. This was in collaboration with the Structures Section.

The principal development over these years was that of a systems approach to the analysis of skeletal structures. The topics considered included automated optimal design, plastic collapse displacements, and the mesh method of elastic and plastic analysis. Of paramount importance was the use made of static-kinematic duality and its allied mathematical techniques.

Research on shear. Two final reports, one covering the analytical and the other the experimental aspects of the study, were submitted to the Construction Industry Research and Information Association (CIRIA) who sponsored the project. This was to become an extremely detailed document reflecting the considerable effort which had been put into the study of this difficult subject.

Prestressed concrete. Work was continued on the fundamental behaviour of prestressed box beams subjected to combined bending and torsion. Three 30 ft span single-cell box beams were manufactured for testing. The finite element programme established earlier for these problems was refined. A complete project of a 1/12

31. Tests on a prestressed concrete beam, *c*. 1974

scale model of a continuous post-tensioned twin-cell box bridge which bifurcated into two single cell boxes was constructed for test. It occupied an area of 45 ft × 25 ft of the laboratory. The Department of Transport also contracted the College to test several thin-webbed prestressed box beams, especially to find the shear capacity of their webs. These experiments only formed part of the large programme carried out during the years 1970–78.

Panel construction. The investigation was asked for by the Department of the Environment in 1971 and completed with a final report by 1974. Design formulae were proposed governing the many-sided facets of this type of construction. Special attention was paid to floor-to-wall jointing. The Ronan Point accident brought this construction sharply into public notice and resulted in this project being contracted to the Department.

Concrete materials research. This was continued from the previous period obtaining data to enable design criteria to be applied by practising engineers. Tests were made to compare prediction and experiment. A testing machine was developed capable of applying biaxial stresses up to 10,000 p.s.i. and an ultra-high pressure triaxial cell was manufactured to apply confining pressures up to 20,000 p.s.i., and axial stresses up to 100,000 p.s.i.

Effects of very high or very low temperatures. The range of temperatures considered was −180°C to 650°C. A large testing programme was commissioned by the Science Research Council in connection with their offshore programme.

Durability of concrete in a marine environment. Again, further testing was contracted to the laboratory by the Science Research Council in connection with Offshore Technology. As would be inevitable, the parameters to be investigated included aggregate/cement ratio, water/cement ratio, cement and aggregate types, air entrainment, admixtures, curing, salinity of water, wetting and drying, and freezing and thawing.

(8) *Research since 1977*

Structural analysis. Work continued on the nonlinear analysis of concrete members in the post-cracking range using finite elements. This began in 1968 for the analysis of box girders. Very good agreement with both the average and the spread of experimental crack widths has been observed.

On the purely theoretical side, a special interest in plates was being developed with respect to vibration and buckling theory. A variety of boundary conditions was covered in these investigations. Other topics included beam-columns on elastic foundations, stability of mild steel struts having plastic pre-strains, and numerical truss models for thin elastic shells to provide ways of improving shell design by limited bending stresses. The inelastic behaviour of slabs, plates and shells was being studied by means of a single layer yield surface instead of the multi-layer method.

Concrete materials and thermal research. This research came under three headings: (i) durability of normal and special concretes, (ii) behaviour of concrete under simple and complex states, and (iii) effects of temperature and various environments on concrete.

In (i) over 400 prismatic specimens of concrete were tested for freeze/thaw behaviour with a temperature range −40°C to 120°C. A considerable amount of automation was used in order to cope with the quantity of data needed.

For (ii), on the complex stress side again, many tests were carried out with the hope of devising a realistic approach to design work.

Finally, in (iii), experiments were carried out on concrete subjected to extreme thermal conditions from −200°C to 600°C. The aim of the cryogenics research is to investigate the effects of liquefied natural gas (LNG) on various concretes. It was hoped to explore the possibility of the construction of LNG containers without inner steel containers. Special apparatus was designed and constructed to test for the parameters covering a large number of characteristic concrete properties.

Composite joints for tubular steel structures. A series of static tests on straight grouted connections was completed and analysed for both straight and complex connections. It was anticipated that the next series of tests would involve prestressing methods to increase the efficiency of the connections.

Response of prestressed concrete slabs to impact loading. Model slabs 1.5 m square, 60 mm thick and simply supported were tested, using a long steel billet as an impact striker. Considerable instrumentation was needed for the determination of the loading and its

32. Model of a bifurcated elevated motorway interchange in prestressed concrete, 1974

effects. This work is associated with marine investigations of this Section and the Structures Laboratory.

High performance concrete elements. The project was concerned with the construction of massive offshore structures. There were three phases: (i) small scale specimens were to be tested under various multiaxial loadings, (ii) large scale elements were to be tested under service conditions and (iii) design criteria were to be proposed for elements of sub-sea structures and for relevant portions of floating or gravity platforms.

Studies of a 1/12 scale prestressed concrete bifurcated bridge model. This most elaborate model was completed and fully tested in the elastic range by applying separate and combined lane/span loads. These were in various stages up to dead load plus 2 × HA lane load and then taken through to full collapse under a blanket UDL over the entire bridge. The loading test rig construction, because of the size of the model, was quite as involved as the model itself. All this work has turned out to be a triumph in concrete model testing and very useful in application.

The laboratory staff who performed such an important function included research assistants Ashdown, Prentis, Creed, Gwynn, Waldron, Dougill and Regan together with Moncrieff seconded from Kier and French. The senior technicians were Loveday, Turner, Mortlock, Glen, Jellis and Baxter.

The academic staff are listed below alongside the work for which they were most responsible.

(a) Reinforced concrete: Baker, Mattock, Edwards, Yu and Perry.
(b) Prestressed concrete: Baker, Gifford, Mattock, Edwards, Harris and Burgoyne.
(c) Indeterminate structures (theoretical): Henderson, Munro and Smith.
(d) Shells: Baker, Henderson, Munro and Pavlovic.
(e) Concrete materials: Gifford, Mattock, K. Newman, Yu, Sullivan, J.B. Newman and Dougill.

Soil Mechanics

As described earlier, Skempton was invited by Pippard in 1946 to form a new Section of Soil Mechanics. He immediately recruited A.W. Bishop, as his assistant. Bishop had already spent some time with Skempton at the Building Research Station (BRS) on secondment from the Metropolitan Water Board.

The first ten years, 1945–55

Initially, undergraduate teaching and research were undertaken, utilising facilities already available in the Highways Section. The first PhD (J.J. Kolbuszewski—who went to teach Soil Mechanics at the University of Birmingham) was awarded in 1948, and the first MSc by research (A. Lund) in 1949. Pippard had planned the new development with postgraduate teaching in mind, and the first full-time one year course leading to the DIC was given in 1950–51. D.J. Henkel, an old aquaintance from BRS days, who had started research under Skempton in 1948, joined the staff in 1950 to assist with the new course. A further important addition to the Section was R.E. Gibson, who took his PhD in 1950, but remained as a research assistant supported by DSIR until 1953. Gibson brought a valuable analytical power to the group.

Eleven students obtained the DIC between 1951 and 1953. By 1953 the course was well established, with thirteen students attending in that year. Full-time students were almost entirely from overseas, with a large contingent from Canada. There was no government support for students of postgraduate courses from Britain. However, a large number of British engineers attended the lecture courses as part-time students.

In 1955, Skempton was appointed to the newly created Chair of Soil Mechanics. A further landmark was the appointment of David Evans as the Section's first full-time technician. Ten PhD degrees had been awarded by the end of 1955, and nine MSc degrees by research.

Skempton was greatly concerned with the application of soil mechanics and applied geology to practical engineering, and much of the early research work reflects this. While fundamental aspects were not neglected, research covered a wide range of applied subjects. A survey of reports, published papers and research theses indicates the following topics: the porosity and packing of sands; the study of drained and undrained strength of sands, clays and compacted fills in terms of effective stress; sampling equipment; filter design; bearing capacity in clays; piles in sands and clays; properties of recently deposited soft clays; allowable settlements of buildings; settlement prediction; the stability of natural and excavated slopes and retaining walls and the development of new methods of circular and non-circular stability analysis; accelerated consolidation by drainage of embankment foundations and fills; and the initial application of plasticity theory to the behaviour of clays. Forty-five technical papers had been published by the end of 1955, nine in the Second International Conference on Soil Mechanics in Rotterdam in 1948, and six in the Third Conference in Zurich in 1953. Skempton played an important role in the formation in 1948 of *Géotechnique*, the first European journal for Geotechnical Engineering, in which sixteen papers from Imperial College had been published by 1956.

Two aspects of the early work seem to deserve special mention. Bishop, as seen earlier, was exceptionally gifted in the design and manufacture of testing equipment, carrying out much of the machining on his own lathe in the laboratory. The Department's excellent workshops were also utilised. A full range of triaxial testing equipment, shear boxes and consolidation frames was devised and manufactured, together with constant pressure sources, model piles, footings, field equipment, and so on. The designs, fully proven in use, were subsequently used in manufacture by several firms specialising in laboratory equipment, and have formed the basis of a business, largely for overseas sale, which continues today with a multi-million pound turnover. Bishop applied the equipment to his important and fundamental studies of the principle of effective stress, among many other uses, and Henkel conducted the studies on the properties of normally and overconsolidated reconstituted clays in the triaxial test, which formed the basis for the application of plasticity theory to the properties of soils which followed during the next decade, primarily at Cambridge. The developments in laboratory testing were covered in the book *The Measurement of Soil Properties in the Triaxial Test* by Bishop and Henkel, published in 1957, which remained the standard text on the subject for the next 20 years.

The Section was also heavily involved in consulting work. Skempton kept meticulous job files during the early years, and by 1956 they had reached No. 176. The close contact with industry which was involved stimulated much of the research carried out and provided much important data for the research effort.

The second decade, 1955–65

The next decade involved much development of the previous work. Gibson rejoined the staff in 1956 and his analytical work, mainly on consolidation theory, added a new and unusual dimension to the work of the Section, up to his departure in 1965 to King's College, London where he became Professor of Engineering Science.

In 1957 the Fourth International Conference of Soil Mechanics and Foundation Engineering was held in London. Five papers were presented from the College, and the Section was involved in the organisation. At this conference Skempton became the second International President in succession to Terzaghi, reflecting the international standing of both him and his group. In this year Skempton was also created Professor of Civil Engineering and succeeded Pippard as Head of Department. The year 1957 also saw the expansion of postgraduate teaching in Geotechnical Engineering at Imperial College with the start of the course in Engineering Geology in the Geology Department under J. Knill.

In 1958, N.N. Ambraseys joined the staff. Ambrasey's appointment initiated the interest in earthquake engineering in the Department, which has continued to the present time. N. Morgenstern arrived as a research student from Canada in 1958 and joined the staff in 1960, characteristically immersing himself in a wide range of interests and activities. Henkel left for IIT, New Delhi in 1963. Gibson resigned in 1965. New staff additions were N.E. Simons, from the Norwegian Geotechnical Institute, in 1963; J.N. Hutchinson, after his work on the stability and geomorphology of Britain's coasts at Cambridge and BRS, in 1965; and G.E. Green, after completion of his research in the Section in 1965. In 1965 Bishop succeeded Skempton as Professor of Soil Mechanics.

A major event in the life of the Section was the move to the new building in 1963. The three new laboratories were largely equipped with new apparatus, and their wide open spaces when compared with the previous cramped accommodation caused a minor cultural shock. However, within a few years they were almost as crowded as the old laboratories had been.

The one-year postgraduate course continued to flourish. Between 1955 and 1965, 149 full-time students attended, 26 of them from Canada. Increased financial support in Britain allowed the attendance of 51 home students. The introduction of field trips by Henkel proved a valuable and popular addition to the course.

Twenty PhD degrees were awarded in the period, together with nine MSc degrees by research. Topics covered included design of bored piles in clay; field studies in rock mechanics; grouting; the development of methods for measuring pore water pressures correctly in the laboratory and field; the study of effective stress in partly saturated soils; the development of laboratory equipment for K_0 testing in the triaxial apparatus, for high pressure testing, for testing in plane strain and with independent control of the intermediate principal stress; work on residual strength in clays; extensive field and laboratory studies of the in-situ properties of the London Clay, including in-situ lateral stresses and the effect of discontinuities; the effect of sampling disturbance; theoretical and laboratory studies of undrained slope failures in clays; the development of slope stability coefficients for analysis in terms of effective stress; theoretical and laboratory studies of consolidation, field studies on the long-term stability of natural slopes; the development and interpretation of field measurements in embankment dams; and the study of the properties of weathered granite. Ambraseys was extensively involved in field studies of earthquakes, and in the earthquake resistance of embankment dams and foundations in terms of displacements, a technique developed during his sabbatical year at the University of Illinois in 1963. The technician staff under Evans expanded during the period, numbering four by its end.

The Section remained extensively involved in consulting work. The interest in the residual strength of clays and weak mudstones arose from the field observations at the Walton's Wood landslide, involved in the construction of the M6 motorway, and the slightly later discovery of similar shear zones of tectonic origin in the foundations of the Mangla Dam in Pakistan. Other problems arising from the new national road construction programme began to feature in the Section's work.

The annual Rankine Lecture was founded by the British Geotechnical Society in 1961 to be given in alternate years by an overseas and a British lecturer. Skempton became the second British lecturer in 1964, on the subject of residual strength and slope stability.

Recent history, 1966–1983

The period from 1966 to the present mainly involves consolidation of the previous progress. Soil mechanics research and postgraduate teaching were by then established in many other British universities. More government funds became available for the support of research and of postgraduate students. The period has also seen a revolution in the laboratory, with the introduction of electric sensors and electronic data acquisition and processing equipment.

In 1967 A.E. Skinner joined the staff and in the same year Ambraseys formed a separate Section for Engineering Seismology.

Morgenstern left in 1968 to return to Canada and become Professor of Civil Engineering at the University of Alberta, and Simons also left in 1968 to take the Readership and, later, the Chair of Soil Mechanics, at the new University of Surrey. R.J. Chandler joined the staff in 1968 after extensive laboratory and field studies of the properties of the Keuper Marl at Birmingham University, and P.R. Vaughan rejoined the Section in 1969 after five years in industry. Green returned to professional practice in the United States in 1975. A period of financial stringency prevented his replacement until 1978 when D.W. Hight joined the staff from the consulting world. The title of Professor of Engineering Geomorphology was conferred on Hutchinson in 1977, in recognition of his extensive work in the field of stability and evolution of natural slopes.

In 1979, after a period of ill-health, Bishop retired as Professor of Soil Mechanics. D.M. Potts joined in 1979, to bring long-needed analytical and numerical skills to the staff, and, in 1980, Bishop was succeeded by J.B. Burland, who had been head of the Geotechnical Division at the Building Research Station, much involved with their continuing programme of field observations,

33. The disastrous slide at Aberfan in October 1966. Professor Bishop led the team of investigators at the Aberfan Tribunal

and a major figure in British geotechnical engineering. A great sadness occurred in 1981 when Evans died after a long illness to which he had refused to give in. Typically, he was at work a week before he died. He was succeeded as chief technician by S. Ackerley. The total technician staff now numbers six.

A major development in geotechnical engineering at Imperial College occurred in 1966 with the formation of an Interdepartmental Rock Mechanics Project under Professor E. Hoek in the Department of Mining and Mineral Resources. The postgraduate course in Rock Mechanics started in 1969.

In 1975 further interdepartmental cooperation occurred in the postgraduate teaching of Geotechnical Engineering when the Civil Engineering, Mining and Geology Departments created a Geotechnical Engineering Steering Committee. A larger element of common teaching had been progressively introduced, particularly between the Soil and Rock Mechanics groups, such that, at the present time, some 40% of the compulsory courses in Soil Mechanics cover Rock Mechanics aspects and are jointly given, with most of the other Rock Mechanics courses available as non-examined options. Similar arrangements are available to Rock Mechanics students.

An important change occurred in postgraduate teaching in 1964–65 when the university regulations were changed and the MSc degree was awarded, in addition to the DIC, for successful completion of the one-year course now including university examinations.

Between 1965 and 1974, 226 students attended the nine MSc classes in Soil Mechanics and 263 attended the nine joint courses with Engineering Seismology up to 1983–84. The major increase in fees required by Government in 1980 reduced applications substantially, but, since the courses were previously oversubscribed, the number of students attending was maintained, and even increased slightly in response to financial stringencies. Present numbers approach 35 per year, and thus, with students in Engineering Geology and Rock Mechanics there are nearly 70 postgraduate students studying Geotechnical Engineering at Imperial College.

Research has continued at a high level, with 55 research degrees awarded in Soil Mechanics in the last eighteen years. Earlier programmes which have continued in the laboratory are high-pressure testing, and testing in plane strain and with independent control of the intermediate principal stress. New developments have in-

34. The hollow cylinder torsion shear apparatus, made in the main workshop by C. Pitches, a workshop technician, in 1977

cluded large diameter triaxial and oedometer equipment, mainly for testing model rockfill; creep testing with test durations up to four years; the ring shear apparatus for residual shear studies; hydraulic loading systems for stress path testing; computer controlled systems for cyclic and rapid loading; model piles and footings; load cells, probes and strain meters for the accurate measurement of load, and pore pressures and strains on the boundaries of samples under test; and the development of a new large hollow cylinder apparatus for the study of principal stress rotations, which was the last piece of equipment designed by Bishop before his retirement. Field equipment has been developed, mainly for in-situ and field measurements, including settlement gauges for oil production platforms.

Extensive studies have been made of the properties of the Upper Lias Clay, and studies of the in-situ London Clay have continued. Soft Thames Alluvium was involved in studies for the Thames

Flood Protection Scheme, and large-scale field studies were made. Major studies were also made in connection with the Empingham Dam, on weak Upper Lias Clay foundations. There has been increasing interest in natural slopes, geomorphology and the influence of the Quaternary, and a number of full-scale slope studies have been made including Folkestone Warren, Hadleigh Castle in Essex, the south coast of the Isle of Wight and various coastal mud flows. Much work has been done in connection with marine technology, including extensive studies of actual North Sea sediments. Computational methods have been developed and applied to a wide range of problems, including dams and embankments, piles, footings, tunnels and deep excavations.

The period has seen a substantial reduction in internal funds for research, but a greater availability of external funds. Generous support has been received from the Construction Industry Research and Information Association (CIRIA) for studies on rockfill, and London Clay; from the Science Research Council (SRC) and the Science Engineering Research Council (SERC) for extensive studies on creep, for field observations on dams and embankments, for laboratory testing of stiff clays, for stress strain behaviour of sands and of clays at high pressure, for pile and footing model studies and soil-structure interaction, for cyclic loading for ring shear testing and for the development of the hollow cylinder. Support has also been received from the Water Resources Board, Transport and Road Research Laboratory, the National Environment Research Council (NERC), the American Army European Research Office, the Shell Oil Company, and British Petroleum.

Consulting work has continued to play an important part in the work of the Section, and, with the recent reduction in civil engineering activity in Britain, more overseas work has been undertaken in South and Central America, in Greece and Cyprus, in the Middle East, Pakistan, Africa, South East Asia and the Pacific.

Envoi

The Section has existed now for nearly forty years. From being one among very few, it has become one among many, with centres of excellence elsewhere often staffed by those trained at Imperial College. Other countries are now more active in geotechnical engineering than Britain and have a much wider range of primary projects on which to practice their skills. However, the combined group at Imperial College in the Civil Engineering, Geology and

Mining Departments is one of the largest and most widely based in the world, and, given adequate financial support and continuity, it can continue as a centre of international excellence for the foreseeable future.

Its present position in Britain and in the world may be shown by some simple illustrations. Nearly 700 students have studied Soil Mechanics and Engineering Seismology at postgraduate level since 1946; with 41% from Britain; 15% from Europe and Scandinavia; 8% from North America, from South and Central America, and from the Far East; 6% from the Indian Subcontinent; 5% from Africa, and from Australasia; and 4% from the Middle East.

At the International Conference on Soil Mechanics and Foundation Engineering in Stockholm in 1981, some 90 out of 1,600 delegates had been at Imperial College in some capacity, as had over 10% of the selected platform speakers. Of twenty-four Rankine Lectures given to date, twelve by British and twelve by overseas lecturers, four of the British choices have fallen on the first four members of staff: Skempton in 1964, Bishop in 1966, Gibson in 1974 and Henkel in 1982. A further British choice was A.C. Meigh, who obtained the MSc degree by research in 1950 and gave the lecture in 1976. Morgenstern was the choice for overseas lecturer in 1981.

Public Health Engineering (1949–1977)

To assist in the running of the postgraduate course, to be established with Rockefeller Foundation support, as previously described, the College formed a Public Health Engineering Advisory Committee, composed of representatives of relevant professional institutions together with the academic staff, under the chairmanship of Mr M.T. Tudsbery. It met annually until 1967, when it was considered to have fulfilled its function and was disbanded. In the meantime, following discussions between the two Schools, a Joint Academic Committee was formed in 1960 with academic representatives only.

Staff

From the preparatory period of 1949–50 until the end of the 1952–53 session, Bruce was the only member of staff in the Section. When the Rockefeller Foundation's three-year period of support ended in September 1952, the University took over full responsibility for its continued financing. Bruce was appointed University Reader in Public Health Engineering in January 1953.

In July 1953 G.T.J. Fox, who had worked in the City of Birmingham Water Department and in the Middlesex Main Drainage Department, was appointed lecturer, and A.L. Dowley, with both academic and consulting experience, and a Master's degree in Sanitary Engineering from Northwestern University, Illinois, USA, was appointed research assistant in February 1960 becoming a lecturer in 1962. Dowley left in 1969 to return to a post at University College, Dublin, but for several months travelled weekly to the College to continue his series of lectures.

In May 1970 R. Perry was appointed lecturer. Whereas Bruce, Fox and Dowley were all engineers, Perry was, as described earlier, a chemist with a considerable background of chemical engineering research at Birmingham University. He was therefore well qualified to take over the running of the Public Health Engineering Laboratories, to introduce advanced instrumental methods of analysis, and to build up a programme of research, with a number of research assistants on outside funding.

From 1950 to 1963, the laboratory had been something of a makeshift, and, without a technician, it was operated under some difficulty. The larger laboratory in the new building merited the appointment of a technician in 1964.

Bursaries

In each of the first two years of the postgraduate course, the Rockefeller Foundation provided funds for three bursaries to be awarded to applicants at the discretion of the College. From 1953 it extended the bursary scheme by allotting funds to the Institution of Civil Engineers for the award of bursaries to applicants wishing to study or undertake research in public health engineering at any UK university having suitable facilities. The Imperial College course continued to benefit from these awards, with the result that from 1950 to 1960, when the Foundation's support ended, a total of 49 Rockefeller Bursaries had been held by students on the course.

From 1958 Advanced Course Studentships were available from the Department of Scientific and Industrial Research (DSIR) (later from the Science Research Council (SRC)) and other sources of financial support for students on the course came from international organisations, British Council and local authorities in the UK.

The postgraduate syllabus and its development

The most important consideration in designing the syllabus for the postgraduate course was the multi-disciplinary nature of the subject, which necessitated introducing qualified civil engineers to the microbiology of water and developing their usually scanty knowledge of chemistry. It was considered essential that they should have laboratory experience in both sciences to enable them to understand the natural and induced changes which occur in water quality, and to appreciate the work of the microbiologists and chemists with whom they would work subsequently.

For the teaching of these subjects, willing co-operation was received from members of other Departments of the College, too many to mention all by name, but these first contributors should be remembered: S.E. Jacobs (Bacteriology); J.A. Barnard and J.T. Hannen (Chemistry); W.F. Jepson (Zoology); Professor F.A. Barnard (Statistics) and F.G.H. Blyth (Geology). They set the pattern for those who followed.

Within the Civil Engineering Department, the course covered water collection, storage, treatment and distribution, the design of sewerage systems, the treatment of sewage and industrial effluents, control of water pollution, solid waste disposal and air pollution. Assistance was given by the Hydraulics Section and there was close collaboration with the hydrologists under P.O. Wolf. Numerous visits were made to works and research laboratories, and outside lecturers were invited to speak on special subjects.

To provide a background understanding of public health problems, the students attended the London School of Hygiene and Tropical Medicine (LSHTM) one day a week to attend lectures on Public Health, Tropical Hygiene, Epidemiology and Occupational Hygiene with tutorials by Dr R.F. Guymer. The lecturers included Professor J.M. Mackintosh, Dean of the School and Professor of Public Health, and Professor G. Macdonald, Director of the Ross Institute, and one of the leading figures in malariology and tropical medicine.

Dr Guymer resigned from his post at the London School in 1955, but continued to serve on the PHE Advisory Committee. He was replaced as Tutor by Dr A.D. Robertson, and subsequently several members of the LSHTM staff took over this work, the longest serving being Mr G. Graham Don.

The general pattern of the postgraduate course lent itself to gradual expansion as the staff of the Section grew with the appointments of Fox, Dowley and Perry. During the 1950s and 1960s the field of water management was attracting more attention world-wide. In particular, the basic scientific principles of water quality control were becoming clearer, so that within a more or less unchanged layout, the teaching of the engineering side of the course, particularly with regard to treatment processes and quality control, developed greater depth.

Experience showed that the engineers were not always able to derive full benefit from some of the lectures at the LSHTM, which were directed mainly at medically-trained people. From 1965, therefore, it was arranged that instead of the students travelling to the School, the School's staff would give lectures at Imperial College especially for the engineers. This proved to be a more satisfactory arrangement, though unfortunately reducing the contact between engineers and doctors, which had been one of the objectives of the original proposals.

International impact

Bruce interpreted his mission in starting the postgraduate course in Public Health Engineering as primarily to spread the gospel of engineering for health as widely as possible, particularly in what were then described as undeveloped or emergent countries. In keeping with the traditions of the College, a large proportion of overseas students were attracted to the new course, most of them from the Commonwealth, but many also from foreign countries. For example, during the first ten years, a total of 119 students took the course, of whom 66 were from Commonwealth countries and 21 from other overseas countries. Many came from universities and returned to start or develop Public Health Engineering courses of their own.

Bruce was able to supplement the teaching given in the courses by taking part in many activities of the World Health Organisation, e.g., in the Seminars for European Sanitary Engineers, meetings of the Expert Committee on Environment Sanitation, and a Seminar on Rural Water Supplies in the Western Pacific Region, held in Singapore. He also undertook consultancies for the World Health Organisation and other bodies in many countries, to advise on the teaching of Public Health Engineering, and on water supply and sanitation problems. The countries involved included Australia, Bulgaria, Greece, India, Kuwait, Lebanon, Poland, Sri Lanka and Turkey.

In 1960, Bruce was appointed to the Faculty Committee for the new International Course in Sanitary Engineering in the Technological University of Delft, and lectured there for several years.

Fox gave courses at Ahmadu Bello University, Zaria, Nigeria, and from 1970 onwards, Perry travelled extensively in the Far East, North & South America and European countries as a consultant and to take part in Conferences. He was the invited distinguished lecturer to the Association of Environmental Engineering Professors of the United States visiting some fifteen universities specialising in Environmental Engineering.

Research

Although the emphasis in the early years of the Section was on teaching the one-year postgraduate course, a programme of research was started in 1952 on flow in a model rectangular sedimentation tank, and the use of inclined planes to accelerate settlement, which established useful guidelines on the optimum angle of the inclined planes.

Dowley carried out comparative flow tests on three sedimentation tanks over a range of sizes. The object was to study scale relationships and to ascertain how far laboratory experiments can be extrapolated to full-scale tanks.

Sedimentation studies were extended to circular tanks in 1959–62 with the study of the effect of spiral motion in a tank in which a forced vortex flow is imposed, and the principle was followed up by a detailed theoretical analysis.

Besides these studies, primarily on the sedimentation process, some work on sand filtration was started in 1954, with examination of head losses in a model filter and an investigation of the variations in porosity of a filter at different depths as a result of various back-washing procedures. The mechanism of back-washing of a rapid sand filter was studied in greater detail in 1964–67. In the meantime Fox was taking a great interest in the use of multi-media filters. He carried out research on filters with two, three or four layers of different materials, and co-operated with the National Coal Board on the use of anthracite as the most useful and widely-used material after sand.

With the arrival of Perry in 1970, many new lines of research were opened up. Emphasis was given to the formation of a multidisciplinary team capable of working in the main areas of Public Health Engineering including air pollution control, water and waste water treatment, and the management and control of solid, toxic and hazardous wastes.

Analytical facilities in the laboratory were greatly improved by the addition of equipment for gas-liquid chromatography, atomic adsorption spectrophotometry and mass spectrometry. The sensitivity of some of the new instruments was improved by special adaptations devised in the laboratory. The research topics included the pollution of ground and surface water from solid waste tips with special attention to organic materials, the separation of heavy inorganic solids from organic wastes in domestic sewage, the multilayer filtration of waters heavily loaded with suspended matter, and the effects of heavy metals on the activated sludge process. This last project initiated a long-term programme of research into the distribution and adverse effects of heavy metals in the environment. In the study of air pollution caused by the burning of petrol, diesel and other fuels to form aromatic polynuclear hydrocarbons, techniques for identifying specific hydrocarbons at very low concentrations were developed. These techniques enabled assessments to be made of the relative contributions of the different pollutants to the atmosphere, e.g. in establishing the spread of aircraft exhaust emissions around London Airport. The much discussed lead pollution from car exhaust fumes inspired the development of a method of determining organic lead alkyls at the nanogram level, thereby reducing necessary sampling times. Air samples for analysis were collected regularly at a number of points in London to assess levels of atmospheric pollution in an urban area. Much of the field work and on-site measurements were facilitated by the use of a mobile laboratory, adapted from a converted ambulance. Such early work led on to detailed environmental studies of each of London's three major airports.

Hydrology (1955–76)

As seen earlier, the appointment of P.O. Wolf in 1949 with a special interest in Hydrology led eventually to the establishment of a postgraduate course in 1955. The course was administered by Wolf, assisted by H. Underhill, under the general supervision of White as Professor of Fluid Mechanics and Hydraulic Engineering. Lectures and practical work for this interdisciplinary subject were supplemented by help from the Departments of Meteorology, Geology, Botany, Geophysics and Mathematics. Opportunities for practical field work were provided at the College field station at

Silwood Park and with the engineers of the Thames Conservancy at Reading. In the first two years, the students came principally from developing countries, such as Burma and Sudan, together with United Kingdom graduates who had been working in hydrology overseas. A number of part-time students and research students also attended selected lecture courses.

The session 1957–58 saw several significant developments, with the appointment in October 1957 of Wolf to the newly established Readership in Engineering Hydrology. Home students on the course became eligible for the Advanced Course Studentships introduced that year by the Department of Scientific and Industrial Research (DSIR). Three graduates in Geography were awarded studentships, thus encouraging the training of non-civil engineers in the application of hydrology to the solving of water engineering problems. The overseas students were generously supported by the British Council as part of its overseas aid programme.

The tradition of a continental study tour was initiated in 1957 with the first visit to Switzerland. The principal host there was the Chief Engineer of the Swiss Federal Bureau of Water Resources, Emil Walser, a renowned figure in European water affairs, who organised special demonstrations of all types of river discharge measurement techniques by his teams of expert gaugers. Visits were also made to the E.T.H., Zurich, to the hydrogeologists at the University of Neuchatel and in neighbouring France to Sogreah in Grenoble and to the hydropower works of Electricité de France. To the continental study tour in later years were added visits to the Rijkswaterstaat in the Netherlands at the invitation of another famous international hydrologist, Professor A. Volker. Eminent visitors to Imperial College during that early period were Professor E.J. Gumbel (of extreme value statistics fame) and Professor R.K. Linsley, the American engineering hydrologist of world renown, who gave a stimulating series of 21 lectures.

During the late 1950s and early 1960s, the course content gained greater cohesion and benefited from the absorption of wider experiences particularly when senior practising engineers attended as full-time students. Wolf spent a year at Stanford University and there was an infusion of new blood in the appointment in 1959 of T. O'Donnell, who replaced Underhill on his move to the Food and Agricultural Organisation (FAO) in Rome. Valuable contributions were provided in hydrometeorology by Dr J. Glasspoole and his colleagues at the Meteorological Office and in hydrogeology by Dr S. Buchan and Dr J. Ineson from the Institute of Geological Sciences. International names continued to figure in the list of occasional lecturers who never failed to visit Imperial College as they passed through London. Of these, those notably recorded are Alexander, Amorocho, Dooge, Laurenson, Matalas, Midgley, Munro, Nash and Raudkivi. Their courses and seminars contributed greatly to the advancement of the subject in the reporting of their research activities and of hydrology in practice in many different parts of the world.

Research

The research activities of the departmental hydrologists were focussed in two directions. The first employed physical models in the Hydraulics Laboratory to establish the optimum dimensions for intakes, tunnels or spillways of controlling structures, e.g. dams in Scotland, New Zealand, Iraq and Uganda. For the reconstruction works following the Lynmouth flood in 1952, a model of part of the Lyn valley was made in order to estimate the levels which would be reached by flows of known magnitudes.

The second field of research was in the application of digital computers to simulate hydrological processes and thereby to derive catchment outputs (river discharges) from measured rainfalls. The fitting of conceptual catchment models to real catchments led to the investigation of automatic optimisation techniques for determining model parameters. Linear systems techniques were developed for the derivation of unit hydrographs. These computer-based researches made substantial advances during O'Donnell's sabbatical year (1963–64) with the Water Resources Division of the U.S. Geological Survey.

The idea of the cross-fertilisation of physical modelling and mathematical modelling approaches to the study of catchment behaviour led to plans for a laboratory catchment facility. The first stages resulted in the successful design of a system of nozzles for the generation of artificial rainfall. This long-term research project suffered many setbacks before finally producing highly valuable detailed data of rainfall and runoff for a variety of catchment configurations.

Teaching

A major development in the teaching of Hydrology occurred in the 1964–65 session when suitably qualified students on successful completion of the course became eligible for the award of the MSc degree of the University of London. Previously, the course had led only to the award of the DIC. The new university regulations called for more stringent examination procedures and in 1966–67, written papers were introduced as an addition to the assessments of coursework and of a dissertation or project report. During this period, there were several staff changes. Miss R.J. More, who had been specifically engaged as lecturer to undertake analyses of Captain W. McClean's data archive, as an adjunct to normal teaching commitments, was replaced in November 1965 by Miss E.M. Shaw, a hydrologist with the Devon River Authority. M.J. Hall, having recently completed his laboratory catchment rainfall simulation research, was appointed as a lecturer to the permanent staff.

In 1966, the leadership of the team of hydrologists within the Hydraulics Section devolved on to O'Donnell, who was appointed to the readership vacated by Wolf on his appointment as Professor of Civil Engineering and Head of Department at the City University. The group expanded yet again with the appointment to a lectureship of P.E. O'Connell from University College, Galway. However, the teaching responsibilities also grew with the introduction of an undergraduate option in the third year and with the steadily increasing number of full-time postgraduate students. The growth in postgraduate numbers resulted from increased demand for places both from overseas and from home students supported by the Natural Environment Research Council (NERC) which replaced DSIR.

The expansion of Hydrology in the United Kingdom, due in part to the requirements of the Water Resources Act, 1963, also encouraged consulting engineers and river authorities to send staff on the course for advanced training in the subject. Many of the course students stayed on to do research; projects were still undertaken in the laboratory, e.g. a study of groundwater flow with a Hele-Shaw model, but the use of the College computer facilities became an increasing attraction (e.g. optimization studies for conceptual catchment models and the application of deterministic models to motorway drainage design). The years of the late 1960s saw the growth of stochastic modelling of hydrological data series. O'Connell achieved his doctorate in this expanding field and subsequently supervised a number of research students following up related topics.

In 1970, the staff gave a successful short course on Hydrological Time Series for practising engineers. In addition, they applied their expertise to solving problems for consulting engineers. Analysis of flood discharges (R. Wey and R. Vardar), urban drainage design (Crawley New Town and coastal towns in Libya), land drainage for agricultural development (Waghi valley in New Guinea) and enhancement of water resources (sugar cane irrigation in the Ivory Coast) were all demanding of careful hydrological studies, and the latest techniques were used in providing answers to the various problems. The annual pattern of teaching, study tours, project and research supervision and examinations was disturbed in 1972 by the departure of O'Donnell to a Chair of Hydrology and Hydrogeology at the University of Lancaster. With a restructuring of the lecturing commitments, the course continued to flourish and valuable support was received from the new Head of Section, Professor Francis.

The postgraduate course in Engineering Hydrology celebrated its 21st anniversary in the summer of 1976 with a very successful party for old students and staff. The only regret of the organisers was that the large number of overseas students could not be more fully represented. Alas, it was also the end of an era since the course had to be discontinued that year. Hall and O'Connell left the College to further their careers, Hall with Sir William Halcrow and Partners and O'Connell with the Institute of Hydrology. The latter has since become Professor of Water Resources in the University of Newcastle upon Tyne. University financial cutbacks precluded their immediate replacement.

Timber Structures and Technology

Although the main thrust of the Department's work on timber did not begin until the introduction of the MSc course in Timber Structures and Technology in 1965, the College has been involved in timber since its foundation at South Kensington.

As early as 1894 Unwin undertook tests on Empire timbers for the Department's nearest neighbour, the Imperial Institute. The Institute had no test machines of its own and Unwin performed strength tests in his laboratory on timbers from, amongst others, Ceylon, South Africa, Australia and the West Indies. His laboratory books covering the period 1894 to 1900 were subsequently included in the Unwin Collection in the College Library and are now in the Department's Civil Engineering History

Collection; the work was fully reported in the Institute's Journal and was later summarized in Unwin's standard text book on *The Testing of Materials of Construction.*

Dixon, as seen earlier, continued the Department's interest in timber testing by acting as a member, and sometime Secretary, of the Institution of Civil Engineers Committee on the Deterioration of Structures in Sea Water. A series of tests was performed at the College on Empire timbers treated with various preservatives in order to investigate their resistance to teredo attack. Dixon also served on the British Standards Institution (BSI) Committee on the testing of timber.

It would appear that Imperial College's first appointment in timber was not in the Civil Engineering Department, but in the Royal College of Science's Biology Department, where P. Groom was appointed in 1908 as lecturer (and subsequently Professor) in the Technology of Wood and Fibres. During the First World War Groom led the search for suitable timbers for the rapidly expanding aircraft industry and tests were performed under his direction at Farnborough at what was later to become the Royal Aircraft Establishment. His reports went to the Ministry of Munitions where they were analysed by a young structural engineer, A.J.S. Pippard, who of course later became Professor of Civil Engineering at Imperial College.

Pippard's early interest in the strength of timber and plywood is well illustrated by his collecting some twenty reports on these topics: the reports were subsequently bound together in a number of volumes which are now in the Department's Library.

Pippard's interest in timber lasted throughout his life and when he became Professor Civil Engineering he continued the tradition that the Civil Engineering Department students should have a working knowledge of the properties of timber. As early as 1910 Groom was giving a course of lectures and laboratory demonstrations entitled Timber for Engineering Students and he taught this course until his retirement in 1931, when responsibility for it fell to F.Y. Henderson, then a lecturer in the Biology Department. Henderson became Reader in Timber Technology in 1944 and almost immediately moved to Princes Risborough to become the Director of the Forest Products Research Laboratory (FPRL). Pippard insisted that the course on timber for his young civil engineers should continue and J.F. Levy, then a demonstrator in the Botany Department, was offered the chance to learn the subject whilst Dr W.P.K. Findlay of FPRL filled the breach. The choice proved to be inspired and Levy served his own and the Civil Engineering Department for nearly forty years as lecturer, senior lecturer, reader and finally, in 1981, as the College's first Professor of Wood Science.

For some fifteen years Levy taught the course alone, and naturally as a botanist, the emphasis was on wood structure and the important topics of preservation against fungal and insect attack.

In the early 1960s, at the time that the College was expanding rapidly, L.G. Booth's appointment in 1963 changed the direction of the teaching of timber in the Department. In 1963 he gave a short course on Timber Structures and Technology as part of the DIC course on Structural Engineering. Many of the students on this course came from parts of the world with unlimited supplies of timber, but most of them had graduated with little knowledge of timber as an engineering material. The course was well received and, encouraged by its success, Booth, with the support of Sparkes, proposed to the Ministry of Overseas Development that they should sponsor a full time one-year postgraduate course on Timber Structures and Technology. The proposal was enthusiastically accepted by the Ministry and the first MSc course began in October 1965.

The staff of the new Timber Structures and Technology Section was completed when F.H. Potter was appointed in 1965 as a lecturer. Potter had graduated from Manchester University in 1949 and after a period in industry had joined the staff of the then Portsmouth College of Technology.

The course was designed for engineers, although suitably qualified timber technologists, foresters, builders and architects were also accepted: it was aimed primarily at overseas students from the developing countries.

During the first term all the students attended the same lectures on the basic properties and utilisation of timber but during the second term a limited amount of specialisation was introduced: the engineers concentrated on the design of structural components, whereas the occasional timber technologist and forester studied the biodeterioration of timber.

The lectures on the engineering aspects of the material were undertaken by Booth (on mechanical properties and the structural analysis of components) and by Potter (on jointing methods and the manufacture of industrialised timber building components). The botanical aspects and problems of biodeterioration and preservation of timber were dealt with in the Botany Department by Levy, who was assisted from 1974 by D.J. Dickinson.

In 1972 the seven year agreement with the Ministry of Overseas Development came to an end and the Department of Civil Engineering assumed the financial responsibility for the course.

Towards the end of the 1970s several of the postgraduate courses in the Civil Engineering Department were moving towards increased specialisation. Timber Structures and Technology followed the pattern and, although the title of the course did not change, from 1979 its intake was restricted to engineers. This proved to be an unpopular move and, at the time of writing, it has been decided to revert to an expanded form of the original format of the course under the new title Timber Technology: Timber Engineering and Wood Protection, a title which emphasises the increasing cooperation with the Botany Department.

The course was attended by a small number of UK students, but the majority came from overseas: during the first seventeen years (1965–1982) it attracted 98 students from 29 countries.

Most of the overseas students were sponsored by the UK Ministry of Overseas Development and returned immediately after the course to their original positions in government service, industry and universities with the aim of applying their specialised knowledge of timber to the immediate benefit of their countries. Several, however, were sponsored by their own government to remain at the College, or to return later, and undertake research leading towards their PhD degree either in the Civil Engineering Department or the Botany Department. O.M.E. Fageiri undertook work on the ultimate load behaviour of plywood web box beams, whilst J.A. Ofori and P. Vinden worked with Levy on problems associated with the preservation of timber.

Not all the research students attended the MSc course, particularly if they already had a background in timber. The linking theme of most of the research work was the interaction of solid timber and plywood in structural components. In the mid-1960s PhD degrees were obtained by several students: E.J. Amana, from Nigeria, who studied the behaviour of stiffened plywood panels subject to slip at the interface between the plywood skin and the timber ribs; K.A. Segun, also from Nigeria, who worked on timber hyperbolic paraboloid shell roofs; and C.K.A. Stieda, from Canada, who researched the lateral stability of plywood web box beams. In the late 1970s M.K. Surendranath investigated the ultimate load behaviour of stiffened plywood panels.

The behaviour under load of structural timber components reflected Booth's main research interest and in addition to the topics mentioned above he worked on shear deflection of components and the ultimate load behaviour of curved glued laminated members. He also believed that the study of the history of structural engineering often illuminated current problems and frequently led to a greater understanding of the subject: in this field he undertook research on the early strength testing of timber, on the work of Thomas Tredgold (1788-1829), the earliest writer on timber engineering in Britain, and on I.K. Brunel (1806-1859), arguably the greatest timber engineer that this country has produced. Potter, who for many years acted as Senior Tutor in the Department and also as a Warden of one of the College's Halls of Residence, had a special interest in the behaviour of structural timber joints and wrote particularly on multiple nailed joints.

The tradition established by Unwin and Dixon of involvement in BSI Committee work was continued by Booth and Potter. Booth sat for over twenty-five years on the Committee responsible for drafting the British Standard Code of Practice on the Structural Use of Timber, and wrote with P.O. Reece, formerly Director of the Timber Development Association, the official Commentary on the Code: he also acted as chairman of committees that prepared standards on the manufacture of glued laminated timber members and on the strength testing of plywood. Potter continued his interest in joints with the chairmanship of committees responsible for standards on structural finger joints and the testing of mechanical joints.

Although the main effort of the Timber Structures and Technology Section went into the postgraduate course, the Section relieved Levy of part of the burden he had borne for nearly twenty-five years by taking over the responsibility in 1971 for the third-year undergraduate course. Originally the course, entitled Properties of Timber, had been taken by all the undergraduates but pressure of time in the third year led to a reappraisal of the undergraduate syllabus and the course became one of four options to be chosen in the final year. Since Booth's arrival in 1963 the course had included increasing amounts of Timber Engineering and in 1971 its title reflected this change by becoming Timber Structures & Technology. Although the emphasis was now on structural utilisation, Levy's contribution on preservation still formed an important part of the course. Further changes of the third year syllabus took place in 1979 when students had to choose two options from a list of twelve, one of which was entitled Timber Engineering. The new title of this expanded course reflected the gradual change of emphasis that had occurred since Booth's appointment in 1963: the course is still given in conjunction with the Botany Department and Levy's lectures on the preservation of timber contribute to its all-round nature.

After one hundred years at South Kensington, the Department and the College's involvement in timber is greater than ever before. The century began with Unwin testing Empire timbers for the Imperial Institute and continued with Dixon's work on marine structures. The middle of the period was remarkable for Pippard's insistence that a knowledge of timber was vital to the all-round education of a civil engineer: this insistence led to the cooperation with the Botany Department, with a decade of lectures by Henderson, followed by forty years of close collaboration at both undergraduate and postgraduate level with Levy. The last twenty-five years have seen the re-establishment of the study of timber in the Department through the introduction of postgraduate and undergraduate courses on Timber Engineering. The Unwin tradition is being maintained.

Engineering Seismology

The Section began in 1967 under Ambraseys alone, but he was later joined by J.S. Tchalenko. A graduate in Geology of Nancy, Tchalenko had worked for the engineering firm Soletanche in Paris before coming to the Soil Mechanics Section as a research student. He joined the Engineering Seismology Section after his appointment to the staff and worked for several years with Ambraseys, mainly in the field, on active tectonics. He left in 1975. In 1973, S.K. Sarma, a graduate of the Indian Institute of Technology, Kharagpur, joined the Section, having taken his PhD in the Department in 1968 on the stability of earth dams during strong earthquakes.

From the start, Ambraseys and staff and students were involved in field missions sponsored by UN and UNESCO to areas where strong earthquakes had recently occurred. This took them over the years to Turkey, Iran, Pakistan, Nicaragua, Romania, Jugoslavia and Italy.

A postgraduate DIC course was offered for the first time in 1967, jointly with the Soil Mechanics and Structures Sections and with the Geology Department. Difficulties of funding for students led to its closing in 1975, but by then eighty students had obtained this diploma. The subject then became an option in the Soil Mechanics MSc course, but the situation was regularised in 1978–79 when a separate MSc degree in Soil Mechanics and Engineering Seismology was started, and is still running.

The research programme has encompassed work on basic design principles for structures in seismic zones, establishing the need for provision of sufficient ductility in the structure to absorb the earthquake energy that is required to cause foundation failure through sliding. The need for 'fail safe' techniques in design was recognised very early.

Much work, with which Sarma has been closely associated, has been done on the stability analysis of earth dams. A design method based on plastic yield of the body of the dam was developed and has been used in the design of a number of dams in earthquake areas. Recent work has developed designs based on 'displacement' rather than 'stress' criteria.

A good deal of effort has gone into the retrieval and analysis of strong motion seismic recordings obtained from various parts of the world. This has been accompanied by seismic mapping of countries in seismically active areas. Such data are an addition to historical data of the last 2000 years which have been recovered through research on regional seismicity in the Middle and Near East. This historical research was carried out over a number of years with the support of NERC, UNESCO and the collaboration of several archaeological and geological institutes. This compilation of data will contribute enormously to the understanding of the long-term pattern of earthquake hazard. Currently, the Section is collaborating with the SERC London Centre of Marine Technology in respect to risk assessment.

Other research has included the study of the formation and development of shear zones in soils and soft rocks, and the evaluation of the upper bound of ground motions as a function of the foundation properties. The recent acquisition of a 4-tonne biaxial shake table, built in the Department with the collaboration of industry, offers a powerful tool for the verification of the post-yield behaviour of foundation and building materials subjected to prototype ground motions.

Twelve research degrees were awarded in the Section between 1966 and 1983. The title of Professor of Engineering Seismology was conferred on Ambraseys in 1973.

Civil Engineering Systems and Mechanics

Formative influences

During the 1960s a group of senior academics in the Department began to give expression to a growing fear that the mathematical and computational aspects of civil engineering were receiving insufficient attention. A major factor contributing to the neglect, it was thought, was the strict division of the Department into Sections which had become autonomous and isolated from one another.

On the other hand, there was good reason for this organisation. Each Section represented a separate professional discipline—steel structures, concrete structures, soil mechanics, hydraulics, etc—supported an associated postgraduate course and recruited staff to service this course. Consequently, each Section acquired a considerable expertise in its own discipline. This very outcome was Pippard's objective in organising the Department on sectional lines—to create a 'centre of excellence' in postgraduate education.

Nevertheless, there was a clear call for the loosening of the boundaries between the Sections. While the technological aspects of each professional discipline are different, and need a separate development, the underlying mathematical representation is largely common, as are the numerical techniques by which solutions are obtained to specific problems. Part of that fund of mathematical commonality between the professional disciplines is the subject of mechanics—particularly continuum mechanics which, in the 1960s, received the impetus for rapid development and consequently gained wider interest. In the Department, at that time, it became the focus for some inter-sectional activity in the form of postgraduate lecture courses and research seminars.

In October 1969 J. Munro was asked to give a new and contrasting pair of optional courses to third-year undergraduate students. He chose to present 'Mechanics'—an elementary account of the continuum mechanics of solids and fluids—and 'Systems Engineering'—a subject entirely new to the civil engineering curriculum in British universities.

Systems Engineering goes right to the heart of the mathematical ground common to all professional disciplines in civil engineering: the fundamental activity of the civil engineer as decision-maker. Whether he undertakes the design of a structure or a foundation, the operation of a sewage treatment plant or a traffic management scheme, or even the organisation of a construction schedule, the engineer's approach is substantially the same, and each case may be described in similar mathematical terms. A decision that leads to the satisfactory performance of the system is often said to be feasible; however, the engineer may not be satisfied with this decision, and may choose to seek further for one that will optimise performance in some way.

The techniques for establishing optimal decisions, are part of the realm of Systems Engineering. It is inseparably related to computing: its methods are algorithmic, and its roots are embedded in simple logic.

The formation of the Section

From 1971, the responsibility for teaching first year students devolved entirely on the departments in which they were registered. A first year civil engineering student who in the common course would have taken the single subject Applied Mechanics and Structures would now be required to take the two subjects Structures and Engineering Mechanics. The new subjects were, of course, to be specialised for the needs of a civil engineer.

Munro was given responsibility for teaching Engineering Mechanics and permission to appoint a new lecturer to service this course. D. Lloyd Smith, one of Munro's own research students, was appointed in August 1971. Smith, a graduate in Civil and Structural Engineering of the University of Sheffield, had previously been employed as a steelwork designer in the G.E.C. Automation Division, and in 1969 had come to Imperial College to take the postgraduate course in Concrete Structures.

A little later, it was agreed that the responsibility for the computer education of undergraduate students should no longer be vested in the College Computer Centre, but should be returned to the individual departments. Munro was asked to set up a first year course to be called Computer Methods.

C.J. Hogger, a computer science specialist, was appointed in September 1971 to a new post of lecturer. An Imperial College Chemistry graduate, Hogger had remained at the College in 1969 to take the postgraduate course in Computer Science. Upon leaving the Department of Computing and Control, he worked as a programmer with a computer software consultancy.

Teaching and research in Systems

Systems Engineering, paired with Mechanics as an option course for third-year undergraduates, was first given in 1969 by Munro. It proved exceedingly popular with students, largely through that part of its content which may be called 'management science'. However, it also set out to show how the systems approach could influence the development of the technology of civil engineering, particularly in structural design. The topics discussed were linear programming, games theory, utility theory, statistical decision analysis and networks, each being illustrated by application to practical civil engineering problems.

Soon after the founding of the Section, Munro was encouraged to offer the service of lectures on relevant concepts of systems engineering to the postgraduate courses in Transport, Hydrology and Public Health Engineering.

In October 1974 the staff of the Systems and Mechanics Section was augmented by the appointment of P.W. Jowitt to a temporary lecturership. Jowitt was a graduate of the Department, during his final year discharging the onerous duties of President of the City and Guilds College Students' Union. In 1972 he had joined Munro as a research student to work on the development of the maximum entropy formalism in statistical decision analysis. This work was subsequently broadened to include the statistical mechanics of particulate media. As temporary lecturer he assisted Munro in developing the Systems courses and also played an active role in mechanics teaching. In January 1977 he was appointed lecturer in the Hydrology group—soon to become part of the expanding Public Health and Water Resource Engineering Section—where his enthusiastic application of systems methods has continued.

P.F. Perry replaced Jowitt in October 1978 as lecturer in the Systems and Mechanics Section. With degrees in Engineering and Economics from Trinity College, Dublin, Perry moved to Cambridge, where he obtained a doctorate in Systems Engineering and Water Resources. He was then appointed Assistant Professor of Civil and Urban Engineering at the University of Pennsylvania, where he remained for three years before joining the staff at Imperial College. Although able to offer some support in Mechanics teaching, Perry's immediate duty in 1978 was to develop a new Systems course. The pair of final-year options, Systems Engineering and Mechanics, were replaced by two optional courses in Systems. It was decided that the first course should deal with systems for which the input and system parameters are known with certitude; it contained an increased coverage of network concepts and the study of linear programming was broadened to encompass the

Kuhn-Tucker theory of nonlinear programming. The treatment of systems with uncertain data was to form the basis of the second course. In 1979 the first course (Systems) was made mandatory for all third year undergraduates, the second course (Systems Engineering) remaining elective.

Munro's research in decision analysis began to lay emphasis on the distinction between two types of uncertain data or information. Random data may be collected in statistical form through repeatable experiments and decisions made through the maximum entropy formalism. Imprecise data in the form of subjective assessments—usually verbal and descriptive—may constitute the equally valid expert information from which decisions must be made. A scientific appraisal of this latter data has necessitated the development of the logic associated with fuzzy sets.

At the same time, Perry's research work also involved uncertain data, largely of a random nature. Perry left Imperial College in September 1981 to return to his native Ireland and to a lecturership at University College, Dublin.

In April 1980 the title Professor of Civil Engineering Systems was conferred on Munro, who on becoming Head of Department in 1982 resigned as head of Section and Smith became the new head.

Perry's place was taken by M.B. Beck as lecturer in October 1982. A chemical engineer, graduating from Exeter University, he became a research student in Control Engineering at Cambridge in 1970. After receiving a doctorate for his work on the application of systems theory to river pollution control, he held research fellowships at Lund Institute of Technology, Sweden, and Cambridge University. Then, in 1977 he became Research Task Leader at the International Institute for Applied Systems Analysis in Laxenburg, Austria, where he worked prolifically until tempted to take the vacant lecturership at Imperial College.

Teaching and research in Computing

Upon his appointment as lecturer in 1971, Hogger replaced Munro as Departmental Computer Representative, with responsibility for advising on investment in computing resources. Initially, however, all energies had to be channelled into working up the new first year undergraduate course in Computer Methods. This course was given by Hogger, with minor improvements, until 1977, when it was decided to replace it in October 1979 with a second year course.

Hogger developed several courses for the special needs of a large postgraduate school involved in advanced courses and research, and also became responsible for instituting and maintaining the departmental collection of terminals.

In research, Hogger maintained a close working relationship with members of the Department of Computing and Control, particularly R.A. Kowalski. His work primarily occupied the arena of computing science: rules of procedure for the derivation of algorithms and the development of logic as a high-level procedural programming language formed the main objectives in a long-term programme of research. In October 1983 he was appointed to one of the new Information Technology Lecturerships tenable in the expanding and reorganised Department of Computing.

The mantle of Departmental Computer Representative then passed to R.D. Wing, the possessor of remarkable practical skills in electronics and instrumentation. After graduating from Imperial College in Mechanical Engineering, Wing departed for the University of California at Berkeley. Here he was awarded the MS degree for research into the detonation of explosives in free space, a contribution to the Apollo Program for Lunar Exploration. In 1964 he returned to the Mechanical Engineering Department of Imperial College as a research assistant, receiving a doctorate for work on combustion and lubrication problems in highly rated engines. With the contraction of the British motor industry, Wing joined the Civil Engineering Department in 1978 to work on instrumentation problems in the Hydraulics Laboratory. He was appointed research fellow in 1980, and, since his special expertise was used to provide a departmental service related to computing, it seemed entirely appropriate that he should also join the Systems and Mechanics Section.

In October 1983 the Head of Department demanded a concerted effort to establish computer education as an integral element of the undergraduate curriculum. Through the efforts of C.J. Burgoyne, Hogger and Wing, a teaching laboratory—based on the BBC microcomputer—was founded.

Teaching and research in Mechanics

The third year undergraduate option course in Mechanics—started by Munro in 1969, and from 1972 given by Smith—ran until 1978 when, due partly to an increased coverage of mechanics in the second and third years and partly to a desire to increase undergraduate exposure to systems theory, it was terminated. Its emphasis had changed over the years from continuum mechanics to discrete mechanics through finite element methods and the application of linear programming to the plastic collapse of structures.

The first year course in Engineering Mechanics was begun by Smith in 1971. Its aim was to contrast the vectorial and variational approaches to the statics and dynamics of particles, rigid bodies and systems of particles by illustrating the general principles through a variety of engineering applications. For the first two years the course included an introduction to incompressible fluid dynamics given by B. MacMahon, and from 1974 Jowitt gave lectures on statics and kinematics; but 1977 saw its demise with the reorganisation of the undergraduate curriculum.

Prior to 1972, the theory of vibrations and the strength of materials were taught in a second year combined course by members of the Department of Mechanical Engineering. It was replaced by a new course initially called 'Mechanics of Materials and Vibrations', which in 1975 became simply 'Mechanics'. Munro taught the theory of vibrations—being replaced in 1975 by Jowitt; Smith gave the mechanics of materials lectures; and MacMahon lectured on fluid dynamics.

In 1977, to ease the burden on second year students, the vibrations lectures were removed to the third year, there to constitute a separate and mandatory course called 'Vibrations' given first by Munro and later by Smith. The course was enlarged in 1980 under the title 'Mechanics' to include the linear programming content of the abandoned third year option courses. Fluid dynamics was dropped from the second year course in 1978 due to the founding of a separate third year option course in that subject. So, in 1979, the second year course became 'Mechanics of Materials', and some new lectures on plates and shells were contributed by M.N. Pavlovic, a newly appointed lecturer in the Concrete Structures Section. In 1983 Munro began a new and brief first year course on the dynamics of structures, which included demonstrations of the new shake-table facility.

When Munro left the Concrete Section to found the Systems Section, he continued to teach the Indeterminate Structures and Structural Dynamics courses for Concrete Structures postgraduate students. Munro's one-year tenure of a Visiting Professorship at the University of California at Berkeley in 1963 was the primary agent which inspired his development of the course in Structural Dynamics. Then, in 1967, he was asked to give a course on random vibrations for postgraduate students of Seismology: this structural mechanics interest in statistics led him directly to the study of Bayesian decision analysis.

Munro's course on Indeterminate Structures owed a considerable debt to the matrix techniques developed by the far-sighted R.S. Jenkins—a former student (1927-30)—and to J.C. de C. Henderson who had given the first course to be based on Jenkins' methods. By 1971, Munro had significantly developed the course so that the theory of plastic structures could be presented in a similar manner to that for elastic structures. The special similarity between the relations of statics and those of kinematics, termed contragredience by Jenkins, became the founding axiom in Munro's view of plastic structures: he gave it a new name—static-kinematic duality (SKD).

From 1971, further developments in Munro's lectures on the plastic theory of structures reflected the vigorous programme of research being pursued in the Systems and Mechanics Section. In 1967 he had begun to lecture on optimal plastic design using linear programming. Then, in 1970, Smith became his research student, working on the use of linear programming and related mathematical systems for describing the theory of structural plasticity. The important role of SKD was emphasised through the duality theory of mathematical programming, which itself gives expression to all the complementary variational principles of the plastic theory of structures.

In 1972, Smith began an introductory course on Finite Element Methods applied to elastic and plastic systems, a course for postgraduate students of Concrete Structures, Timber Structures and Soil Mechanics. Over the years, however, these lectures became more specialised to the needs of structural engineers; so in 1978, when Smith inherited the Structural Dynamics course, and with the more recent support of Pavlovic, stronger links were formed between the two courses.

A succession of able research students has enabled Munro and Smith to undertake a long-term exhaustive survey of the use of mathematical programming in the plastic theory of structures—in particular for plates and slabs, three-dimensional frames with interactive plastic yielding in bending, twisting and thrust, reinforced concrete frames with plastic softening, elastoplastic buckling of spatial truss systems, elastoplastic plane frames with very large displacements and deformations, bearing problems and slope stability in geomechanics and vibrations in elastoplastic structures. In addition, fuzzy programming has been applied to problems where the data are known only imprecisely.

In research, as the old paths become well-trodden, there is always the excitement of exploring the new: the development of 'expert systems' in the field of civil engineering has now begun.

Environmental Studies

In 1971, the opportunity which existed of creating a new first-year course encouraged T.A. Wyatt to propose a new course for inclusion in the first year curriculum. Wyatt, a graduate of the Department, had taken his PhD degree in the Structures Section in 1955. After practical experience with Freeman Fox & Partners, he returned to the College as a lecturer in 1962. Concern for the environmental effects of technology was growing rapidly, and Wyatt felt strongly that Imperial College graduates should have their undoubtedly excellent technical education complemented by an understanding of the effects of their work both on the natural environment and on the community. Accordingly, he had introduced a series of tutorial classes in 1970, and obtained Departmental agreement that a new course of this nature merited the appointment of a new member of staff. M.W. Baldwin, a Cambridge graduate, was chosen and started duties as a lecturer in 1971. Baldwin had worked with Mott, Hay & Anderson for five years on a variety of transport projects, and had come to the Department in 1970 to take an MSc degree in Soil Mechanics. They set up the framework of the course, and were joined the following year by Miss J.M. Brown, a graduate of St Andrews University, where she had read English and History. After several years of teaching, Brown had come to the Department as an assistant to Professor Skempton, and had worked with him for several years, aiding him in his historical work, prior to her appointment as a lecturer.

The course then established was initially based on coursework only, but was subsequently expanded to become a Part I examination subject. Its basic philosophy is to demonstrate that civil engineering problems are frequently not merely problems in applied mechanics, but require solutions which take account of social and environmental factors too. It is not sufficient for the engineer to concern himself merely with whether he *can* build, but to ask himself as well whether he *ought* to build. Drawing board and calculator are no longer the only tools; to these must be added the environmental impact assessment, and cost benefit analysis, for the engineer must place his work in the wider context of the community in which he works.

The interactions between the work of the civil engineer and the environment are without number; therefore, to tackle the subject within the confines of a single course for first year students necessitates a highly selective approach. It was decided to give the students a basic grounding in the rudiments of the history of the profession, and engineering economics. These two elements then provide a background against which a number of specific subjects can be examined more closely. The areas chosen for this more detailed work vary from year to year, but typically include studies on energy resources, water supply, waste-water treatment, urban transport and noise. With such a spread, it is particularly appropriate to enlist the support of other Sections to provide expert assistance, and this ability to call upon the skills available within the Department is an important feature of the course.

To date, the teaching effort has been concentrated within the first year syllabus, although an environment option was also provided for second year students until 1983.

Research

Wyatt has continued to divide his time between Environmental Studies (here and in the interdepartmental Centre for Environmental Technology) and the Structures Section. His research has been based in the latter Section and, as such, is described elsewhere.

Baldwin's major research interest has grown directly out of his involvement with the environmental aspects of engineering. He has concentrated on studies of transport planning, with particular reference to the use of inland waterways for freight carriage. This has led to appointments to a number of professional and trade committees. He is currently an elected member of the British National Committee of the Permanent International Association of Navigation Congresses, and a Vice-Chairman of the National Waterways Transport Association. Recently, the Institution of Civil Engineers invited him to give the 1984 Vernon-Harcourt lecture.

Brown has continued the research interests in the history of engineering commenced under Skempton and, among other topics, she has spent several years studying the building and organisation of the great nineteenth-century irrigation systems of Northern India.

Public Health and Water Resource Engineering

The establishment of the Public Health and Water Resource Engineering Section in 1977 was well founded in terms of both the advanced research activities initiated in the 1970s by Perry and of the valued tradition of the specialist postgraduate teaching in the Engineering Hydrology and Public Health Engineering MSc courses. The linking of the two subjects was very timely in relation to the state of water engineering in practice, following the recent reorganisations in England and Wales and the growing demand for specialist water resources engineers in developing countries. Although developments in hydrology have stemmed mainly from fluid mechanics and hydraulics, contemporary applications of hydrological techniques are now closely connected with aspects of water quality. Hydrologists in water authorities are currently concerned with the management of water resources in which water quality standards of supplies and effluents have become as important as water quantities.

Public Health Engineering

The first priority of the new Section was the building up of the complement of academic staff to cope with the postgraduate teaching and with the direction and supervision of the research projects. For the latter it was particularly important to retain continuity and thus it was gratifying to be able to appoint J.N. Lester to a lectureship after his invaluable two years as research assistant. Lester's initial qualifications in the life sciences added to the interdisciplinary nature of the teaching and made the Section less dependent on outside expertise in microbiology. The other research assistant, a chemist, R.J. Young, served as a temporary lecturer until his appointment in 1979 as a lecturer in the Civil Engineering Department of the University of Dundee. The strength in engineering in the Section was partially supplied by the appointment in 1977 of N.J.D. Graham, who had just completed the postgraduate course after several years of experience with a firm of consultants. At the same time, added weight to the leadership of the Section was gained by Perry's promotion to reader.

With such major staff changes, it was inevitable that the postgraduate course in Public Health Engineering should take on a new look. The fundamental aims of the founders remained intact, but developments in the subject also called for inclusion in the modified syllabus. The first term's series of basic lecture courses continued to cover applied chemistry, introductory zoology and bacteriology, but was widened to include introductory meteorology, rainfall analysis and an introduction to systems analysis with strong encouragement to attend the computer programming course in the Christmas vacation. The standard courses on water supply, sewerage systems and practical analysis of water and water-borne wastes laid the foundations for advanced considerations, in the second term, of the unit processes of water and waste-water treatment and of the problems of public health engineering in tropical climates. A design project for a water supply treatment works or for a waste-water treatment plant was also included in the second term's programme. The students were also given a choice between taking air pollution control and solid waste disposal or systems analysis in water resources management given jointly with the Engineering Hydrology class. Following a study tour of water authorities and research institutes during the Easter vacation and written examinations, the students embarked upon individual projects for the rest of the year. The projects could be laboratory-based, could entail an engineering design with or without the aid of computer analyses or be associated with one or other of the several research topics under investigation. The project reports form a major part of the examination for MSc and DIC.

The Public Health Engineering course continues to have well over a hundred applicants each year. In the first year after reorganisation, there were 21 students of whom 8 were home students and 13 from overseas. The emphasis of post-experience specialist training was evident in that 18 out of the 21 students attending had some form of postgraduate industrial experience. However, in more recent years, there has been an increase in applications from new graduates, especially from home students. The overseas applicants tend to remain those with previous engineering experience.

The course syllabus continues to be updated each year according to the availability of teaching staff. The strength in engineering returned to its former level with the appointment in 1979 of J.P. Lumbers, a product of the Birmingham Public Health Engineering course, with considerable design experience with civil engineering consultants. The successful fulfilment of numerous outside research contracts and the consolidation of the teaching and research activities in the Public Health and Water Resource Engineering Section was recognised in the appointment in 1981 of Perry, the head of Section, to a chair.

The scope of the research in Public Health Engineering widened considerably with the expansion of the laboratory facilities. The former all-purpose laboratory has been refurbished for research only and extra bench space has been made by constructing a mezzanine floor along one side of the room. The postgraduate course drawing-office has been converted into a dual-purpose room with enhanced arrangements for formal lecturing and with three walls fitted with benches to provide teaching laboratory space. A new mobile laboratory built and equipped to in-house specifications is used for remote site sampling and on-site analysis. A permanent large-scale pilot sewage treatment plant at a sewage works also allows much on-site study of the various aspects of process design and performance. The research laboratories now include the most advanced techniques for monitoring the physical, chemical and biological parameters of waters and waste-waters

35. The Public Health Engineering mobile laboratory for environmental sampling

and the pollutants of the atmosphere. Mass spectrometric, atomic adsorption and gas-liquid chromatographic techniques have been developed for the determination of specific pollutants in gaseous and aqueous samples from the environment. Unfortunately, it has been possible to engage only one extra qualified and experienced technician to manage and maintain all the advanced equipment. In any one year, there are on average a dozen research students engaged on a wide range of projects under the guidance of three or four post-doctoral fellows who have obtained research assistant appointments on completion of their theses. Funding is arranged on an annual basis from research contracts with government departments, research councils and institutes, water authorities and industry.

The advanced analytical techniques are being applied in the study of polycylic aromatic hydrocarbons and heavy metals from urban surface runoff and halogenated organic substances in lowland waters abstracted for potable supplies. The research into multi-layer filtration in water treatment has advanced into mathematical models applicable to the function of grains of any material in filters. In waste-water treatment, particular attention is being paid to both toxic elements (including heavy metals) and specific organic substances of concern in effluent waters. The composition of sewage sludges is also being investigated with respect to the treatment required for their safe disposal to agricultural land. In the air pollution studies, air quality surveys have been made at Gatwick and Stansted Airports as part of the investigations associated with their considered expansion. Co-ordinated research in waste-water treatment modelling and control links the work of the public health engineers with the expertise in systems engineering to improve process understanding and design in order to reduce operating costs and to increase efficiency and treatment capacity of waste-water treatment plants.

Engineering Hydrology

From 1977, Hydrology continued to be taught at the undergraduate level in the final year option, but stimulated by a four-month visit to Australia, Miss Shaw proposed an introductory course in the subject for the first year Civil Engineering students. This was successfully incorporated into the new undergraduate syllabus in the session 1977–78 and has run satisfactorily for six years. However, the need for postgraduate hydrological training was still manifest, particularly in overseas countries, and it was considered important to restart the Engineering Hydrology MSc course as soon as possible. New staff members were recruited into the Section. First came P.W. Jowitt in 1977, bringing systems and statistical expertise from the Civil Engineering Systems and Mechanics Section of the Department. He was soon followed in 1978 by H.S. Wheater, a research hydrologist from the Civil Engineering Department of Bristol University. The part-time appointment of a former student and senior engineer, T.G. Davis, brought invaluable overseas practical experience to the teaching at all levels. The postgraduate course began again in the session 1978–79 with the renewed support of the Geology Department and with special temporary assistance from Professor D.R. Cox for Time Series Analysis and Professor A.J. Rutter for Plant Water Relations. The encouragement and helpful criticism of the external examiners, first Professor J.E. Nash and then Professor T. O'Donnell, during these years has ensured the reinstatement of the previous high academic standards.

Within the restructured Sectional framework, the expansion of research has been most marked. In any one year, the number of research students in full-time attendance has been on a par with the number of postgraduates attending the course. The advancement of the knowledge of hydrological processes is being actively pursued in field studies at Silwood Park, where considerable instrumentation for the measurement of meteorological and soil moisture variables has been installed. The instrumental data are being used to test theoretical models of rainfall/evaporation/soil moisture fluxes under different weather, crop and soil characteristics. The application of these studies is in improving methods of estimating groundwater recharge, in catchment balance studies and in irrigation scheduling. Studies of the rainfall-runoff process are proceeding in order to define methods of accounting for the nonlinear catchment response to rainfall. A distributed nonlinear rainfall-runoff model is being used to evaluate the sensitivity of flood runoff to storm dynamics particularly for urban catchments. Stochastic techniques continue to be actively researched, particularly with regard to real-time flood forecasting and control. Statistical models are being applied to problems of water quality and to waste-water treatment process forecasting and control. Systems analysis and decision theory are being applied to the problems of operational/real time water resources management and particular emphasis is laid on the consideration of costs and benefits of forecasting and control schemes. The problems of uncertainty and risk are being incorporated into the planning and design of water resource systems. For non-numerical information, 'fuzzy set' theory offers a technique for its interpretation and inclusion in any decision-making. In all aspects of the hydrological research, close cooperation is fostered with water authorities, research institutes and consulting engineers where the main aim is to solve real practical engineering problems.

Water Technology and Environmental Technology

In addition to the merged responsibilities for Engineering Hydrology and Public Health Engineering, the new Section has further teaching commitments under the above headings.

The recent changes in the undergraduate Civil Engineering syllabus have brought an alteration in student requirements for optional subjects in the third year. Since a prime request was for engineering applications in the water industry, a course entitled 'Water Technology' was devised, bringing together the practical aspects of the evaluation of water quantities, water treatment for potable supplies and the treatment processes necessary to make the various waste waters into effluents acceptable to the environment.

In the session 1977–78, the newly established interdisciplinary Imperial College Centre for Environmental Technology introduced an MSc course in Environmental Technology. In addition to participating in the core course in the first term, the Public Health and Water Resource Engineering Section makes substantial contributions to the Pollution Option and is fully responsible for the Water Resources Management (subsequently renamed Water Management) option.

The youngest Section in the Department is thus seen to be vigorously active and hard-working, contributing to increasing teaching at the undergraduate level, to the running of two successful postgraduate courses and to the advancement of the subject through the considerable volume of research undertaken for a wide range of sponsors.

~ 8 ~

The history of the support services

The Departmental Library

The establishment of a departmental library was an integral part of the development plans which were being formulated in the late 1950s, and it is largely due to Skempton's recognition of the vital rôle which could be played by such a service in supporting the Department's research and teaching needs, and his enthusiastic encouragement during its early years, that the Civil Engineering Library today not only fulfils its intended purpose but has also become nationally renowned.

Prior to the formation of the departmental libraries, the literature requirements of the College's engineering departments had been met in the main by the City and Guilds Library (later to form part of the Lyon Playfair Library) and by the Science Museum Library. The Department itself possessed a small collection of textbooks which was housed in the Common Room and served as a staff library, access to which was occasionally permitted to research students; collections of books of specific interest were also held by some departmental Sections, notably Public Health Engineering, which had been provided with funds for this purpose by the Rockefeller Foundation.

The beginnings of an organised library service can be traced back to 1960, when Miss J. Troy, previously a member of the City and Guilds Library staff, transferred to the Department. Miss Troy took charge of the staff library, cataloguing its stock and setting up a formal loan system; she also became actively involved in the plans for the new library and selected much of its furniture and equipment. At the end of 1962, however, she resigned from the College in order to take up a post in the library of the Engineering Laboratories, Oxford.

As the move to Imperial College Road was now imminent, the appointment of a Departmental Librarian became a priority and Skempton invited Mrs M. Carter, a member of the Institution of Civil Engineers' library staff, to apply for the position. It is rare that an opportunity to participate in the creation of an entirely new library is presented and this offer was readily accepted. Mrs Carter entered the Department in February 1963 as its Librarian, an appointment she was to hold for nearly twenty years.

A Departmental Library Committee, consisting of three members of staff, had already been formed and, on being joined by Mrs. Carter, set about acquiring basic library stock. It had been agreed that the Public Health collection should be absorbed into the new library and, although for a time it seemed there might be a disproportionate provision of books on the Black Death, yellow fewer and sewage treatment, this was a welcome addition. Runs of journals which had been kept in various parts of the old building now came to light and many personal donations of books and other material were made at this time by members of staff. Moving day also provided an opportunity for clearing out bookcases and cupboards, the sometimes surprising contents of which were directed to the Librarian's new office. Unfortunately, there were as yet no shelves in the Library to house the rapidly growing stock, and the office floor became the depository for a rising tide of books. During the busy summer which followed the move, the Head of Department and the Chairman of the Library Committee were often to be seen with sleeves rolled up, assisting the Librarian in the task of organisation.

The Civil Engineering Library at last opened its doors in October 1963, with a stock of about 1,700 textbooks (mostly uncatalogued at the time), 730 volumes of periodicals and a collection of 1,200 reprints and pamphlets. Originally 279 m of shelving were provided, but as the stock steadily expanded, additional bookcases began to be installed. A stackroom was constructed in the adjacent corridor in 1969 and further storage space subsequently found in other parts of the Department. By 1983, shelving had increased to 630 m, and the stock consisted of 8,400 textbooks and conference proceedings; 3,300 volumes of periodicals; 4,200 reprints and pamphlets; 11,300 serial reports; 1,700 theses and dissertations; and 550 maps.

When the Library was established, it was assumed that its main function would be to support the research work of the Department, an expectation which has been successfully fulfilled. One of its unexpected achievements, however, has been its growing contribution to undergraduate education and training. Today, when so much undergraduate coursework involves intensive use of library resources, it is strange to recall that the undergraduates of twenty years ago were not expected to do more than consult recommended textbooks in the Library, and were certainly not encouraged to take material away to read—to quote from the Library Committee's first policy circular: 'Undergraduates will be permitted to borrow books only in exceptional circumstances, when their supervisors can make a request on their behalf and will accept responsibility for the return of borrowed items'. In practice, of course, it was impossible to prevent their taking full advantage of the Library's services, and the system of obtaining a tutor's written authority for each book borrowed soon became a source of irritation to all concerned. Full borrowing rights were therefore granted to final year students in 1967 and to all undergraduates in 1969.

Personal assistance, offered as the need arises, has always been an integral feature of the library service, but as demand increased it became evident that new students, both undergraduate and postgraduate, would benefit from some formal instruction in efficient library use. In 1976, the Librarian instituted a series of lectures for this purpose at the beginning of the academic year. Practical sessions on information retrieval methods, appropriate to the needs of third year students, were introduced a few years later.

The importance of the Librarian's contribution to the Department's activities was recognised in 1967 when this post was given para-academic status. A full-time library assistant was provided from the beginning and originally held a fairly junior grade, but with the increasing volume of work this became a position of considerable responsibility, attracting professionally qualified applicants. Eventually, soon after the appointment of Mrs K. Crooks in 1976, it was decided that elevation to the para-academic grade of Assistant Librarian was merited. Mrs Crooks, who came to the Department from the Library of Queen's University, Belfast, succeeded Mrs Carter as Departmental Librarian in October 1982.

In addition to the Library's modern stock, a special collection of particular interest to the engineering historian is maintained, and is administered by a small sub-committee of the Library Committee. Known as the Civil Engineering History Collection, this consists of about 700 works published during the last 250 years on applied science and engineering, many of them classic texts. Books acquired from the Institution of Civil Engineers in 1961 form the basis of the Collection, but important additions have occasionally been purchased and many gifts have been received: notable among these was Skempton's own collection of early works on soil mechanics, presented to the Department in 1981. The aim of the Collection is to preserve the key works of the past and influential publications of more recent times, thus providing a unique record, through contemporary literature, of the development of civil engineering from the eighteenth century onwards. Exhibitions of material from the Collection are mounted in the Library, and a detailed catalogue, intended for publication, is in progress.

The Library's readers, staff and students alike, have always been liberal in their gifts of publications, and these have been especially welcome in lean financial years. Literature is also presented by many individuals and organisations outside the College; approximately half the annual intake of periodicals is received in this way. Miss L. Chitty's generous bequest to the Department is to be used to create the Chitty Reading Room as an annexe to the Library.

It is on record that the Civil Engineering Library Committee was once described as the most civilised library committee in the College, and it still retains the quality of an informal discussion group. Its most cherished tradition is the sherry party given by the Librarian just before Christmas—those working in the Library's normally studious environment are often puzzled by the unusual sounds of merriment coming from the office on these occasions. The Committee's main purpose is to formulate the Library's policy and to oversee its budget; professional and administrative decisions rest with the Librarian, who is also responsible for all expenditure. The opinions of the members of the Department are always sought on major policy decisions, to gain the widest possible representation of interests. The original three academic Committee members eventually increased to six, including the Librarian, and since 1971 one postgraduate and one final year undergraduate have been elected each year to participate in the Committee's work. A senior member of the Lyon Playfair Library staff is also invited to attend Committee meetings, to liaise in matters affecting the College library system as a whole; in recent years the College Librarian has been welcomed in this capacity.

Members of the Civil Engineering Library Committee, 1962–1982

R.E. Gibson	1962–65	(Chairman 1962–65)
P. Minton	1962–77	(Chairman 1968–77)
A. Edwards	1962–75	(Acting Chairman 1970)
M. Carter	1963–82	(Librarian 1963–82)
N. Morgenstern	1963–68	(Chairman 1965–68)
L.G. Booth	1965–	

J. Munro	1965–75	
J.N. Hutchinson	1968–	(Chairman 1977–)
G. Owens	1975–	
D.L. Smith	1975–	
A. Scott-Moncrieff	1977–	
K.M. Crooks	1982–	(Librarian 1982–)

Representatives of the Lyon Playfair Library:
G.M. Paterson; J. Morcom; A. Whitworth

The years have seen the evolution of the Civil Engineering Library from a small collection of books into an efficient information service, closely integrated with the work of the Department but also attracting visitors from all part of the country and overseas. It is now taken for granted, which is perhaps a measure of its success. The traditional library principles on which it was founded are now becoming allied to modern technology, thus ensuring that the Departmental Library continues to develop in step with the needs of future generations of civil engineers.

Technical Services

When the Department of Civil and Mechanical Engineering opened in 1884, Unwin had two members of staff to assist him, one of whom was H. Gillett, described as 'Principal mechanic', although he was later promoted to 'Workshop Superintendent'. His job was the care of the machines and engines with which the laboratory was equipped. A few years later, two other members of staff joined him, one described as 'Carpentry Instructor' and the other 'Workshop Instructor'. They are listed under Gillett's name and their job seems to have been to work in the laboratories and workshops and help with instruction on the use of tools and machines which formed an important part of Unwin's course. At the time of the separation of Civil and Mechanical Engineering subjects in 1913, there were 18 employed in the workshops, 7 of them skilled mechanics. Gillett was still there and indeed remained in the Department of Mechanical Engineering and Motive Power from 1913 until his retirement in 1920.

Dixon began work in 1913 with three members of academic staff and one member of technical staff, T. Bryce, described as a 'draughtsman', although he later performed the function of laboratory and workshop superintendent. The interruption of the war delayed the engagement of more staff, but in 1918–19, the following are listed: T. Bryce (draughtsman), Miss E. Redway (tracer), A. Brew (fitter), H.G. Fisher (labourer), and three boys. This staff gradually built up and the lists in the mid-1920s show four workshop staff, two or three labourers and three or four boys. By the end of Dixon's headship there were seven in the workshop and four boys as well as the draughtsman and tracer.

The technicians' work was by this time more varied. Obviously they had to continue to look after plant, but Dixon's own experimental work involved the building in the laboratory of items such as the 20 ft span concrete arch resting on brick abutments referred to in research reports. The vertical rig for testing the wire ropes used in mines was also built by technical staff in connection with Dixon's work for the Safety in Mines Research Board.

Pippard's interest in small models and his later interest in the testing of the voussoir arch and model dams required more advanced skills to be developed in the technicians. The same is true of White's experimental work in the Hydraulics Laboratory where, for example, special glass-sided flumes were built to exhibit different phenomena of fluid mechanics.

In addition to the laboratories, separate workshops gradually developed for electrical, carpentry and machine work. These performed a service function for the Department as a whole and the laboratories. The workshops were at the north end of the Goldsmiths' Extension. The Welding Shop was at basement level beneath the Electrical and Carpenters' Workshops, which were at ground level. Above them was the Machine Shop overlooking the Structures Laboratory. The majority of the machine tools were driven by overhead belting.

In the immediate post-Second World War period, the numbers of technicians rose to about a dozen with a sharp rise in the period of the expansion of the College in the late 1950s and early 1960s. By 1959 there were twenty-seven technicians; four years later, at the time of the move to the new building in April 1963, there were forty. Their numbers went on growing, reaching a peak of sixty-seven in 1971. By this period, a fair number were on contract work for government bodies and industrial organisations, their salaries paid out of the grant for specific pieces of research. The skills required by this stage had made it necessary for the College to establish an apprenticeship scheme, with boys admitted to it and taking their City and Guilds Certificates or other qualifications while in full- or part-time work. The apprenticeship system still exists, alongside day release schemes.

Under Sparkes and Baker, model-testing in the Structures and Concrete Laboratories entered a new phase with much larger models constructed. A number of model dams, for example, were made by technicians, who cast the concrete for the arch dam models of the Verwoerd, El Atazar, and Monar dams, among others.

Other work in which they have been actively involved includes all the steel work on plated structures, box girders, the Thames Barrier, and a bifurcated motorway section. The test specimens are designed in the Department, and the components constructed by specialist firms. The work of erecting them, applying strain gauges to them, and testing them is usually done in the Department.

For many years in the 1920s and 1930s the laboratory was staffed by the same small group of men, most of whom stayed until retirement forced them to leave. Throughout the thirties this group was made up of T. Bryce, draughtsman and laboratory Superintendent (1914–44), H.G. Fisher (1918–54), G.G. Pirie (1919–64), A.S. Amos (1919–58), W.A.V. Bryan (1920–60), E. Sinfield (1920–59), E.J. Howe (1926–54), H.R. Thomas (1927–50) and J. Watt (1930–60).

The rapid build-up of staff since 1945 makes it impossible to list all, but many appointed post-war were here for more than twenty years: W. Bryan (1948–79), N.D. Scott (1948–71), F.H. Crawley (1949–81), G. Harvey (1950–78), D.T. Evans (1955–82), H.G. Wilson (1955–77) and J.W. Pickering (1959–81).

In the present generation of technicians, those with thirty or more years service include J.E. Neale (1948), J.R. Turner (1950), L.F. Spall (1952), and P.F. Clifford (1954); and with twenty years or more G.R. Scopes (1958), J.C. Finn (1959), C.D. Mortlock (1960), R.A.J. Philpott (1962), G. Thomas (1962), P.J. Jellis (1963) and H.R. Clements (1964). Among recent superintendents, noteworthy was R. Brannan, appointed to the staff in 1949 and superintendent in 1962. His premature death in 1980 removed from us a cheerful and likable man. The post of Departmental Superintendent has been filled recently, with the appointment of R. Loveday, who joined the staff in 1950.

Superintendents
Civil and Mechanical Engineering Department

H. Gillett	1884–1920	'Principal mechanic' 1884–97. Workshop Superintendent 1897–1920 (in Department of Mechanical Engineering from 1913).

Civil Engineering Department
Laboratory Superintendents

T. Bryce	1914–1944	Always described as 'Draughtsman'.
A. Hall	1946–1949	Joined staff 1944.
A.S. Amos	1949–1958	Joined staff 1919.
R. Brannan	1958–1962	Joined staff 1949. Acting Superintendent.

*Departmental Superintendents**

R. Brannan	1962–1980	
R. W. Loveday	1984–	Joined staff 1950.

Secretarial Services

At the beginning of our history it seems to have been a luxury for staff to have any secretarial assistance. The establishment of the College allowed for a Chief Clerk to keep the records of the Board of Studies. The status of this person is now rather obscure, but he probably was not the equivalent of to-day's College Secretary, a senior administrative post. In 1911 we find a clerk listed in the Department of Civil and Mechanical Engineering's establishment and Dalby's Department went on employing such a person from that date. In the Department of Civil Engineering it took longer for such an appointment to be made, and it was 1917 before a 'tracer' was appointed. This person probably combined tracing and clerical duties, but she was formally replaced by a 'professor's secretary' in 1935. An early tracer who gave long service was Miss H. Doezy (1920–32). She was succeeded by Miss

* The title changed, and the scope of duties widened to include general departmental service. In the period 1980–84, the Department was organised by a Technical Services Working Party, with R. Loveday as Executive Secretary.

M. Wingate (1932–35), who appears in the group photograph of staff in 1935.

The first 'professor's secretary' was Miss C.E. Mackay (1935–40). Only one secretary was employed up till 1945, when a second person was appointed as secretary to the Concrete Section. By the late 1940s there were three, but bearing in mind that there were still comparatively few academic staff, they managed to cope between them with the work. It was only after the development of Sections that the secretarial staff increased. By 1957 there were five, but their numbers were increased rapidly to fifteen or sixteen by the 1960s, in line with the general expansion of the Department at that time. The numbers have stayed at about this level and currently we have seventeen.

In addition to secretarial assistance, Pippard was able in 1946 to appoint an administrative assistant. The first of these was J.E. Duncan (1946–53) (died 1953), followed by O.W.F. Leach (1953–55) and F.C.G. Cutcliffe (1955–56). Out of this office evolved the post of Assistant Director.

The duties of the first secretaries were in essence much as they are now, except that the technology of the office has changed dramatically. The typewriter was, naturally, in use for correspondence and the typing of papers, with much use of carbon paper to make several copies—oh, the horror of making corrections on several sheets using an ink eraser! Early duplicating-machines involved the production by the secretary of a 'master' sheet on specially coated paper so that the message appeared in reverse on the back of it. The back was then brought into contact with some fluid or jelly and the imprint transferred onto clean paper by a pressing or rolling mechanism. Staff who were in the Department in the 1950s will remember the famous 'Banda' machine, which consumed large quantities of spirit in a rather drunken way before it did its work, producing a purple imprint on the sheet of greater or lesser intensity according to its mood. Many a thesis was produced (slowly) this way. The Banda gave way eventually to an increasing use of ink duplicating-machines. The process of reproduction involved the cutting of a waxed sheet by typing without the ribbon in the typewriter. Correction of errors involved a good deal of pink correcting fluid, and operating the machine was an inky business, with a great show of temperament on the part of the machine. It was a huge relief to secretarial staff when duplicating tasks were largely taken over by photo-copying machines in the mid-1960s. These have become more and more elaborate;

the newest ones installed carry out automatic collation and stapling functions, and our latest installation has a reduction and enlarging capacity which has revolutionised the use that can be made of graphic material for teaching and other purposes.

During the 1960s manual typewriters gave place to electric ones and the Department even had one or two 'golf-ball' type machines. The more recent typewriters are able to carry out automatic correction of errors at the touch of a button, and some have a one-line display panel and memory to allow correction rather on the same principle as a word processor. We have recently also installed several of this last item, and the secretary's traditional skills of accuracy and high speed are less important now than her expertise in grappling with 'the manual' and learning to make 'the commands'. The speed with which corrections, additions and deletions can be made to the text has made this an invaluable office tool, while the potential of using it in combination with the computer opens up a whole new area of activity.

One of the remaining traditional skills still in demand is shorthand, as the dictaphone has never really caught on in popularity. Our romance with one in the Department in the 1960s was of the briefest. Shorthand writers are, however, becoming increasingly rare, and if voice-sensitive machines eventually become widely available, the secretary's role will indeed have changed in respect of her tools. It will not be easy, however, to replace what she offers in personal service in running the office, assisting with the administration of postgraduate courses, telephoning, keeping the engagement diary, organising the files (or discs) and fending off the unwanted visitor. The Department will be the poorer if we ever decide that secretaries are a luxury we can no longer afford.

~ 9 ~

Some distinguished alumni

In continental Europe the prestige, in their respective countries, of the alumni of the technical institutions is unchallenged. It has been said that Guildsmen constitute the only comparable body in Britain. Certainly Guildsmen occupy positions of influence in all branches of civil engineering, although it is easier to find examples in the upper ranks of government and political influence when one looks at Guildsmen overseas.

It would be an invidious task to attempt any coordinated roll of honour. It has, however, seemed worthwhile to demonstrate the extent to which we have contributed to the achievements of the profession by viewing some of these achievements in perspective and recording a few of the names associated therewith.

From the outset, Guildsmen showed themselves able to reach senior posts at home and abroad. Eminent surveyors included A.E. Young (1887–90), Surveyor-General of Jamaica, and E.M. Dowson (1895–98), Director-General of the Survey of Egypt. Several reached the highest level in irrigation engineering in India, men such as G. Lacey (1904–07), G.W.M. Ball (1904–07), A.B. Buckley (1893–96), and A.M.R. Montagu (1911–13). Others became Directors of Public Works in farflung parts of the world, among them H.G. Peake (1907–10) in Zanzibar, W. Wise (1907–09) in Fiji and A.S. Clay (1909–12) in Iraq. Those who took up academic life included A. (later Sir Alfred) Chatterton (1885–87), who became Professor of Engineering at the Government College of Engineering, Madras, and F.H. Hummel (1889–92), who became Professor of Engineering at Queen's University, Belfast. Very interesting for us now is the fact that one of Unwin's first four students, H.M. Martin (1885–87), in his book *Statically Indeterminate Structures and the Method of Least Work* (1895), drew attention to the ideas of Castigliano, which were to have such a profound effect on methods of structural analysis when they became widely known.

The importance attached to a university education in civil engineering rose sharply in the period following the First World War. War-time advances perhaps had greatly extended the scope and detail of analytic calculations. When Ralph Freeman (senior)

(1897–1900) embarked on the Sydney Harbour Bridge project in 1922, the work was remarkable not only for its scale of the structure, but also for the extent of solutions evaluated of elastic stress distribution in multiply-indeterminate structures. Gilbert Roberts (1920–22) was responsible for this, which called for many, many hours of operation of mechanical calculators.

H. Shirley Smith (1919–23) and Charles Crosthwaite (1920–23) joined the group of bridge engineers. Crosthwaite brought Timoshenko's thinking on suspension bridge theory to this country and extended it, making it a simple design office procedure. There is personal continuity through our Guildsmen to the great 'streamlined' suspension bridges of the last 25 years, Humber bridge being currently the world's longest span.

When the McRobert Awards for innovation engineering were inaugurated in 1971, the first award was divided between the Harrier aircraft and the Severn Bridge. Both teams were headed by Guildsmen; four out of the six of the Severn Bridge team had first or second degrees from the Department, namely, Roberts and Crosthwaite already mentioned, as well as W.C. Brown (1951–52) and T.A. Wyatt (1949–52).

The twenties and thirties also saw the widespread development of reinforced concrete construction. No one in Britain had a wider range of activity than Oscar Faber (1903–06), who had received the DSc from the University of London as early as 1909 for a thesis on concrete beams in bending and shear, and continued his activities through to the Mulberry Harbours of 1944 and beyond. In parallel with his practical achievements, Oscar Faber contributed greatly as a publicist for reinforced concrete construction.

Danish engineers also made great contributions to the development of concrete construction in Britain, not least Ove Arup. Although to our regret not an Old Centralian, he, and his firm, have maintained exceptionally close links with the Department; two of its current directors, for example, are Guildsmen, namely P.R. Rice (1957–58) and M. Shears (1964–65). We have benefited greatly when experience in that practice has been followed by recruitment to the staff of Imperial College. In the forties the lead in techniques of elastic analyses passed to this group, notably through the work of R.S. Jenkins (1927–30). A particularly significant result was the much improved practical design capacity for shell structures, exploited in a number of buildings that attracted much attention in the fifties. John Henderson (1947–48;

staff 1948–78) and John Munro (1955–57; current staff) were closely associated with this. There is no need to catalogue the distinguished structures designed by the Arup group. The tallest building in the UK comes from another hand, however; the Natwest Tower, designed by W.W. Frischmann (1953–55).

Prestressed concrete construction had been advanced in France. Alan Harris introduced much of this to Britain; again not a student here, but certainly to be counted amongst us by virtue of his more recent association! C.W. Yu (1950–54, staff 1963–74) is now a partner with Harris and Sutherland. Dudley New (1929–32) and E.O. Measor (1924–27) were also in the forefront of this technology in Britain, initially with the Heathrow hangar, and Festival of Britain (1951) structures. Britain's first major prestressed bridge, carrying the M2 over the Medway, again owed much to the highly competitive enterprise of the Danish entrepreneurs, but their project manager (becoming a Director of J.L. Keir Ltd) was Guildsman J.A. Dunster (1943–45).

The pressure vessels for the nuclear reactors at Oldbury represent the seminal application of concrete in that field, and the name of John Derrington (1946–47) must be foremost. Prestressed containment vessels for the generation of power stations currently proposed follow directly from this design. Segmented prestressed concrete construction draws attention to another major consultancy with which the Department maintains close links: Maunsell and Partners. Their most striking bridges are in the antipodes, but J.W. Baxter (1933–36) and David Lee's (1953–54) work on the Mancunian Way (and elsewhere, including Hammersmith) has set the pattern of viaduct construction for many urban expressways.

The final development of numerical techniques for hand computation lay in 'relaxation'. Although this had considerable research application, and owed much to the Department's collaboration with Richard Southwell and D.N. de G. Allen, as has been recounted earlier, the future lay with electronic computation. The finite element technique is today applied in many fields, not simply to the solution of elastic stress distributions, and its development this side of the Atlantic is inseparable from the name of Olgierd Zienkiewicz (1940–45). More recently, Peter Bettess (1964–68) has become an active member of that team.

A different approach is represented by dynamic relaxation, which was dramatically developed by J.R.H. Otter (1923–26), at first for the tidal flow computations required for the feasibility study for the Thames Barrier, but extended to many structural applications. Otter was the first civil engineer to be appointed a Visiting Professor in the Department.

The Thames Barrier brings us to the interface between structures and the field of fluid mechanics and water engineering. The design of the steel barrier gates owes most to Peter Clark (1952–55), following the school of neat welded platework pioneered by Roberts and Bernard Wex (1947–50) (for power station and similar structures) and W.C. Brown (1951–52) (for bridges). The senior partner in Rendel, Palmer and Tritton, responsible for the Thames Barrier, was P.A. Cox (1940–42), and this firm is yet another of the major consultants who maintain very close links with the Department.

Of the many activities of Sir William Halcrow and Partners we can highlight the offshore engineering, and mention especially C.J. Antonakis (1942–45) and Patrick Godfrey (1964–67). The Royal Sovereign lighthouse showed that the concrete gravity structure, floated to site, was a practical means of providing a secure fixed platform in the toughest marine environment. The offshore field has proved a fruitful employment in recent years, although the size of the project teams makes it invidious to single out any one or two names. The role of Guildsmen in the major research and development laboratories set up by the Wimpey group must, however, be recorded, especially the roles of Jack Chapman (1940–42 and 1946–48; staff 1948–71) in setting the pace, which has been maintained by Colin Billington (1965–73); the latter is now Deputy Managing Director of Wimpey Offshore Engineers and Contractors.

The world's biggest project in the field of water resources development, control and utilisation is the Indus Basin Project. Associated with it are two dams which can each claim world record dimensions on the basis of measurement: Mangla and Tarbela. The Mangla development came first, in the sixties, and represents the climax of British achievement in this field in many respects, and a major step in ongoing technical and scientific development as well. Binnie and Partners were responsible overall, yet another of the firms having very close long-term links with the Department; in this case, R.T. Gerrard (1934–37) was a partner with major responsibility. It would be invidious to draw detailed comparisons with the Tarbela project that followed under American direction. But certainly some of the Department expertise, especially on the damage of concrete by cavitation, could beneficially have been applied to the latter before, rather than after, the event.

Mangla gave a very great stimulus to the geotechnical work of the Department, in specific soils testing (including extension of slow testing techniques) and in analysis; seismology was also an important issue. Tarbela produced some further developments, including some record-breaking triaxial test cells over one metre diameter, designed here and set up on site by S.G. Tombs (1964–67).

Elsewhere in the field of geotechnics it has proved more difficult than (for example) in structures to separate the work going on within the Department, belonging properly in Sectional history, from developments outside. It makes no sense to expand here on the work and contracts of present or recent members of staff, but many may not have realised that F.G.H. Blyth (1921–25) was a renegade Guildsman. One other among the founders of understanding, and of entrepreneurial skills in this field, was H.J.B. Harding (1919–22).

Alan Meigh (1945–50) carries this forward as a Director of Soil Mechanics Ltd. From the learned society angle, currently we can add claim to the General Secretary of the International Society of Soil Mechanics and Foundation Engineering, R.H.G. Parry (1954–57). Our long-term links with *Géotechnique* have been mentioned; the writer of this chapter, not being a worker in this field, can perhaps endorse the prestige of that journal with less inhibition!

The current United Nations International Drinking Water Supply and Sanitation Decade has focused renewed attention on these problems. In addition to the close links of college staff with the World Health Organisation, some half-dozen Guildsmen hold influential appointments in that body. In terms of actually getting the job done, it is claimed that the Cairo waste-paper project is presently the world's largest, joint British–USA funded and engineered; Taylor–Binnie carrying our flag with Ted Flaxman (1949–52 and 1956–57) representing Binnie's on the Board of Control and David Kell (1973–74) managing the project team in London.

Hydrology is another field where it is relatively difficult to distinguish between stages in the practical design of a scheme. In few major schemes is the hydrologist the determining participant, although in many his may be the vital quantitative input. We can quote the pumping of the Tugela over the watershed between the Indian and Atlantic Oceans, and the part played by Peter Herbst (1966–67) at the Republic of South Africa Department of Water Affairs. However, there is a newly founded learned society in this field which is well guided by us, with Michael Mansell-Moulin (1955-56) as its President, and Michael Hall (1962-65, staff 1965-76) as its Secretary.

Transport is not only a field of engineering operations, but conspicuously a field of public participation and the meeting point of a number of professional disciplines with the public. This cannot be better illustrated than by the person of Colin Buchanan (1924-27, 1928-29) and in the influence of *Traffic in Towns*; a Guilds graduate in civil engineering, but a past President of the Town Planning Institute, Buchanan also had links with architecture, and this integration of his interests is demonstrated by the part played by him in establishing the School of Advanced Urban Studies at Bristol, which he directed when he left us for the second time. The youth of this branch of the profession in its present form is reflected in the growth of specialist transport consultancies. Buchanan and Partners shares the field not only with some of the older general consultants, but with men from both undergraduate and postgraduate courses, who have advanced rapidly to operating their own firm—Brian Martin (1957-60), via Martin, Voorhees and Associates to Logica; J. Steer (1971-72) and J. Davies (1970-71) of Steer, Davies and Gleave.

No less influence is exerted through the public sector, although our dominance of the career grade that used to be unequivocally 'County Engineer/Surveyor' has diminished at home. This is perhaps balanced by the number overseas—Abu Dhabi, Bombay, Mombasa ... The same applies to national agencies and ministries; a specially interesting policy role is played by Jorge Kogan (1973-74) on the national transport plan of Argentina. Meanwhile, Guildsmen in academic life overseas include Nigel H.M. Wilson (1962-65), Head and Professor, of the Transportation Systems Division in the Department of Civil Engineering at M.I.T.; David Briggs (1963-64; staff, 1966-72), Professor of Transportation Engineering at COPPE Federal University of Rio de Janeiro, Lauchlan Millar (1963-64), Head of Department of Civil Engineering, Western Australia Institute of Technology; and George Gramopoulos (1968-72), Professor of Transportation Engineering, University of Salonika, Greece.

Transport engineers often have to face the glare of the Public Enquiry, but they are not alone in this. Few major civil engineering enquiries are conducted without the advice of Guildsmen. The enquiry into the disaster at Aberfan placed its heaviest reliance on Alan Bishop (staff 1947-80). Tony Flint (1942-45; staff 1953-72) played a crucial role in the enquiry into the design of box-girder bridges, following the sad failures in that field. The Ronan Point enquiry was unusual in that the Guildsman at the top cannot be claimed by this Department, namely, Sir Owen Saunders. In the field of commercial enquiries into specific failures, names such as Flint frequently occur.

Not all enquiries are post-hoc; we also exert influence on enquiries directed to public policy. Although we do sometimes find ourselves dissenting from the majority opinion, this is no less of public value. The marathon Third London Airport enquiry (the Roskill Report), and Colin Buchanan's role therein is one major example. The more recent Serpell Report on the future of the railways is another, where the minority report of Alfred Goldstein (1944–47) has given the whole a much sharper focus.

The list of alumni rising to senior appointment in other universities is very long and some are mentioned in Sectional histories. Only a handful of those who have become university professors are named here: E.L. Kemp (1954–56) at Virginia, USA; P. LaRochelle (1956–60) at Laval, Canada; I.B. Donald (1958–61) at Monash, Australia; G.E. Blight (1958–61) at Witwatersrand, South Africa; B. de V. Batchelor (1960–63) at Queen's University at Kingston, Canada; J.C. Scrivener (1960–62) at Melbourne, Australia; M.A. Ward (1960–63) at Calgary, Canada; J.A. Teixeira de Freitas (1974–78) and J.A. da S. Appleton (1975–78), both at Lisbon, Portugal; E.L. Mello (1977–80) at Brasilia, Brazil; while B. Aalami (1963–69) became Vice-Chancellor at Arya-Mehr University, Tehran. Mention may also be made of some alumni who became members of the staff of the Department before moving on to take university chairs, some as Head of Department: W.T. Marshall (1926–29; staff 1936–45) at Glasgow University; R.E. Gibson (1943–45 and 1947–50; staff 1956–65) at King's College, London; D.J. Henkel (1949–50; staff 1950–63) at the Indian Institute of Technology, New Delhi, and later at Cornell University, USA; Z.S. Makowski (1950–51; staff 1951–62) at the University of Surrey; A.D. Edwards (1956–57; staff 1957–80) at Heriot-Watt University, Edinburgh; N.R. Morgenstern (1956–58; staff 1959–68) at the University of Alberta, Edmonton; and P.E. O'Connell (1970–72; staff 1968–76) at the University of Newcastle.

The direction of specialist technical institutions (very often, starting from their foundation) is another field where it is impossible to attempt to be complete, but we should mention a few names to illustrate its diversity. Organisations like CIRIA in UK, which will long remember A.R. Collins (1930–33), are a long step from the International Centre for Earthquake Engineering at Skopje where J. Petrovski (1969–70) played a similar seminal role. On other continents we have O.M.E. Fageiri (1970–74) at the Building and Road Research Institute at Khartoum, T. Kubo (1959–60) at the Japan Sewage Works Agency, and C.K.A. Stieda (1966–68) at the Council of Forest Industries of British Columbia. Back home, we can point out the external links of academics; Peter Hills (1957–61; staff 1963–72) directing the Transport Operations Research Group, and Patrick Dowling (1961–66; staff since 1968) chairing Eurocode 3. We should also remember the importance of academic links overseas, not least our link with the Indian Institute of Technology, Delhi, and mention S.R. Sparkes (staff 1934–73), B.M. Ahuja (1958–61) and A.K. Basu (1959–64; staff 1964–69).

Entrepreneurial activity takes many forms. In the top league of international contracts we have Terrel Wyatt (1956–57), who is Chairman of the Costain Group. Senior men with other contractors have also been mentioned (although we did not point out that John Derrington, as well as being a Director of Sir Robert McAlpine, is also chairman of the Advisory Board of the National Maritime Institute). We can mention Ken Newman's (staff 1954–66) role with the British Ready-Mixed Concrete Association. Jorge Kogan we have mentioned once; he is also a Director of Aerolineas Argentinas. Don Williams (1964–69) is Chairman of Australia National Railways ... At the time of writing, the most recently recognised Guilds face on the writer's television screen was that of Rick Wharton (1961–64 and 1965–66, Mechanical Engineering); but the public appearance is the tip of an iceberg of achievement in underwater operations by Wharton, Williams and Taylor. It is clear that Guilds continue to turn out engineers who are not simply well trained in the classical disciplines of the profession, but are very ready to innovate, to develop, and to enter the commercial fray.

~ *10* ~

Looking backwards—and forwards

Looking back to our origins, we can see that Unwin's success was to establish a successful Engineering course which formed a solid basis for further and rapid development and enhancement. His own distinction as an engineer did much to strengthen the place of engineering in technical education and his particular reputation in the field of civil engineering improved its status as a specialist subject.

Within sixteen years of its opening, the Central Institution was worthy of incorporation in the University of London, and much credit for this must rest with Unwin. Dalby further advanced the status of the College, when through his efforts and administrative skills the College's diploma, the ACGI, was recognised by the University as comparable in standard with the BSc(Eng).

The conversion of the Central Technical College to a specialist Engineering College in 1907 and its incorporation with Imperial College seemed a natural consequence of the prestige its teaching of engineering had gained for it in a relatively short span of time. The separation of civil and mechanical engineering subjects in 1913, less than thirty years after the opening of the Central Institution, was the culmination of a period of steady progress made in civil engineering education at the College.

Most of our development since 1913 has been achieved under three long-serving heads of department: Dixon (20 years), Pippard (23 years) and Skempton (19 years). This long tenure of office gave a continuity to each period and a certain flavour to the Department's work. The credit for the establishment of the Department in a university mode, with large and well-equipped laboratories and fundamental research being undertaken, rests with Dixon. His gift for creating an atmosphere of cheerful co-operation was important in establishing a tradition we have managed to maintain, even if it looks a little frayed at the edges sometimes. Pippard's ability as a structural analyst established his subject on its modern basis, while his instinct for picking 'good men' led to the appointment of many able teachers and research workers. Under him the framework of the Department in specialised Sections was established. The period of Skempton's headship, coinciding with the period of rapid expansion of Imperial College in the 1960s, brings us into recent times with many new special areas of interest encouraged by him and the introduction of many new postgraduate courses. His reputation as a scholar did much to attract a high calibre of research worker to the Department. All these heads of department were backed up by the excellence of many of the Sectional heads, and the many gifted people we have had on our staff.

Now that the office of head of department has become a limited term, less opportunity exists to reshape the Department nearer to the heart's desire, but in Neal's six years he overhauled the undergraduate curriculum to make its content more relevant to the needs of the modern professional engineer. His establishment of a new special study area in Marine Technology is important in the spectrum of departmental development. History will record the achievements of our new head, Munro. In his first two years his equipping of the Department with expanded computing facilities is an indication of his determination to keep civil engineers abreast of changing modern practice. If during his headship we also establish a four-year course, this will also be a contribution to satisfying the needs of the profession for more specialised graduates.

The undergraduate course has evolved slowly, the study of heat engines only slowly superseded by subjects closer to the civil engineer's interests. As civil engineering itself has grown in complexity, our course has had to try to reflect this, and in recent times to include subjects which would once have been thought useful but not essential to an engineer's equipment—those, for example, intended to heighten his awareness of his role in the community and to equip him with the confidence to write and speak effectively about his subject. In the same way, postgraduate courses have kept abreast of what the modern engineer needs to know, both here and in the developing world. A review of the growth in student numbers over the years shows a steady build-up:

	1933–34	1955–56	1977–78	1983–84
undergraduate	68	161	181	215
postgraduate	27	86	126	140
research	10	45	39	40

As for the students themselves, the photographs of them as late as the 1950s depict a sombre group in neat grey flannel suits, a far

36. Staff group 1984

cry from today's students in their jeans and jumpers. Their ranks now also include women, their numbers growing in the last ten years from two or three in each year to a total of 33 in the current undergraduate course. For the first time also, a woman Civil Engineering student, Miss M. Anderson, has been elected President of the City and Guilds Union for the session 1984–85, only the third woman in the City and Guilds College to hold this office. We also have considerably more overseas students in the undergraduate course than we had say ten years ago, a group representing some 25% of the total. All the same, I suspect that those young men in grey suits were in heavy disguise and that students then were as exuberant as they are now, with the same cheerfulness and optimism about their future work in the profession.

Corresponding to the growth in student numbers, the staff has grown greatly from the handful with which the Department began, particularly in the years since 1963. In our current session, we have a staff of 119, made up of 51 members of academic staff and a support staff of 68, of whom 52 are technical staff. We also have 39 research assistants, some of whom are registered for higher degrees.

Our research has always been concerned with the fundamental nature and behaviour of materials. Later work encompassed the design and analysis of complete structures, at first on a small scale, later on a scale intended to simulate the behaviour of full-scale individual units. Many new areas of study have been added to our repertoire, many new techniques have been absorbed into our competence. Each generation has shown itself willing to respond to the demands of the problems posed by industry and society and to serve the professional bodies in their task of evolving Codes of Practice. Looking back, there seems to be a natural evolution. It is all in the same tradition and part of the same process which began one hundred years ago in this College.

~ *Appendix A* ~

Staff Lists

Academic Honours of Members of Staff

Fellowship of the Royal Society

1886 W.C. Unwin
1913 W.E. Dalby
1954 A.J.S. Pippard
1961 A.W. Skempton
1975 R. Weck (Visiting Professor)

Fellowship of Engineering

1976 A.W. Skempton
1976 R. Weck (Visiting Professor)
1980 B.G. Neal
1981 J.B. Burland
P.J. Dowling
1983 J.J. Bobrowski (Visiting Professor)
T.A. Wyatt

Appointments of the University of London

Professors

1900 W.C. Unwin, Civil & Mechanical Engineering
1904 W.E. Dalby, Civil & Mechanical Engineering
1913 S.M. Dixon, Civil Engineering and Surveying
1929 R.G.H. Clements, Maybury Professor of Highway Engineering
1933 A.J.S. Pippard, Civil Engineering and Surveying
1945 A.L.L. Baker, Concrete Technology
1945 C.M. White, Fluid Mechanics and Hydraulic Engineering
1955 A.W. Skempton, Soil Mechanics
1957 A.W. Skempton, Civil Engineering
1958 S.R. Sparkes, Engineering Structures
1963 C.D. Buchanan, Transport
1965 A.W. Bishop, Soil Mechanics
1966 J.R.D. Francis, Hydraulics
1971 E.H. Brown, Structural Analysis
1973 N.N. Ambraseys, Engineering Seismology
A.J. Harris, Concrete Structures and Technology
B.G. Neal, Engineering Structures
1977 J.N. Hutchinson, Engineering Geomorphology
1979 P.J. Dowling, Steel Structures
1980 J.B. Burland, Soil Mechanics
J. Munro, Civil Engineering Systems
1981 R. Perry, Public Health and Water Technology
1983 J.W. Dougill, Concrete Structures and Technology
1983 P. Holmes, Hydraulics

Readers

1933 M.K. Rice-Oxley, Civil Engineering
C.M. White, Civil Engineering
1946 A.W. Skempton, Soil Mechanics
1947 S.R. Sparkes, Civil Engineering
A. Stephenson, Surveying
1950 B.G. Manton, Highway Engineering
1953 R.J. Ashby, Civil Engineering
F.E. Bruce, Public Health Engineering

1957	A.W. Bishop, Soil Mechanics
	P.O. Wolf, Hydrology
1958	J.R.D. Francis, Fluid Mechanics
	A.R. Flint, Structural Steelworks (British Steel Corporation Readership)
1959	E.H. Brown, Structural Analysis
1960	J.C. de C. Henderson, Reinforced Concrete Structures
1962	R.E. Gibson, Civil Engineering Analysis
	J.C. Chapman, Structural Engineering
1966	T. O'Donnell, Engineering Hydrology
1969	N.N. Ambraseys, Engineering Seismology
1971	J.N. Hutchinson, Soil Mechanics
1974	J. Munro, Civil Engineering Systems
	T.A. Wyatt, Structural Design
	P.J. Dowling, Structural Steelwork (British Steel Corporation Readership)
1977	R. Perry, Public Health Engineering
	A.C. Cassell, Structures
	P.R. Vaughan, Soil Mechanics
1981	R.J. Chandler, Soil Mechanics
1982	L.G. Booth, Timber Engineering

Former Academic Staff

Notes

Apologies are made for any inaccuracies or omissions in the following list. The dates of appointments for the period 1884–1911 have been reconstructed from the College Calendars, which are not completely in step with resignations and new appointments. The period after 1911 has been reconstructed from the *Minutes of the Delegacy of City and Guilds College* and *Board of Studies Minutes*.

In the early days, the posts of Demonstrator, Laboratory Assistant and Research Assistant were teaching posts. Student Demonstrators have not been listed, nor junior staff who were in the Department for only one year.

Modern Research Assistantships are shown only when they were of considerable duration or where the person concerned was later appointed to the teaching staff.

Qualifications have been edited to the extent of citing the higher of two degrees where more than one degree is held, unless the first was awarded in a different faculty. The qualifications shown are those held by staff while members of the College. Many afterwards acquired further qualifications and awards.

Square brackets round the date indicate the end of service in the Department of Civil and Mechanical Engineering, but continuation in the Department of Mechanical Engineering and Motive Power.

Department of Civil and Mechanical Engineering, 1884–1913

Unwin, W.C. BSc, LLD, MICE, FRS	1884–1904	Professor of Engineering; Emeritus Professor 1904–32
Sharp, A. BSc, AMICE	1885–1898	Instructor in Mechanical Drawing and Engineering Design
Taylor, J.	1887–1893	Laboratory Assistant
Middleton, R.E. MICE, FSI	1889–1897	Instructor in Surveying
Burls, G.A.	1891–1897	Assistant Instructor 1891: Laboratory Assistant 1893
Ackerman, A.S.E. ACGI, AMICE	1892–1897	Assistant Instructor
Gilbert, W. AMICE	1897–1899	Instructor in Surveying
Lea, F.C. BSc, ARCS, AMICE	1898–1911	Instructor in Mechanical Drawing and in Engineering Design 1898; Instructor in Engineering Design and

		Applied Mechanics 1900; Lecturer and Instructor in Engineering Design and Applied Mechanics 1905 (1871-1952)
Hewson, W. BSc, ARCS, AMICE, MIMechE	1898-[1913]	Laboratory Assistant 1898; Instructor in Engineering Drawing and Design 1900; Lecturer and Instructor in Engineering Drawing and Design 1905; Lecturer and Instructor in Engineering Design and Applied Mechanics 1906; Assistant Professor 1911 (Died 1925)
Powell, J.R. BSc	1898-1902	Assistant Instructor 1898; Laboratory Assistant 1900
Russell, G.M. ARCS	1898-1902	Laboratory Assistant
Ashcroft, A.G. MICE	1899-1911	Assistant Professor (Died 1911)
Hayward, J.W. MSc	1902-1906	Laboratory Assistant 1902; Assistant Instructor and Laboratory Demonstrator 1903; Instructor and Laboratory Demonstrator and Lecturer on Workshop Accounts 1905
Smith, P.H.	1902-1904	Junior Lecturer and Laboratory Assistant
Dalby, W.E. BSc, MA, MICE, MIMechE, FRS	1904-[1913]	Professor of Civil and Mechanical Engineering 1904-13 (Professor of Mechanical Engineering and Motive Power 1913-31; Emeritus Professor 1931-36)
Day, W.H.	1904-[1913]	Junior Lecturer and Laboratory Assistant 1904 (Left 1937)
Margetson, A.J. MSc	1905-[1913]	Lecturer and Instructor in Engineering Drawing and Design 1905; Instructor and Demonstrator in Engineering Laboratory 1906; Assistant Professor 1911 (Left 1914)
Witchell, E.F.D. BSc (Eng), FCGI, MIMechE	1905-[1913]	Instructor in Engineering Drawing & Design 1905; Demonstrator in Engineering Laboratory 1906; Lecturer and Instructor in Engineering Design and Applied Mechanics 1911 (Left 1946; died 1956)
Cruickshank, A. MIMechE	1906-[1913]	Instructor in Engineering Drawing & Design 1906; Assistant Professor 1911 (Left 1942)
McKay, R.F. MSc	1906-[1913]	Instructor in Engineering Drawing & Design 1906; Lecturer and Instructor in Engineering Design and Applied Mechanics 1911 (Left 1919)
Chappell, E. BSc, ACGI, AMICE	1911-[1913]	Lecturer in Engineering Design and Applied Mechanics (Left 1915)
Whittaker, H. BSc, ARCS, AMICE, AMIMechE	1912-[1913]	Demonstrator (Left 1923)

Howard, J.V. DSc(Eng), MIMechE	1912–[1913]	Instructor & Demonstrator (Left 1951; died 1954)
Wells, G.C. ACGI	1912–1913	Instructor and Demonstrator
Newton, K. MC, BSc, ACGI, AMICE, AMIMechE	1912–[1913]	Junior Assistant (Left 1923)
Deuchar, W.R. BSc, ACGI, AMICE	1912–1919	Draughtsman and Drawing-Office Assistant (advanced courses). Transferred to Civil Engineering Department.

Department of Civil Engineering

Dixon, S.M. MA, MSc, MICE	1913–1933	Professor of Civil Engineering & Surveying
Purser, J.W. BAI, MSc, AMICE	1913–1933	Assistant Professor 1913; Reader 1931
Tullis, J. BSc	1913–1920	Demonstrator
Wickenden, A.F. AMICE, ARIBA	1919–1926	Draughtman & Drawing-Office Assistant 1919; Lecturer 1920
Rice-Oxley, M.K. ACGI, MICE, MIStructE	1919–1942	Lecturer 1919; Assistant Professor 1921; Reader 1931 (Died 1956)
Manton, B.G. BSc(Eng), DIC, AMICE	1920–1963	Demonstrator 1920; Lecturer 1929; Senior Lecturer 1943; Reader 1950–57; Special Lecturer 1957
Moorsom, C.J. FRAS	1920–1926	Assistant Demonstrator
Fitzgibbon, G. BAI	1924–1934	Research Assistant
Gibbs, E.F. MSc, ACGI, DIC	1925–1937	Assistant Demonstrator 1925; Demonstrator 1929; Assistant Lecturer 1931
Shearer, W.V. BSc, MIMechE	1926–1938	Lecturer
Blyth, F.G.H. PhD, MSc, ACGI, DIC	1926–1932	Assistant Demonstrator 1926; Demonstrator 1928 (In Department of Geology 1932–64)
Clements, R.G.H. MC, MICE	1928–1945	Professor of Highway Engineering (1880–1953)
Chilton, O.H. MSc, ACGI, DIC, AMICE AMIStructE	1931–1939	Demonstrator 1931–34; Assistant Lecturer 1934–38; Lecturer 1938–39
Jacobsen, C.F.J. BSc	1931–1933	Assistant Demonstrator
McHugh, J.N. BSc, BE	1931–1932	Demonstrator
Pippard, A.J.S. MBE, DSc, HonACGI, MICE, FRAeS, FRS	1933–1956	Professor of Civil Engineering
White, C.M. PhD, DSc(Eng), HonACGI	1933–1966	Assistant Professor & Reader 1933; Professor of Fluid Mechanics and Hydraulic Engineering 1946
Redshaw, S.C. MSc, AMICE	1933–1936	Demonstrator 1933; Assistant Lecturer 1934

Hill, H.V. MSc	1934–1935	Demonstrator
Sparkes, S.R. PhD, HonACGI, DIC, MICE, MIStructE	1934–1973	Demonstrator 1934; Assistant Lecturer 1936; Lecturer 1939; Senior Lecturer 1946; Reader 1947; Professor of Engineering Structures 1958 (1910–1976)
Chitty, Miss L. MA, DIC, AMICE, FRAeS	1934–1962	Research Assistant 1934; Lecturer 1943 (1897–1982)
Marshall, W.T. PhD, ACGI, DIC, AMICE, AMIStructE	1936–1945	Assistant Lecturer 1936; Lecturer 1942
Stephenson, A. OBE, MA, FRICS	1937–1971	Assistant Lecturer 1937; Lecturer 1943; Reader 1947
Yates, A.H. BSc	1937–1945	Assistant Lecturer
Gayed, Y.K. PhD	1940–1944	Temporary Demonstrator 1940; Temporary Assistant Lecturer 1942; Temporary Lecturer 1943
Baker, A.L.L. DSc(Eng), HonACGI, MICE, MIStructE	1945–1973	Professor of Concrete Technology
Ashby, R.J. MSc(Eng), ACGI, DIC, CEng, FICE	1946–1977	(Research Assistant 1937–38); Lecturer 1946; Reader 1953; Assistant Director 1957
Hutton, S.P. MEng, AFRAeS	1946–1949	Lecturer
Francis, J.R.D. MSc, CEng, FICE, FIWES	1946–1961 1966–1979	Lecturer 1946; Reader 1958; (Rejoined staff as Professor of Hydraulics 1966–79) (Died 1979)
Duncan, J.E. BSc(Eng), AMICE	1946–1953	Lecturer (Died 1953)
Ainsworth, H. MA, ARICS	1946–1971	Lecturer 1946; Senior Lecturer 1960 (Died 1971)
Ashdown, A.J. AMIStructE	1947–1961	Senior Research Assistant
Chapman, J.C. PhD, ACGI, DIC, CEng, FICE, FIStructE	1948–1971	Research Assistant 1948; Senior Lecturer 1961; Reader 1962
Henderson, J.C. de C. AADip, DIC, ARIBA	1948–1978	Assistant Lecturer 1948; Lecturer 1949; Reader 1960
Clarke, D.A. BSc(Eng), ACGI	1948–1951	Assistant Lecturer
Falconer, B.H. PhD	1949–1951	Assistant Lecturer
Gifford, F.W. PhD, DIC, AMIStructE	1949–1952	Assistant Lecturer
Wolf, P.O. BSc(Eng), CEng, MICE, MIWE	1949–1966	Lecturer 1949; Reader 1957
Bruce, F.E. MSc(Eng), SM(Harvard), ACGI, DIC, CEng, FICE, FIPHE, FRSH	1949–1977	Rockefeller Fellow in Public Health 1949; Reader 1953
Henkel, D.J. PhD, AMICE	1950–1963	Lecturer 1950; Senior Lecturer 1960

Gibson, R.E. PhD, DSc,ACGI, DIC, CEng, AMICE	1950–1965	Research Assistant 1950; Lecturer 1956; Reader 1962
Makowski, Z.S. DipEng, PhD,DIC, AMICE	1951–1962	Assistant Lecturer 1951; Lecturer 1952; Senior Lecturer 1960
Kent, D.H. BA	1951–1954	Assistant Lecturer 1951; Lecturer 1953
Mattock, A.H. PhD	1952–1957	Lecturer
Fox, G.T.J. BEng, CEng, MICE, MIWES, AMIWPC	1953–1980	Lecturer
Leach, O.W.F. AMICE	1953–1955	Lecturer and Personal Assistant to Professor
Flint, A.R. PhD, CEng, FICE, FIStructE	1953–1972	Lecturer 1953; Reader 1958
Kenn, M.J. BSc, MASc, CEng, MICE, MIMechE, MIWES, MEIC	1954–1955 1962–1983	Lecturer (Rejoined staff in 1962 as Senior Lecturer)
Newman, K. BSc(Eng), CEng, AMICE	1954–1966	Lecturer
Bunting, F.B. BSc(Eng), DIC	1954–1955	Lecturer
Underhill, H.W. MA, AICE	1955–1959	Lecturer
Cutcliffe, F.C.G. BA	1955–1956	Administrative Assistant
Minton, P. BSc(Eng), ACGI, CEng, MRAeS, MICE	1956–1983	Lecturer 1956; Senior Lecturer 1967; Assistant Director 1977–83
Taylor, P.F. BSc	1956–1966	Research Assistant
Edwards, A. D. PhD, DIC, CEng, MICE	1957–1980	Lecturer 1957; Senior Lecturer 1966
Morgenstern, N.R. BASc, PhD, DIC	1958–1968	Research Assistant 1958; Lecturer 1960
Agnew, R. BSc, PhD	1958–1961	Lecturer
O'Donnell, T. MA, CEng, MICE, MIWE	1959–1972	(Research Assistant 1951–53); Lecturer 1959; Reader 1966
Basu, A.K. PhD, DIC	1960–1969	Research Assistant 1960; Lecturer 1964
Szwajkajzer, Z.M. DipArch, DIC	1961–1963	Assistant Lecturer
Yu, C.W. PhD, DIC	1961–1974	Research Assistant 1961; Lecturer 1963; Senior Lecturer 1967
Dowley, A.L. BE, MS	1962–1969	Lecturer 1962
Buchanan, Sir Colin CBE, BSc(Eng), ACGI, CEng, AMICE, MTPI, ARIBA	1963–1972	Professor of Transport
Hills, P.J. MSc(Eng), ACGI, CEng, MICE, AMInstHE	1963–1972	Lecturer
Simons, N.E. MA, MSc(Eng), PhD, CEng, AMICE	1963–1968	Lecturer

More, Miss R.J.M. MA, PhD, AICE	1963–1965	Lecturer
Wong, G.C.K.M. PhD, DIC	1963–1964	Assistant Lecturer
Khalil, M.B. PhD, DIC	1963–1964	Lecturer
MacEwen, Mrs A. AADIP, ARIBA, AMTPI	1963–1966	Research Fellow
Crompton, D.H. AADip, ARIBA, MRTPI	1963–1981	Research Fellow 1963; Senior Lecturer 1967
Carter, Mrs M.	1963–1982	Departmental Librarian
Wright, D.E. PhD, ACGI, DIC, CEng, AMICE	1964–1969	Lecturer
Green, G.E. BSc, MS, PhD	1965–1975	Lecturer
Hall, M.J. PhD, DIC, CEng, MICE	1965–1976	Lecturer
Tchalenko, J.S. DipENSG, PhD, DIC	1965–1975	Research Assistant 1965; Lecturer 1969
Holland, J. BSc, DIC, CEng, AMIStructE	1966–1967	Lecturer
Briggs, D.A. MSc(Eng), DIC, DipTP, AMTPI, AMInstHE	1966–1972	Lecturer
Clark, P.J. BSc, ACGI, CEng, MICE	1966–1973	Lecturer
O'Connell, P.E. BE, PhD, DIC	1968–1976	Assistant Lecturer 1968; Lecturer 1969
Head, C.R. BSc, CEng, MICE, MIWE	1970–1974	Lecturer
Hogger, C.J. BSc, PhD, DIC, ARCS	1971–1983	Lecturer
Neal, B.G. MA, PhD, ScD, HonACGI, FEng, FICE, FIMechE, FIStructE	1973–1982	Professor of Engineering Structures 1973; Head of Dept 1976–1982; Head of Structures Section 1973–1981
Harris, Sir Alan CBE, BSc(Eng), FEng, FICE, FIStructE, MConsE	1973–1981	Professor of Concrete Structures and Technology
Bunce, J.W. DIC, CEng, MIStructE, MSocICF	1973–1976	Lecturer
P.A. Mantz MSc, PhD, DIC, CEng	1973–81	Research fellow
Perry, P.F. BAI, BA, PhD	1978–1981	Lecturer

Academic Staff 1984

Head of Department

J. Munro
PhD, DIC, CEng, FICE, FIStructE

Head of Department 1982; Professor of Civil Engineering Systems 1980; (Lecturer 1957; Senior Lecturer 1967; Head of Systems and Mechanics Section 1971–82; Reader in Civil Engineering Systems 1974)

Administration

B. Chiat BSc, ARICS	Assistant Director 1983; Senior Lecturer, Surveying
F.H. Potter BScTech, AMCT, CEng, MICE, FIWSc	Senior Tutor 1973; Careers Adviser 1983; Senior Lecturer, Timber Structures
A.R. Gent PhD, CEng, MICE	Admissions Tutor 1970; Senior Lecturer, Structures
Mrs K. Crooks, BA, DipLib	Librarian 1982 (Asst. Librarian 1976)
R.W. Loveday	Departmental Superintendent 1983 (Joined Department 1950)

Senior Research Fellows

A.W. Skempton DSc(Eng), FCGI, DIC, FEng, FICE, FRS	Emeritus Professor 1981; (Reader in Soil Mechanics 1946; Professor of Soil Mechanics 1955–57; Professor of Civil Engineering 1957–81; Head of Department 1957–76)
A.W. Bishop MA, PhD, DSc(Eng), CEng, FICE	Emeritus Professor 1980; (Asst. Lecturer 1946; Lecturer 1947; Reader in Soil Mechanics 1957; Professor of Soil Mechanics 1965–80)

Visiting Professors

P. Ackers MSc, FCGI, FEng, FICE	Appointed 1973, Hydraulics
J.J. Bobrowski PhD, FEng, FICE, FIStructE, MConsE	Appointed 1982, Concrete Structures
R.F. Packham PhD, FRCS, FIWES, MIWPC	Appointed 1983, Public Health Engineering
T.M. Ridley BSc, MS, PhD, CEng, FICE, FCIT, MITE	Appointed 1981, Transport
R. Weck CBE, PhD, FEng, FICE, FMechE, FWeldI, FRS	Appointed 1975, Structures

Sections

Civil Engineering Hydraulics

P. Holmes PhD, CEng, MICE	Professor of Hydraulics 1983; Head of Section 1983
K. Anastasiou DiplEng, MSc, PhD	Lecturer 1983
J.D. Hardwick BASc, PhD, DIC	Lecturer 1961
B. MacMahon BE, IngEIH (Grenoble)	Lecturer 1964
A. Scott-Moncrieff BASc, PEng, MEIC	Lecturer 1968 (Asst. Lecturer 1966)

Civil Engineering Systems and Mechanics

D.L. Smith BEng, MSc, PhD, DIC, CEng, MICE	Senior Lecturer 1984; Head of Section 1982; (Lecturer 1971)
M.B. Beck BSc, MA, PhD	Lecturer 1982
R.D. Wing BSc(Eng), MS, PhD, ACGI, DIC, CEng, MIMechE	Research Fellow 1978; (Computer Operations Supervisor 1976)

Concrete Structures

J.W. Dougill MSc(Eng), PhD, DIC, CEng, FICE	Professor of Concrete Structures and Technology 1981; Head of Section 1981 (Research Asst. 1961–64)
J.B. Newman PhD, ACGI, DIC, CEng, MIStructE	Senior Lecturer 1982 (Research Asst. 1965; Lecturer 1966)
C.J. Burgoyne MA, MSc, PhD, DIC, CEng, MICE	Lecturer 1978 (Research Asst. 1974)
M. Pavlovic BEng, MEngSc, PhD	Lecturer 1978
S.H. Perry PhD, CEng, MICE, MIStructE	Lecturer 1974
P.J.E. Sullivan BEng, MA, PhD, DIC, CEng, FICE, FIStructE	Lecturer 1967 (Research Asst. 1966)

Engineering Seismology

N.N. Ambraseys DiplEng, PhD, DSc(Eng), CEng, FICE, FGS	Professor of Engineering Seismology 1973; Head of Section 1967 (Lecturer 1958; Reader in Engineering Seismology 1969)
S.K. Sarma BTech, PhD, DIC	Lecturer 1973

Environmental Studies

T.A. Wyatt PhD, ACGI, DIC, FEng, FICE	Reader in Structural Design 1974; Head of Section 1971 (Lecturer 1962; Senior Lecturer 1973)
M.W. Baldwin MA, MSc, PhD, DIC, CEng, MICE	Lecturer 1971
Miss J.M. Brown MA, DipEd	Lecturer 1972 (Research Asst. 1962)

Public Health and Water Resource Engineering

R. Perry BSc, PhD, FIPHE, MIWES, MIWPC, FRSH	Professor of Public Health and Water Technology 1981; Head of Section 1977; (Lecturer 1970; Reader in Public Health Engineering 1977)
N.J.D. Graham MA, MSc, PhD, DIC, CEng, MICE, MIPHE, MIWPC	Lecturer 1977
P.W. Jowitt PhD, ACGI, DIC	Lecturer 1974
J.N. Lester BTech, MSc, PhD, DIC, MIWES, MIBiol	Lecturer 1977 (Research Asst. 1975)
J.P. Lumbers BSc, MSc, CEng, MICE	Lecturer 1979
Miss E.M. Shaw BSc, MSc, MIWES, FRMetS	Lecturer 1965
H.S. Wheater MA, PhD, CEng, MICE	Lecturer 1978

Soil Mechanics

J.B. Burland MSc, PhD, DSc(Eng), FEng, FICE, MIStructE, FGS	Professor of Soil Mechanics 1980; Head of Section 1980

J.N. Hutchinson PhD, CEng, FICE, FGS	Professor of Engineering Geomorphology 1977 (Senior Lecturer 1965; Reader in Soil Mechanics 1971)
R.J. Chandler MSc, PhD, CEng, MICE, FGS	Reader in Soil Mechanics 1981 (Lecturer 1969)
P.R. Vaughan PhD, ACGI, DIC, CEng, FICE, FGS	Reader in Soil Mechanics 1976 (Temporary Lecturer 1962–64; Lecturer 1969; Senior Lecturer 1973)
D.W. Hight MSc, DIC, CEng, MICE	Lecturer 1978
D.M. Potts PhD	Lecturer 1979
A.E. Skinner PhD, DIC, CEng, MICE	Lecturer 1967

Structural Engineering

P.J. Dowling PhD, DIC, FEng, FICE, FIStructE, MRINA	Professor of Steel Structures 1979; Head of Section 1981 (Research Fellow 1968; Reader 1974)
E.H. Brown PhD, DIC, CEng, MICE	Professor of Structural Analysis 1971 (Assistant Lecturer 1948; Lecturer 1950; Reader in Structural Analysis 1959; Dean of City and Guilds College 1979–82)
A.C. Cassell PhD, DIC, MICE	Reader in Structures 1977 (Assistant Lecturer 1952; Lecturer 1954; Senior Lecturer 1965)
T.A. Wyatt PhD ACGI, FEng, FICE	Reader in Structural Design 1974 (Lecturer 1962; Senior Lecturer 1973; Head of Environmental Studies Section 1971)
A.R. Gent PhD, CEng, MICE	Senior Lecturer 1972 (Lecturer 1957; Admissions Tutor 1970)
R.E. Hobbs PhD, DIC, CEng, MIStructE	Senior Lecturer 1983 (Lecturer 1970)
M.J. Baker BSc(Eng), ACGI, DIC, CEng, MICE, MIStructE	Lecturer 1978 (Research Asst. 1966)
J.E. Harding MSc, PhD, ACGI, DIC, CEng, MIStructE	Lecturer 1979 (Research Asst. 1971)
G.W. Hunt MSc(Eng), PhD, DIC	Lecturer 1978
G.W. Owens MSc, PhD, DIC, CEng, MICE, MWeldI	Lecturer 1973 (Research Asst. 1970)

Surveying

B. Chiat BSc, ARICS	Senior Lecturer 1972; Head of Section 1972 (Assistant Director 1983)
S.K. Sharma MSc, MPhil, ARICS	Lecturer 1973

Timber Structures and Technology

L.G. Booth MA, PhD, DIC, CEng, FICE, FIStructE, FIWSc	Reader in Timber Engineering 1982; Head of Timber Structures Section 1965 (Lecturer 1963; Senior Lecturer 1974)
F.H. Potter BScTech, AMCT, CEng, MICE, FIWSc	Senior Lecturer 1980 (Lecturer 1965; Senior Tutor 1973; Careers Adviser 1983)

Transport	
G.P. Crow BSc(Eng), DipTE, CEng, MICE, MIMunE, MIHT	Senior Lecturer 1965; Head of Section 1973 (Lecturer 1963)
D.A.M. Gilbert MSc(Eng), DIC, CEng, MICE, MIMunE, MIHT, MITE	Lecturer 1975 (Research Asst. 1967)
A. Tzedakis MA	Lecturer 1973
P. Rice MSc, PhD, CEng, MICE	Research Fellow 1978

Support Staff 1984

Date of first appointment

Senior Technical Staff	
S.K. Ackerley	1971
P.F. Clifford	1954
C.D. Mortlock	1960
J.E. Neale	1948
R.A.J. Philpott	1962
C.L. Pitches	1965
G. Thomas	1962
Technical Staff	
D. Alleyne	1979
J. Audsley	1967
R.A. Baxter	1965
K.H. Bhatt	1980
S.J. Blackaller	1979
W.P. Bobinski	1979
A.P. Bolsher	1974
A.W. Boxall	1979
E.W. Bristow	1984
A.J. Chipling	1979
I.W. Clark	1978
H.R Clements	1964
Mrs M. Cole	1976
C.R. Day	1966
S.R. Finch	1966
J.C. Finn	1959
Mrs E.M. Gibbs	1967
C. Gordon	1979
F.J. Gould	1969
S.S. Gupta	1966
J.A. Hall	1978
P.S. Hart	1979
P.J. Jellis	1963
K.J.S. Jenkins	1976
B.M. Johnston	1978
S.W.R. Keir	1966
Mrs A. Langford	1979
A.J. Leete	1967
J. Mires	1972
K.W. Mitchell	1979
D.D. Morris	1966
R.C. Packer	1983
D.R. Pretty	1972

V.J. Rebello	1979	
A.J. Roberts	1979	
H. Rouse	1972	
P.S. Scanlon	1983	
G.R. Scopes	1958	
E.J. Seeker	1966	
L.F. Spall	1952	
D. Stride	1979	
B.R. Surry	1977	
E.W. Toohey	1967	
J.R. Turner	1950	
J.R.P. Williams	1966	
G.W. Wilson	1971	
R.J. Wilson	1977	

Clerical Staff

Miss J. Barritt	1974	
Miss P.J. Carter	1963	Joined Civil Eng. 1983
Miss V.H.E. Collins	1980	
Miss K.M. Evans	1983	
Miss L. M. Gallen	1978	
Mrs E. Gorham	1983	
Mrs K.H. Guile	1980	
Miss L.L.L. Hayes	1972	Joined Civil Eng. 1975
Miss A. Hikel	1978	Joined Civil Eng. 1980
Ms R.S. Lee	1982	
Mrs F. Miller	1984	
Miss P. O'Connell	1983	
Miss D. Ovens	1977–80, 1983	
Mrs C.E. Potter	1980	
Mrs M.J. Treadaway	1982	
Miss C.J. Wells	1982	
Mrs S. Wright	1966	Joined Civil Eng. 1978

Library Assistants

Mrs E. Boden	1983	
Mrs E.A. Gibson	1982	
Miss J.F. Underhill	1982	

Messenger

R.G. Elliot	1961	Joined Civil Eng. 1963

~ Appendix B ~

Research Degree Titles, 1923–1983

The degree of PhD(Eng) awarded by London University

1927	**M. Amin**	The flow of water in canals fitted with Venturi flumes
1928	**L.G. Brazier**	On the flexure of thin cylindrical shells and other thin sections
1935	**R.V. Burns**	A study of river bed erosion with special reference to the protection of spillway dams
	I. Moyal	Accelerated flow past rough surface and allied problems in open channels
	B. Set	Stress distribution in the web of a plate girder
1936	**K.H. Chu**	A theoretical and experimental study of the stress distribution in an electrically welded steel Vierendeel truss
	S.C. Redshaw	An investigation into the elastic instability of certain compression members
1937	**C.F. Colebrook**	Laminar and turbulent flow in parallel and converging pipes with smooth and rough walls
	E.F. Gibbs	Cavitating flow past cylinders and other obstacles
	R.M. Vadhelvala	Linear shrinkage of cements during setting
	R.P. Wallis	Flow in nests of tubes
1938	**P. Srichamara**	Studies of the actions of fluids flowing over movable granular beds
1939	**W.T. Marshall**	1. An experimental investigation into the torsional rigidity of plain and reinforced concrete and the application in problems of design 2. An experimental study of the strength of thin isolated column bases in reinforced concrete
1941	**N.N. Bhandari**	A study of the turbulence created by the discharging of a jet into a mass of the liquid and its bearing on the design of hydraulic structures in river control problems
	Y.K. Gayed	The mechanics of dispersion and suspension
	J. Gimpel	An experimental study of a reinforced concrete square slab subjected to impact
	D.F. Orchard	A study of various factors influencing skidding on roads with special reference to the effect of surface films
1942	**M.S.M.A.B. Quraish**	Silt movement in running water

1944	**R.A. Collacott**	Liquid flow through obstructed passages with special reference to the influence of the approach on the discharge through orifices and nozzles
1945	**S.R. Sparkes**	An analytical and experimental investigation of the behaviour of the webs of plate girders
	O.C. Zienkiewicz	Classical theories of gravity dam design in the light of modern analytical methods
1948	**C.S. Chao**	Density currents and the desilting of reservoirs
	J.J. Kolbuszewski	Research on packing and density of sands
	Y.S. Li	A theoretical and experimental study of the behaviour of thin flanged box girders in pure bending, with special reference to the deflected form and stress distribution in the compression flange
	M. Smolira	An analytical and experimental investigation of the behaviour of thin cylindrical shell roof structures
	P.S. Wang	A theoretical and experimental investigation into the stresses at the rim of a reinforced circular hole in a flat strip under tension
1949	**S.J. Mazur**	An analytical and experimental treatment of the problem of sway in complex rigid frames and its application to inter-connected bridge girders and a discussion on the use of timber bridges in Poland with proposals for their more economical design and construction
1950	**J.C. Chapman**	A theoretical and experimental study of the behaviour in pure bending of box girders having thin webs
	D.F. Denny	1. On hydraulic seals 2. On waves: their generation, measurement and impact
	M.A. Hafiz	Strength characteristics of sands and gravels in direct shear
	K.M. Malouf	The movement of detritus around models of river and channel bends
	R.D. Northey	An experimental study of the structural sensitivity of clays
	P. Selvanayagam	An analytical and experimental investigation of the distribution of stress in shell structures
	A.A. Yassin	Model studies on bearing capacity of piles
1951	**M.M Darhouse**	Tar as a soil stabilizing agent for highway subgrades
	B.H. Falconer	Box girders in torsion
	E.A.K. Gamal-Eldin	Some fundamental factors controlling the shear properties of sand
	M.A.H. Gouda	Experimental and analytical investigation of stresses in reinforced concrete cylindrical shell roofs

	Y.C. Lao	Investigations on the ultimate strength of prestressed concrete beams
	J.M. Plowman	The vibration of concrete
	A. Shaker	Experimental and analytical investigation of the stresses in prestresed reinforced concrete cylindrical shell roofs
1952	**A.W. Bishop**	The stability of earth dams
	K.A. Everard	Moment redistribution in statically indeterminate structures due to inelastic effects in steel and concrete
	R.E. Gibson	An investigation of the fundamental shear strength characteristics of clays
	F.W. Gifford	An analysis of the factors governing the economic design of prestresed concrete
	R. Sadek	The propeller as applied to pumps and fans
	R.W. Smithies	Stress–strain relationships in concrete by bending simulation
1953	**E.H. Brown**	The application of photoelasticity to stress–diffusion problems
	S. Chandrangsu	A theoretical and experimental study of the bowstring arch
	M.T.M.W. El-Katib	An analytical and experimental investigation of the bending moment distribution in continuous prestressed concrete beams
	Z.S. Makowski	Theoretical and experimental stress analysis of braced domes with special reference to the Dome of Discovery
1954	**L.G. Booth**	An analytical and experimental investigation of the elastic and rupture theories in the design of reinforced concrete shells
	W.W. Chan	An investigation of the characteristics of plastic hinges in reinforced concrete
	S.K. Datta	Reflection of water waves from nearly vertical walls
	A.R.H. El-Ramli	Shear strength of compacted materials
	M.A-E-S.M. Fahmy	A study of soil-cement stabilisation of heavy clays with particular reference to London Clay
	G.D. Gilbert	The basic shear strength properties of Weald Clay
	A.A. Halim	Flow in a spiral casing
	S.P. Hutton	Analysis of the flow through propeller pumps and turbines in terms of blade characteristics
	S. Mikhail	Three-dimensional flow in axial pumps and fans
	A.L. Moss-Morris	An analytical and experimental investigation of the factors influencing the collapse load of reinforced concrete frames
	M.A. Sinbel	Flow in conical passages
	C.W. Yu	An analytical investigation of the ultimate load design of reinforced concrete framed structures

	V.M.S. Ziauddin	Ultimate strain distribution in concrete beams reinforced with high tensile steel, with special attention to the effects of prestress and bond
1955	**Z.B. Abdalla**	Investigations in continuous flow sedimentation with special reference to the use of models
	K. Arumugam	Surface characteristics of fast-moving water emerging from a sluice
	D.H. MacDonald	The settlement of buildings
	A.H. Mattock	A study of the ultimate moment of resistance of prestressed and reinforced concrete beams, with special reference to bond conditions
	T.A. Wyatt	A comparison of experimental and analytical studies of the behaviour of spherical shell domes
1956	**G. Ghosh**	The effects of the physical characteristics of media used in the filtration of water
	A.K.E.M. Labib	An analytical and experimental investigation on the elastic and ultimate behaviour of reinforced concrete cylindrical shells under uniformly distributed load
	T.M. Prus-Chacinski	The secondary flow in a meandering channel
	H.C. Visvesvaraya	An experimental and analytical study of prestressed concrete beams made continuous by local post-stressing, with particular reference to ultimate moment distribution
1957	**A.Q.K.K. Afghan**	The effect of particle-size distribution on the strength of soil cement mixes
	P. Chaudhuri	A critical study of factors governing the accuracy of various analytical treatments of interconnected girder systems
	F.A. De Lory	Long-term stability of slopes in overconsolidated clays
	A.M. Fraser	The influence of stress ratio on compressibility and pore pressure coefficients in compacted soils
	J. Lonergan	An analytical and experimental investigation of the shear strength of prestressed concrete beams
	R.H.G. Parry	Strength and deformation of clay
	S. Suvunnetr	A theoretical and experimental study of landing mats for temporary airfields
	G.T. Wadekar	Secondary flow in curved channels
	K.C.F. Wong	The behaviour of building frames of composite construction
1958	**L. Aadnesen**	An experimental and theoretical study of compressed chords for through-bridges
	M.S. Fayyad	Hydraulic problems of rock-fill dams
	D.J. Henkel	The correlation between deformation, pore water pressure and strength characteristics of saturated clays

	D.J. Kluth	An experimental study of an idealised arch dam in a V-shaped valley to determine the adequacy of suggested approximate solutions together with a study of the effect of Poisson's ratio on the axially symmetrical relaxation analysis
	B. Mohanrao	Flow patterns downstream of a sluice and their influence on scour
	B. Richmond	An experimental and theoretical study of an idealised arch dam in a rectangular valley with special reference to the effect of a variation in Poisson's ratio
	C.C. Wood	Shear strength and volume change characteristics of compacted soil under conditions of plane strain
	D.E. Wright	Seepage patterns arising from laminar transitional and turbulent flow through granular media
1959	**A.O. Adekola**	Interaction between steel beams and a concrete floor slab
	S.N. Ahmad	The influence of grading and the energy of compaction on density and strength of soil cement mixes
	I. Alpan	A study of the principles of effective stress in partly saturated soils
	N.N. Ambraseys	The seismic stability of earth dams
	S.P. Sharma	Application of photoelasticity to shells of revolution
1960	**S.K. Baruah**	Periodic action at the interface between water and a granular bed
	K.S. Iyer	Heat of hydration and strength development of soil cement
	P. La Rochelle	The short-term stability of slopes in London Clay
	M.S. Perera	An experimental and analytical investigation of the internal stress deformation and failure characteristics of concrete
	K. Poologasoundra-Nayagam	An analytical and experimental investigation of the formation and behaviour of plastic hinges in prestressed reinforced concrete frames
	B. Singh	Transport of bed-load in channels with special reference to gradient and form
1961	**B.M. Ahuja**	Stress distribution in shells of negative Gaussian curvature
	S.K. Al-Naib	Diffusion of a sluice-way jet
	G.E. Blight	Strength and consolidation characteristics of compacted soils
	D.H. Cornforth	Plain strain failure characteristics of a saturated sand
	I.B. Donald	The mechanical properties of saturated and partly saturated soils with special reference to the influence of negative pore water pressures

1962	**C.C. Agbim**	The use of glass fibre as reinforcement for thin concrete structures, with particular reference to shell structures
	D.S. Bondale	The effect of concrete encasement on eccentrically loaded steel columns
	A.C. Cassell	The structural behaviour of a building of composite construction
	S.M.A. Perera	Inlet baffles and their effect on the velocity distribution and turbulence in a pipe
	J.C. Scrivener	An investigation of reinforced concrete hyperbolic paraboloid shells
	S. Tonsiengsom	A study of the flow characteristics in a circular sedimentation tank under the influence of a forced vortex
1963	**M. Anson**	An investigation into a hypothetical deformation and failure mechanism of concrete
	S. Balakrishnan	The behaviour of composite steel and concrete beams with welded stud shear connectors
	B. de V. Batchelor	Stress distribution in some shells of negative Gaussian curvature with particular reference to edge effects
	A.M. El-Dujaili	The effect on free-surface percolation of misalignment of horizontal line sinks
	A.I.A. El-Gawhary	Turbulent flow past rough walls, and the movement of grains on stream beds
	M.B. Khalil	Mechanics of bed-load transport and the characteristics of rippled-beds with special reference to channel roughness
	E.L. Matyas	Compressibility and shear strength of compacted soils
	J. Munro	An analytical and experimental investigation of the stress distribution in reinforced concrete shell roofs, with particular reference to longitudinal continuity
	V.A. Sowa	A comparison of the effects of isotropic and anisotropic consolidation on the shear behaviour of clay
	M. Sulaiman	Soil stabiliation with bitumen emulsion and rubber latex
	N.H. Wade	Plane strain failure characteristics of a saturated clay
1964	**A. Basu**	The theory of orthotropic plates under lateral pressure and its application to corrugated plates
	S. Gogoi	Interaction phenomena in composite beams and plates
	D. Ho	The buckling of perforated web plates
	P. Krishna	Analysis of funicular suspension systems
	N. Morgenstern	The limit equilibrium method of slope stability analysis
	G.S. Robinson	The failure mechanism of concrete with particular reference to the biaxial compressive strength

	B.P. Walker	Experiments on model pile foundations in sand
	M.A. Ward	The testing of concrete materials by precisely controlled uni-axial tension
	G.C.K.M. Wong	Investigation of a square-based pyramidal-sheet roof system
1965	**A.D. Edwards**	The elastic behaviour and ultimate strength of reinforced and prestressed concrete frames
	C.C. Hon	The interaction between slab and columns in flat slab construction
	C.M. Lee	The geotechnical properties of a decomposed granite
	P.J. Moss	The stability of thin shells
	O.T. Sigvaldason	Failure characteristics of concrete
	P.R. Vaughan	Field measurements in earth dams
	G.W.D. Vile	Behaviour of concrete under simple and combined stresses
1966	**B. Aalami**	Non-linear behaviour of rectangular orthotropic plates under transverse and in-plane loads
	A.M.N. Amarakone	Limit design of reinforced concrete skeletal structures
	S. Arthanari	Influence of temperature and biaxial stresses on creep in concrete
	C. Ciray	Turbulence, its measurement and calculation: the engineering approach
	R.E. Hobbs	Dynamic relaxation and model techniques applied to arch dams
	T.C. Kenney	Shearing resistance of natural quick clays
	K.Y. Lo	The stress-strain pore-pressure relationship of normally consolidated clays
	H.R. Milner	The elastic-plastic stability of stanchions bent about two axes
	D.J. Petley	The shear strength of soils at large strains
	V.K. Raina	Ultimate moment distribution in continuous prestressed concrete beams
	S.P. Sarna	Local stresses in plated structures
	M.T.M. Soliman	Ultimate strength and plastic rotation capacity of reinforced concrete members
	S.Z. Uzsoy	Certain aspects of the stress analysis of shells of revolution
	D.L. Webb	The mechanical properties of undisturbed samples of London Clay and Pierre shale
1967	**K.B. Agarwal**	The influence of size and orientation of sample on the undrained strength of London Clay
	Z.A-R. Al-Dhahir	Correlation between field and laboratory measurements on earth dams
	E.J. Amana	Application of orthotropic plate theory to stiffened plywood plates

	P.G. Fookes	Site investigation of the Siwalik clay bedrock, Mangla Dam project
	D.A. Gunasekera	Numerical analysis of thin shells
	B.K. Gupta	The ultimate strength of statically indeterminate prestressed concrete structures
	M.J. Hall	Artificial rainfall in laboratory hydrology
	H.J. Memon	Resistance to flow in open channels
	M.L.A. Moncrieff	Temperature effects in a spherical prestressed concrete pressure vessel
	P.K. Neogi	Concrete filled tubular columns
	P.E. Regan	Combined shear and bending of reinforced concrete members
	K.A. Segun	Timber hyperbolic paraboloid shells supported on flexible edge members
	J.S. Tchalenko	The influence of shear and consolidation on the microscopic structure of some clays
	S.E. Uluğ	The backwashing of rapid sand filters
	L.C.P. Yam	Ultimate-load behaviour of composite T-beams having inelastic shear connection
1968	**A.F. Asfari**	Secondary flows in river bends
	M. Bailey	Reinforced concrete columns subject to large lateral deformations
	A.K. Chatterji	The distribution of stress-strain resultants in prestressed concrete portal frames
	P.J. Dowling	The behaviour of stiffened plate bridge decks under wheel loading
	S.H. Gadre	Vibrations of guyed masts
	D.R. McCreath	Fracture mechanics of concrete
	K.C. Michael	Approximate solutions of certain shallow shell problems
	A.L.T. Phukan	Non-linear deformation of rocks
	S.K. Sarma	Response characteristics and stability of earth dams during strong earthquakes
	N.T. Som	The effect of stress path on the deformation and consolidation of London Clay
	C.K.A. Stieda	The lateral stability of timber beams and arches
	S.B. Tan	Consolidation of soft clays with special reference to sand drains
	J.S. Teraszkiewicz	Static and fatigue behaviour of simply supported and continuous composite beams of steel and concrete
1969	**A.F.S.A. Aowal**	The analysis of mixing in continuous flow systems
	N.M. Awan	The moving water table in tile drain systems
	G.E. Green	Strength compressibility of granular materials under generalised strain conditions
	J.D. Hardwick	Periodic vibrations in model sluice-gates
	S.Krishnamoorthy	Thermal creep behaviour of concrete portal frames

	N.K. Kumapley	Triaxial tests on clays and silts at elevated cell pressures
	H.T. Lovenbury	Creep characteristics of London Clay
	P.A. Lowe	Prediction of loadings causing unserviceability of reinforced concrete and composite highway bridges
	P. Natarajan	Sand movement by combined action of waves and currents
	B.E. Palmer	The ultimate strength of reinforced concrete space frames
	Y. Pigeon	The compressibility of rockfill
	A. Placas	Shear failure of reinforced concrete beams
	K.M. Price	Fatigue characteristics of bonded post-tensioned concrete I-beams
	H.K. Sen	Triaxial effects in concrete-filled tubular columns
	S.G. Tombs	Strength and deformation characteristics of rockfill
	D.G. Williams	Analysis of a doubly plated grillage under in-plane and normal loading
1970	**N.N. Anis**	Shear strength of reinforced concrete flat slabs without shear reinforcement
	V.K. Garga	Residual shear strength under large strains and the effect of sample size on the consolidation of fissured clay
	M.A. Gill	Bed erosion around obstacles in rivers
	R.P. Ibbitt	Systematic parameter fitting for conceptual models of catchment hydrology
	P.M. James	Time effects and progressive failure in clay slopes
	H.I. May-Matwiejew	A study of the effect of yield on the dynamic response of tall structures to wind loading
	U. Nahhas	The inelastic behaviour of reinforced concrete sway frames with special reference to instability
	N. Remedios	Stresses in reinforced composites
	S. Selvalingam	Fluid motions in axially oscillating pipes
	J.C. Sharp	Fluid flow through fissured media
	A. Stamenkovic	Local strength of flat slabs at column heads
	G.D. Stefanou	A theoretical and experimental investigation into the perforated zones of nuclear reactor pressure vessels
	P.J.E. Sullivan	The structural behaviour of concrete at elevated temperature
	A.T. Tankut	The behaviour of the reinforced concrete flat plate structures subjected to various combinations of vertical and horizontal loads
	A.C. Visvalingam	Flow through partly-lined conduits
	P.T. Wong	The non-linear behaviour of elastic frames

1971	**G.M. Ayoub**	Dispersion of buoyant jets in a flowing ambient fluid
	H.C. Bara	Investigation of the effect of axial loads on the shear strength of reinforced concrete beams
	R.K. Bhandari	Mudflows in stiff fissured clays
	J.W. Dougill	The effects of high temperature on the strength of concrete with reference to thermal spalling
	J.M. Laing	A finite element method for investigating cracking in embankment dams
	T.K. Lim	Elastic analysis of bridge structures by the finite element method
	E.A.W. Maunder	Topological and linear analysis of skeletal structures
	A. Mitra	Effects of shear on moment/rotation characteristics of continuous reinforced concrete beams
	M. Moayer	Shear and torsion in prestressed concrete beams
	N. Narasimhan	Shear reinforcement in reinforced concrete column heads
	D.M. Osborne-Moss	Limit states of composite steel-concrete bridges
	D.J. Papastamatiou	Ground motion and response of earth structures subjected to strong earthquakes
	A. Picard	The fatigue and bond characteristics of prestressing strand
	I.C. Pyrah	The calculation of deformations in earth structures using numerical methods
	C.J. Swinnerton	Hydrological design for motorway stormwater drainage systems
	D.N. Trikha	Analytical and experimental investigation of post-tensioned single-cell concrete box-girders
	W.M. Ying	Fully-developed flow with swirl in non-circular ducts
1972	**T.A.I. Akeju**	Dynamic analysis of shells of revolution
	C.S. Krishnamoorthy	Optimal limit design of reinforced concrete frames
	S.J. Maddox	A fracture mechanics analysis of the fatigue strength of welded joints
	J.D.G. de Oliveira	Dynamic analysis of translational shells
	D.W. Reades	Stress-strain characteristics of a sand under three-dimensional loading
	A.M.A. Salih	Entrained air in an accelerating water flow
	B.Z. Sha'al	The behaviour of cohesionless soils in simple shear under cyclic loading
	D. Stephen Sandegren	The experimental and analytical investigation of plastic hinges in a reinforced concrete space frame
	K. Tharmaratnam	Structural behaviour of external horizontal joints in large panel buildings

	M. Zahedi	The behaviour of reinforced concrete columns under lateral loads due to earthquakes
1973	**A.A. Akhtaruzzaman**	The effect of transient and stationary temperature on concrete
	J.H. Atkinson	The deformation of undisturbed London Clay
	J.A. Charles	Correlation between laboratory behaviour of rockfill and field performance with particular reference to Scammonden Dam
	M. Clamen	Pulsating flow in an oscillating pipe
	M.M. Ghaderi-Tafreshi	Earthquake resistance design of reinforced concrete columns
	G.A. Giannopoulos	A dynamic traffic assignment model for assessing traffic management schemes
	H. Gross	Computer aided thermal creep analysis of concrete continua
	S.A.R. Owainati	Behaviour of reinforced concrete beams under tension, bending and shear
	R.J. Sobey	Flow patterns in lakes and reservoirs
1974	**J.E. Abbott**	The dynamics of a single grain in a stream
	C.J. Billington	The theoretical and experimental elastic behaviour of box girder bridges
	O.M.E. Fageiri	A theoretical and experimental investigation of the ultimate load behaviour of glued and nailed plywood-web I-beams
	T. Gostelow	Slope development in stiff overconsolidated clays
	M. Inzuka	Flexural behaviour of reinforced concrete members at high temperatures
	A. Kaveh	The application of topology and matroid theory to the analysis of structures
	L.E.M. de Melo Magalhaes	The merging of flow from a sluice gate with a parallel stream
	K.R. Moffatt	Finite element analysis of box girder bridges
	T. Nasseri	Non-linear behaviour of elastic space-frames
	J.B. Newman	Deformation behaviour, failure mechanisms and design criteria for concretes under combinations of stress
	P.E. O'Connell	Stochastic modelling of long-term persistence in stream flow sequences
	S. Sakthikumar	The stability of external walls in panel construction
	Z. Sen	Small sample properties of stationary stochastic models and the Hurst phenomenon in hydrology
	D.L. Smith	Plastic limit analysis and synthesis of structures by linear programming
	K.D. Virdi	Inelastic column behaviour—its application to composite columns in biaxial bending and stiffened plates in compression

	M.L.G. Werneck	Field observations of the behaviour of the Upper Lias clay at the Empingham Dam site
1975	**B. Bandypadhyay**	Computer analysis of skeletal structures with special reference to deterioration due to fire
	P. Davies	Creep characteristics of three undisturbed clays
	J.A. Dean	The collapse behaviour of steel plating subject to complex loading
	A.A. El-Ruwayih	Stress-strain characteristics of rockfill, and of clays under high pore water tension
	J.E. Harding	Bolted spliced panels and stress redistribution in box girder components up to collapse
	M. Kotsovos	Failure criteria for concrete under generalised stress states
	P.A. Mantz	Low transport stages by water streams of fine, cohesionless, granular and flakey sediments
	K. Ramachandran	Compatibility linear analysis of skeletal structures with an extension to the finite element method
	M. Raz-Nahan	The ultimate load behaviour of structures under the action of wind
	A.E. Skinner	The effect of high pore water pressures on the mechanical behaviour of sediments
	J.K. Ward	Structural interaction between arch dam and valley with special reference to the El Atazar Dam
	R.A. Wellings	Studies of polynuclear aromatic hydrocarbons in water treatment processes
1976	**A.Y. Abu-Sayf**	The stability of stones in steep shallow streams
	P. Alexa	The analysis of geometrically non-linear elasto-plastic frames by mathematical programming
	K.N.M. Amin	Forced vortex flow as a means of separating suspensions
	A. Armaghani	The failure of reinforced concrete beams and slabs subjected to fire
	M.U. Ergun	Study of generalised strength characteristics of granular soils in a three-dimensional apparatus
	P.A. Frieze	Ultimate load behaviour of steel box girders and their components
	M.M.A.F. Hamza	The analysis of embankment dams by nonlinear finite element method
	A-M. Jowharzadeh	The large deflection elasto-plastic behaviour of beam-columns and simple frames
	F. Labib	Nonlinear analysis of the bond and crack distribution in reinforced concrete members

	J.N. Lester	The influence of specific components of trade effluents upon mixed bacterial populations of sewage origin
	G.A. Lopez-Valadez	Response of soil deposits to earthquake disturbances: a time-history approach
	W.M. Maguire	The undrained strength and stress behaviour of brecciated Upper Lias Clay
	M.G.W. Millais	A dual approach to the linear analysis of elastic structures
	T. Mirata	Short-term stability of slopes in Ankara clay
	F.M. Moolani	Ultimate load behaviour of steel box girder stiffened compression flanges
	M. Rad	The deposition of silt in reservoirs by density currents
	T.K. Sen	Inelastic H-column performance at high axial loads
	H.J. Walbancke	Pore pressures in clay embankments and cuttings
	L.D. Wesley	Influence of stress path and anisotropy on the behaviour of a soft alluvial clay
	P.J. Yannopoulos	Fatigue, bond and cracking characteristics of reinforced concrete tension members
1977	J.P. Apted	Effects of weathering on some geotechnical properties of London Clay
	R.F. Danesi	Prestressed concrete box girders of deformable cross-section
	P. Djahani	Large-deflection elasto-plastic analysis of discretely stiffened plates
	R.A. Falconer	Mathematical modelling of jet-forced calculation in reservoirs and harbours
	K. Ghavami	The interaction between cross-sectional distortion and the fatigue behaviour of box girder corner welds
	J.M. Labani	The short-term structural behaviour of a lightweight aggregate concrete at elevated temperature
	P. Leinster	Some effects of vehicle and industrially generated emissions on the environment
	T.D. Lekkas	The use of two- and three-layer granular filters in the treatment of stored water
	L.P.R. Lyons	A general finite element system with special reference to the analysis of cellular structures
	P.S. McCreath	The scour of sand by an impinging jet
	C. Memos	Diffraction of waves through a gap between two inclined breakwaters
	S.S. Sandroni	The strength of London clay in total and effective stress terms
	E.G. Truscott	Behaviour of embankment dams
1978	J.E. Aguirre Romano	Flow-induced, in-line vibrations of a circular cylinder
	M.W. Baldwin	The post-1948 development of, and prospects for, inland waterway transport in Britain

	P.B. Buri	Influence of secondary consolidation and overconsolidation on the behaviour of a soft alluvial clay
	S. Chatterjee	Ultimate load analysis and design of stiffened plates in compression
	O. Daramola	The influence of stress-history on the deformation of a sand
	M-M. Davachi	Finite element analysis of footings and embankment dam cores
	F. Dibsi	The creep of triaxially stressed concrete at high temperature
	P.K. Gorf	The behaviour of a prototype form-reinforced bridge deck slab under static and repeated loading
	H. Javaherian	A finite element analysis of crack propagation problems with application to seismology
	P.W. Jowitt	Decision-making in civil engineering systems
	K.H. Littlebury	Nonlinear stochastic systems: dynamic excitation of stayed masts by wind turbulence
	E. Mardiross	Response of soil deposits on the deformable bed-rock during earthquakes and the consequent pore-water pressure dissipation
	R.S. Pugh	The strength and deformation characteristics of a soft alluvial clay under full scale loading conditions
	S. Stoveland	An investigation of some factors which influence the removal of heavy metals by an activated sludge developed in a synthetic sewage
1979	**J.A. da S. Appleton**	Elastoplastic analysis of skeletal structures by mathematical programming
	M.J.T. Carrondo	The influence of zeolite type A on the removal of heavy metals in waste water treatment processes
	M.K.A.K. El-Ghamrawy	A sandy clay till—some properties measured during consolidation and shear
	T. Ganendra	Real-time forecasting and control in the operation of water resource systems
	F.H.S. Javadi	Joints of composite construction in marine structures
	A.R.G. Lamas	Influence of shear lag on the collapse of wide-flange girders
	F. de R. Lopes	The undrained bearing capacity of piles and plates studied by the finite element method
	S.M. Metcalf	Aspects of practical multi-layer filtration
	G.W. Owens	Experimental non-linear modelling for composite structures, applied to a bifurcated bridge
	P. Rocha Filho	Behaviour in cone penetration tests in saturated sands
	J. Sioris	Hydrodynamic characteristics of floating annular structures

	J. Stefanakos	Entrained air in decelerating water flows
	J.A. Teixeira de Freitas	The elastoplastic analysis of planar frames for large displacements by mathematical programming
1980	**K.G. Abdel Nasser**	Factors affecting the choice of mode for the journey to work
	A.R. Bokaian	Fast water streams deflected by transverse walls
	L. de M. Costa Filho	A laboratory investigation of the small strain behaviour of London Clay
	M. Eetemaadi-Idgaahi	Foundation effects on free-field strong ground motions
	A.E. McIntyre	Organic substances of concern in sewage treatment processes
	M.C.R. Martins	Large model footing tests on a sandy clay till
	E.L. Mello	Some applications of generalised inverse theory to structural problems
	T.P. Nicholls	The environmental implications of the heat treatment of sewage sludge
	C.J. Peters	Trihalomethane formation arising from the chlorination of potable waters
	E.S. Tsani Bazaca	Vehicle associated air pollutants
	P. Waldron	The analysis of concrete structures including the effects of warping restraint
	P.A. Warren	Composite box girders loaded to collapse
1981	**E.N. Bromhead**	Steady and transient seepage in soils with non-linear permeability characteristics
	M.J. Brown	Metal removal by bacterial extracellular polymers in activated sludge
	I. Egeli	Pore pressures and volume changes in undrained, unsaturated clays
	A.M.A. da Fonseca	Plastic analysis and synthesis of plates and shells by mathematical programming
	J.F. Lupini	The residual strength of soils
	U.R. Madi	The elastoplastic analysis of pin-jointed spatial structures
	L.A. Obeng	Detergent builders in the activated sludge process
	H. Okafor	Bonded prestressed concrete square slabs subjected to concentrated loading
	H.B. Ooi	A numerical model for fire resistance of concrete structures
	A.C. Rossin	Influence of detergent builders on heavy metals in waste water treatment
	R.M. Sterritt	Heavy metals in biological waste water treatment
	M. Taha	Concrete deep beams with web openings
	M. Takahashi	Transient and cyclic behaviour of a sandy clay
	S.E. Webb	Stiffened plating under combined in-plane and lateral loading
1982	**C.J. Burgoyne**	The non-linear behaviour of elastic beams and beam columns

	A.F. Dier	Collapse of metal plates
	C.B. Echeta	Semi-rigid connections between concrete-filled steel columns and composite beams
	P.W.W. Kirk	Treatment and disposal of sewage sludge containing nitrilotriacetic acid
	M.K. Surendranath	Ultimate load behaviour of plywood stressed-skin panels
	C.P. Tsatsanifos	Effective stress method for dynamic response analysis of horizontally layered soils
1983	**C.P. Abbiss**	Shear wave measurements of deformation properties of soil
	J.B.O. Adewumi	Systems modelling and control in irrigation
	W.E. Armstrong	Axially loaded concrete prisms with lateral confinement
	C. Bédard	Non-linear finite element analysis of concrete structures
	M. Bull	Anaerobic treatment of high strength wastewater in fluidized bed reactors
	A.I.W. Clark	Air quality impact assessment of transport-related air pollutants
	S.C. Cook	Systems identification and control of waste water treatment processes in river management
	B. Einarsson	Ultimate load behaviour of rectangular steel box girder diaphragms
	A. Garcia Gutierrez	Significance and removal of organochlorine micropollutants in primary sedimentation
	A. Gens	Stress-strain and strength characteristics of a low plasticity clay
	N.J.D. Graham	Significance of filter pore particle flocculation in direct filtration
	D.W. Hight	Laboratory investigations of sea-bed clays
	P.M. Jones	A new approach to understanding travel behaviour and its implications for transportation planning
	G.A. Khoury	Transient thermal creep of nuclear reactor pressure vessel type concretes
	P.S. Lawson	The uptake of metals in the activated sludge process
	T.V. Luong	Halogenated organic materials in water supplies
	J.P. Martins	Shaft resistance of axillary loaded piles in clay
	G.G.K. Ngirane	Influences of storm dynamics on flood hydrographs
	M.Raoof	Interwire contact forces and the static, hysteretic and fatigue properties of multi-layer structural strands
	T. Rudd	Heavy metal complexation by extracellular polymers of activated sludge bacteria

	T. Stephenson	Behaviour of nitrilotriacetic acid during biological waste water and sludge treatment
	M.J.P.R. Symes	Rotation of principal stresses in sand
	U. Trueb	Stability problems of elasto-plastic frames and shells by finite elements

The degree of MSc(Eng) awarded by London University

1923	**A. Dean**	An investigation of the effects of replacing Portland cement by ground sand in cement mortars
1926	**H.D. Morgan** (*with* **C.H. Peppiatt**)	Cinder concrete and the temperature changes in cement and mortars
	C.H. Peppiatt	*See* H.D. Morgan
	R.S. Read	Aerated concrete
1927	**E. Burke**	The constitution of Portland cement with special reference to its microscopy
1928	**R.Edgar**	Increasing the dependability of winding ropes in mines
	K.C. Wu	Discharge of syphons
1929	**S.S. Kumar**	The effect of consistency and voids on the strength of cements and mortars
	S.D. Lash	Movable crest weirs, with special reference to Walton Gates
1930	**A. Alfes** (*with* **S.R. Gadhoke**)	Research on the properties of aero-concrete plain and with different aggregates
	S.R. Gadhoke	*See* A. Alfes
	M.L.X. Kambhu	Flow through mouthpieces and rise of pressure in pipe line when jet issuing from its mouthpiece impinges on a rigid normal plane
	K.G. Shaikh	The modulus of elasticity of concrete under compression
1931	**N.H. Taylor**	Asphalt paving mixtures
1932	**F.E. Draddy**	Analysis of concrete road failures and the determination of values for coefficient of expansion of concrete of varying mixes and aggregates in relation to such failures
	T.B. Hli	Standing waves and standing wave flumes
1933	**A.G. Boorman**	Concrete, plain and reinforced
	O.H. Chilton	Welded steel structures
	F.V.A.E. Engel	Problems and phenomena of non-uniform flow of water in open channels with side contractions (External)
	W.H. Evans	An investigation into the strength and efficiency of steel arches for use in mines
	E.F. Gibbs	Tests of uniformly loaded concrete arches
	H.T. Horsfield	An investigation into the physical properties of bitumen and sand

	R.C. Marc	The relative thermal conductivities of various concretes
	A.V. Paes	Effects of hydrated lime on the properties of Portland cement concrete
1934	**M.B. Chablani**	Volume changes in concrete and shrinkage stresses
	H.Y. Chiao	A study of broad-crested weirs
1935	**R.N. Dogra**	Tar concrete paving mixtures
	T.K. Jones	A study of the coefficient of discharge of rounded V-notches
	A.E. McClelland	Wire ropes for colliery purposes
	R.W. Pearson	The bond between mortar and brick
1936	**M.M. Bilaney**	An experimental investigation of the flexural rigidity of reinforced concrete beams
	A.W. Skempton	A study of reinforced concrete columns subject to flexure
1937	**P.Y. Ho**	Experiments on terminal velocity of sand and on erosion in a model river
	J.R. Ramchandani	The absorption of bitumens by road aggregates
	T.H. Tung	A theoretical and experimental investigation of the stresses in open spandrel arches
1938	**R.J. Ashby**	An experimental study of the masonry voussoir arch
	F.E. Bruce (*with* **E.W. Cuthbert)**	An experimental verification of the strain energy theory of the arch rib
	A.R. Collins	The workability of concrete in relation to the grading of the aggregate
	E.W. Cuthbert	*See* F.E. Bruce
	H.U. Makhijani	An experimental investigation of the flexural rigidity of doubly reinforced concrete beams
	L-.R. Robertson	The skidding properties of pneumatic tyres and road surfaces with special reference to their measurement in the laboratory
	F.J. Sanger	Foundations research
	N.R. Tembe	Experimental investigation of the torsional rigidity of plain and reinforced concrete members
	T.M. Yu	Theoretical and experimental study of electrically welded rigid joints
1939	**R.F. Davis**	The mechanics of flame and air jets
	J.P.A. De Waele	1. An analytical and experimental study of a Vierendeel cantilever with non-parallel chords 2. The loading of interconnected bridge girders
	A.G. Gowers	The collapse of thin steel tubes under external pressure
	P. Hartley	Bituminous jointing materials
	N.N. Purandare	1. The effects on the strength of tee beams of casting the flange and the rib separately

		2. The effects of revibration on the strength of concrete
	R.P. Verma	An experimental investigation of the behaviour of reinforced brickwork
	B.C. Wearn	Axial and non-axial loads on props
1940	**Y.H. Kefeli**	Theoretical and experimental study of an electrically welded single-bay double-storey model portal
	C.M. Patel	An experimental study of concrete slabs supported on 4 edges
	M.V. Yazici	Redistribution of stress in a truss when one of the members yields
1941	**G.M. Cornfield**	The buckling of the webs of plate girders
	G.B. Marriott	Bituminous joints in concrete
	J.G. Thon	Investigation of the stresses in a plate of finite width with a circular hole by means of rubber models
1942	**M.I.M. Khan**	An experimental investigation of prestressed reinforced concrete columns
1945	**J.F. Douglas**	Adhesion between binders and road aggregates
	J.C. King	An experimental investigation into the structural features of a corrugated construction smooth wing
1947	**W.Y. Wan**	A critical examination of the analysis of wind stresses in tall building frames
1948	**C.W. Liu**	Multi-storey building foundations: the relation between the strength and flexibility of rafts and the yielding capacity of ground
	C.G. Swaminathan	Stability testing of asphalt paving mixtures
1949	**A. Firth**	Flow in a spiral case
	G.M. Gidwani	An experimental study into the behaviour of cold twisted steel bars for concrete reinforcement, and recommendations for the design methods and stresses in bending
	K. Krishnamacharyulu	A study of the use of expanding cements in prestressed concrete design
	A. Lund	An experimental study of graded filters
	A.H. Mattock	A study of design methods for 'end-anchored' prestressed concrete beams
	T.M. Menon	The effect of curing conditions on the compressive strength of cement-stabilised soils
	H.H.S. Mygind	Shear forces in reinforced concrete beams with special reference to electric wire strain gauges
	H.D. Stead	A study of plastic theories for the ultimate strength of reinforced concrete beams in bending
1950	**D.N. Barbora**	Model tests on a discharge regulator for open channels
	A. Hassan	The study of reinforced concrete flat-plate structures

	P.H. Lam	The effect of mixing-time on the properties of bituminous stabilized soils
	P. Lumb	The effect of grading on the mechanical stabilization of soils
	A.C. Meigh	Model footing tests on clay
	V.M.S. Ziauddin	Ultimate strength of prestressed concrete beams with reference to plastic theory
1951	**E.R.P. Chunnet**	Flow over a step
	D.A. Wright	A theoretical and experimental study of the behaviour of thin box girders in pure bending
1952	**P.J. Madan**	Changes in the properties of a clay soil effected by the addition of lime
	I. Revesz	The behaviour of prestressed beams
1953	**J. de C. Gray**	The influence of bond on neutral axis position and crack spacing in reinforced concrete beams
	F.A. Kilner	Local scour in river models due to spurs
	M.P. Poucher	An experimental investigation of the factors affecting the flow and compaction of concrete in reinforced structures
1954	**P.A.D. Allsopp**	Stabilization of a tropical clay for highway construction
	K.G. Bassi	Plastic hinges in long columns, with reference to the plastic theory of reinforced concrete structures
	S.R. Chokhavatia	The behaviour of the segmental voussoir arch under distributed loads
	V.K. Collinge	Floods: some hydrological and hydraulic studies
	J.J. Davis	Investigation of the flow of air through a duct of non-circular cross-section
	U.D.N. Desai	Stability analysis of earth dams with special reference to pore pressures
	M.M.N. Dhar	An experimental and theoretical comparison of light prefabricated steel-framed structure with one of orthodox design
	J.C. Howe	Bed movement in a model tidal estuary
	H.W. Leung	The influence of grouting on neutral axis position and crack spacing in prestressed concrete beams
	J.G. Lewis	The sloping core principle for earth and rock-fill dams
	D.W. Murray	An experimental and analytical investigation of an arch dam model
	O.S. Sahgal	A study of the mechanical testing of sand-bitumen mixes
	P.G. Valvis	An experimental and analytical approach to the problem of the arch dam
	A.J. Watt	Shear strength and pore pressure characteristics of six compacted soils
1955	**B. Chaudhary**	Compressibility characteristics of compacted soils
	J.E. Feir	On the action of a stream in lifting grains from its bed

	B. Hanson	Shear strength and pore pressure characteristics of compacted soils
	N.M. Khan	An experimental investigation of the shear strength of plastic hinges in reinforced concrete members
	D.R. Kohli	The mechanical testing of soil-cement mixtures for highway subgrades
	B. Lamarre	An experimental investigation of the distribution of stress in reinforced concrete beams by bending simulation and other methods
	J.R. Plant	Shear strength properties of London clay
	M.S.M. Venkoba Rao	The influence of road design on traffic flow and accident occurrence
1956	**D. Criticos**	Experimental investigation of the shear strength of 'plastic hinges' of pretensioned beams
	M.N. Gogate	The theoretical stress analysis of encastre parabolic arch-ribs and experimental verification by models
	T.C. Kenney	An examination of the methods of calculating the stability of slopes
	J. Kolosowski	A theoretical and experimental study of the castellated girder
	S. Narasinham	Wave patterns in rapid flow
	G.E.V. Panas	An experimental investigation of stresses in a reinforced concrete north light shell roof
	M.C. Pundarika Row	An experimental study of the effects of prestressing on a Pratt truss
	B.V. Ranganatham	Investigation of the stress-strain properties of sand-clay mixtures in relation to pavement design
	A.Q.A.J. Saif	An analytical and experimental investigation of the optimum form of edge beams for cylindrical shells
1957	**G.C. Gupta**	Design and testing of sand-bituminous base course mixes for Indian conditions
	A.B. Hicks	The influence of shear span and concrete strength upon the shear resistance of prestressed pretensioned concrete beams
	H.L.A.M. Levelt	The effect of aggregate absorption on concrete mixes
	W.R. MacKechnie	The shearing resistance of a partially saturated sand under repetitive loading in a triaxial cell
	P.K. Som	An experimental and analytical study of the behaviour of light-alloy angles used as structural members in tension
1958	**P. Ackers**	The hydraulics of side-spillways with special reference to super-critical flow
	A.S. Arshad	Variation of porosity with depth in a laboratory scale rapid sand filter
	H.-ud-D. Bangash	The action of boundaries near a free vortex
	F.M. El Moosa	The effect of compaction on the strength and pore pressure characteristics of a boulder clay

	E.L. Kemp	An investigation of prestressed concrete knee joints
	P.J. Prasad	An experimental and analytical investigation of post-tensioned joints in continuous prestressed concrete frames
	R. Sethunarayanan	An experimental and analytical investigation of the ultimate strength of pretensioned thin webbed I-beams, under combined bending and shear
	T.M.N. Sinha	Behaviour of bituminous road mixtures under repeated loads
1959	**R.C. Ballance**	An experimental study of the effect of inclined baffles in sedimentation tanks
	B.S. Benjamin	The analysis of Schwedler domes
	A.J. Das Daniel	The fairing of conduit entrances with reference to separation and cavitation
	J.H. Dastur	An analytical and experimental investigation of the EI values of prestressed and reinforced concrete beams
	R. Fisher	Turbulent diffusion in an artificially roughened channel
	A.E. Insley	The behaviour of bored foundation piles in London Clay
	S.N. Manohar	An experimental and theoretical analysis of braced barrel vaults with particular reference to the effect of edge conditions
	C.I. Mathew	The effect of some approximations on the analysis of a structural grid
	R. Narayanan	An investigation of maturity-strength relationships of normal-cured and accelerated-cured concrete
1960	**P. Brahmachari**	Stress relaxation owing to creep in concrete under sustained working loads and overloads
	S. Chattopadhyay	Plastic collapse of bow girders
	P. Mukhopadhyay	Structural analysis of double-layer grids
	A. Ramirez Rivera	Load analysis of hexagonal grids
	G. Saint-Pierre	An experimental investigation of the ultimate behaviour of a longitudinally continuous reinforced concrete cylindrical shell
	K. van Dalen	An analytical and experimental investigation of the shear strength of prestressed concrete Tee beams
1961	**L. Adsett**	The shear strength of prestressed concrete I-beams with web reinforcement
	J.D. Brown	The stability of clay slopes
	M.S. Jalundhwala	Load distribution in a geodesic dome
	J.A. Kozlowski	The leakage through annular gaps in journal bearings
	B.J.D. Manning	The use of the digital computer in the analysis of arch dams
	K.C. Wilson	The connection between Froude number and the transportation of bed-load
1962	**P.A. Banks**	Flow from a vertical shaft into a horizontal tunnel

	S.L. Chow	Analysis of a double curvature shell by photoelasticity
	F.R.W. Clarke	The action of submerged jets on moveable material
	L. Lachance	The effect of end restraint, shape and size on the elastic properties and failure characteristics of concrete specimens under compression
	J.B. Martins	Some factors controlling the consolidation of saturated soils
1963	**S. Ahmad**	A strategically indeterminate truss mechanism for reinforced concrete beams failing by shear
	A.M.N. Amarakone	Deformation characteristics of reinforced concrete columns subject to bending
	E.M. Aziz	The design of continuous prestressed concrete bridge girders by computer
	T.W. Bremner	The influence of the reinforcement on the elastic and inelastic properties of reinforced concrete members
	E.F.P. Burnett	The ultimate load design of statically indeterminate concrete structures
	R.H. Ferahian	Shear lag and buckling in plated grids
	D.H.W. Hykin	The displacement of grid structures
	H.L. Kheng	The effect of valley stiffness on the behaviour of an arch dam
	A.K. Lal	The flexural failure of reinforced concrete continuous beams and portal frames
	D. Laplante	The design of shells to predetermined stress distributions
	B.C.A. Obi	Cement stabilisation of a tropical laterite for highway construction
1964	**D.N. Acharya**	The influence of shear force on the ultimate strength of flexural members in reinforced concrete structures
	P.A.K. Awotwi	The interaction between an arch dam and its valley
	J. Normand	One-dimensional consolidation of saturated clays with large strains
	J.M. Salmon	Effects of remoulding soil cement
1965	**M. Ben-George**	Analysis of arch dams with particular reference to the boundary sections
	J.G.C. Chinwah	The strength and deformation characteristics of eccentrically loaded reinforced concrete columns
	R.M. El-Debouni	Steady and unsteady groundwater flow with a free surface
	M.E. Ibbitt	Studies in hydrology: arid regions
	T. Mirata	Deformations in compressible foundations on embankments
1967	**A. Kizideli**	An arch gravity dam on an anisotropic foundation

The degree of MPhil(Eng) awarded by London University*

1967	**F. Ekman**	The calculation of displacements and stress in an arch dam
	P.C. Ledi	Split-ring connectors in timber structures
	A. Mitra	Guide to model testing of spherical pressure vessels
	D.D.O. Paranagama	Pretensioned prestressed beams under repeated overloads
1968	**F.H.N. Sayani**	Influence of axial tension on the shear strength of reinforced concrete beams
1969	**M.H. Khan**	Shear strength of concrete beams reinforced under bent-up bars
	M.Pigeon	The process of crack initiation and propagation in concrete
1971	**B.K. Chadha**	The seismicity of northern Iran
1973	**M.S. Navabi**	Seismicity of Iran
1974	**M.D. Pachakis**	An investigtion of five long-term failures on embankments founded on landslipped soils
	V.G. Sodha	The stability of embankment dam fills of plastic clay
	G.C. Tobia	Towards a simplified trip distribution model
1975	**R. Can**	Seismotectonics of the North Anatolian fault zone
	K. F. McCue	Seismicity and seismic risk in Australasia
	M. Tosic	Ground motion characteristics of strong earthquakes
1976	**A.M. Memon**	An experimental investigation into the consolidation characteristics of gap-graded soils
1977	**R.P. Herbertson**	A model test facility for soil-structure interaction
1978	**E.V. Ingimundarson**	Vehicle emission control technology: a correlation of emissions in relation to source
	A. Roussopoulos	Seismic regionalisation techniques and strong motion recordings
	V.K. Shebini	Approximate analysis of multi-box systems
1979	**S.J. Robinson**	Hydraulic modelling of circulation in reservoirs
1980	**H.F. Soares**	Experiments on the retention of soils by filters
1981	**R.R. Ponte Ramirez**	Storm rainfall and runoff in Venezuela
1982	**J.C. Nicholls**	On the determination of structural system reliability

*The degree of MSc(Eng) for research was superseded by MPhil(Eng) in 1967 when the MSc(Eng) could be obtained by examination

Index of Higher Degrees 1884-1983

Aadnesen, L.	PhD	1958
Aalami, B.	PhD	1966
Abbiss, C.P.	PhD	1983
Abbott, J.E.	PhD	1974
Abdalla, Z.B.	PhD	1955
Abdel Nasser, K.G.	PhD	1980
Abu-Sayf, A.Y.	PhD	1976
Acharya, D.N.	MSc	1964
Ackers, P.	MSc	1958
Adekola, A.O.	PhD	1959
Adewumi, J.B.O.	PhD	1983
Adsett, L.	MSc	1961
Afghan, A.Q.K.K.	PhD	1957
Agarwal, K.B.	PhD	1967
Agbim, C.C.	PhD	1962
Aguirre Romano, J.E.	PhD	1978
Ahmad, S.	MSc	1963
Ahmad, S.N.	PhD	1959
Ahuja, B.M.	PhD	1961
Akeju, T.A.I.	PhD	1972
Akhtaruzzaman, A.A.	PhD	1973
Al-Dhahir, Z.A-R.	PhD	1967
Al-Naib, S.K.	PhD	1961
Alexa, P	PhD	1976
Alfes, A	MSc	1930
Allsopp, P.A.D.	MSC	1954
Alpan, I.	PhD	1959
Amana, E.J.	PhD	1967
Amarakone, A.M.N.	MSC	1963
Amarakone, A.M.N.	PhD	1966
Ambraseys, N.N.	PhD	1959
Amin, K.N.M.	PhD	1976
Amin, M.	PhD	1927
Anis, N.N.	PhD	1970
Anson, M.	PhD	1963
Aowal, A.F.S.A.	PhD	1969
Appleton, J.A.daS.	PhD	1979
Apted, J.P.	PhD	1977
Arumaghani, A.	PhD	1976
Armstrong, W.E.	PhD	1983
Arshad, A.S.	MSc	1958
Arthanari, S.	PhD	1966
Arumugam, K.	PhD	1955
Asfari, A.F.	PhD	1968
Ashby, R.J.	MSc	1938
Atkinson, J.H.	PhD	1973
Awan, N.M.	PhD	1969
Awotwi, P.A.K.	MSc	1964
Ayoub, G.M.	PhD	1971
Aziz, E.M.	MSc	1963
Bailey, M.	PhD	1968
Balakrishnan, S.	PhD	1963
Baldwin, M.W.	PhD	1978
Ballance, R.C.	MSc	1959
Bandyopadhyay, B.	PhD	1975
Bangash, H.-ud-D.	MSc	1958
Banks, P.A.	MSc	1962
Bara, H.C.	PhD	1971
Barbora, D.N.	MSc	1950
Baruah, S.K.	PhD	1960
Bassi, K.G.	MSc	1954
Basu, A.	PhD	1964
Batchelor, B. de V.	PhD	1963
Bedard, C.	PhD	1983
Ben-George, M.	MSc	1965
Benjamin, B.S.	MSc	1959
Bhandari, N.N.	PhD	1941
Bhandari, R.K.	PhD	1971
Bilaney, M.M.	MSc	1936
Billington, C.J.	PhD	1974
Bishop, A.W.	PhD	1952
Blight, G.E.	PhD	1961
Bokaian, A.R.	PhD	1980
Bondale, D.S.	PhD	1962
Boorman, A.G.	MSc	1933
Booth, L.G.	PhD	1954
Brahmachari, P.	MSc	1960
Brazier, T.W.	MSc	1928
Bremner, T.W.	MSc	1963
Bromhead, E.N.	PhD	1981
Brown, E.H.	PhD	1953
Brown, J.D.	MSc	1961
Brown, M.J.	PhD	1981
Bruce, F.E.	MSc	1938
Burgoyne, C.J.	PhD	1982
Buri, P.B.	PhD	1978
Burke, E.	MSc	1927
Burnett, E.F.P.	MSc	1963
Burns, R.V.	PhD	1935
Can, R.	MPhil	1975
Carrondo, M.J.T.	PhD	1979
Cassell, A.C.	PhD	1962
Chablani, M.B.	MSc	1934
Chadha, B.K.	MPhil	1971
Chan, W.W.	PhD	1954
Chandrangsu, S.	PhD	1953
Chao, C.S.	PhD	1948
Chapman, J.C.	PhD	1950
Charles, J.A.	PhD	1973
Chatterjee, S.	PhD	1948
Chatterji, A.K.	PhD	1968
Chattopadhyay, S.	MSc	1960
Chaudhary, B.	MSc	1955
Chaudhuri, P.	PhD	1957
Chiao, H.Y.	MSc	1934
Chilton, O.H.	MSc	1933
Chinwah, J.G.C.	MSc	1965
Chokhavatia, S.R.	MSc	1954
Chow, S.L.	MSc	1962
Chu, K.H.	PhD	1936
Chunnet, E.R.P.	MSc	1951
Ciray, C.	PhD	1966
Clamen, M.	PhD	1973
Clarke, F.R.W.	MSc	1962
Colebrook, C.F.	PhD	1937
Collacott, R.A.	PhD	1944
Collinge, V.K.	MSc	1954
Collins, A.R.	MSc	1938
Cornfield, G.M.	MSc	1941
Cornforth, D.H.	PhD	1961

Costa Filho, L. de M.	PhD	1980
Criticos, D.	MSc	1956
Cuthbert, E.W.	MSc	1938
Danesi, R.F.	PhD	1977
Daramola, O.	PhD	1978
Darhouse, M.M.	PhD	1951
Das Daniel, A.J.	MSc	1959
Dastur, J.H.	MSc	1959
Datta, S.K.	PhD	1954
Davachi, M-M.	PhD	1978
Davies, P.	PhD	1975
Davis, J.J.	MSc	1954
Davis, R.F.	MSc	1939
De Lory, F.A.	PhD	1957
De Weale, J.P.A.	MSc	1939
Dean, A.	MSc	1923
Dean, J.A.	PhD	1975
Denny, D.F.	PhD	1950
Desai, U.D.N.	MSc	1954
Dhar, M.M.N.	MSc	1954
Dibsi, F.	PhD	1978
Dier, A.F.	PhD	1982
Djahani, P.	PhD	1977
Dogra, R.N.	MSc	1935
Donald, I.B.	PhD	1961
Dougill, J.W.	PhD	1971
Douglas, J.F.	MSc	1945
Dowling, P.J.	PhD	1968
Draddy, F.E.	MSc	1932
Echeta, C.B.	PhD	1982
Edgar, R.	MSc	1928
Edwards, A.D.	PhD	1965
Eetemaadi-Idgaahi, M.	PhD	1980
Egeli, I.	PhD	1981
Einarsson, B.	PhD	1983
Ekman, F.	MPhil	1967
El-Debouni, R.M.	MSc	1965
El-Dujaili, A.M.	PhD	1963
El-Gawhary, A.I.A.	PhD	1963
El-Ghamrawy, M.K.A.K	PhD	1979
El-Katib, M.T.M.W.	PhD	1953
El Moosa, F.M.	MSc	1958
El Ramli, A.R.H.	PhD	1954
El-Ruwayih, A.A.	PhD	1975
Engel, F.V.A.E.	MSc	1933
Ergun, M.U.	PhD	1976
Evans, W.H.	MSc	1933
Everard, K.A.	PhD	1952
Fageiri, O.M.E.	PhD	1974
Fahmy, M.A-E-S.M.	PhD	1954
Falconer, B.H.	PhD	1951
Falconer, R.A.	PhD	1977
Fayyad, M.S.	PhD	1958
Feir, J.E.	MSc	1955
Ferahian, R.H.	MSc	1963
Firth, A.	MSc	1949
Fisher, R.	MSc	1959
Fonseca, A.M.A.da	PhD	1981
Fookes, P.G.	PhD	1967
Fraser, A.M.	PhD	1957

Frieze, P.A.	PhD	1976
Gadhoke, S.R.	MSc	1930
Garga, S.H.	PhD	1968
Gamal-Eldin, E.A.K.	PhD	1951
Ganendra, T.	PhD	1979
Garga, V.K.	PhD	1970
Gayed, Y.K.	PhD	1941
Gens, A.	PhD	1982
Ghaderi-Tafreshi, M.M.	PhD	1973
Ghavami, K.	PhD	1977
Ghosh, G.	PhD	1956
Giannopoulos, G.A.	PhD	1973
Gibbs, E.F.	MSc	1933
Gibbs, E.F.	PhD	1937
Gibson, R.E.	PhD	1952
Gidwani, G.M.	MSc	1949
Gifford, F.W.	PhD	1952
Gilbert, G.D.	PhD	1954
Gill, M.A.	PhD	1970
Gimpel, J.	PhD	1941
Gogate, M.N.	MSc	1956
Gogoi, S.	PhD	1964
Gorf, P.K.	PhD	1978
Gostelow, T.	PhD	1974
Gouda, M.A.H.	PhD	1951
Gowers, A.G.	MSc	1939
Graham, N.J.D.	PhD	1983
Gray, J. de C.	MSc	1953
Green, G.E.	PhD	1969
Gross, H.	PhD	1973
Gunasekera, D.A.	PhD	1967
Gupta, B.K.	PhD	1967
Gupta, G.C.	MSc	1957
Hafiz, M.A.A.	PhD	1950
Halim, A.A.	PhD	1954
Hall, M.J.	PhD	1967
Hamza, M.M.A.F.	PhD	1976
Hanson, B.	MSc	1955
Harding, J.E.	PhD	1975
Hardwick, J.D.	PhD	1969
Hartley, P.	MSc	1939
Hassan, A.	MSc	1950
Henkel, D.J.	PhD	1958
Herbertson, R.P.	MPhil	1977
Hicks, A.B.	MSc	1957
Hight, D.W.	PhD	1983
Hli, T.B.	MSc	1932
Ho, D	PhD	1964
Ho, P.Y.	MSc	1937
Hobbs, R.E.	PhD	1966
Hon, C.C.	PhD	1965
Horsfield, H.T.	MSc	1933
Howe, J.C.	MSc	1954
Hutton, S.P.	PhD	1954
Hykin, D.H.W.	MSc	1963
Ibbitt, M.E.	MSc	1965
Ibbitt, R.P.	PhD	1970
Ingimundarson, E.V.	MPhil	1978
Insley, A.E.	MSc	1959
Inzuka, M.	PhD	1974

Iyer, K.S.	PhD	1960
Jalundhwala, M.S.	MSc	1961
James, P.M.	PhD	1970
Javadi, F.H.S.	PhD	1979
Javaherian, H.	PhD	1978
Jones, P.M.	PhD	1983
Jones, T.K.	MSc	1935
Jowharzadeh, A.-M.	PhD	1976
Jowitt, P.W.	PhD	1978
Kambhu, M.L.X.	MSc	1930
Kaveh, A.	PhD	1974
Kefeli, Y.H.	MSc	1940
Kemp, E.L.	MSc	1958
Kenney, T.C.	MSc	1956
Kenney, T.C.	PhD	1966
Khalil, M.B.	PhD	1963
Khan, M.H.	MPhil	1969
Khan, M.I.M.	MSc	1942
Khan, N.M.	MSc	1955
Kheng, H.L.	MSc	1963
Khoury, G.A.	PhD	1983
Kilner, F.A.	MSc	1953
King, J.C.	MSc	1945
Kirk, P.W.W.	PhD	1982
Kizideli, A.	MSc	1967
Kluth, D.J.	PhD	1958
Kohli, D.R.	MSc	1955
Kolbuszewski, J.J.	PhD	1948
Kolosowski, J.	MSc	1956
Kotsovos, M.	PhD	1975
Kozlowski, J.A.	MSc	1961
Krishna, P.	PhD	1964
Krishnamacharyulu, K.	MSc	1949
Krishnamoorthy, C.S.	PhD	1972
Krishnamoorthy, S.	PhD	1969
Kumapley, N.K.	PhD	1969
Kumar, S.S.	MSc	1929
La Rochelle, P.	PhD	1960
Labani, J.M.	PhD	1977
Labib, A.K.E.M.	PhD	1956
Labib, F.	PhD	1976
Lachance, L.	MSc	1962
Laing, J.M.	PhD	1971
Lal, A.K.	MSc	1963
Lam, P.H.	MSc	1950
Lamarre, B.	MSc	1955
Lamas, A.R.G.	PhD	1979
Lao, Y.C.	PhD	1951
Laplante, D.	MSc	1963
Lash, S.D.	MSc	1929
Ledi, P.C.	MPhil	1967
Lee, C.M.	PhD	1965
Leinster, P.	PhD	1977
Lekkas, T.D.	PhD	1977
Lester, J.N.	PhD	1976
Leung, H.W.	MSc	1954
Levelt, H.L.A.M.	MSc	1957
Lewis, J.G.	MSc	1954
Li, Y.S.	PhD	1948
Lim, T.K.	PhD	1971

Littlebury, K.H.	PhD	1978
Liu, C.W.	MSc	1948
Lo, K.Y.	PhD	1966
Lonergan, J.	PhD	1957
Lopes, F.deR.	PhD	1979
Lopez-Valadez, G.A.	PhD	1976
Lovenbury, H.T.	PhD	1969
Lowe, P.A.	PhD	1969
Lumb, P.	MSc	1950
Lund, A.	MSc	1949
Luong, T.V.	PhD	1983
Lupini, J.F.	PhD	1981
Lyons, L.P.R.	PhD	1977
McClelland, A.E.	MSc	1935
McCreath, D.R.	PhD	1968
McCreath, P.S.	PhD	1977
McCue, K.F.	MPhil	1975
MacDonald, D.H.	PhD	1955
McIntyre, A.E.	PhD	1980
MacKechnie, W.R.	MSc	1957
Madan, P.J.	MSc	1952
Maddox, S.J.	PhD	1972
Madi, U.R.	PhD	1981
Maguire, W.M.	PhD	1976
Makhijani, H.U.	MSc	1938
Makowski, Z.S.	PhD	1953
Malik, I.M.K.	MSc	1942
Malouf, K.M.	PhD	1950
Manning, B.J.D.	MSc	1961
Manohar, S.N.	MSc	1959
Mantz, P.A.	PhD	1975
Marc, R.C.	MSc	1933
Mardiross, E.	PhD	1978
Marriott, G.B.	MSc	1941
Marshall, W.T.	PhD	1939
Martins, J.B.	MSc	1962
Martins, J.P.	PhD	1983
Martins, M.C.R.	PhD	1980
Mathew, C.I.	MSc	1959
Mattock, A.H.	MSc	1949
Mattock, A.H.	PhD	1955
Matyas, E.L.	PhD	1963
Maunder, E.A.W.	PhD	1971
May-Matwiejew, H.I.	PhD	1970
Mazur, S.J.	PhD	1949
Meigh, A.C.	MSc	1950
Mello, E.L.	PhD	1980
Melo Magalhaes, L.E.M.	PhD	1974
Memon, A.M.	MPhil	1976
Memon, H.M.	PhD	1967
Memos, C.	PhD	1977
Menon, T.M.	MSc	1949
Metcalf, S.M.	PhD	1979
Michael, K.C.	PhD	1968
Mikhail, S.	PhD	1954
Millais, M.G.W.	PhD	1976
Milner, H.R.	PhD	1966
Mirata, T.	MSc	1965
Mirata, T.	PhD	1976
Mitra, A.	MPhil	1967
Mitra, A	PhD	1971
Moayer, M.	PhD	1971

Moffatt, K.R.	PhD	1974
Mohanrao, B.	PhD	1958
Moncrieff, M.L.A.	PhD	1967
Moolani, F.M.	PhD	1976
Moore, W.N.C.	PhD	1971
Morgan, H.D.	MSc	1926
Morgenstern, N.	PhD	1964
Moss, P.J.	PhD	1965
Moss-Morris, A.L.	PhD	1954
Moyal, I.	PhD	1935
Mukhopadhyay, P.	MSc	1960
Munro, J.	PhD	1963
Murray, D.W.	MSc	1954
Mygind, H.H.S.	MSc	1949
Nabavi, M.S.	MPhil	1973
Nahhas, U.	PhD	1970
Narasimhan, N.	PhD	1971
Narasimhan, S.	MSc	1956
Narayanan, R.	MSc	1959
Nasseri, T.	PhD	1974
Natarajan, P.	PhD	1969
Neogi, P.K.	PhD	1967
Newman, J.B.	PhD	1974
Ngirane, G.G.K.	PhD	1983
Nicholls, J.C.	MPhil	1982
Nicholls, T.P.	PhD	1980
Normand, J.	MSc	1964
Northey, R.D.	PhD	1950
Obeng, L.A.	PhD	1981
Obi, B.C.A.	MSc	1963
O'Connell, P.E.	PhD	1974
Okafor, H.	PhD	1981
Oliveira, J.D.G.de	PhD	1972
Ooi, H.B.	PhD	1981
Orchard, D.F.	PhD	1941
Osborne-Moss, D.M.	PhD	1971
Owainati, S.A.R.	PhD	1973
Owens, G.W.	PhD	1979
Pachakis, M.D.	MPhil	1974
Paes, A.V.	MSc	1933
Palmer, B.E.	PhD	1969
Panas, G.E.V.	MSc	1956
Papastamatiou, D.J.	PhD	1971
Paranagama, D.D.O.	MPhil	1967
Parry, R.H.G.	PhD	1957
Patel, C.M.	MSc	1940
Pearson, R.W.	MSc	1935
Peppiatt, C.H.	MSc	1926
Perera, M.S.	PhD	1960
Perera, S.M.A.	PhD	1962
Peters, C.J.	PhD	1980
Petley, D.J.	PhD	1966
Phukan, A.L.T.	PhD	1968
Picard, A.	PhD	1971
Pigeon, M.	MPhil	1969
Pigeon, Y.	PhD	1969
Placas, A.	PhD	1969
Plant, J.R.	MSc	1955
Plowman, J.M.	PhD	1951
Ponte Ramirez, R.R.	MPhil	1981
Poologasoundranayagam, K.	PhD	1960
Poucher, M.P.	MSc	1953
Prasad, P.J.	MSc	1958
Price, K.M.	PhD	1969
Prus-Chacinski, T.M.	PhD	1956
Pugh, R.S.	PhD	1978
Pundarika Row, M.C.	MSc	1956
Purandare, N.N.	MSc	1939
Pyrah, I.C.	PhD	1971
Quraishy, M.S.M.A.B.	PhD	1942
Rad, M.	PhD	1976
Raina, V.K.	PhD	1966
Ramachandran, K.	PhD	1975
Ramachandani, J.R.	MSc	1937
Ramirez Rivera, A.	MSc	1960
Ranganatham, B.V.	MSc	1956
Raz-Nahan, M.	PhD	1975
Read, R.S.	MSc	1926
Reades, D.W.	PhD	1972
Redshaw, S.C.	PhD	1936
Regan, P.E.	PhD	1967
Remedios, N.	PhD	1970
Revesz, I.	MSc	1952
Richmond, B.	PhD	1958
Robertson, L.R.	MSc	1938
Robinson, G.S.	PhD	1964
Robinson, S.J.	MPhi	1979
Rocha Filho, P.	PhD	1979
Rossin, A.C.	PhD	1981
Roussopoulos, A.	MPhi	1978
Sadek, R.	PhD	1952
Sahgal, O.S.	MSc	1954
Saif, A.Q.A.J.	MSc	1956
Saint-Pierre, G.	MSc	1960
Sakthikumar, S.	PhD	1974
Salih, A.M.A.	PhD	1972
Salmon, J.M.	MSc	1964
Sandroni, S.S.	PhD	1977
Sanger, F.J.	MSc	1938
Sarma, S.K.	PhD	1968
Sarna, S.P.	PhD	1966
Sayani, F.H.N.	MPhi	1968
Scrivener, J.C.	• PhD	1962
Segun, K.A.	PhD	1967
Selvalingham, S.	PhD	1970
Selvanayagam, P.	PhD	1950
Sen, H.K.	PhD	1969
Sen, T.K.	PhD	1976
Sen, Z.	PhD	1974
Set, B.	PhD	1935
Sethunarayanan, R.	MSc	1958
Sha'al, B.Z.	PhD	1972
Shaikh, K.G.	MSc	1930
Shaker, A.	PhD	1951
Sharma, S.P.	PhD	1959
Sharp, J.C.	PhD	1970
Shebini, V.K.	MPhi	1978
Sigvaldason, O.T.	PhD	1965
Sinbel, M.A.	PhD	1954
Singh, B.	PhD	1960

Sinha, T.M.N.	MSc	1958
Sioris, J.	PhD	1979
Skempton, A.W.	MSc	1936
Skinner, A.E.	PhD	1975
Smith, D.L.	PhD	1974
Smithies, R.W.	PhD	1952
Smolira, M.	PhD	1948
Soares, H.F.	MPhil	1980
Sobey, R.J.	PhD	1973
Sodha, V.G.	MPhil	1974
Soliman, M.T.M.	PhD	1966
Som, N.N.	PhD	1968
Som, P.K.	MSc	1957
Sowa, V.A.	PhD	1963
Sparkes, S.R.	PhD	1945
Stamenkovic, A.	PhD	1970
Stephenson, T.	PhD	1983
Srichamara, P.	PhD	1938
Stead, H.D.	MSc	1949
Stefanakos, J.	PhD	1979
Stefanou, G.D.	PhD	1970
Stephen Sandegren, D.	PhD	1972
Stephenson, T.	PhD	1983
Sterritt, R.M.	PhD	1981
Stieda, C.K.A.	PhD	1968
Stoveland, S.	PhD	1978
Sulaiman, M.	PhD	1963
Sullivan, P.J.E.	PhD	1970
Surendranath, M.K.	PhD	1982
Suvunnetr, S.	PhD	1957
Taha, M.	PhD	1981
Takahashi, M.	PhD	1981
Tan, S.B.	PhD	1968
Tankut, A.T.	PhD	1970
Taylor, N.H.	MSc	1931
Tchalenko, J.S.	PhD	1967
Teixeira de Freitas, J.A.	PhD	1979
Tembe, N.R.	MSc	1938
Teraszkiewicz, J.S.	PhD	1968
Tharmaratnam, K.	PhD	1972
Thon, J.G.	MSc	1941
Tobia, G.C.	MPhil	1974
Tombs, S.G.	PhD	1969
Tonsiengsom, S.	PhD	1962
Tosic, M.	MPhil	1975
Trikha, D.N.	PhD	1971
Truscott, E.G.	PhD	1977
Tsani Bazaca, E.S.	PhD	1980
Tsatsanifos, C.P.	PhD	1982
Tung, T.H.	MSc	1937
Turner, T.W.	PhD	1974
Ulug, S.E.	PhD	1967
Uzsoy, S.Z.	PhD	1966
Vadhelvala, R.M.	PhD	1937
Valvis, P.G.	MSc	1954
Van Dalen, K.	MSc	1960
Vaughan, P.R.	PhD	1965
Venkoba Rao, M.S.M.	MSc	1955
Verma, R.P.	MSc	1939
Vile, G.W.D.	PhD	1965
Virdi, K.S.	PhD	1974
Visvalingam, A.C.	PhD	1970
Visvesvaraya, H.C.	PhD	1956
Wade, N.H.	PhD	1963
Wadekar, G.T.	PhD	1957
Walbancke, H.J.	PhD	1976
Waldron, P.	PhD	1980
Walker, B.P.	PhD	1964
Wallis, R.P.	PhD	1937
Wan, W.Y.	MSc	1947
Wang, P.S.	PhD	1948
Ward, J.K.	PhD	1975
Ward, M.A.	PhD	1964
Warren, P.A.	PhD	1980
Watt, A.J.	MSc	1954
Wearn, B.C.	MSc	1939
Webb, D.L.	PhD	1966
Webb, S.E.	PhD	1981
Wellings, R.A.	PhD	1975
Werneck, M.L.G.	PhD	1974
Wesley, L.D.	PhD	1976
Williams, D.C.	PhD	1969
Wilson, K.C.	MSc	1961
Wong, G.C.K.M.	PhD	1964
Wong, K.C.F.	PhD	1957
Wong, P.T.	PhD	1970
Wood, C.C.	PhD	1958
Wright, D.A.	MSc	1951
Wright, D.E.	PhD	1958
Wu, K.C.	MSc	1928
Wyatt, T.A.	PhD	1955
Yam, L.C.P.	PhD	1967
Yannopoulos, P.J.	PhD	1976
Yassin, A.A.	PhD	1950
Yazici, M.V.	MSc	1940
Ying, W.M.	PhD	1971
Yu, C.W.	PhD	1954
Yu, T.M.	MSc	1938
Zahedi, M.	PhD	1972
Ziauddin, V.M.S.	MSc	1950
Ziauddin, V.M.S.	PhD	1954
Zienkiewicz, O.C.	PhD	1945

~ Appendix C ~

Diploma of Membership of Imperial College (DIC)

Note: The DICs in this list are those awarded for successful completion of one year's post-graduate study. In the earlier years the DIC was awarded for one year's advanced study; in the later years the DIC was given for one-year specialist postgraduate courses.

Those receiving research degrees were also awarded the DIC, and their names may appear only in Appendix B.

The dates cited are taken from the Calendars and Annual Reports and may vary by one year from the date of the award.

Abbreviations:

From 1948 the appropriate specialist Section has been named.

C Concrete Structures
H Civil Engineering Hydraulics
Hi Highway Engineering
Ho Engineering Hydrology
Hy Hydro-power
P Public Health Engineering
S Structures
Se Engineering Seismology
So Soil Mechanics
T Transport
Ti Timber Structures and Technology

1909
Oliff-Lee, W.N.
Russell, C.H.
Stock, W.H.
Swan, J.B.R.
White, W.

1910
Airey, J.
Naz, J.L.
Rodriguez y Ramon, M.
Stephens, T.A.

1911
Chester, A.B.
Gabb, A.H.
Morau, M.J.L.
Morgan, G.E.
Pallister, A.W.B.
Sanders, J.L.
Tomblings, E.H.G.
Wallis, N.L.

1912
Begg, A.J.
Burkhardt, J.E.
Carter, B.C.
Chang, C.R.
Dass-Kochhar, T.
Eley, H.J.
Faber, S.E.
Hornblower, T.J.
Johnstone, T.W.
Knight, R.A.
Maringe, T.H.J.
Mawson, H.
Morris, F.
White, A.J.
Yang, C.Y.

1913
Boyes, F.T.
Buddle, G.A.
Campbell, W.L.
Chassereau, J.D.
Cook, J.W.D.
Corwin, B.L.
Dannhorn, A.J.
Davis, W.J.
Dew, M.T.
James, R.
Limbourne, C.W.
Maunder, W.R.
Peake, R.W.
Potter, J.E.B.
Turner, W.G.A.
Wark, D.

1914
Elderton, E.F.

1915
Earnshaw-Wall, E.E.

1917
Walsh, H.N.

1920
Menon, K.P.P.
Messer, W.G.

1921
Budgett, F.la.T.
Hogan, M.A.
James, R.T.
Jones, E.M.R.
Morphy, D.W.
Oosthuizen, E.A.
Redmond, F.A.
Ryves, F.D.M.

1922
Dean, A.
Fogg, W.
Gayes, C.E.
Glynne, E.E.
Gowring, G.I.B.
Hamilton, W.E.
Harding, H.J.B.
Holbein, A.M.
Hunter, J.K.
Pitt, G.A.
Reeves, H.C.

1923
Braikevitch, M.
Bundock, W.H.
Crosthwaite, C.D.
Davis, R.F.
Howes, C.F.
Lewis, J.W.
Narbeth, R.G.
Rogers, C.E.
Smith, H.S.

1924
Dixon, E.J.C.
Docker, C.E.
Evans, J.T.
Finlayson, R.W.
Kershaw, J.B.
Packshaw, S.
Piper, G.H.
Robertson, S.A.
Rowe, N.E.
Sandifer, D.A.N.
Shneerson, M.

1925
Adlington, R.E.
Bell, T.E.S.
Blyth, F.G.H.
Boorman, A.G.
Circé, A.
Coyle, D.E.
Gibbs, E.F.
Illiff, E.
Whitehead, J.I.

1926
Amin, M.
Berridge, P.R.S.
Burke, E.
Chatterton, K.
Cochrane, J.N.
Fourniss, W.H.
Howell, R.H.S.
Jenkins, H.G.
Morgan, H.D.
Otter, J.R.H.
Peppiatt, C.H.
Read, R.S.
Wright, H.E.
Wu, K.C.
Zinovieff, L.

1927
Barker, B.H.
Berg, C.L.
Crouch, A.S.
d'Avary, A.M.
Fitt, R.L.
Godfrey, D.A.
Godwin, J.S.
Lowe, R.M.W.
Murti, M.J.K.
Newton, H.L.
Pearson, R.F.
Sharp, H.J.
Tayler, E.S.P.
Wakley, T.G.

1928
Bates, P.D.
Bean, D.C.
Chester, J.M.
Clerke, R.W.G.
Cohen, B.J.M.
Coulson, S.E.
Goddard, R.T.W.
Heaton-Armstrong, R.C.
Johnson, H.R.
Kumar, S.S.
Lash, S.D.
Nazareth, C.V.J.C.
Pfeil, B.B.
Sanger, F.J.
Squires, H.J.

1929
Broomfield, R.E.
Downs, R.A.
Gadhoke, S.R.
Hooper, G.N.
Ittihadieh, A.
Kambhu, M.L.X.
Marshall, W.T.
Porter, A.R.
Talintyre, E.C.

1930
Bhatia, H.R.
Bingham, J.E.
Bushell, G.E.
Clenshaw, W.C.
Hogan, P.J.
Jenkins, R.S.
Johnstone, J.M.
Malkani, T.M.
Manthei, R.A.
Sardi, C.A.
Shahani, G.P.
Shaikh, K.G.

1931
Claxton, E.C.
Draddy, F.E.
Hli, J.B.
Kenwood, T.T.
King, L.N.
Paes, A.V.
Tolhurst, J.R.
Tsui, L.K.

1932
Birkhead, J.E.
Brown, J.A.
Browne, T.P.
Busher, R.A.
Chablani, M.B.
Davies, V.C.
Dogra, R.N.
Fowler, R.J.
Gomez, A.
Govindakrishnayya, P.
Grunberg, S.
Harrison, J.R.
Horsfield, H.T.
Lawley, W.
Lee, W.R.
Marc, R.C.
New, D.H.
Sahgal, G.

1933
Ballantine, K.C.
Boykin, H.P.
Campbell, D.H.
Chatham, C.G.
Chiao, H-Y.
Clarke, A.C.
Colebrook, C.F.
Collins, A.R.
D'Souza, D.C.
Engel, F.V.A.E.
Fetto, N.D.
Greenhouse, W.J.
Hill, A.W.
Matthews, N.W.L.
Parker, T.F.
Pearson, R.W.
Pinto, W.L.
Spencer, H.J.
Varma, P.L.
Visvanathan, M.S.

Whittell, E.A.
Wingfield, G.G.

1934
Appasamy, C.S.
Bent, C.R.
Biggs, R.C.
Crockett, J.H.A.
Duncan, J.S.
Forster, F.D.B.
Gardner, S.V.
Hopkins, D.A.
Howdill, N.
Mahy, J.H.
Menon, K.B.
Nayler, J.J.
Plunkett, W.R.
Sharples, J.
Smith, F.J.R.
Srichamara, P.
Tongudai, C.
Vadhelvala, R.M.
Wallis, R.G.

1935
Atherton, T.W.
Bilaney, M.M.
Booth, G.C.
Bright, D.J.
Burns, R.V.
Chen, Y-L.
Chilton, O.H.
Chu, K.H.
Coles, G.R.
Hedgcock, J.H.
Hsia, C-P.
Manton, B.G.
Moyal, I.
Nankivell, K.
Set, B.
Tung, C-L.
Turner, L.E.
Wang, C-C.
Wren, W.G.

1936
Allwright, E.S.
Boardman, G.
Bruce, F.E.
Cheong, K.T.
Chitty, L.
Cohen, S.
Cuthbert, E.W.
Gan, K.P.
Ho, P.Y.
Jacobson, M.
Lanham, K.
Lee, T-F.
McClelland, A.E.
Orchard, D.F.
Reatchlous, R.
Robertson, L.R.
Shivdasani, H.B.
Skempton, A.W.
Sparkes, S.R.
Tung, T.H.

1937
Banwet, D.N.
Bresciani, M.
Harpman, G.D.
Makhijani, H.U.
Ng, C.L.
Ramchandani, J.R.
Silbert, A.C.
Tembe, N.R.
Yu, T-M.

1938
Ackerley, G.E.
Ashby, R.J.
Bingham, T.G.
Chang, W.
de Weale, J.P.A.
Douglas, J.F.
Garside, D.
Jaedicke, J.
Lee, C.R.
Leigh, J.V.
Marriott, G.B.
Taiber, M.

1939
Adams, C.A.
Aston, A.C.
Bentley, J.B.
Chang, W-C.
Chu, C.J.
da Silva, A.L.N.
Gayed, Y.K.
Gimpel, J.
Glen, J.A.
Gowers, A.G.
Hawker, A.M.
Khan, M.I.M.
Lee, Z-D.
Patel, C.M.
Purandare, N.N.
Sidhpura, H.B.
Skelt, G.J.
Tan, E.K.
Thon, J.G.
Tye, S-C.
Verma, R.P.

1940
Emerton, R.F.
Fahmy, I.S.M.
Kefeli, Y.H.
Yazici, M.V.

1941
Bhandari, N.N.
Cornfield, G.M.
Gawlinski, S.

1942
Saleh, Q.M.

1944
Rowe, N.E.

1947
Andrew, P.H.F.
Goldstein, A.
Large, J.E.
Levy, J.F.
Miners, J.B.
Smallman, A.J.
Steventon, G.L.

1948
Alderman, D. (C)
Briggs, J.R. (C)
Burrill, N.E. (C)
Hafiz, M.A.A. (So)
Hassani, J. (C)
Henderson, J.C. de C. (C)
Liu, C-W. (C)
Menzies, G.S. (S)
Ogden, L.D. (C)
Powlesland, J. (C)
Wan, W-Y. (S)
Wang, P-S. (S)

1949
Adler, G.F.W. (Hy)
Antony, C.M. (Hy)
Askin, F.R. (H)
Barbora, D.N. (Hy)
Bengali, M.T. (Hy)
Chao, C-S. (H)
Chaturvedi, D.C. (C)
Crook, D.E. (Hy)
Edwards, J. (Hy)
Firth, A. (Hy)
Gamal-Eldin, E.A.K. (So)
Hassan, A. (C)
Jathal, M.N. (Hi)
Kolbuszewski, J.J. (So)
Krishnamacharyulu, K. (C)
Li, Y-S. (S)
Lloyd, D.G. (Hy)
Mathews, R.V. (Hy)
Mazur, S.J. (S)
Mukherjee, N.C. (C)
Newman, W.M. (C)
Pasha, A.W. (Hy)
Pengilly, A.H. (S)
Razmara, R. (Hy)
Sandover, J.A. (C)
Skinner, D.J. (C)
Smolira, M. (S)
Swaminathan, C.G. (Hi)
Toki, G.S. (Hi)
Whitham, L.S. (Hy)
Whittaker, J.H. (C)
Wilmot, A. (Hy)

1950
Bartholomew, P. (Hy)
Bennell, B.M.U. (So)
Bigwood, G.M.C. (C)
Bulman, J.P. (Hy)
Chapman, J.C. (S)
Chunnett, E.R.P. (Hy)
Clarke, C.L. (Hy)
Cox, A.R. (Hy)
Dempsey, J.A. (Hy)
Dholakia, B.G. (Hy)
Dickens, W.J. (Hy)
Dorey, M.R. (Hy)
Fleming, J.H. (Hy)
Gelibter, A.A. (C)
Gidwani, G.M. (C)
Gifford, F.W. (C)
Harman, A.B. (C)
Humphries, E.F. (C)
Kilner, F.A. (Hy)
Lumb, P. (Hi)
Malouf, K.M. (H)
Mattock, A.H. (C)
Menon, T.M. (Hi)
Mulligan, C.G. (Hy)
Pathak, K.S. (Hy)
Redlich, W. (C)
Rodger, J.L. (C)
Sadleir, N.A. (C)
Sedgwick, R.H. (Hy)
Shaw, J.B. (Hy)
Tsai, Y-P. (C)
Wray, L.M. (Hy)

1951
Brown, D.H. (Hy)
Butterfield, R. (C)
Clare, R. (C)
Darhouse, M.M. (Hi)
Falconer, B.H. (S)
Fitzpatrick, P.A. (Hi)
Gouda, M.A.H. (C)
Halim, A.M.A. (Hy)
Harrison, R.E. (C)
Hinde, G. (C)
Isaac, G. (C)
Keast, G.T. (Hy)
Lam, P-H. (Hi)
Lao, Y-C. (C)
Lau, Y.S. (C)
Lewis, H.E. (C)
Martinez, P.A. (C)
Mears, D.D. (Hy)
Meigh, A.C. (So)
Mellor, C. (C)
Moller, K. (C)
Morris, D.A. (C)
Neiva, F.C. (Hi)
Ortega Vaca, N.G. (Hi)
Selvanayagam, P. (C)
Shaker, A. (C)
Sharrock, W.G. (C)
Smith, J.L. (C)
Stead, H.D. (C)
Thomas, W.J.H. (C)
Wearne, S.H. (Hy)
Whidborne, R.F. (C)
Williams, M.S. (Hi)
Wilson, J.F. (C)
Wright, D.A. (S)
Yassin, A.A. (So)

1952
Abdalla, Z.B. (P)
Advani, C.T. (Hy)
Banks, R.B. (H)
Bazett, D.J. (So)
Berger, J. (S)
Bolton, R.S. (Hy)
Brown, W.C. (S)
Campbell-Little, D.J. (P)
Cassell, A.C. (S)
Chandrangsu, S. (S)
Devereux, W.F. (P)
Dhar, M. (S)
Dubhashi, J.D. (H)
Dunton, D.A. (C)
Eid, Y.M. (P)
El-Salman, J.A.W. (C)
Everard, K.A. (C)
Foster, B.K. (S)
Franklin, J.E. (C)
Gibson, R.E. (So)
Graff, S. (C)
Grimaldi B., L.J. (P)
Hassid, S. (S)
Hobbs, N.B. (So)
Hobden, S.L. (So)
Holroyd, F.G. (C)
Hsiung, C.Y. (S)
Jackson, J.K. (C)
Kakish, F.I. (P)
Kale, M.R. (Hy)
Kirec, Y. (So)
Langdon, J. (C)
Leibowitz, B. (C)
Levy, G.H. (C)
Martin, P.F. (P)
Munasinha, M.A.L.E.I. (Hy)
Nawy, E.G. (C)
Oehler, L.R.T. (C)
Plowman, J.M. (C)
Pun, Y.K. (C)
Rahimtoola, M.H.A. (P)
Rahman, L. (P)
Révész, I. (C)
Roberts, D.V.N. (So)
Ruyabhorn, P. (S)
Sadek, R. (H)
Savoie, A.P. (P)
Sinbel, M.A. (Hy)
Sneller, A.T. (P)
Sullivan, T.S. (P)
Thomas, D.H.W. (P)
Vallet, L.A.P. (P)
Wood, R.E. (C)
Ziauddin, V.M.S. (C)

1953
Advani, T.R. (C)
Arah, R.M. (Hy)
Astorga, R.W. (C)
Bassi, K.G. (C)
Boucherat, F.J. (Hy)
Briggs, W.R. (Hy)
Brown, E.H. (S)
Chatterji, A.K. (C)
Chokhavatia, S.R. (S)
Chooi, T-K. (C)
Chow, S.K. (S)
Chowdhry, B.A. (C)
Desai, K.P. (Hy)
Desai, U.D.N. (So)
De Silva, M.S.M. (So)
Faundes, R.A. (S)
Fellows, A.G. (C)
Fells, J.N. (Hy)
Franklin, D.H. (S)
Gadish, I. (C)
Garrod, A.D. (Hy)
Gray, J. de C. (C)
Gray, K.J. (Hy)
Gunn, C. (Hy)
Jabbar Khan, S.A. (C)
Kar, R.N. (Hy)
Kedar (Shwartz), M. (C)
Lau, F.S. (So)
Lee, T.W. (C)
Lethbridge, J.A. (C)
Leung, H-W. (So)
Lewis, J.G. (So)
Longhorn, P.T. (C)
MacKay, R.S. (Hy)
McLean, G. (C)
Madan, P.J. (Hi)
Mamoojee, A.K. (Hy)
Mane, P.M. (Hy)
Mayor, S.P. (Hy)
Nissen, P.B. (Hy)
Schonhut, D.L. (Hi)
Schreier, D. (C)
Smallridge, C.G. (Hy)
Smithies, R.W. (C)
Song, P. (S)
Taylor, G. (Hy)
Webb, N.K. (Hy)
Windsor, J.S. (Hy)
Woloszczuk, Z.L.J. (C)
Wright, R.A. (Hy)
Ziman, M. (C)

1954
Acheson, M.A. (P)
Advani, I.T. (Hy)
Bates, R.K. (P)
Blanchard, J.C. (C)
Boonsukha, B. (C)

Brill, H. (C)
Bunting, F.B. (C)
Campbell, P.L. (C)
Chamberlain, G.R. (C)
Chow, P.Y.W. (C)
Collinge, V.K. (H)
Cooper, B.W. (C)
Darracott, J.M. (C)
Davidson, R. (Hy)
de Marassé-Enouf, M.L.J. (P)
Dick, D. (Hy)
Donaldson, G.W. (So)
Doran, D.K. (C)
Doshi, J.J. (C)
Dowerah, T.C. (Hy)
El-Katib, M.T. (C)
El Ramli, A.R.H. (So)
Fahmy, M.A-e-S. (So)
Faye, J.T. (C)
Ferner, M.H. (C)
Fung, Y-S. (C)
Ghosh, G. (P)
Gilbert, G.D. (So)
Goldstein, S.M. (C)
Hall, A.S. (C)
Hamlin, M.J. (P)
Han, S. (C)
Ho, C.H. (Hy)
Hollings, J.P. (C)
Johnston, G.R. (P)
Jolly, R.C. (C)
Joshi, A.V. (S)
Kerr, J.A. (Hy)
Kjaernsli, B. (So)
Knill, M.W. (P)
Kullavanijaya, C. (Hi)
Lambert, J.C. (P)
Lee, D.J. (C)
Lovell, J.S. (P)
Lownds, P. (C)
Lye, T.F. (P)
Mackay, E.B. (So)
McKiernan, B.A. (Hy)
MacSweeney, J.J. (P)
Mak, W-K. (S)
Makowski, Z.S. (S)
Mallick, P.K. (Hy)
Mikhail, S. (H)
Millar, G.A.I. (C)
Moini, S.Q. (P)
Mondal, A.A. (P)
Moore, B.G. (P)
Morris, R.W. (C)
Moss-Morris, A.L. (C)
Murray, D.W. (Hy)
Nandi, S. (C)
Ng, P.K. (S)
Orme, D.H. (C)
Pearce, R. le B. (Hy)
Perez Arteta, L. (P)
Phoenix, J.R. (C)
Piette, I.R. (Hy)
Plant, J.R. (So)
Porter, D.M. (C)
Poucher, M.P. (C)
Powell, D.S. (C)
Powell, T.F. (Hy)
Price, R.L. (C)
Pugh, C. (P)
Quirke, D.F. (C)
Raichur, A.R. (C)
Reyes, E.R. (S)
Rogers, A.D. (P)
Rosenhaupt, S. (C)
Rosewarne, J.R. (C)
Saif, A.Q.A.J. (C)
Sanderson, J.G. (P)
Santa-Maria, J. (C)
Scholnick, G. (C)
Shahrabani, S.G. (Hi)
Sinha, D.P. (S)
Smith, G.R. (C)
Subramanian, R. (Hy)
Taylor, E.G. (Hy)
Taylor, L.E. (P)
Tsou, H.H. (C)
Valvis, P.G. (Hy)
Varadarajan, M.B. (Hy)
Varma, G.K.R. (Hy)
Vaswani, H.P. (S)
Venkatarama Reddy, D. (S)
Visvesvaraya, H.C. (C)
Waller, D.H. (P)
Watt, A.J. (So)
White, K.F. (C)
Williams, A.A.B. (So)
Winful, H.F. (P)
Wong, M-K. (Hi)
Yip, S-P. (S)
Young, D.I.B. (P)

1955

Adler, D.J. (C)
Alexander, J.F. (S)
Ali, S.B. (Hy)
Bakker, J.J. (C)
Bamford, G.E. (C)
Banerji, B. (S)
Barman, K. (C)
Biviji, S.A. (S)
Booth, L.G. (C)
Britt, G.B. (C)
Chan, W.W.L. (C)
Clements, A.C. (C)
Corbett, R.E. (H)
Coxon, R.E. (Hy)
Criticos, D.M. (C)
Cushion, E.A.L. (C)
Datta, S.K. (H)
DeLory, F.A. (So)
Dunn, A.G. (C)
Dutta-Munsi, T.K. (S)
Evans, G.H. (C)
Fahmy, M.A-E-S.M. (Hi)
Farrington, P. (So)
Feir, J.E. (H)
Fort, G.B. (C)
Frischmann, V. (C)
Galloway, R.D. (C)
Gendron, M. (S)
Gogate, M.N. (S)
Grant, E.J. (C)
Haseltine, B.A. (C)
Hazell, M.D. (C)
Hosking, A.D. (So)
Howley, M. (S)
Huang, C-L. (C)
Joshi, S.P. (S)
Kemp, E.L. (C)
Kenney, T.C. (So)
Khan, N.M. (C)
Kierulf, H. (C)
Kirkor, A. (C)
Kramer, A.E. (Hy)
Kynaston, R.F. (Hy)
Labib, A.K.E.M. (C)
Law, T.H. (C)
Levelt, H.L.A.M. (C)
Low, E. (So)
Lowe, J.F. (So)
McAdam, F.L. (C)
MacDonald, D.H. (So)
Mittal, L.K. (So)
O'Connell, W.N. (C)
Panas, G.E.V. (C)
Pundarika Row, M.C. (S)
Rensaa, A.J. (C)
Ridley, T. (C)
Rindl, W.S. (C)
Santa Maria Alvarez, J. (S)
Sharan, S. (C)
Suvunnetr, S. (S)
Taylor, D.K. (So)
Taylor, R. (C)
Temple, R.A. (S)
Teo, C.H. (C)
Townsend, D.L. (So)
Turner, F.H. (C)
Weston, R.F. (C)
Winiarski, M.S. (C)
Wong, K.C.F. (S)
Wyatt, T.A. (S)
Yap, C.L. (C)
Yu, C.W. (C)

1956

Afghan, A.Q.K.K. (Hi)
Amanullah, N. (Hi)
Anderton, J.E. (Hy)
Arumugam, K. (H)
Astete, F.B. (Hy)
Ballance, R.C. (P)
Barber, D.G. (Hi)
Bhatia, H.S. (Hi)
Bradbury, J.N. (C)

Burdett, J.F. (C)
Casinader, R.J.T. (Hy)
Chaudhary, B. (So)
Crozier, A.C. (Hy)
Daranandana, N. (Hy)
Desai, H.J. (Hy)
Dowling, P.J. (So)
Dun, U.T. (Hi)
Dyer, J.H. (Hy)
Engmann, E.Y.S. (P)
Freer, R. (Hy)
Gale, M. (Hi)
Gupta, G.C. (Hi)
Hanson, B. (So)
Hlaing, U.K. (Hi)
Hourvitz, Z. (Hi)
Howard, M.N. (C)
Jones, D.T. (P)
Kathirgaman, K. (So)
Khair, F.A. (Hi)
Khan, A.L. (P)
Kohli, D.R. (Hi)
Kumarasuriar, C. (P)
Lamarre, B. (C)
Lee, T.C. (P)
Levy, S.J.D.G.Q.V. de Q. (P)
Lewis, K.W. (P)
Longley, G.W. (Hy)
Luxon, A.M. (C)
Mackechnie, W.R. (So)
Marshall, W.J. (C)
Mandez, H.P. (Hy)
Morgan, G.C. (So)
Narasimhan, S. (Hy)
Papo, I. (Hi)
Patel, B.S. (Hi)
Peaker, K. (Hi)
Pritchard, D. (P)
Prus-Chacinski, T.M. (H)
Ranganatham, B.V. (So)
Rausti, U.F.V. (P)
Roberge, J.P.A. (C)
Schwartz, H.I. (P)
Seychuk, J.L. (So)
Souza-Okpofabri, D.S. (P)
Staynes, B.W. (P)
Thomas, I.E. (P)
Türkeri, M.N. (Hy)
van Heerden, A. (P)
Venkoba Rao, M.S.M. (Hi)
Wildt, R.H. (C)
Wint, D.H. (Hi)
Wolpert, L. (So)
Wood, C.C. (So)
Wythes, J.M. (Hy)

1957
Aadnesen, L. (S)
Ahmad, S.N. (S)
Ambraseys, N. (So)
Annan, C.K. (P)
Auger, G.C.B. (C)
Banerji, H.D. (Hi)
Bangash, H-u-D. (Hy)
Benson, F.R. (C)
Brettle, H.J. (C)
Cadavid Lopez, J.L. (S)
Campbell, G.A. (C)
Campbell, J.E. (S)
Chatterjee, M.K. (Hy)
Chaudhuri, P.K. (S)
Cheah, T.S. (P)
Chin, K.K. (P)
Chuan, C.N. (P)
Cobb, J.L. (C)
Cruz Molina, C.R. (C)
Desai, S.V. (P)
Dutta, A. (C)
Eadie, D.M. (C)
Edwards, A.D. (C)
El-Khayatt, A.M.H. (C)
Elliott, C.D. (Hi)
El-Moosa, F.M. (So)
Evans, G.L. (C)
Eyers, G.K. (C)
Fairley, A.T. (Hy)
Fong, C-W. (S)
Fraser, A.M. (So)
Fraser, E.M. (C)
Furst-Hepburn, M. (C)
Gandhi, M.M. (S)
Ghosh, A.K. (S)
Ghosh, M.M. (C)
Ghosh, S. (S)
Hasan, A.A.Z. (S)
Hicks, A.B. (C)
Huang, J.W.L. (C)
Jarosz, J.W. (C)
Jones, R.C. (Ho)
King, S.F. (S)
Kluth, D.J. (S)
Koh, K.E. (P)
Kolosowski, J. (S)
Kozminski, A. (S)
Kyi, B. (Ho)
Labonté, R.J-L. (P)
Langeman, P. (S)
Leung, T.K. (S)
Lirios, J.F. (Ho)
Lonergan, J. (C)
Low, A.E. (C)
Lyndon, A. (So)
McDermont, J.L. (C)
McDermott, A.A.G. (P)
Maddocks, D.C. (C)
Mahajan, K.D. (C)
Maisel, B.I. (C)
Manohar, S.N. (S)
Mansell-Moullin, M. (Ho)
Misra, P.N. (S)
Moran, P.J. (C)
Munro, J. (C)
Murray, D.R. (C)
Muscat-Fenech, G. (C)
Nadarajah, A. (P)
Najaraj, C.N.S. (So)
Nath, S. (Hi)
Nettleton, A.F.S. (So)
Ng, L-H. (S)
O'Callaghan, W.C. (C)
O'Rafferty, S. (P)
Palmer, D. (S)
Palmer, P.M. (C)
Paré, J-J. (C)
Pearce, P.T. (C)
Power, L.B. (C)
Prasad, K. (C)
Prasad, P.J. (C)
Prashad, S.N. (Hi)
Puller, M.J. (So)
Ramakrishnan, V. (Hy)
Ray, P.K. (S)
Richards, J.A. (C)
Richmond, B. (S)
Rogers, B.A. (P)
Rohatgi, N.N. (Hi)
Rook, H. (C)
Ryalls, P.J. (C)
Sachidanand, N. (Hy)
Sahgal, O.S. (Hi)
Samanta, K.K. (S)
Sanyal, S.K. (S)
Sarkar, S.K. (S)
Sharma, B. (P)
Sharma, S.P. (S)
Shaw, K.W. (C)
Shields, D.H. (So)
Shushtarian, A. (S)
Singh, M. (C)
Sinha, T.M.N. (S)
Smith, W.T. (Hy)
Smollett, D.M. (S)
Soderman, L.G. (So)
Som, P.K. (S)
Strongman, C.P. (Hy)
Sutcliffe, F.H. (C)
Tso, K.S. (S)
Turner, C.P.O. (Hy)
Tymms, R.S. (P)
Vafai Tabrizi, M.S. (P)
Vaidya, G.M. (S)
Villeneuve, J.E. (C)
Wadekar, G.T. (H)
Wallace, R.R. (C)
Waller, J.A. (C)
Weddell, T.W. (C)
Westwood, P.D. (C)
Wills, R.F. (P)
Wilson, B.H. (Ho)
Wright, A.E. (C)
Wyatt, C.T. (C)
Yap, E-S. (C)

1958
Adams, R.H. (C)

Azmeh, M.M. (Hy)
Baxter, D.A. (C)
Bushell, A.J. (C)
Carneiro, A.G. d. R. (P)
Condon, J.J. (C)
Cowie, C.A. (P)
Cowie, F.L. (P)
Daniel, A.J.D. (Hy)
DaRocha, E.M. (So)
De Souza, F.X. (C)
Ellul-Sullivan, P.J. (C)
Fayyad, M.S. (H)
Fernandez, X.V. (C)
Fernando, E.P.C. (C)
Flaxman, E.W. (P)
Fraser, G.J. (Hy)
Goepel, R.F.J.K. (C)
Henkel, D.J. (So)
Irani, S.N. (C)
Jahina, K.B. (C)
Kaushik, C.P. (P)
Kemp, A.A. (Hy)
Knight, W.A. (C)
Lee, G.J.B. (Hy)
Machado, J. (So)
Mackenzie, B.J. (C)
Mageed Ahmed, Y.A. (Ho)
Meader, R.J. (Hy)
Mills, H.B. (C)
Mohanrao, B. (H)
Müller, G. (C)
Odedairo, E.O. (So)
Olliver, P.R. (P)
Paré, J-J. (So)
Parry, R.H.G. (So)
Patel, M.N. (C)
Pawar, P.V. (C)
Perera, C.M.S. (C)
Poologasoundra-nayagam, K. (C)
Price, D.C. (C)
Ramakrishnan, V. (C)
Rothwell, M.A. de W. (C)
Saghayroon, S. el Z. (Ho)
Sethunarayanam, R. (C)
Shahani, P.J. (Hy)
Stigter, J. (C)
Subieta Otalora, A. (C)
Tokarski, E.W. (C)
Wise, E.V.A. (So)
Wright, C.J. (So)

1959
Adekola, A.O. (C)
Ali, S.A. (P)
Almeida Ribeiro, E.A.B. (C)
Arnaud, M.D. (Hy)
Azzopardi, G. (C)
Balasunder, N.K. (Ho)
Banerjee, N.C. (Hi)
Barnard, B.J.S. (P)
Bawa, N.S. (C)
Beckett, D. (C)
Beg, M.D. (Hy)
Benjamin, B.S. (S)
Benson, W.D. (P)
Body, D.O. (C)
Bondale, D.S. (C)
Brett, P.R. (C)
Brooke-White, J. (So)
Byrne, J.G. (C)
Chattopadhyay, S. (S)
Chua, T.G. (P)
Clark, B.E. (C)
Clarke, M.F. (Ho)
Crawford, C.B. (So)
Cunge, J.A. (S)
Dalvi, D.R. (C)
Dastur, J.H. (C)
Davies, Y.M. (Hi)
Degaetano, J.C. (P)
Dennett, M. (C)
Evans, T.E. (P)
Farooqui, R. (Ho)
Fisher, R. (H)
Guhabiswas, S.M. (S)
Gupta, P.K.S. (S)
Gupta, P.S. (S)
Haekal, H. (Hy)
Hanby, N.H.E. (P)
Hatcher, E.W. (S)
Haugland, C. (C)
Heffernan, F.J. (So)
Hunt, P.M.J. (C)
Hussain, Z. (C)
Hyslop, P.J. (Hi)
Kalali, B.M. (P)
Kiwana, A.S.N. (Hi)
Kufuor, J.A. (Hi)
Ladduwahetty, N.S. (C)
Li, Y-T. (H)
Low, W.I. (So)
McKinnell, P.B. (C)
Maris, A.J. (C)
Mathew, C.I. (S)
Menzenbach, E.A. (So)
Mookerjee, M.K. (S)
Mulroy, T.M. (Hi)
Narayanan, R. (C)
Neysadurai, A. (P)
Ng, S.K. (Ho)
Ng, Y.B. (C)
Oldfield, J.B. (C)
Olwoch, N. (P)
Onysko, D.M. (C)
Pandit, A.V. (C)
Parkinson, F.E. (Hy)
Parvez, J.A. (So)
Patil, P.B. (C)
Pereira-da-Silva, L. (P)
Phelps, H.O. (H)
Pigott, B.B. (C)
Pillar, I.D. (Ho)
Prabhakar, D.R. (Ho)
Ramirez-Rivera, A. (S)
Rice, P.R. (C)
Rolfsen, E.N. (So)
Rosenak, S. (C)
Salmon, J.M. (Hi)
Scott, W.J. (Ho)
Shawkan, M. (C)
Stone, D.M. (Hy)
Strmac, A. (So)
Sulaiman, M. (Hi)
Thomas, R.H. (P)
Tocher, J.L. (S)
Tomalak, M. (C)
Tomalak, M. (C)
van Dalen, K. (C)
Vaughan, L.T. (S)
Vorster, P.J.C. (Ho)
Walimbe, B.G. (P)
Williams, P.A. (C)
Wojakowski, A.W.S. (C)
Wong, Y. (C)
Wright, D.E. (H)
Wright, W.H.C. (C)
Yousaf, M. (Ho)

1960
Adsett, L. (C)
Agbim, C.C. (C)
Ahuja, B.M. (C)
Alavi, N.A. (P)
Alpan, I. (So)
Baker, C.J. (S)
Balakrishnan, S. (S)
Baruah, S.K. (H)
Basu, A.K. (S)
Bates, R.K. (C)
Bhandari, D.A. (C)
Bird, E.H. (So)
Brahmachari, P. (C)
Brody, R. (C)
Buxton, L.A. (C)
Calder, D.G. (S)
Chan, S-W. (P)
Chen, D.B. (So)
Choudhuri, M.K. (S)
Chow, S.L. (S)
Cook, A.H. (C)
Crawford, J.C. (S)
Crawley, A.F.D. (C)
Dasgupta, B.R. (S)
Davies, R.M. (S)
Dekany, A. (S)
Desmond, H.F. (P)
Dickens, P.J. (So)
Dougill, J.W. (C)
Dunleavy, J.F. (C)
Ehaliotis, D. (P)
El Agib, A.A.R. (Hy)
Ferrier, D.A. (P)
Fisher, D.I. (P)
Forsyth, J.K. (C)

Gay, P. (S)
Gillson, I.P. (C)
Gogoi, S.D. (S)
Gomes, A.H.C. (P)
Gouge, R.L. (P)
Harris, E. W. (C)
Hartley, A. (C)
Hewitt, G. (C)
Hill, G. (P)
Hillis, S.F. (So)
Hira, C.G. (S)
Ho, D. (S)
Hodgson, F.T. (C)
Hollington, M.R. (C)
Hotten, L.J. (So)
Innes, K.W. (S)
Insley, A.E. (So)
Iyer, K.S. (Hi)
Jalundhwala, M.S. (S)
Jarman, D.A. (S)
Kamalzai, S. K. (C)
Keenan, C.J. (P)
Keogan, D. St J.B. (C)
Khan, M.M.R. (P)
Kirch, J.B. (P)
Kubo, T. (P)
Küsgen, H. (S)
Lachance, L. (C)
Lakin, D.G. (C)
Langlois, A.P. (Hy)
Leung, B. (S)
Lew, D. (C)
Liauw, T.C. (C)
Livneh, M. (S & So)
Lo, K.Y. (So)
Lobo, U. (S)
Mathias, M.P.A. (Hy)
Mears, T.F. (S)
Meyer, B. (C)
Miles, J.R. (C)
Mohandessi, P. (P)
Mukhopadhyay, P.K. (S)
Nandi, B.C. (P)
Nankivell, J.L. (C)
Nassim, V.H. (S)
Nedderman, J.M. (Hy)
Neumann, B. (Hy)
Nwariaku, C. (Hi)
Nzeako, G.N. (C)
O'Callaghan, M.J. (S)
Ogundiya, E.O. (P)
O'Higgins, M.W. (C)
Osibamowo, J.O. (P)
Owen, W.G. (Ho)
Perera, S.M.A. (Hy)
Poplett, T. (C)
Powell, E.R. (P)
Pun, P.Y-S. (So)
Reith, I.H. (C)
Ryan, P.W.S. (P)
Saint-Pierre, G. (C)
Sandoy, D.F. (C)
Sarkar, A.K. (S)
Saunders, J.W. (C)
Scarlett, P.H. (C)
Shaukat, A. (P)
Sheffield, P. (C)
Short, J. (S)
Shukla, M.L. (C)
Siddiqui, A.A. (C)
Singh, B. (H)
Singh, R.C. (P)
Stone, P.B. (S)
Swan, F.W.F. (S)
Tahir, M.A. (P)
Tonsiengsom, S. (P)
Trigg, R.T. (C)
Usmani, H.H. (So)
van Blankenstein, L. (C)
van Duuren, F.A. (P)
Webster, P.T. (So)
Wells, G.P. (C)
Whiteley, H.R. (Ho)
Zikusoka, J.M.N. (P)

1961
Ah-Chin, L. (Hi)
Anson, M. (C)
Ballantyne, J.L. (C)
Banasiak, M.K. (C)
Beale, R.A. St J. (C)
Berlyn, R.W. (So)
Blight, G.E. (So)
Burnell, A.J. (S)
Butler, D.J.R. (Hi)
Campion, A. (C)
Carnie, W.C.G. (C)
Casey, T.J. (C)
Cawley, C.J. (Hi)
Ceballos, E.A. del R. (Hi)
Chan, G.L. (P)
Collins, P.J. (C)
Comninos, T.M. (So)
Das, S.B. (P)
Dastidar, N.R.G. (C)
Davey, D.J. (C)
Denloye, S.M.O. (Hi)
Dhar, P.R. (C)
Dodd, V.A. (P)
Donald, I.B. (So)
Drybrough, D.A. (C)
Dutch, W.G. (C)
Elia, P. (C)
Evans, J.E. (Hi)
Ferland, C. (So)
Fok, W.K. (C)
Folkestad, O.G. (So)
Foster, E. (Hi)
Goyal, S.P. (Hi)
Gudgeon, D.L. (So)
Hamilton, I. (Hi)
Herbstein, M. (C)
Ho, C. (So)
Holland, J. (C)
Imrie, P.G.M. (So)
Jackson, J.M. (P)
Jacob, P.P. (So)
Jolliffe, M.J.A.H. (C)
Khalil, M.B. (Hy)
King, E. (C)
Kirpalani, M.B. (C)
Lazenby, D.W. (C)
Lemos, F. (P)
Lyew, T.G. (C)
Mahesan, T. (P)
Manning, B.D.J. (C)
Manocha, H.S. (P)
Mirza, R.M. (C)
Moon, R.B. (C)
Nicoll, D.J. (C)
Pan, S.D. (C)
Phillips, K.A. (So)
Prabhu, S.S. (C)
Roy, P.K. (C)
Rudgley, J.E.M. (C)
Salam, A. (C)
Sandbeck, S.O.E. (C)
Sen Gupta, S.K. (C)
Seth, M.M.D. (C)
Siddiqui, I.A. (C)
Smith, H. (P)
Smith, I.C. (C)
Smith, P. (Hi)
Spiteri, C. (P)
Sposito, B. (Hi)
Srodzinski, A.H.N. (C)
Talapatra, S. (C)
Trevisan, S.J. (So)
Trochalakis, T. (C)
Trudeau, B. (C)
Walford, H.W. (C)
Walker, G.W.B. (C)
Watson, G.H. (So)
Weaver, J. (C)
Webb, B.H. (C)
Weeks, A.G. (Hi)
Zaidi, S. A.K. (Hy)

1962
Abbasi, A.S. (S)
Ahmad, S. (C)
Airaksinen, J.U. (Ho)
Al-Naib, S.K. (H)
Amin, A.Z. el A.H. (P)
Andu, J.A. (Ho)
Aquilina, C.V. (S)
Awotwi, P.A.K. (S)
Aziz, E.M. (C)
Banerjee, B.K. (S)
Banks, P.A. (Hy)
Basith, S.A. (C)
Batchelor, B. de. V. (C)
Bates, B.H. (C)
Bell, D.J. (C)
Benaim, R. (C)
Ben-George, M. (S)

Bishop, B.A. (S)
Bowyer, C. (C)
Bremner, T.W. (C)
Brett, D.E. (C)
Brown, T.C. (P)
Burhouse, P. (C)
Burnett, E.F.P. (C)
Cattan, L.H. (S)
Chan, H.C. (S)
Chattopadhay, A.K. (S)
Clarke, F.R.W. (H)
Cook, D.A. (So)
Deb, B.C. (C)
Douglas, R.E. (C)
Dowling, P.J. (S)
Drinkwater, B.J. (Hy)
Duncan, M.A.G.R.E. (S)
Edwards, J.J. (S)
Estrada, J. (Hy)
Evans, E.P. (C)
Ferahian, R.H. (S)
Ferland, C. (S)
Frost, B.D. (C)
Gallacher, D. (C)
Ghosh, S. (C)
Gidvani, J.H. (Hy)
Girgis, A.K. (So)
Haberman, L.P. (Hy)
Hadid, H.A. (C)
Hagenbach, P. (C)
Hayward, D.G. (Hy)
Higson-Smith, D.J. (C)
Hill, I.D. (C)
Hue, L.E. (So)
James, B.T. (S)
Jenkins, J.L. (S)
Johnson, H.G. (Hy)
Kassar, T.F. (C)
Kizildeli, A. (S)
Korn, H.G. (C)
Kozlowski, J.A. (H)
Kshirsagar, S.S. (C)
Kukadia, B.P. (C)
Lainez-Lozada, P. (C)
Lal, A.K. (C)
Lau, K.H. (S)
Ledesma, M.M. (Hy)
Loh Teh Kang, P. (C)
Lwegarnlila, F.K. (Ho)
McCalla, J.H. (S)
Malla, S.K. (Hy)
Martins, J.B. (So)
Matz Ulloa, S. (Hy)
Maya, H. (S)
Mitra, R. (So)
Mobed, Y.N. (C)
Mohan, G.V. (Hy)
Morton, K. (So)
Moses, G.W. (C & S)
Nooshin, H. (S)
Outhwaite, F.M. (C)
Panayidos, P.T. (C)
Paton, J.M. (C)
Pinfold, G.M. (C)
Puplampu, A.B. (So)
Ranawake, K.R. (S)
Rao, V.V. (Hy)
Remedios, C.A. (C)
Richardson, R.T. (C)
Ross, P.S. (C)
Rossaak, T. (C)
Rymill, F.M. (S)
Saakwa-Mante, O. (S)
Sarkar, T.K. (S)
Sarna, S.P. (S)
Sheehan, J.V. (So)
Silva-Fajardo, A. (C)
Sladek, G.L. (C)
Smith, T.C. (C)
Stainsby, R. (C)
Suen, L. (C)
Suttar, T. (Hy)
Szwajkajzer, Z. (S)
Tagore, S.B. (P)
Taylor, E.H. (Hy)
Teraszkiewicz, J.S. (S)
Thomson, I.M. (C)
Thurairasasingam, J.V. (C)
Todeschini, C.E. (C)
Wagialla, O.H. (P)
Wahid, S.A. (C)
Ward, M.A. (C)
Watt, W.E. (Hy)
Weare, F.E. (S)
Whitworth, K.M. (C)
Wilson, G. (C)
Wilson, K.C. (H)
Wong Kong Ming, G.C. (S)
Yam Chung Pong, L. (S)

1963

Acharya, D.N. (C)
Acharyya, N.P. (C)
Airaksinen, U.L. (So)
Akinde, J.I. (Hi)
Akoto, B.G.A. (P)
Alexandrou, A.A. (C)
Allgrove, M.A.L.J. (Hi)
Amarakone, A.M.N. (C)
Anderson, A.F. (C)
Angadi, B.C. (So)
Aquilina, A.C. (C)
Axell, J.P. (P)
Bertok, J. (So)
Bickerdike, J. (So)
Binnie, C.J.A. (So)
Birdy, J.N. (C)
Cege, O.S. (P)
Chan, K.Y. (C)
Chandhuri, B.K. (C)
Crowe, W. (C)
Dasgupta, D. (Hy)
Doherty, J.P. (P)
Duncanson, J.K. (P)
Dussault, R. (Ho & So)
Dutton, A.R. (C)
El-Gawhary, A.I.A. (H)
Faluyi, B.A. (P)
Farquhar, G.F. (C)
Flett, J.H. (C)
Ford, D.J. (Hi)
Giller, C.A. (C)
Gowans, I.A.T. (Hy)
Hagan, G.R. (P)
Hall, G. (Hi)
Harris, G.M. (So)
Hayes, J.A. (So)
Herbert, H.J. (C)
Hernandez, C.A. (C)
Inayatullah (C)
Khan, A. (So)
Khan, M.A. (C)
Kinley, J.M. (Hi)
Lane, R. (Hi)
Laplante, D. (C)
Larsen, G.H. (So)
Lau, H.S. (Hi)
Lau, T.H. (C)
Leslie, W.G. (C)
Lewis, J.A. (C)
Liu, H.A. (C)
Longworth, C.R. (So)
Maya, O.L. (C)
Melling, J.A. (C)
Mirata, T. (So)
Moore, B. (C)
Moss, P.J. (C)
Nakase, A. (So)
Ng, S.H. (C)
Normand, J. (So)
Obi, B.C.A. (Hi)
Owusu, F. (Hi)
Panesar, S.S. (Hi)
Perera, T.G. (P)
Piper, H. (Ho)
Pontin, K. (C)
Pontin, R.A. (P)
Portfors, E.A. (Hy)
Rahman, M.S. (C)
Regan, P.E. (C)
Reid, A.G. (So)
Rigney, M.P. (So)
Robinson, G.S. (C)
Round, R.P.D. (Hy)
Salam, E.R.A. (Ho)
Samuel, P. (C)
Scrivener, J.C. (C)
Selman, J.E. (Hi)
Shen, F.K. (P)
Sigvaldason, O.T. (C)
Smith, A.C. (C)
Som, N.N. (So)
Tarafdar, M.M.R. (Ho)
Tawil, A.H. (Hi)
Taylor, K.A. (Hy)
Thompson, J.L. (P)

Tung, H.S.S. (C)
Vile, G.W.D. (C)
Webb, D.L. (So)
Wilson, G. (So)
Yap, C.T. (Hi)
Zelkha, J.H.S. (P)

1964
Alam, A. (C)
Amir-Tahmasseb, I. (So)
Anketell, B. (C)
Au, Yiu-Tong (C)
Ayoub, G.M. (P)
Ayub, M. (Ho)
Ballard, P.C.V. (Hi)
Bermudez, R.I. (C)
Bridgman, T.G. (C)
Caldwell, M.J. (P)
Chambers, J.A. (S)
Chandavimol, P. (S)
Chinwah, J.C.G. (C)
Choudhury, S. (C)
Chow, C.L. (So)
Cotton, C.J.N. (Ho)
Cudmani, R.O. (C)
Dunstan, T. (So)
Erskine, T.A. (C)
Evans, D.G.R. (C)
Farquharson, K.G. (C)
Feather, D. (C)
Felzmann, V.J.A.V. (S)
Finney, M.R. (So)
Folie, G.M. (C)
Gabru, M.S. (C)
Ganguly, H.K. (S)
Ghanem, N.D. (P)
Gibb, M.W.G. (P)
Gomez Upegui, F.J. (C)
Gupta, R. (C)
Hall, M.J. (Ho)
Harding, L.R. (S)
Haswell, J.F.S. (S)
Heath, P. (C)
Henderson, C.J. (S)
Hernandez, C.A. (S)
Hill, P.N. (So)
Hirianniah, B.S. (H)
Hooper, J.A. (So)
Hunter, O.W. (C)
Jeffries, J.E. (S)
Jolly, S.H. (C)
Kanoo, A.L. (C)
Kennedy, F.E. (C)
Khokher, M.A. (C)
Khoo, C.L. (So)
Landine, R.C. (P)
Laplante, D. (S)
Lawrence, J.D. (Hy)
Liddell, W.I. (C)
Limna, T. (S)
McCleary, P. (C)
McCormack, A.H. (S)
Mallick, W.A. (P)
Matyas, E.L. (So)
Menon, M.G.K. (C)
Mitra, A.C. (C)
Moore, P. (So)
Naylor, D.J. (So)
Neogi, P.K. (S)
Oztürk, Y.F. (P)
Painter, W.T. (So)
Papageorgiou, O. (So)
Patten, B.J.F. (C)
Pike, J.G. (Ho)
Pope, D.L. (C)
Potter, K.E.D. (Ho)
Prasad, N.K. (C)
Puleston, L.P. (P)
Ramachandran, K.N. (C)
Ray, M.H. (C)
Roy, T.K. (C)
Saia, J. (C)
Sansom, M.J. (C)
Sarjeant, B.W.D. (C)
Segun, K.A. (S)
Sen, S. (C)
Sobey, J.H. (C)
Soliman, M.T.M. (C)
Sowa, V.A. (So)
Spitz, I. (C)
Stigter, M. (C)
Tattersfield, J. (Ho)
Uzsoy, S.Z. (C)
Vigneux, B. (C)
Wade, N.H. (So)
Warner, E.W. (P)
Watkins, W. (C)
Webster, A.T. (So)
White, R.B. (S)
Yalames, A. (C)
Yankson, B. (P)
Yeoh, K.P. (P)
Yrjänä, M.K.I. (So)

1965
Abdullahi, I.F. (C)
Ahmed, S. (C)
Ali, M.M. (C)
Arès, R. (So)
Armstrong, I.C. (C)
Au, Y.T. (C)
Barton, M.E. (So)
Barton, P. (C)
Basu, S.K. (S)
Basu, T.K. (P)
Beeby, M.I. (So)
Bhakta, A.K. (S)
Bisono Pichardo, G.R. (So)
Bommer, C.M. (C)
Brown, I.E.W. (C)
Bruton, M.J. (T)
Butler, A.T. (S)
Chaderton, A.F. (C)
Channer, G.F. (C)
Chaudhari, M.A. (So)
Chaudhary, A-U-R. (So)
Cheng, H.K. (C)
Chin, T.H. (P)
Chraibi, M. (P)
Clapham, H.G. (So)
Cochran, W.D.M. (C)
Conyette, C.S. (P)
Couch, R.L. (Ho)
Crowe, P.J. (Ho)
Daniels, S.B.M. (P)
Dasgupta, M. (S)
Deck, W.R. (C)
Dorman, A.P. (C)
Dunne, C.R. (P)
Fearn, M. (S)
Franklin, A.J. (C)
Gadre, S.H. (S)
Gallagher, J.E. (C)
Gangopadhyay, G. (S)
Gunasekera, D.A. (C)
Hidaytalla, A. (Hy)
Hung, S.C. (S)
Hussain, A.I. (C)
Hyde, T.R. (Hy)
Kelleher, P.F. (C)
Khan, M.U. (P)
Khan, S.A. (P)
Krishna, P. (S)
Laryea, A. (P)
Ledi, P.C. (S)
Legg, R.A. (C)
Lester, P.D. (C)
Lim, L.G. (T)
Lucks, A.S. (S)
Martel, N.J. (C)
Martin, R.T. (So)
Millar, L. (T)
Mirza, S.H. (C)
Morgenstern, N. (So)
Morris, L.J. (S)
Morton, J.D. (So)
Mould, K.F. (T)
Moussa, M.A.S.A. (Hy)
Paterson, G.V. (C)
Pattanaik, A.B. (Hy)
Perkins, J.A. (Hy)
Priestley, J.D. (S)
Purcell, W.E. (C)
Raina, V.K. (C)
Rizvi, S.A.H. (C)
Robinson, D.L. (S)
Roy, S.C. (C)
Saha, S.K. (C)
Sahgal, R.K. (C)
Saravanapavan, A. (P)
Sargin, M. (C)
Sarmecanic, S. (C)
Senna, J.C.M. (S)
Sharan, D. (Hy)
Smith, A.W. (C)
Smith, D.C. (C)

Smith, R.H. (C)
Snell, E.F.A. (Hy)
Somalya, A.R. (C)
Stamatou, G. (C)
Stephens, P.G. (C)
Symonds, D.A. (C)
Taylor, S.J. (C)
Trippner, G. (Hy)
Vaughan, P.R. (So)
Vijayaraghavan, N. E. (C)
Vine, M.J. (P)
Wackman, H.E. (Hy)
Waggott, J.G. (C)
Walker, B.P. (So)
Warburton, H.B. (C)
Ware, P.H. (P)
Welch, D.E. (So)
Wells, E.C. (Hy)
Wemah, K. (P)
Whittle, R.H. (T)
Wiebe, P.A. (Hy)
Wilson, C.B. (S)
Yau, E.S.F. (S)

1966
Anderson, D. (S)
Appan, A. (P)
Appleby, F.V. (Ho)
Bagchi, G. (S)
Bailey, M. (S)
Bamber, T.O. (So)
Banerjee, P.K. (C)
Barocio Ramirez, R. (C)
Brown, J.R. (C)
Brown, M.G. (C)
Burnard, A.P. (C)
Calder, A.C. (So)
Carrington, R.W.M. (So)
Chai, K.H. (C)
Chakrabarti, S. (S)
Chambers, D.L. (C)
Charles, J.A. (S)
Chee, K.Y. (So)
Cheng Shing Yuen, A. (C)
Constantine, P.P. (So)
Dajani, M.H.M. (P)
Dalal, S. (S)
Davis, T.G. (Ho)
Delaney, J.D.P. (C)
De Marco, G. (So)
Eaton, C.H. (So)
El-Debouni, R.M. (So)
El-Dujaili, A.M. (H)
Finigan, A.B. (C)
Gascon, G. (C)
Giddens, E.P. (Hy)
Gilbert, D.A.M. (T)
Gilchrist, H.G. (So)
Green, C.S. (C)
Hafiz, M.A. (P)
Hardcastle, B.J. (Ho)
James, P.M. (So)
Khuma, Z. (S)
Kilford, J.T. (S)
Lee, C.M. (So)
Lobo, A.C. (C)
Lowing, M.J. (Ho)
Lowther, G. (So)
Loya, A.R. (C)
McCreath, D.R. (C)
McNeely, P.A. (C)
Marais, G.R. (P)
Martin, K.W. (T)
Matheson, R.G. (C)
Maunder, E.A.W. (C)
Michael, K.C. (C)
Milner, H.R. (S)
Morin, N. (S)
Nag, K. (C)
Nene, M.G. (S)
Newman, J.B. (C)
Nie, P. (C)
O'Hara, I.J. (Ho)
O'Riordan, D.J.P. (C)
Pao, W.K. (P)
Paranagama, D.D.O. (C)
Parker, C.H.M. (C)
Parkinson, J.J. (So)
Paul, S.C. (S)
Pekau, O.A. (S)
Porteous, A. (S)
Potter, P.D. (C)
Pratt, F.Y. (So)
Purandare, A.N. (S)
Rao, K.V. (H)
Reid, A.U. (T)
Ross, N.I.R. (C)
Russell, A.J.O. (C)
Sanmuganathan, K. (H)
Saxena, K.R. (So)
Schuster, R.L. (So)
Selvadurai, A.P.S. (So)
Shakespeare, K.J. (C)
Shears, M. (C)
Shome, A. (S)
Sivaloganathan, K. (C)
Skinner, R.J. (T)
Smith, G.C. (S)
Steven, H.O. (C)
Tan, S.B. (So)
Taylor, I.P. (So)
Telling, R.M. (So)
Thomason, S.R. (C)
Thompson, P.J. (C)
Wesley, L.D. (So)
Wheeldon, G.B. (S)
White, C.S. (C)
Widdis, T.F. (So)
Yousif, K.N. (P)

1967
Aalami, B. (S)
Acharjyya, A.R. (S)
Ahmad, A.U. (P)
Ahmed, S.N. (S)
Akbar, M.A. (P)
Ali, H. (C)
Amana, E.J. (S)
Andrew, W.S. (C)
Anis, N.N. (C)
Anwer, Z. (C)
Aowal, A.F.S.A. (P)
Arthanari, S. (C)
Ashiabor, W.K. (Ti)
Babar, N.Y. (So)
Babazadeh, K.V. (P)
Bagchi, D. (S)
Baird, N.A. (So)
Baker, M.J. (C)
Barnes, J.A.L. (C)
Bell, W.C. (T)
Bjorksten, L.E.W.
Boneh, A. (Ho)
Briggs, D.A. (T)
Brindley, J.S. (So)
Brookes, M.A. (C)
Brown, A.D. (Ho)
Burney, S.Z.U.H. (S)
Chakravorty, S. (S)
Chan, F.C. (C)
Chong, S.C. (C)
Christsen, C.J. (S)
Ciray, C. (H)
Clark, R.D.S. (Ho)
Crowther, F. (P)
Dafalla, A.A. (P)
Deans, R.M. (T)
Denness, B. (So)
Devlin, J.P. (T)
Devon, M.R. (Ti)
Ekman, F. (S)
El Nimeiri, M.M. (S)
Er, K.C. (P)
Ernest, H.M. (Ho)
Fernando, A.P. (S)
Fiddes, D. (Ho)
France, R. (T)
Gerada-Azzopardi, J.A. (P)
Gosling, P.A. (S)
Gulliksen, C.C. (So)
Gür, A. (P)
Harris, E.W. (So)
Hart, R.W. (So)
Hepworth, A.J.W. (C)
Hill, W.F. (S)
Hobbs, R.E. (S)
Howard, N. (P)
Howkins, W. (So)
Hunt, C.G. (T)
Hutchings, C.B. (C)
Hyslop, J.S. (C)
Ibbitt, M.E. (Ho)
Icekson Frydland, A. (Ti)
Irwin, W. (C)
Jenkins, E.V. (C)
Justo, J.L. (So)

Kamal, R.B. (S)
Karkanis, A.G. (Ti)
Kattan, F.D. (T)
Keech, B. (T)
Kinsey, P.J. (S)
Knowles, N.C. (S)
Kumapley, N.K. (So)
Kwei, G.C.S. (C)
Lai, H.L. (C)
Laing, J.M. (So)
Lashine, A.K.F. (So)
Leach, M.H. (C)
Lee, E.L. (Hy)
Loukola, E.J. (So)
Lowe, P.A. (S)
MacDonald, A.K. (Ho)
MacLennan, C.B. (T)
Maidment, W.J. (C)
Mander, R.J. (Ho)
Marlon-Lambert, J.R. (S)
Martin, P.J. (C)
May-Matwiewjew, H.I. (S)
McCann, J.P. (P)
Meehan, R.L. (So)
Morgan, M.K. (S)
Mustafa, Z.A. (P)
Ng, T.S.L. (Ti)
Nicholds, R.M. (Ho)
Okigbo, L.C. (Ti)
Oluwande, P.A. (P)
Palmer, B. (C)
Paul, P.N. (P)
Pearce, G.A. (P)
Petley, D.J. (So)
Pigeon, Y. (So)
Price, K.M. (C)
Qureshi, B.M. (P)
Reitz, M.F.W. (C)
Roberts, J.D. (S)
Rooke, G.F. (C)
Ryan, M.J. (C)
Salem, M.N. (So)
Sankeralli, M.A. (Ho)
Sargent, M.D. (T)
Sefton, D.J. (S)
Seidel, G. (Ho)
Self, G.F. (T)
Setya, S.P. (C)
Shakir, B.A. (C)
Sinha, S. (C)
Sutcliffe, M.A. (So)
Taylor, D.A. (C)
Taylor, P.J.B. (C)
Tchalenko, J.S. (So)
Threlfall, A.J. (C)
Tipler, T.J. (C)
Tremblay, D. (C)
Turner, T.E. (C)
Ulug, S.E. (P)
Venetis, C (Ho)
Voysey, J.A. (P)
Wainwright, D.A. (So)
Warren, G.D. (Ho)
Warren, J.P. (S)
Williams, H.L. (C)
Yeates, J.A. (So)

1968

Abankwah, J.M. (Ti)
Adeosun, A. (So)
Adraktas, K.E. (S)
Agarwal, K.B. (So)
Ahsan, S.K. (C)
Alatzas, D.Z. (T)
Al-Dhahir, Z.A.R. (So)
Aleong, G.L. (C)
Amegashie, E.C.K. (Ti)
Asmah. J. (Ti)
Baku, E.S.K. (Ti)
Banks, R.G. (C)
Beshir, B.A.G. (S)
Bliss, P.J. (P)
Branchaud, M. (T)
Brave-Boy, G.K. (C)
Brown, A. (C)
Brown, D.W. (C)
Brown, W.P. (C)
Brynildsen, O.A. (Ti)
Buck, A.B. (C)
Cano Delgado, J.C. (Ti)
Carter, T.H. (P)
Cashman, P.M. (Ho)
Chainarong, L. (P)
Chawdhary, A.L. (C)
Chen, H. (P)
Cheng Siu Wan, S. (Hy)
Chien, Y.H.G. (So)
Clifton, A.W. (So)
Cocksedge, J.E. (So)
Cooper, A.T. (C)
Croft, D.D. (C)
De Faria, A.S.L. (P)
Economou, N. (C)
Edwards, L.S. (S)
Espiloy, E.B. (Ti)
Fisher, R. (Ho)
Gardner, J.E.S. (C)
Garga, V.K. (So)
Ghose, M.K. (C)
Gibb, H.G. (C)
Gordon, R.W. (C)
Graterol-Monserrate, J. (So)
Gupta, B.K. (C)
Henry, W.J. (S)
Herbertson, P.W. (Ho)
Herbst, P.H. (Ho)
Hong, S.M. (Ti)
Jaccarini, J.M. (P)
Jensen, G.T. (Ti)
Johnson, M.F. (So)
Johnson, P.R. (P)
Jones, H.H. (Ho)
Jones, M.V. (S)
Jones, R.A. (T)
Kashatri, J.S. (C)
Kasriel, A.T. (C)
Kaul, B.L. (P)
Khayat, L. (C)
Kirmani, A.A.S. (C)
Kulkarni, A.D. (C)
Lake, L.M. (So)
Latif, M. (C)
Lauricio, F. (Ti)
Levy, J. (So)
McKenna, J.M. (So)
Mallick, B.C. (C)
Marchetti, S. (So)
Martinian, A. (C)
Maung, H.W. (P)
Mejia-Gomez, O. (So)
Memon, H.M. (H)
Millais, M.G.W. (C)
Mineiro, A.J.C. (So)
Myers, R.S.A. (C)
Mynard, P.J. (C)
Nahhas, U. (C)
Nazaré, M.F. (C)
Nielsen, N.M. (So)
Odewusi, P.O. (P)
O'Leary, W. (Ho)
Pathmanathan, P. (P)
Pau, M.K. (So)
Plant, D.M. (S)
Pole, E.L. (So)
Pope, G.A. (P)
Potter, M.M.A. (C)
Pranno, G. (T)
Rainford, E.C. (C)
Rose, J.G. (T)
Sackeyfio, C.W.O. (Ti)
Samartin Quiroga, A. (C)
Sarma, S.K. (So)
Saunders, C.R. (T)
Sayani, F.H.N. (C)
Senaratne, M.J.F.R. (So)
Sommerville, W. (S)
Stathatos, X.P. (S)
Stefanou, G.D. (C)
Syn, W.H. (So)
Tamakloe, E.K.A. (T)
Tamuly Phukan, A.L. (So)
Taylor, G.H. (S)
Thilaganathan, K. (P)
Thompson, C.J.G. (P)
Turvey, G.J. (S)
Ullon, J.V. (Ti)
Wijayatilleke, M.G.C.P. (So)
Wong, H.F. (P)
Yung, Y.H.E.H. (So)
Zand, M.B. (H)

1969

Adu-Nyako, F. (Ti)
Ahari, M.H. (So)
Ahmed, E.F.H. (P)

Al-Khudhairy, W.K. (C)
Al-Mashidani, G. (Ho)
Anderson, R. (So)
Andrews, J. (So)
Arulambalam, T.G. (P)
Asfari, A.F. (H)
Bannaga, H. (C)
Bara, H.C. (C)
Beardsell, R.E. (P)
Berre, T. (So)
Bettess, P. (S)
Boyce, B.T. (So)
Brett, C.A. (C)
Brown, L.H. (C)
Brown, R.L. (So)
Buddhadasa, S.V.A. (Ho)
Chaudhry, A.M. (P)
Collings, A.G. (C)
Cooper, F. (So)
Curtis, D.J. (S)
Dawson, J.M. (S)
D'Elia, B. (So)
Densley, R.J. (P)
D'Souza, J.J. (C)
Evans, N.R. (C)
Fernandez, V.A. (Ti)
Fisher, G.A. (Ho)
Fletcher, M.S. (So)
Francis, C.M.G. (So)
Francis, G.V.H. (S)
Ghosh, S.K. (S)
Gilman, S. (S)
Gittus, R.W. (C)
Goff, R.D. (C)
Goh, T.E. (P)
Goonaratne, G.W.D.M. (C)
Grace, M.F. (So)
Gunawardana, O.M. (H)
Gunawardane, G.J.P. (Ho)
Haider, G. (C)
Haq, F. (P)
Harding, G.T. (C)
Harrington, E.J. (So)
Healy, P.L. (C)
High, R.A. (Ho)
Hill, M.A. (C)
Hollingdale, R.R. (C)
Holman, C.E. (C)
Housden, C.S. (C)
Howard, B.H.A. (S)
Hunt, A.E. (S)
Hunt, G.W. (S)
Ilden, M.Y. (So)
Iles, D.C. (S)
Jabry, Z. (C)
Jones, W.T.F. (P)
Jordan, D.O. (So)
Joseph, A.P. (So)
Juliao, C.A. (C)
Kee, R. (So)
Khan, M.H. (C)
Kow, R. (P)
Kudu, H.Y. (Ho)
Kyei, K.G. (Ti)
Lee, P.B.T. (C)
Lovegrove, G.W. (So)
Luck, A.F. (S)
McRoberts, E.C. (So)
Mann, G.C.A. (C)
Marsh, P.D. (So)
Marshall, K.R. (S)
Martin, W.C.C. (C)
Miciano, R. (Ti)
Miller, M.D. (C)
Monga, M.S. (Ho)
Naim, M. (Ti)
Nair, K.B. (P)
Narasimhan, N. (C)
Nash, A.C. (C)
Neal, F.R. (S)
Neira Combariza, H. (H)
O'Brien, W.T. (S)
Osborne-Moss, D.M. (S)
Osman, K.E.D.H. (P)
Ottway, T.J. (So)
Palomino Infante, A. (S)
Park, J.B. (C)
Peek, J.D. (Ti)
Pells, P.J.N. (So)
Phillipson, N.G. (C)
Pigeon, M. (C)
Ranatunga, D.G.L. (Ho)
Reader, A.J. (S)
Richardson, D. (C)
Robertson, J.N. (S)
Roberts-Wray, R.C. (C)
Rosenberg, D.J. (S)
Roxburgh, I.E. (C)
Sangster, A.A. (C)
Savage, J.E. (S)
Sekarajasekaran, A. (P)
Sharpe, D.J. (C)
Shrestha, R.M. (P)
Simon, E. (Ho)
Skelsey, D.V. (C)
Sowden, G.H. (C)
Stieda, C.K.A. (S)
Swinnerton, C.J. (Ho)
Tan, T.H. (P)
Thant, N.N. (Ti)
Thomson, G.R.D. (C)
Tombs, S.G. (So)
Touma, A. (C)
Urquiola, R.T. (Ti)
Walbancke, H.J. (So)
Ward, B.S. (C)
Ward, J.K. (S)
Winokur, A. (S)
Woods, A. (So)
Wright, L.F. (C)
Zahedi, M. (S)
Zaidi, S.F.A. (Ho)

1970
Albert, L.F. (So)
Antonopoulos, J. (Se)
Aragon-Morales, F. (T)
Arroyo, J. (C)
Artemis, C.C. (So)
Awan, N.M. (Ho)
Bajaj, A.N. (Ti)
Balchin, B.A. (C)
Banisadr, M. (Se)
Barutcu, A.M. (T)
Belloni, L. (So)
Bennett, T.H. (T)
Berg, J.H. (C)
Bhartari, R.K. (Ti)
Billington, C.J. (S)
Bitarakwate, A.L.M. (Ti)
Bobie, J.K. (So)
Bolger, T.A. (So)
Boyd, T.M. (C)
Bramley, M.E. (H)
Buluk, O.E.A.A. (P)
Bungey, J.H. (C)
Choudhury, A.R. (T)
Coster, R.C. (C)
Dart, J.R. (T)
Davidson, J.H. (C)
Davies, P. (So)
De Groote, K. (S)
Dukes, M.T. (So)
Duvivier, N.S. (C)
Dyson, S.W. (S)
Elamin, M.A.E.R. (P)
Elliott, T.G. (C)
Evans, J.S. (So)
Evison, J.A. (C)
Flynn, B. (H)
Foster, J.E. (T)
Fox, P.D. (C)
Fullard, M.H. (T)
Gamble, R. (C)
Giannopoulos, G.A. (T)
Gill, M.A. (H)
Goodwin, R.P. (T)
Green, G.E. (So)
Gross, H. (C)
Gugulovski, M. (Se)
Gunadi, A. (Ti)
Guy, R.R. (S)
Hall, D.L. (P)
Hall, P.W. (T)
Hammond, R. (S)
Harding, C.P. (C)
Hardwick, J.D. (H)
Harris, I.D.H. (T)
Harvey, R.M. (T)
Holder, A.R. (T)
Hopper, P.E. (T)
Horta da Silva, J.A. (So)
Ibbitt, R.P. (Ho)
Islam, M.R.U. (Ti)
Jeffery, R.P. (So)

Jones, A.A.A. (C)
Khalifa, A.M. (S)
Krishnamoorthy, S. (C)
Kundu, A.K. (P)
Lavender, P.A. (P)
Lee, M.S.Y. (C)
Leggeat, R.J. (C)
Liang, K.Y. (P)
Lovenbury, H.T. (So)
Lyons, L.P.R. (S)
McCann, B.J. (S)
McCracken, M.H. (C)
McKee, W.A. (T)
Manning, R.E. (C)
Mansell, P.F. (C)
Maritz, G. (C)
Merrony, B.J. (C)
Miles, R.A. (C)
Mills, W.R. (S)
Mortimer, G.H. (C)
Murray, A.D. (C)
Naranjo Arango, A. (So)
Nasseri, I. (Ho)
Nasseri, T. (S)
Newton, R. (S)
Nisanci, I.E. (H)
Njie, E.A. (So)
O'Hea, R.S. (C)
Ojiako, G.U. (P)
Oliver, R.S. (C)
Özden, S.Y. (T)
Papadopoulos, D.N. (So)
Patel, B.H. (So)
Pateman, A.S. (H)
Pelton, F. (H)
Pemberton, M.W. (T)
Pierce, C.B. (Ti)
Placas, A. (C)
Pratt, E.J. (T)
Raaff, C.B. (P)
Raghupathi, M. (S)
Rahman, M.F. (Ti)
Read, N.S.L. (T)
Rigden, W.J. (So)
Roberts, R.J.F. (S)
Robinson, M. (C)
Roscoe, G.H. (So)
Rosenberg, P.H. (So)
Rosenthal, G.N. (So)
Rowland, A.D. (C)
Rutherford, A.R. (C)
Saifu, W. (P)
Sarosh, D. (P)
Selvalingam, S. (H)
Sen, H.K. (S)
Sheerman-Chase, A. (So)
Shelton, J.C. (So)
Shimali, A.A. (P)
Smith, G.C. (C)
Somohano Nunez, A. (So)
Stables, J.F. (H)
Stamenkovic, A. (S)
Tankut, A.T. (C)
Taylor, R.D. (C)
Tharmaratnam, K. (C)
Thompson, D.M. (C)
Tonge, F.L. (C)
Visvalingam, A.C. (H)
Watkins, D.J. (So)
Wedden, R. (T)
Weltman, A.J. (So)
Wiesner, I.R. (S)
Williams, D.G. (S)
Wrigley, M.J. (T)
Yates, M.L. (H)
Yu, B.K. (C)
Zahedi, F. (C)
Zerrate Sierra, G. (S)

1971
Akram, M. (P)
Alagiah, D.R. (P)
Aleem, A. (C)
Allouni, S.A.K. (C)
Ansah, E.L. (Ti)
Arlaban, J.M. (So)
Atkinson, J.H. (So)
Au, C.L. (C)
Azarm, N.P. (T)
Bailey, S.S. (T)
Balmond, C.H.I. (C)
Baranowski, N. (C)
Barnor, F.A. (Ti)
Beal, D.L. (C)
Belton, G. (C)
Beng, K.A. (P)
Bilgin, R. (Ho)
Binder, P.F. (C)
Boga, S.K. (C)
Bond, P.D.R. (C)
Brand, R.E. (C)
Bridle, R.C. (So)
Bubb, C.T.J. (Se)
Bunce, J.W.F. (S)
Burford, D. (So)
Carr, P. (S)
Carroll, B.C. (C)
Chambers, D.W. (C)
Cheung, T.L. (C)
Clark, A.H. (S)
Coe, R.H. (So)
Convery, D.J. (So)
Davenport, J.F. (C)
Dewhurst, W.L. (C)
Doruk, M. (So)
Effirim, K.K. (Ti)
Engku, A.R. (Ti)
Farrell, C.F. (S)
Fernando, D.M.M. (C)
Finch, T.D.A. (So)
Frost, J.R. (Ho)
Garrett, C. (So)
Gilbertson, A.L. (C)
Goh, H.S. (H)
Goodhew, R.C. (Ho)
Goodson, M.G. (P)
Goren, A. (C)
Grant, J.M. (C)
Greenfield, B.J. (Ho)
Grey, J.F. (C)
Grillo, G. de. Q. (So)
Groundsell, M. (C)
Guthrie, J.E. (T)
Harris, R.E. (C)
Harrison, J.B. (C)
Harwood, G.R. (C)
Hayaud Din, M.A. (C)
Hegan, R.J. (Ho)
Hegarty, G. (T)
Hickling, D. (C)
Hill, N.A. (Ho)
Hillman, D. (C)
Hirzallah, B.S.E. (Ho)
Hossein-Javaheri, J. (Se)
Htay, T. (Ti)
Hume, I.J. (C)
Hurst, A.J. (H)
Hussain, N. (C)
Kaveh, A. (S)
Kee, K.P. (S)
Kelkka, A.A. (So)
Kempton, G.T. (C)
Khan, J-Z. (H)
Kin, P.S-C. (So)
Kinstler, F.L. (So)
Klemencic, B. (So)
Knight, R.G.W. (C)
Krikorian, A.K. (H)
Kristiansen, R. (S)
Kyriacou, A.T. (C)
Laborde-Basto, C.A.N. (C)
Latham, D.C.F. (C)
Lavan, S. A. (C)
Lawson, L.A.L. (P)
Leonard, M.S.M. (So)
Leung, D.Y-L. (C)
Lim, E.C. (S)
Longworth, T.I. (So)
Lwin, L. (C)
MacDonald, E.A.D. (H)
McLoughlin, J. (C)
Mandeville, A.N. (Ho)
Manion, R.B. (P)
Mann, P.R. (T)
Martin, P.L. (So)
Martinez. L. (Ti)
Mitchell, G.B. (C)
Mittra, D. (P)
Moayer, M. (C)
Mock, R.A. (C)
Money, M.S. (So)
Mudallal, U.H. (Ho)
Mutsuddi, D.K. (C)
Narasimham, P.L. (Se)
Natarajan, P. (H)
Oliver, E.R. (C)

Owens, G.W. (S)
Papaioannou, I.C. (C)
Patel, A.U. (C)
Paton, J.L. (C)
Phelps, R.M. (C)
Pook, M.J. (So)
Pritchard, G.T. (C)
Pyle, F.G. (C)
Pyrah, I.C. (So)
Rahman, M.A. (So)
Ramsay, R.B. (C)
Raymond, I.D. (C)
Raz-Nahan, M. (S)
Razvi, S.F.H. (C)
Reed, J.E. (T)
Reichert, H. (T)
Remy, J.P.P. (So)
Rojo, R. (Ti)
Rupasinghe, K.A.W.D.C. (C)
Silcock, D.T. (T)
Singh, S. (S)
Smith, D.G.E. (C)
Smith, D.L. (C)
Spasic, B. (C)
Spingler, J.R. (T)
Stanford-Smith, O.C.H. (P)
Suarez, J.A. (So)
Sutton, G.A. (C)
Swann, A.B. (H)
Sweeney, M. (So)
Tadlaoui, M.A. (C)
Thei, A. (C)
Thomas, W.C. (C)
Thompson, S.B. (C)
Tite, A.P. (C)
Trangrathpit, S. (Ti)
Tsang, K.Y. (P)
Turner, F.H. (C)
Uriel, A.O. (So)
Valenzuela, J. (Se)
Wanjohi, I.G. (T)
Ward, J.H. (C)
Williams, T.R. (C)
Wilson, J.S. (C)
Wong, P.W. (C)
Wynne, A.A. (H)
Zand, M.J. (S)

1972
Adhya, A.K. (P)
Akeju, T.A.I. (C)
Alfy, G.G. (P)
Alis, P.W.S. (So)
Aryan, G.R. (Se)
Aurola, R.H.E. (P)
Baldwin, M.W. (So)
Barrell, D.W.F. (T)
Braune, E. (Ho)
Butterworth. N.R. (P)
Carr, D.P. (Ho)
Chadha, B.K. (Se)
Cioppa, I.B. (T)
Constant, B.D. (So)
Cox, G.C. (P)
Craft, J.R. (So)
Daley, P. (So)
Davies, J.A.G. (So)
Davies, T.J.K.L. (T)
De Las Casas Pasquel, J. (Se)
de Oliveira, J.D.G. (C)
de Oliveira, L.F.V. (T)
Desai, B.B. (P)
Digby, R.P. (H)
Douglas, J.T. (H)
El Awad, H.A.R. (P)
Fageiri, O.M.E.H. (Ti)
Flanagan, P.J. (H)
Fortnum, B.C.H. (H)
Goldston, W.F. (So)
Goodram, L.W. (So)
Grandis, I. (So)
Grayson, M.R. (T)
Guerra Penco, A. (So)
Hamza, M.M.A.F. (So)
Hartley, P.M. (T)
Hegg, U.W. (So)
Hight, D.W. (So)
Ho, K-H (Ho)
Hollingworth, B.E. (H)
Hrudey, S.E. (P)
Hughes, G.M. (T)
Juneidi, A.A. (Ho)
Kay, M.G. (H)
Kesse, G.O. (T)
Khan, J.A. (Ti)
Kim, J.S. (Ho)
Kirkham, D.G. (Ti)
Kobayashi, Y. (P)
Langdon, D.S. (So)
Lason, J. (P)
Lee, C.J. (T)
Lim, T.K. (S)
Loughlin, P. (Ti)
Lucas, E.B. (Ti)
McKenzie, H.S. (T)
Maksimovic, M. (So)
Medd, R.G. (P)
Megraw, B.P.A. (T)
Moya Barrios, J.E. (So)
Mpala, A.S. (H)
Munoz Gilabert, J.R. (Se)
Nash, D.F.T. (So)
Nasroun, T.E.D.H. (Ti)
Nelson, J.A. (H)
Nicol, S.M. (H)
Oyiro-Ayoro, B.I. (T)
Papastamatiou, D. (Se)
Parent, M.E. (P)
Peatfield, A.M. (H)
Pengprecha, N. (Ti)
Picard, A. (C)
Rahim, A. (So)
Rein, J.O. (So)
Robb, J.L. (T)
Rumsey, P.B. (So)
Runnacles, T.V. (T)
Sammons, C.J. (So)
Satari, I.H. (Ho)
Sawi, F.E.T. (P)
Sellahewa, G. (So)
Sha'al, B.Z. (Se)
Shende, E.D. (Se)
Shihab, H.A.G. (P)
Slator, V.C. (Ho)
Smith, T.A. (T)
Somani, A.H.M. (P)
Sutcliffe, G. (So)
Sweeney, D.J. (So)
Tapiaillanes, C. (So)
Tobia, G.C. (T)
Trikha, D.N. (C)
Tuli, J.M. (P)
Twelftree, P.D. (T)
Wan Kee Cheung, W.S.W. (Ho)
Warman, P.R. (T)
Westaway, E.J. (T)
Willoughby, P.J. (T)
Wright, C.J.H. (T)
Yee, K.H.J. (T)
Yousif, E.R.M. (P)
Zaboli, S. (S)

1973
Abdul, R. (C)
Abro, A.A. (P)
Adali, H. (P)
Adamson, C.J. (So)
Ahmadzai, M.K. (P)
Algeo, R.G. (S)
Al-Hassan, A.R. (Ti)
Amico-Ramos, A. (C)
Anderson, W.V. (S)
Arguelles Petit, A. (T)
Atraghji, D.G. (So)
Bakht, B. (S)
Barlow, B.J.F. (C)
Barrack, J.W. (C)
Barrett, R.L. (P)
Bates, D.N.J. (S)
Bawa, A.S. (S)
Bhachu, M.S. (H)
Bhatia, S.A. (S)
Blackie, J.R. (Ho)
Bleek, J.M. (Ho)
Bogetti, F.E.G. (So)
Bolat, H. (So)
Brody, S.J. (C)
Bromhead, E.N. (So)
Bucher, K. (S)
Budd, C.G. (C)
Bugeja, J.V. (P)
Burgoyne, C.J. (S)
Campbell, S.C. (P)
Cassar, A. (So)

Charrett, J.A.M. (C)
Chatterjee, S. (S)
Child, S.C. (Ho)
Christophides, A. (C)
Cracknell, C.J. (C)
Crowhurst, M.G. (T)
Demetracopoulos, A. (C)
De Silva, B.V.S.K. (S)
Dhir, V.K. (So)
Dickens, W.R. (H)
Dracopoulos, G. (S)
Eadie, H.S. (S)
Ealey, T.A. (C)
Eatessami, Z.S.A. (C)
Ellis, D.S.M. (C)
Eze, A. (Ho)
Ferrando, P.P.C. (P)
Foot, B. (T)
Frankland, J.W. (C)
Frieze, P.A. (S)
Ghavami, K. (Se)
Green, A. (H)
Groves, G. (H)
Hallowes, G.R. (So)
Hamedi, N. (Se)
Harding, J.E. (S)
Hill, P.V. (C)
Hocker, R.G. (Ho)
Holleyoak, J.P. (H)
Hooton, T.S. (P)
Hunt, T. (So)
Irgens, E. (T)
Isaza, E. (C)
Jesudason, J. (So)
Johnston, D.K. (T)
Jones, B.S. (C)
Jones, L.C. (C)
Khudair, R.A. (C)
Klement, T.J. (C)
Knapton, G.C. (H)
Kneebone, G.F. (C)
Knott, T.A. (P)
Krishnamoorthy, C.S. (C)
Kwok, W.P.S. (C)
Labib, F. (S)
Labib, G.A. (C)
Lejeune, J.M. (So)
Lim, K.S. (C)
Liyanage, E.O. (C)
Lynn, P.P. (Ho)
Makonnen, B. (Se)
Malewski, P.D.A. (S)
Mallia, H.J. (P)
Malysovann, C. (So)
Marshall, C. (T)
McDyre, B.C. (T)
Metcalf, S.M. (P)
Minor, P. (H)
Mittleman, M.L. (S)
Moolani, F.M. (S)
Moore, R.V. (Ho)
Moschovidis, Z. (S)
Nabavi, M.S. (Se)
Narayanan, R.S. (S)
Nunoo, J.N.A. (P)
Omisanya, E.O. (Ti)
Owainati, S.A.R. (C)
Papamichael, C.M. (C)
Parker, M.D. (C)
Perera, J.A.A. (C)
Pine, R.J. (So)
Pippet, A.G. (C)
Powrie, D.E. (T)
Puerta Garcia, M. (C)
Pugh, R.S. (So)
Quitt, E. (C)
Qureshi, M.A. (C)
Radukic, V. (So)
Ramachandran, K. (S)
Ramirez Agudelo, J.A. (S)
Ramstad, T. (Ti)
Rayner, D.S. (T)
Reades, D.W. (So)
Rickards, C.M. (P)
Robinson, M.V.C. (H)
Salih, A.M.A. (H)
Sandegren, D.S. (C)
Sanyal, S. (P)
Seager, M. (P)
Sen, Z. (Ho)
Sertmehmetoglu, M.L. (P)
Sharma, Y.K. (So)
Smith, A.J. (S)
Smith, T.E. (Ti)
Sobey, R.J. (H)
Steer, J.K. (T)
Stikas, G.P. (S)
Suphi, H.S. (P)
Tang, C.L. (So)
Traynor, F.S. (P)
Veale, J.R. (C)
Wallace, W.J. (T)
Ward, K.B. (C)
West, M.J. (C)
Williams, M.C. (P)
Willumsen, V.L. (T)
Yannopoulos, P. (C)
Young, R.J. (S)

1974

Abdelgadir, M.A. (C)
Abdel-Qadir, S.A.A. (So)
Abu-Sayf, A. (H)
Acheson, M.A. (P)
Akhtaruzzaman, A.A. (C)
Al-Yassin, Z.A. Miss (So)
Araque Garces, G.A. (H)
Attewill, L.J.S. (So)
Bampfylde, A.P. (T)
Bell, P.W.R. (C)
Bell, W.T. (T)
Birks, F.J. (C)
Calderon, E.B. (T)
Campbell, P.A. (H)
Chan, K.T.L. (P)
Chiverrell, C.P. (So)
Chusri, C. (P)
Clamen, M. (H)
Clark, P.B. (H)
Clayton, C.R.I. (So)
Cole-Baker, J.R. (So)
Costa-Filho, L. de M. (So)
Da Graca, A.N. (So)
Damaskinos, C. (C)
Das, K.N. (P)
Derekas, L. (So)
De Vasconcellos, S.A.W. (T)
Diab, W. (C)
Dick, R.C. (So)
Doughty, G.M. (P)
Duncan-Williams, J.V. (Ti)
Ellis, P. (C)
Evans, P.L. (T)
Fader, S.H. (C)
Fox, H.R.I. (So)
Francis, R.M. (T)
Ganesalingam, N. (C)
Gens, A. (So)
Ghadery-Tafreshi, M.M. (Se)
Glenster, A.G. (C)
Goad, J.E.J. (P)
Goddin, G.W. (T)
Graham, D.J. (T)
Granados, G. (Ti)
Gysi, H.J. (So)
Hamedi, N. (Se)
Hart, A.J. (C)
Hathway, A.G. (T)
Hernandez-Lopez, J. (So)
Hills, E.F. (C)
Hurst, M.K. (C)
Hynd, R.J.A. (H)
Ingold, T.S. (So)
Jones, A.E. (Ho)
Jones, T.S.M. (T)
Kam, S.K. (C)
Karnasudirdja, S. (Ti)
Kitchen, M.W. (C)
Kouzeli, A. (P)
Kraneis, B.H. (T)
Kulavaratharajah, K. (H)
Kwarteng, I.E. (Ti)
Lee, A.J.G. (So)
Lee, P.S. (Ho)
Lee, Y.S. (S)
Magalhaes, L.E.M. de M. (H)
McCulloch, I.R. (C)
Melvin, A.L. (T)
Moffatt, K.R. (S)
Mortazari, S. (Se)
Muhiden, N.A. (C)
Murray, C.G. (C)
Nardone, M.R. (Ho)

Nicholls, T.P. (P)
Nisbet, R.M. (So)
Noyes, A. (C)
Oates, A. (H)
Ohn Maung, U. (Ho)
Okutu, W.N. (Ho)
Olsen, A.J. (So)
Onolaja, L. (P)
Osio, J.H. (Ti)
Pinto-Marques, C.A. (So)
Prastitis, L.M. (T)
Quesnell, C.C. (C)
Raper, A.F. (C)
Ratnayaka, D.D. (P)
Roberts, A. (C)
Saavendra-Yanez, R.M. (Ho)
Sakthikumar, S. (C)
Salameh, A.G. (So)
Salmon, D.E. (So)
Scott, R.H. (C)
Sharp, S.D. (C)
Sherman, W.C. (So)
Skey, S.G.P. (H)
Smith, D.T. (C)
Snow, C.H. (C)
Stanway, R.A. (T)
Sykes, A.W. (H)
Talabi, M.A. (T)
Tan, L.K. (P)
Thakur, K.C. (H)
Thomas, B.D. (T)
Thomas, H.R. (So)
Thompson, A.G. (So)
Thomson, G.K. (T)
Trayner, F.S. (P)
Turnbull, R.D. (T)
Valazco-Linares, J.L. (Ho)
Vaziri, H. (C)
Virdi, K.S. (S)
Webb, S.J. (C)
Webster, P.B. (T)
Westlake, D.W. (T)
Whatling, P.F. (C)
White, D.A. (So)
Whitehead, R.P. (C)
Williams, W.J. (T)
Willis, J.G. (T)
Wright, M. (C)
Zakaria, K.A.A. (C)
Zamir, S. (So)

1975

Abbott, J.E. (H)
Abhayagunawardhana, H.A. (T)
Al-Shami, S. (P)
Ang, B.S. (C)
Anning, M.J. (So)
Arulkumarasan, A.R. (C)
Ashford, G.R. (H)
Balen-y-Valenzuela, C.E. (Se)
Bandyopadhyay, B. (C)
Barlow, R.F. (T)
Barry, A.J. (So)
Barum, K. (C)
Basabe, J.M. (So)
Bashorun, A.A. (C)
Basnayake, I.C. (C)
Bathurst, J.C. (Ho)
Beard, A.S. (C)
Bell, A.J. (S)
Bhula, D.N. (S)
Bone, I.H. (T)
Borrows, P.F. (P)
Bozic, B. (Ho)
Brown, B.J.B. (C)
Brown, C. (T)
Budd, D.V. (C)
Bursey, N.C. (T)
Can, R. (Se)
Cardenas-Gutierrez, A. de J. (C)
Chan, K.M. (P)
Che, P.D. (P)
Cheung, L.Y. (S)
Choi, H.S. (So)
Clark, R.G. (So)
Constas, C. (S)
Craig, M.Q. (T)
Crouch, R.E.A. (C)
Dahlgren, J.A. (So)
Daramola, O. (So)
Darby, A.W. (So)
Dartnell, C.M. (H)
Davachi, M.M. (So)
Davey, R.A. (C)
Davies, P. (T)
Djahani, P. (S)
Dixon, A.J. (T)
El-Hag, Y.E.T. (C)
Ellett, B.G.S. (P)
Fieros, N.M. (S)
Flaschner, P.T. (C)
Flintoff, W.T. (So)
Forhead, B.R. (So)
Garry, R.N. (C)
Ghosh, S. (H)
Gibbs, B.P. (H)
Gonzalez-Garcia, A.J. (So)
Haggett, R.A. (S)
Hammer, M.U. (Ho)
Harris, N.T. (So)
Hasan, K.R. (C)
Hilmy, A.H.M. (C)
Homersham, P.G. (P)
Inglis, D.J. (S)
Ioannou, S.C. (S)
Javadi, F.H.S. (C)
Jayanetti, D.L. (Ti)
Kassabian, A.S.A. (H)
Keer, J.G. (C)
Kell, A.D.K. (P)
Kogan, J.H. (T)
Kong-Hean, C. (So)
Kotsovos, M. (C)
Kwakye, E.A. (T)
Lamas, A.R.G. (S)
Larmour, T.F.C. (Ti)
Legge, M.J. (C)
Lekkas, D.T. (P)
Lewis, P.J. (C)
Logothetis, C.P. (C)
Louis, E.D. (T)
Mackie, C.J. (C)
Mantz, P.A. (H)
May, R.W.P. (H)
McCue, K. (Se)
McGlashan, J.E. (H)
McGlynn, R.F. (T)
Mellios, G.A. (So)
Mitchell, J.M. (So)
Mohamed, O.A. (P)
Morgado, M. de P. (C)
Mortensen, S.E. (So)
Mouyiaris, N. (Se)
O'Connell, P.E. (Ho)
Oni, A.M. (C)
Orton, M. (Ho)
Osara, S.I.O. (Ho)
Osibodu, J.E.D. (C)
Osman, B.E.D.E-S (C)
Osunruku, A. (C)
Pachakis, M. (So)
Packman, J.C. (Ho)
Palmer, D.E. (S)
Papageorgiou, E. (So)
Paraskevopoulos, A. (P)
Parfait, M.J.A. (Ho)
Patel, R.C. (P)
Petrie, S.A. (C)
Pidgeon, J.T. (So)
Pimenta, F.C. (C)
Plathe, D.J.R. (Ho)
Powell, J. (So)
Puri, A.K.D.B. (C)
Ramnaney, A. (P)
Robertson, N.F. (So)
Robson, D.A. (S)
Saha, K.D. (P)
Samuel, H.R. (So)
Sanders, R. (T)
Sandroni, S.S. (So)
Simon, J.A. (Ti)
Sinclair, T.J.E. (So)
Singleton, R. (T)
Sioris, J. (H)
Skandalis, I.D.E. (So)
Smith, B.G.A. (Se)
Smith, D.A.Y. (H)
Sodha, V.G. (So)
Tait, W.B. (T)
Triggs, D.M. (P)
Turner, M.F. (C)
Venables, J. (P)
Vinden, P. (Ti)

Waddington, R. (T)
Warriner, D.L. (T)
Wellings, R.A. (P)
Wild, J. (Ho)
Williams, D.H. (C)
Williams, M.R. (So)
Winter, G.M. (C)
Zarraris, P. (C)

1976

Ahmed, I.E. (C)
Albuquerque, A.J.P. de C.E. (H)
Al-Jamil, M.M. (C)
Andreou, D.A. (C)
Ashford, R.A. (S)
Baghirathan, V.R. (Ho)
Barnes, C.P. (C)
Basher, M.J. (So)
Beesley, L.J. (C)
Bhandari, R.K. (So)
Bitar, G.E. (So)
Callington, H.W.
Carydakis, P. (S)
Casanovas-Rodriguez, J.S. (So)
Chabra, H.L. (So)
Chamberlain, D.A. (S)
Chee. S.C. (C)
Chee-Lin, F.S. (Co)
Coombs, M.L. (S)
Cowland, J.W. (So)
Dale, S.G. (So)
Deen, A.R. (Ho)
Dibsi, F. (C)
Egeli, I. (So)
El-Ruwayih, A.A. (So)
Evans, N.S.D. (C)
Flores Mantilla, L.B. (Ti)
Gammon, J.R.A. (So)
Ganendra, T. (Ho)
Gardner, M.J. (S)
Goddard, J.M. (C)
Gunawardana, A.D.S. (H)
Hach, F.M. (Ti)
Hammond, J.S. (Ho)
Hargreaves, A.C. (S)
Hargreaves, M. (C)
Hartley, A.D. (So)
Ionas, D. (T)
Izugbokwe, I.S. (Ti)
Jaros, M.B. (So)
Jowharzadeh, A.M. (S)
Karatas, A. (C)
Khadem, M. (C)
Lalji, M.N. (C)
Lau, K.L. (C)
Lee, D.H. (C)
Legg, R.A. (Ho)
Leitch, H. (So)
Lerner, D.N. (Ho)
Loewenthal, C.M. (Ho)
Luck, R.C. (So)
Ma, C.S.H. (C)
Ma'adhoor, G.J. (So)
Maguire, W.M. (So)
Malde, K. (Ti)
Maun, K.W. (Ti)
McElwain, G.J. De S. (C)
Michael, O.C.W. (Ho)
Mirza, T.A. (S)
Mohajer-Ashjai, F. (C)
Mori, R.T. (So)
Negro, A. (So)
Nicholson, R.E. (So)
Njagi, T.K. (Ti)
Nuncio, J.B. (H)
Ogunbanjo, O.A. (Ti)
O'Hea, A.R. (Ho)
Pan, Y.F. (So)
Paterson, J.M. (C)
Rad, M. (H)
Rauf, A.Q. (C)
Ray, S. (C)
Revell, D.J. (S)
Rikabi, M. (C)
Roy, G.M. (C)
Saad, H.B. (Ti)
Sargeant, D.M. (Ho)
Sayed, M.S. (C)
Scerri, A.E. (Ho)
Schembri, J.V. (C)
Sewell, M. (C)
Shen, J.M. (So)
Shibuya, H. (So)
Shirke, S.G. (So)
Shrivastava, S.M. (C)
Sidamparanathan, T. (C)
Simmersbach, P.O.P.E. (So)
Skinner, A.E. (So)
Skutsch, J.C. (H)
Starace, R. (So)
Stefanakos, J.P. (H)
Tang, T.Y. (S)
Teixeira de Freitas, J.A. (C)
Ulug, I.B. (C)
Valenzuela Palomi, L.A. (So)
Vergara, R.E. (S)
Walker, B.F. (So)
Williams, T.M. (So)
Wright, F.G.I. (C)
Yeung, T. (C)
Zderic, T. (C)

1977

Algar, R.J. (S)
Alexa, P. (Sy)
Amin, K.N.M. (P)
Annandale, W. (P)
Appleton, J.A. da S. (C)
Armaghani, A. (C)
Artemis, A. (Ho)
Balasundaran, S. (C)
Barr, J.M. (C)
Bell, B.C. (C)
Biscoe, P.A. (C)
Bokaian, A.R. (Ho)
Bolton, D.M. (H)
Bonelli Canabes, P.M. (C)
Braune, C. (C)
Brown, V.C. (Ho)
Buckley, D.S. (P)
Bulumulle, U.G. (H)
Carrondo, M.J.T. (P)
Chiari, F.E. (H)
Chionh, C.K. (C)
Chisnall, P.E. (P)
Chu, H.F. (S)
Cooper, M.R. (So)
Cox, R.J. (C)
De Silva, K.T.R. (S)
Donert, K. (T)
Einarsson, B. (S)
Falconer, R.A. (H)
Ford, R.A. (P)
Garcia-Fragio, A. (So)
Gatt, C.P. (C)
George, G.M. (P)
Ghavami, K. (S)
Giersing, B. (So)
Gregorius, B.H. (Ho)
Gladstone, S.C. (C)
Gnanapala, D.P. (C)
Goddard, R.J. (So)
Goldsworthy, M.H. (So)
Gonsalves, A.T.W.A.R. (C)
Grostein, V.A. (T)
Ho, K.S. (Ti)
Ho, T.K. (S)
Holt, J.J. (C)
Hu Son How, W. (Ti)
Illanes, J.A. (So)
Ingham, F.K.R. (P)
Joyce, R.E. (So)
Kenneally, M.R. (C)
Kerr, A.D. (T)
Kharma, N.N. (S)
Kluttz, Jr., B.E. (C)
Labani, J.M. (C)
Lange Ovalle, J.G. (C)
Lawless, A. (S)
Lee, W.C. (So)
Lopez-Valadez, G.A. (Se)
Lupini, J.F. (So)
Mak, S.L. (C)
Matthew, C.I. (C)
Meletiou, C.C. (C)
Mok, T.K. (P)
Momoya, Y. (So)
Mongiovi, L. (So)
Moreea, G.H.A. (C)
Morgan, J.L. (C)
Morrison, I.M. (So)
Murray, J.G. (P)

Naghshineh, A. (Ho)
Nallaiah, S. (Ti)
Nicolacopoulos, L. (T)
Niles, L. (C)
O'Dea, C.P. (C)
Okafor, H.O. (C)
Oliveira, C.C.D. (T)
Ooi, H.B. (C)
Pavlov, R. (Ho)
Pell, C.M. (T)
Perera, M.A.V. (P)
Perry, A.H. (C)
Pinkney, M.W. (C)
Popper, M.S. (T)
Rocha-Filho, P. (So)
Rodriguez-Guillen, H.J. (So)
Sambanther, B. (C)
Senner, D.W.F. (So)
Siddique, A.H. (P)
Sigalas, I. (C)
Sirju, K. (C)
Smith, J.F. (C)
Smith, T.D. (So)
Sofianos, A. (C)
Song, S.H. (P)
Stott, A.J. (Ho)
Styles, D.W. (S)
Sykes, A.W. (So)
Taha, M. (C)
Teh, K.Y. (C)
Toumazis, T.P. (S)
Tsamis, V. (So)
Tsatsanifos, C.D. (So)
Udoumanah, U.E. (T)
Vago, P. (T)
Vargas-Vargas, E. (P)
Velez-Munera, J.I. (T)
Voelker, L.R. (Ho)
Vouyias, S. (T)
Wai, Y.B. (S)
Warren, C.D. (So)
Watters, W.J. (C)
Wong, Y.K. (C)
Woods, K. (Ho)
Yuen, C.W. (So)

1978

Abdula, A.R. (C)
Aminpour, F. (C)
Anderson, I.W. (S)
Andronicou, A. (S)
Anketell, S. (P)
Apted, J.P. (So)
Araya, R. (So)
Bagnall, J.J. (C)
Beltran-Moreno, L. (So)
Blacker, P. (So)
Bowen, A.J. (C)
Boyce, D.L. (C)
Brown, I. (T)
Buri, P.B. (So)
Campbell, B.R. (T)
Carmichael, A.J. (S)
Chan, P.H. (S)
Charmorro Garcia, P. (C)
Choi, J.T-P. (Se)
Chung, K.H.F. (H)
Coatsworth, A.M. (So)
Corcoran, T. (C)
Crossland, I.B. (P)
Danesi, R.F. (C)
Dean, P.J. (T)
Delle Vedove, E. (C)
Dellow, J.R. (T)
De Mello, L.G.F.S. (So)
Dias, S.P. (C)
Dier, A.F. (S)
Dobie, M.J.D. (So)
Dunmore, R.M. (T)
Eastman, R. (T)
Esfandiari, R. (C)
Evans, N.D. (So)
Evans, S.G. (So)
Fahy, W.G. (S)
French, V.J. (C)
Fung, K.W. (C)
Gahir, J.S. (So)
Gay, D.A. (Se)
Gazal, D.A.R. (C)
Gould, J.E. (H)
Graham, N.J.D. (P)
Gray, G.M. (P)
Gunasingham, K. (P)
Hansen, J.F. (C)
Harridge, S.E. (S)
Helliwell, T. (So)
Heng, A.K. (C)
Herbertson, R.P. (So)
Himawan, J. (C)
Hohberg, J.M. (C)
Hudson, R.R. (So)
Jarukasemratana, S. (T)
Jefferies, M.G. (So)
Kariuki, H.K. (Ti)
Khan, M.A.K. (C)
Kiatiprajuksa, S. (P)
King, N.V.N. (So)
Kojic, R. (So)
Leinster, P. (P)
Lim, H-T. (C)
Limpaseni, W. (P)
Loveless, J.H. (H)
Malenya, C.A. (P)
Mardiross, E. (Se)
Martins, M.C.R. (So)
Masood, K. (C)
Matthews, S.J. (S)
McCreath, P.S. (H)
McMahon, P.A. (C)
Memos, C. (H)
Miralles Claver, E. (T)
Mphonde, A.G. (C)
Nicholson, D.P. (So)
Ofori, J. (Ti)
Pajares, E.E. (So)
Panagopoulos, A. (C)
Patel, P. (P)
Pearce, R.W. (So)
Pereira, J.A. (Se)
Picton, D.J. (C)
Ritchie, J.S. (T)
Robb, B.A. (C)
Rogers, B.T. (So)
Rohani, H.A. (C)
Roussopoulos, A. (Se)
Rowling, R.B. (H)
Rutter, P.A. (S)
Samarasinghe, A.S. (C)
Sayer, A.P. (T)
Schlegel, F. (T)
Shahrestani, F. (C)
Short, I. (H)
Silk, M.D. (T)
Soares, H.F. (So)
Sobers, P.T. (C)
Taiwo, G.B. (So)
Tam, Y.K. (C)
Tang, T.H. (P)
Thomson, R.G. (C)
Tolliday, J.F. (P)
Truscott, E.G. (So)
Van Cauwenberghe, A. (T)
Vanicek, I. (So)
Villate Supelano, G. (T)
West, S.J. (C)
Willson, I.R. (P)
Wilson, T.J. (Ti)
Woo, F.A. (P)
Wu, M.W. (P)
Yassuda, C.T. (So)

1979

Adeola, K.A. (H)
Alves Moreira, J.J.R.G. (C)
Anagnostopoulos, D. (P)
Anagnostopoulos, A. (So)
Andricopoulos, K. (Se)
Ayres, R.C. (C)
Baple, J.P. (So)
Barouki, N. (C)
Baughen, D.J. (S)
Bayne, J.M. (So)
Beake, R.H. (So)
Black, R.D. (T)
Bottom, S.T. (H)
Brindley, C.S. (T)
Bugden, P.S. (H)
Byron-Moore, C.P. (C)
Calhau, J.N. (P)
Cashman, A.C. (So)
Chan, K.H. (C)
Chapman, D.T. (P)
Charnock, G. (P)
Cheah, L.S. (So)

Childs, M. (C)
Chong, Y.P. (Ti)
Clare, D.G. (So)
Crichton, S.C. (S)
Dapre, R.L. (T)
Davies, S.F. (C)
Davis, P.D. (So)
Dawson, A.R. (So)
Donald, R.G. (T)
Echeta, C.B. (C)
Edmonds, J.C. (C)
Ejindu, F.C. (C)
El-Ghamrawy, M.K.A.K. (So)
Essler, R.D. (So)
Evans, T.G. (So)
Finlayson, D.M. (Se)
Fitzell, T.P. (Se)
Ford, D.M. (Ti)
Foulds, N.W. (C)
Fraser, R. (S)
Gadhok, S. (P)
Gibbs, L.T. (P)
Golias, J. (T)
Haile, J.P. (So)
Harrison, I.R. (So)
Hau, J.W. (S)
Heiden, T. (P)
Ho, H.S. (C)
Honarbakhsh, S. (S)
Hughes, L.G.S. (So)
Ip, C.T. (T)
Iqbal, M. (T)
Jahanshabi, J. (S)
Jewell, P.J. (So)
Jobbins, J.W. (C)
Kanitakis, I.M. (C)
Keenan, M.M.M. (T)
Kerr, R.P. (T)
King, C.M. (S)
Knudsen, A. (C)
Kondogeorgi, M. (C)
Krige, G.J. (S)
Krimitas, G. (C)
Kubba, M.M. (C)
Laidler, D.W. (P)
Lawson, C.J. (C)
Lee, V.J. (P)
Lemyre, M. (C)
Leung, S.W. (C)
Lewis, J.S. (T)
Lisboa, C.D.J. (Ti)
Lock, R.R. (P)
Lopes, F.D.R. (So)
Loyer, J.P.E.F. (C)
Lozano, H. (P)
Luscombe, R.W. (C)
Machin, A.G. (C)
Maguiness, J.A. (H)
Mak, K.M.M. (C)
Marino Fernandez, M.G. (P)
Milford, R.V. (C)
Mills, C.A. (C)
Moorwood, L.H.R. (Se)
Nicholson, R.W. (S)
Ogwude, I.C. (T)
Ormerod, S. (H)
Paraskevopoulos, P.N. (H)
Patel, N.S. (P)
Perelberg, S. (So)
Phoon, W.H. (P)
Piper, B.F.F. (S)
Pitrakkos, P.P. (S)
Pitsiava, M. (T)
Poullaides, M.A. (C)
Rajbhandari, L.G. (Ti)
Ramrattan, D. (C)
Rasbash, J.B.J. (P)
Read, G.H. (P)
Robinson, S.J. (H)
Roebuck, I.H. (P)
Rossin, A.C. (P)
Rukkatanyou, T. (So)
Sadka, K.B. (C)
Schmidiger, R.I. (So)
Shaakerin, S. (S)
Shah, B.A. (C)
Sivaloganathan, S. (C)
Snow, M.A. (So)
Sofianos, A. (So)
Sowden, I.M. (C)
Stevens, C. (So)
Tan, H.L. (P)
Tang, N.C. (So)
Tantawi, H.M. (C)
Thomas, D.M. (T)
Towers, D.G. (So)
Townsley, C.H. (T)
Treadgold, P. (H)
Treanor, P. (T)
Troconis, F.-C.-M. (Se)
Tyrimou, R. (Se)
Vazeos, C. (T)
Watt, P.H. (So)
Wickramage, M. (P)

1980

Adebowale, A. (C)
Adesesan, F.A. (P)
Adewumi, J.B.O. (Ho)
Anagnostopoulos, P. (H)
Arabaci, A. (S)
Arbaiza, C.E. (Ti)
Arsenault, L. (C)
Atapattu, D. (Ho)
Ayub, A. (C)
Badger, R.B. (P)
Baker, G. (C)
Balthaus, H. (So)
Bedard, C. (C)
Bier, H. (Ti)
Blower, D.J.G. (So)
Bow, P. (S)
Bracegirdle, A. (Se)
Bradley, I. (So)
Buckton, C.R. (C)
Chan, K.S.R. (So)
Chan, P.W.E. (C)
Chan Chim Yuk, C.W. (So)
Chandler, M.P. (So)
Chipp, P.N. (So)
Choi, K. (Ho)
Conejo, J.G.L. (Ho)
Cowton, N.A. (P)
De Campos, T.M.P. (So)
Demachkie, M.N.M.N. (P)
Devalia, M.M. (P)
Dzam, B.M. (Ti)
Egbeolu, M.A. (T)
Fletcher, P.K. (C)
Fordyce, W.A. (S)
Franca, P.C. (S)
Gardner, K.E. (T)
Glennie, C.E.R. (P)
Goh, H.S. (C)
Griffin, H.G. (C)
Grillo, S.D.Q. (So)
Gupta, R.K. (S)
Hadjistephanou, A. (C)
Ho Kai Ming, L. (H)
Hong, G.M. (S)
Hopkins, P. (P)
Howell, P. (So)
Hui, K.C. (C)
Hunter, A.M. (So)
Hussain, M.B. (C)
Jennings, D.N. (Se)
Jiee, D. (So)
Jukes, A.W. (So)
Kenny, J. (C)
Laporte Pirie, M. (Se)
Leung, W.C. (C)
Liem, S.T. (Ti)
Lie, S.T. (S)
Lighthall, P.C. (So)
Ling, K.W.F. (S)
Luong, T.V. (P)
Mackley, I.C. (P)
Mangan, D.P.A. (So)
Mantzos, D. (Ho)
Maoza, A.A. (P)
Martins, J.P. (So)
Mason, D.K. (P)
Michael, P.D. (S)
Mir, H.A. (C)
Mok, W.H. (C)
Moore, A. (C)
Morrison, M.J.W. (So)
Naing, N.S. (Ti)
Ngirane, G.G.K. (Ho)
Nicol, B.J. (H)
Olia, S.B. (Ti)
Oludare, O. (C)
Palma-Vergara, M.E.L. (T)
Papanastasiou, C. (C)
Pappas, D. (T)

Patel, J.S. (C)
Peters, C.J. (P)
Petsas, I. (T)
Pilitsi, A. (Se)
Pires Santana, F.J. (P)
Ponnampalan, S. (So)
Porter, M.S. (S)
Presern, B. (T)
Rackham, J.W. (S)
Rand, R.P. (C)
Raoof, M. (C)
Riveros Rojas, M.E. (P)
Shum, W.T. (C)
Simoes, L.M.D.C. (C)
Sin, M.T. (C)
Sinnatamby, G.S. (P)
Siu, F.P.M.Y. (Ti)
Somers, N.R. (So)
Spiliopoulos, C. (C)
Stamper, A. (P)
Stillman, A.J. (P)
Swann, L.H. (So)
Tashman-Nurhalim, R.P. (Ti)
Tasou, P.C. (S)
Teoh, S.E. (T)
Tharnthong, L. (C)
Thong, K.H. (S)
Torpiano, A. (C)
Tsani-Bezaca, E.S. (P)
Tsikkos, S. (C)
Tullett, P.J. (T)
Unuigbe, C.A. (T)
Vaziri-Zanjani, H. (So)
Waldron, P. (C)
Watson, A.I. (P)
Wong, M. (T)
Wong Wai Kwong, P. (P)
Yang, C.M. (C)
Zanna, B.G. (Ho)

1981

Abeliuk Rimsky, R.I. (P)
Abraham, J.C. (C)
Adler, M.A. (So)
Almeida, E.D.N.D. (P)
Al-Saidi, N.Z. (C)
Anderson, W.P.D. (So)
Andrews, G.G.C. (C)
Armstrong, B. (S)
Asgian, M.I. (So)
Avril, T.P. (H)
Bamshad, A.R. (C)
Bannister, J. (So)
Barnwell, C.L. (So)
Bell, A.E. (So)
Bhatt, H.R. (T)
Biszewski, P.A. (T)
Bouche, J-H-M (C)
Brazil, A.M.C. (C)
Brown, M.J. (P)
Burnton, P.A. (C)
Cepollina, M. (So)
Chan, C.W.P. (So)
Chang Fong, J. (C)
Cheung, C.H. (C)
Cheung, C.S.M. (C)
Chinas Ramirez, G.E. (So)
Claridge, K. (P)
Clinton, D.B. (So)
Cloke, P.S. (Ho)
Constantacos, M. (So)
Cook, S.C. (P)
De Bono, C. (P)
Dimka, J.B.S. (T)
Donkoh, D.K.N. (C)
Doyle, P.F. (C)
Duffin, M.J. (So)
Edde, R.E.K. (C)
Edmeades, P.M. (Ho)
Eetemaadi-Idgaahi, M. (Se)
Egbulem, A.N. (Ho)
Elnashai, A.S. (C)
El Sawi Mohammed, O. (So)
Ffrench, R.G. (C)
Gaba, A.R. (So)
Garcia Gutierrez, A. (P)
Gerrard, P. (C)
Gill, C.D.C. (C)
Giotis Son of Ioannis, A. (S)
Grant, J.T. (S)
Gruber, T.J.R. (C)
Gunn, N.J. (C)
Harris, A.J. (So)
Harris, M.N. (So)
Haworth, R.G. (S)
Hewavisenthi, A.C. de S. (Ho)
Ho, K.S. (C)
Hodgins, R.M. (P)
Hodgson, R.L.P. (So)
Hollingsworth, P.F. (C)
Hollingworth, G.H. (T)
Hutchison, R.J. (So)
Ioannou, M.A. (So)
Jackson, L.R. (S)
James, C.D. (C)
Jardine, R.J. (So)
Jeanes, M.J.F. (T)
Jenkins, R.D. (So)
Jones, M.O. (P)
Kairis, N. (T)
Kankam, C.K. (C)
Kearney, J.P. (S)
Kkolos, A. (C)
Koullis, C.L. (Ho)
Lam, T.C. (C)
Lam, W.M. (C)
Lau, A.K.U. (S)
Lee, H.K. (C)
Lester, J.N. (P)
Lo, S.C. (C)
Loh, A.T. (P)
Lovell, D.J. (So)
MacInnes, A.I. (T)
Masui, N. (C)
Maswoswe, J. (So)
Mayhew, A.J. (S)
McIntyre, A.E. (P)
McLaughlin, R.S. (So)
McLeod, H.N. (So)
Mello, E.L. (Sy)
Miller, C.J. (So)
Monteith, D.J. (C)
Namasivayam, R. (So)
Newman, R.L. (So)
Obeng, L.A. (P)
O'Canainn, E. (S)
Ofori, D.K. (P)
Olabenjo, O.O. (P)
Parabaran, B. (Ho)
Peerun, S. (T)
Pinho Santos, J.M.D. (P)
Scott, P.A.R. (P)
Seneviratne, P.N. (T)
Shuttleworth, E.P. (C)
Smith, A.P.L. (Ho)
Soothill, J.C. (Ti)
Spink, T.W. (So)
Stamou, A. (P)
Stefanou, N. (C)
Sterritt, R.M. (P)
Tajlil, A. (S)
Taka, A.M. (C)
Thom, M.J. (So)
Thomson, N.A. (P)
Thurairatnam, I.P. (P)
Waboso, D.G. (P)
Walsh, N.M. (So)
Webb, S.E. (S)
Webster, P. (Ho)
Wilkinson, D.J. (C)
Wong, W-H.A. (S)
Yu, K.F. (C)
Zakaria, M.L. (Ti)

1982

Abeysekera, W.A.K.M. (Ho)
Abidi, Y.A. (So)
Adnan, N. (S)
Alibey, J.R. (C)
Alim, S. (C)
Aphamis, P.D. (C)
Augustin, P.C. (C)
Avgerinos, G. (S)
Bealing, P.E. (So)
Bell, N.C. (Ho)
Bodimeade, C.S. (So)
Brennan, M.G. (C)
Buenfeld, N.R. (C)
Bufill, M.C. (Ho)
Burke, J.J. (Ho)
Butler, D. (P)
Calderwood, W.R. (S)
Candler, C.J. (So)

Carney, S.J. (S)
Carolan, J.P. (S)
Caseau, C.J. (T)
Chakrabarti, S. (S)
Chamley, P.J. (So)
Chandra, U.S. (P)
Chan, T.P. (So)
Cheong, H.K. (C)
Cheung, T.C. (C)
Chiu, S.L. (So)
Cripps, J.E. (S)
Davary Dowlatabady, M. (C)
Demetriou, T. (C)
Denner, J.M. (P)
Fawcett, B.N. (P)
Fort, D.S. (So)
Fowler, J.N. (Se)
Guganesharajah, K. (Ho)
Harjono, B. (S)
Hasham, A.J. (P)
Hayakawa, T. (P)
Healy, P.T. (C)
Henley, J.P. (T)
Herbert, J.C. (P)
Hogg, I.G.G. (Ho)
Holloway, M.H.W. (C)
Huggard, R.C.E. (C)
Ibrahim, R.O. (C)
Jarvis, S.T. (So)
Jefferd, C.J. (P)
Jenkins, D.R. (C)
Jones, D.C. (So)
Jones, W. (S)
Kennett, P. (So)
Kufuor, K.G. (C)
Kwan, C.Y. (S)
Lam, S.W. (C)
Langdon, N.J. (So)
Lemos, L.J.L. (Se)
Leroy, Y.M. (C)
Leung, C.H. (So)
Llopiz, C.R. (C)
Madi, U.R. (Sy)
Marriott, M.J. (P)
Matawal, D.S. (So)
Meigh, J.R. (Ho)
Mendez, M.D.P. (So)
Menu, J-M-H (Se)
Miller, A.J.E. (T)
Mirihagalla, P.K. (P)
Mitchell, R.J. (P)
Mo, T.K.A. (S)
Morales, S.E. (T)
Morris, D.R. (C)
Morris, M.J. (S)
Morris, P.M. (P)
Mui, C.K. (C)
Nicholls , J.C. (S)
Nolan, D.K. (So)
Nublat, M.H. (C)
Obayagbonna, E.A. (S)
Ocloo, J.K. (Ti)
Phillips, A.K. (C)
Ponte Ramirez, R.R. (Ho)
Ramirez Piedrabuena, A.(Se)
Roche, M.J. (C)
Rossi, A. (C)
Samarasuriya, K.M. (P)
Santos, M.P.D.S. (T)
Sarshar, B. (T)
Scott, P. (S)
Seghal, K.V. (T)
Seow, K.L. (T)
Skomedal, E. (T)
Smit, E.L. (C)
Stevens, M.G.H. (So)
Stewart, G.M. (Ho)
Sully, J.P. (So)
Szeto, W.Y. (Se)
Takahashi, M. (So)
Tambling, R.F. (P)
Tan, S.L. (Se)
Tchibindat, F. (P)
Teng, K.H. (Ti)
Thomson, R.I. (Ho)
Titus, P.A. (C)
Townsend, G.H. (Ho)
Tsang, S.K. (S)
Valero, F.J. (T)
Vassiades, C.S. (So)
Watson, P.S. (C)
Weldu, F. (Ho)
Wood, S. (T)
Worrell, A.C.J. (S)
Wu, W.S. (C)
Zapitis, S.M. (C)

1983

Abubakar, H.Z. (C)
Allen, S.J. (Ho)
Andoh, R.Y.G. (P)
Andreou, I.I. (So)
Baker, J.M. (P)
Botsford, C.G. (So)
Branter, M.J. (So)
Brown, R.S. (So)
Bulama, M. (C)
Burbidge, M.C. (So)
Burne, S.S. (Ho)
Calkin, D.W. (So)
Chambers, J.J. (C)
Chattopadhyay, A. (So)
Chembi, A.B. (Ti)
Chen, N. (S)
Cheng, K.T. (C)
Cheung, C.M. (C)
Chodorowski, A.R. (So)
Choi, Y-C. (So)
Coulson, J.B. (P)
Cronin, M.M. (C)
Crooks, C.R. (P)
Delahaye, N.A. (So)
Dickson, D.M. (S)
Dina, A.A. (C)
Dinic, G. (C)
Evans, J.J.B. (C)
Firth, I.P.T. (S)
Fletcher, A.M. (Ho)
Futa, M.A. (C)
Germanopoulos, G. (Ho)
Godfrey, P.R. (S)
Haygreen, S.R. (So)
Holden, J.M.W. (So)
Ip, S.P.R. (C)
Jenkins, W.O. (P)
Kanhai, K. (C)
Kelly, J.A. (C)
Kirk, P.W.W. (P)
Kotecha, P. (So)
Lam, A. (So)
Lam, K.W.W. (So)
Lam, N.T.K. (C)
Lee, S.C. (C)
Lewis, C.A.M.A. (C)
Liao, H.J. (So)
Lie, L.T. (C)
Liversidge, P.W. (P)
Luk, P.C.K. (S)
Mak, N.S.C. (Se)
Marangos, C. (C)
Masterton, G.G.T. (C)
McKenzie, A. (So)
Mohammed-Yunus, A.K.B. (Ti)
Newbery, M.J. (So)
Ng, C.L. (So)
Nicolaou, S. (C)
Nsanya, Z.D.M. (C)
Nutt, J.L. (So)
Onabolu, O.A. (C)
Ovando-Shelley, E. (Se)
Parry, L.N. (So)
Pathmanandavel, S. (Se)
Perry, J.R. (C)
Roberts, P.W.D.H. (T)
Rogers, C.C.M. (Ho)
Ronalds, B.F. (S)
Rowlinson, S.M. (C)
Shaaban, M.G.B. (P)
Shepherd, N.B. (P)
Shrestha, P.R. (P)
Surendranath, M.K. (Ti)
Symes, M.J.P.R. (So)
Tam, W.S. (So)
Tang, C.Y. (C)
Tjahyadikarta, F. (S)
Tsatsanifos, C. (Se)
Vijayaratnam, K. (P)
Wilkinson, G.D. (So)
Wright, D.J.M. (S)
Wright, P.M. (So)
Wylie, G.B. (C)
Yau, Y.W.M. (So)
Yeung, S.K. (So)
Zarrabi, F. (Ti)

~ Appendix D ~

Awards of the City & Guilds of London Institute

Fellowship of the City & Guilds Institute (FCGI) Awards

1892	Humphrey, H.A. (C&M 1885–87)
1904	Booth, H.C. (C&M 1889–92)
1907	Young, A.E. (C&M 1887–90)
1912	Chatterton, Sir Alfred, CIE (C&M 1885–87)
1920	Gore, W. (C&M 1893–96)
1925	Ackerman, A.S.E. (C&M 1890–92)
	Bramwell, F.H. (C&M 1906–09)
	Latham, E. (C&M 1900–03)
1928	Buckley, A.B., OBE (C&M 1893–96)
	Cookson, A.C. (C&M 1885–88)
	Tripp, G.W., OBE (C&M 1904–06)
1929	Faber, O., CBE (C&M 1903–06)
	Gibbs, G.J. (C&M 1885–88)
	Wilson, J.S. (C&M 1893–96)
1931	Martin, H.M. (C&M 1885–87)
1932	Carmichael, A. (C&M 1901–04)
	Freeman, Sir Ralph (C&M 1897–1900)
1933	Hicks, G.A. (C&M 1896–99)
	Thornycroft, Sir John E., KBE (C&M 1890–92)
1934	Lacey, S. (C&M 1902–05)
	Price, B., OBE (C&M 1893–96)
	Witchell, Emeritus Professor E.F.D. (C&M 1898–1901)
1935	Dalby, Emeritus Professor W.E. (Honorary)
	Dowson, Sir Ernest M., KBE (C&M 1895–98)
	Hummel, F.H. (C&M 1899–92)
	Mitchell, W.C. (C&M 1908–10)
1936	Hartley, A.C., CBE (C&M 1908–10)
	Walker, E.G. (C&M 1902–04)
1937	Baker, R.F. (C&M 1893–96)
	Lloyd Jones, C.W., CIE (C&M 1897–1900)
1939	Goodwin, L.F. (C&M 1895–98)
1940	Armstrong, H.C., OBE (C&M 1896–99)
1941	van Ryneveld, Sir Pierre, KBE, CB, DSO, MC, DFC (C&M 1911–14)
1944	Bate, E., MC (C&M 1905–08)
	Whalley, F.S., MC (C&M 1903–05)
1946	Pendred, L.StL., CBE (C&M 1886–87)
	Sams, C.E.R. (C&M 1894–95)
	Sproull, A.W., CB, CBE (C&M 1911–14)
1949	Grinsted, H., CBE (C&M 1906–09)
	Lacey, G., CIE (C&M 1904–07)
	Mitchell, Sir Kenneth, KCIE (C&M 1903–07)
1951	Blair, A., CBE (C&M 1906–08)
	Shooshith, H. (C&M 1886–88)
1952	Cronin, H.F., CBE, MC (C&M 1913–14: 1919–20)
	Harding, Sir Harold (Civil 1917–18: 1918–22)
	Roach, W.H.G., MBE (Civil 1919–21)
1953	James, R.T., OBE (Civil 1917–21)
1954	Reed, Sir Ralph (C&M 1902–05)
1955	Pain, J.F., MC (Civil 1916–17: 1918–21)
	Rolt, F.H., OBE (C&M 1906–08)

1956 Montagu, A.M.R., CIE (C&M 1911-13)
1957 Hopewell, G.H. (C&M 1913-14: 1917-19)
1958 Brazier, L.G. (Civil 1919-22)
Duvivier, J. (Civil 1918-21)
Spencer, Sir Kelvin, CBE (Civil 1919-22)
1959 Hawes, C.G., CIE, MC (C&M 1906-10)
Malkani, T.M. (Civil 1926-30)
Morgan, H.D. (Civil 1923-26)
Skempton, Professor A.W. (Civil 1932-36)
1962 Holder, Professor D.W. (Civil 1940-43)
1964 Butten, E.E. (Electrical 1919-21; Civil 1921-22)
Faber, S.E. (C&M 1909-12)
Main, J.F. (Civil 1920-23)
Roberts, Sir Gilbert (Civil 1920-22)
Shirley-Smith, Sir Hubert (Civil 1919-23)
1965 Buchanan, Professor Sir Colin, CBE (Civil 1924-29)
Dean, A. (Civil 1921-23)
1967 Braddick, H.J.W. (Civil 1930-33)
Otter, J.R.H. (Civil 1923-26)
1968 Jenkins, R.S. (Civil 1927-30)
Measor, E.O. (Civil 1924-27)
1969 Fitt, R.L., CMG (Civil 1924-27)
1972 Gowring, G.I.B. (Civil 1918-21)
Payne, N.J., CBE (Civil 1945-49)
Sowden, J.P. (Civil 1935-38)
1975 Coode, D.C., CBE (Civil 1928-31)
Gerrard, R.T. (Civil 1934-37)
New, D.H., ERD (Civil 1929-32)
1976 Baxter, J.W., CBE (Civil 1933-36)
1977 Ackers, P. (Civil 1942-44)
Walton, E.W.K., GC, DSC (Civil 1936-39)
Wood, G., CBE (Civil 1929-31)
1978 Zienkiewicz, Professor O.C. (Civil 1940-45)
1979 Cox, P.A. (Civil 1940-42)
Elliott, A.J. (Civil 1940-42)
Wild, R.M. (Civil 1935-38)
1980 Gibson, Professor R.E. (Civil 1943-45: 1947-53)
1982 Edwards, J.T. (Civil 1937-41)
Makowski, Professor Z.S. (Civil 1951-62)
Neal, Professor B.G. (Honorary)
Wex, B.P., OBE (Civil 1946-49)
1983 Kolbuszewski, Professor J. (Civil 1945-48)
Neal, H.M. (Civil 1950-53)

Associateship of the City & Guilds Institute (ACGI) Awards

1887
Chatterton, A.
Chatterton, B.
Humphrey, H.A.
Martin, H.M.

1888
Coates, G.A.
Cookson, A.C.
Gibbs, G.J.
Jones, H.W.
Jones, J.R.
Shoosmith, H.

1889
Bluck, M.F.N.
Burgess, W.E.
Jones, O.G.
Lewis, A.R.
Stoney, E.D.

1890
Conradi, J.F.
Mayes, G.R.
Young, A.E.

1891
Andreoli, M.
Shelford, F.
Wright, R.B.

1892
Ackermann, A.S.E.
Booth, H.C.
Cooke, C.A.
Hummel, F.H.
Lloyd, G.E.
Thornycroft, J.E.
Wood, H.M.

1893
Digby, K.W.
Drysdale, C.V.
Fry, G.A.
Hadwen, T.L.D.
Heelas, G.H.
Joselin, E.L.
Krall, R.F.
Leake, H.C.
Robinson, H.F.
Roe, R.D.T.

Sonneborn, A.E.H.
Sussman, W.T.W.

1894
Abbott, N.
Aldis, B.S.
Bushell, C.L.
Carter, R.B.
Cautley, A.O.
Hall, A.C.
Hallett, A.
James, J.H.
Lightfoot, C.
Lloyd, H.G.
Maeers, F.
Stubbs, B.T.
Thomas, W.

1895
Andrewes, H.S.
Arnould, G.G.
Chapman, J.E.
Fenwick, H.E.
Hainworth, C.S.
Hainworth, E.W.
Hewett, B.H.M.
Hummel, E.W.
Morgan, F.E.
Reeves, R.E.
Robinson, H.
Wolsely-Lewis, F.T.

1896
Baker, R.F.
Barry, I.
Bayley, D.H.
Buckley, A.B.
Cooper, V.
Gore, W.
Jaffé, D.J.
Jones, J.A.
Kenrick, A.
Kirkby, H.M.
MacColl, A.M.
Mair, G.P.
Perry, G.S.
Price, B.
Salmon, C.E.H.
Saunders, H.J.
Temple, L.
Weekes, M.G.
Wilson, J.S.

1897
Cornish, J.E.
Drury, H.D.
Hanbury, H.W.
Jacomb-Hood, M.
Lewis, A.W.
Malim, J.C.
Rich, T.
Shackle, C.E.
Solomon, R.S.
Unwin, W.P.
Williams, J.W.
Willis, J.B.

1898
Byrde, E.A.
Cantrell, W.C.
Chambers, H.K.
Dowson, E.M.
Dupré, H.A.
Elworthy, A. W.
Fowler, S.M.
Gnosspelius, O.T.
Grant, A.M.
Guttmann, L.
Naz, J.L.
Neild, H.A.
Powell, H.J.B.
Stewart, D.M.
Warner, H.M.
Waters, W.
Waters, W.L.
Winter, E.C.
Wright, C.G.

1899
Ackery, A.P.
Armstrong, H.C.
Arthur, R.
Bryden, C.A.
Cook, E.W.
Craig, W.H.P.
Dunell, H.
Gowan, S.
Hackforth, P.
Hammersley-Heenan, J.
Hicks, G.A.
Hounsfield, A.G.
Hunter, J.I.
Parker, J.A.
Reynolds, A.
Robertson, S.
Schoeberlein, F.
Smith, T.B.
Tisdall, A.D.
Trier, F.N.
Way, E.
White, W.
Whittle, F.E.

1900
Bowrey, J.M.
Bromley-Smith, A.
Butler, J.F.
Clark, A.H.
Clay, W.H.C.
Collins, R.H.
Culley, A.E.
Dennis, F.
Duke, B.M.
Freeman, R.
Jones, C.W.
Knight, A.J.
Leslie, S.
Munro, A.J.
Osbourn, F.
Rusdell, W.J.
Topley, J.W.M.
Unwin, H.B.
Wickham, J.A.

1901
Adams, F.G.T.
Apted, F.E.
Ball, J.D.W.
Brounger, W.H.P.
Cerda, J.E.
Collins, W.A.
Cue, B.F.
Dunell, B.
Gilliland, A.H.
Glanville, E.A.
Jackson, R.H.
Jennings, F.P.
Martin, R.H.
Monk, R.G.
Nisbet, W.S.
Pinel, F.H.
Richards, B.D.
Wessel, H.L.
Whittle, B.A.
Witchell, E.F.D.

1902
Burton, W.A.
Chappell, E.
Crawford, M.N.
Ellis, J.A.
Elsden, F.V.
Esnouf, J.A.
Firmston, E.V.
Folk, S.M.
Hardy, R.G.
Hubbard, A.E.
Leclézio, A.J.A.
Madge, L.G.
Mann, T.H.
Manson, F.P.
Maxwell, G.H.
Moran, H.
Napper, W.E.
Payne, L.T.
Rampal, L.M.
Saxby-Thomas, H.G.

1903
Baxter, H.H.
Bayley, H.F.
Bender, W.E.G.
Biden, S.W.
Borns, G.W.M.
Capito, C.E.

Fox, J.R.
Gatehouse, E.A.
Griffin, J.D.
Guttmann, C.J.
Harley-Mason, V.B.
Hingston, W.H.
Lace, E.W.
Latham, E.
Lautour, E. de
Lehuraux, R.E.
Maynard, F.E.
McGregor, J.E.M.
Munro, R.C.
Ormiston-Chant, T.C.
Porteous, D.A.S.
Rampal, L.F.
Rice-Oxley, M.K.
Salberg, F.J.
Salt, E.A.
Satow, C.F.
Scoones, A.E.
Segrave, J.H.
Smith, C.G.
Smith, V.C.
Thompson, C.E.
Wallace, T.W.

1904
Artola Soruco, J.M. de
Banister, W.G.
Barnes, A.A.
Beggs, G.A.
Bond, F.S.
Bowen, S.
Bowers, L.J.G.
Carmichael, A.
Cory, E.M.
Creedy, H.D.
Daniell, O.C.
Dupré, J.A.V.
Elliott, S.S.
Garforth, T.G.
Gibbs, C.W.
Griffin, G.R.
Liebstein, H.R.
Maas, N.N.
Neuhaus, F.
Newton, H.A.
Osler, R.H.
Peters, R.
Pole, E.F.R.
Robinson, R.B.
Strachan, W.S.
Street, A.H.
Teulon, A.H.
Thomas, O.W.
Udale, S.M.
Van der Meersch, A.E.M.
Vogel, R.F.
Walker, E.G.
Walker, F.E.
Wheaton, H.J.
Wilder, H.H.
Wooding, J.W.

1905
Allen, R.W.
Baissac, C.M.
Balding, C.J.
Beale, A.M.
Bridge, G.E.W.
Buttemer, R.W.
Cooper, F.C.
Denney, J.A.
Guggenheim, L.J.M.
Halse, G.W.
Herbert, C.
Hodgkinson, J.
Job, C.B.
King, L.
Lacey, S.
Laing, A.J.H.
Mitchell, A.R.
Montgomery, J.E.
Newton, K.
Reed, A.R.
Regnard, L.M.
Smith, G.M.

1906
Atchison, C.F.
Barber, C.G.
Bender, H.C.
Betteley, E.S.C.
Blomfield, D.J.
Branch, A.C.
Coles, S.
Daman, J.H.P.
Dani, P.G.
Davis, J.G.
Faber, O.
Farrer, A.W.
Friedrichs, F.
Gaudin, R.F.B.
Hardingham, L.W.
Hilditch, G.W.
Hutton, C.G.
Irens, M.H.
James, E.H.
Kinsey, A.F.StJ.
Lauth, C.H.
Light, R.V.
Maunsell, G.A.
Meier, F.A.
Nightingale, C.E.
Northcote, H.F.
Purday, H.F.P.
Quertier, R.L.
Sayer, S.A.
Stevens, F.K.
Street, F.C.
Tripp, G.W.
Vipan, A.
Vogel, H.E.T.
Willis, T.A.
Wilson, C.M.
Woodbridge, L.A.

1907
Adey, D.F.
Ball, G.W.M.
Barnaby, K.C.
Barrow, F.G.
Bate, E.
Bland, M.G.
Bowers, E.N.
Bowie, P. G.
Bradforth, B.V.
Busfield, J.L.
Butler, S.G.
Clarke, P.
Comber, W.G.
Cooper, H.
Dennes, N.
Dowse, R.J.G.
Fitzherbert, R.A.
Flanagan, J.H.W.
Foster, E.
Francis, H.G.
Gade, F.G.
Geneve, M.C.A.H.
Glennie, S.
Goodfellow, E.A.F.
Gulland, R.G.K.
Haggard, D.A.
Harrison, G.R.
Hickey, P.F.
Hindson, G.C.
Holt-White, W.H.
Hoskings, H.G.
Lace, W.H.
Lacey, G.
Lines, G.E.
Maflin, A.J.G.
Middleton, H.E.
Mitchell, K.G.
Neal, A.M.
North, O.D.
Parker, T.H.G.
Parrott, R.J.
Pearse, J.W.
Piat, A.C.
Pook, S.H.
Shire, L.G.W.
Smith, R.A.B.
Sneyd, R.S.
Stack, G.F.C.
Taylor, H.W.O.
Thieme, H.C.A.
Tildesley, C.E.
Vogel, J.H.
Webb, W.J.
Weeks, S.F.
Whitaker, W.L.

1908
Archer, J. O.

Avery, G.
Bartlett, P.A.B.
Batham, W.S.
Bender, C.A.
Bramwell, F.H.
Burton, T.G.H.
Chadwick, P.M.
Cleaver, C.F.
Collins, A.
Engelbach, R.
English, A.
Fondaumiere, J.L.H.J. de
Forster, F.N.
Furlong, H.W.
Gammon, J.C.
Genève, L.F.C.A.
Gorringe, H.M.
Gregory, M.S.
Grinsted, H.
Haskew, B.B.
Hawdon, C.S.
Hooper, L.D.
Hudson-Spence, E.
Husbands, P.P.
Jones, A.E.
Jones, H.A.
Joscelyne, H.A.
Ker, S.D.
Lear, C.F.
Le Meur, J.J.A.C.
Lindemann, O.A.
Livingstone-Learmonth, A.P.
Low, A.M.
Manes, J.F.L.
Masters, A.H.
Matthews, E.F.
Morris, R.D.
O'Brien, H.M.V.
Olliff-Lee, W.N.
Pilditch, E.
Pook, R.A.
Porter-Makin, J.G.
Richards, E.V.
Ripley, O.H.
Rolt, F.H.
Russell, C.H.
Saker, A.L.
Scheult, L.G.
Selby, A.C.
Smith, E.R.
Swan, J.B.R.
Taylor, R.W.
Unwin, R.B.
Wells, P.H.P.
Woodbridge, W.E.
Wylie, A.F.
Young, S.G.

1909
Beacham, T.E.
Bennett, W.D.
Bevan, A.B.B.
Budden, G.W.
Burdett, H.L.
Castelain, J.J.
Chopra, S.N.
Clarke, H.G.G.
Clougher, N.M.
Cook, H.F.
Coutanceau, L.J.
Cueto, L. del
Cunningham, F.J.
Darwin, G.M.
Deuchar, W.R.
Donkin, C.T.B.
FitzSimon, S.E.
Fraser, A.R.
Gilbert, L.B.
Graham, C.G.
Grundy, F.
Hall, G.F.
Harland, H.B.
Harrington, G.H.
Hepburn, G.
Herford, R.O.
Hitchcock, G.E.W.
Holzapfel, G.L.
Houfton, C.M.
Howe, E.
Hughes, B.A.R.
Hunter, J.W.
Jamieson, C.W.
Jones, H.P.B.
Kent, H.T.M.
Korgaokar, H.K.
Kynnersley, T.R.S.
Laughton, G.C.
MacKinnon, A.
Manes, J.L.E.
Mitchell, C.G.
Morant, A.
Osborn, G.
Osborne, S.H.G.
Pougnet, E.D.
Quinton, W.G.
Rodriguez, M.
Shaw, C.A.
Stephens, T.A.
Sturgess, A.R.
Swain, L.H.
Tann, J.L.
Thomas, W.T.
Thompson, H.M.
Thorpe, H.C.
Travers, L.A.
Vallet, L.J.A.
Vyall, F.S.
Wadia, J.
Wells, G.C.
Whitten, F.R.
Wickham, G.B.
Winckler, L.A.H.
Wise, W.
Wright, W.L.

1910
Askew, H.R.
Bambridge, H.G.
Barton, R.E.
Beit, R.O.
Bird, C. StJ.
Bulloch, M.A.
Bullock, W.E.
Burton, R.
Campbell, E.R.A.
Chester, A.B.
Crofton, E.V.M.
Davis, C.J.
Dicksee, A.P.
Dinwiddie, D.M.
Druitt, C.L.
Ellison, H.F.V.
Forsyth, W.J.
Freeman, F.R.
Gibson, J.C.
Hartley, A.C.
Hawes, C.G.
Hitchcock, G.E.W.
Hoare, E.S.
Jones, E.W.C.
Kemp, L.C.
Langlois, L.A.E.
Mack, R.A.
Masters, H.J.
Mitchell, G.S.
Mitchell, W.C.
Moore, E.
Morau, M.L.J.
Pallister, A.W.B.
Pappanicolaou, P.G.
Paterson, L.M.
Peake, H.G.
Pound, G.T.
Raper, J.H.F.
Raymond, G.A.N.
Richards, H.B.
Richardson, J.
Salmond, H.G.
Sanders, J.L.
Tomblings, E.H.G.
Tonkin, D.C.W.
Turner, A.D.
Wallis, N.L.
Young, T.R.

1911
Abbott-Young, E.C.
Ash, H.W.
Ayres, H.F.
Bacon, W.B.
Beale, H.W.
Blackmore, F.R.
Bradley, G.L.H.
Brown, R.C.
Burns, J.S.

Cole, A.P.
Dass-Kochhar, T.
Davey, F.W.
Davies, J.W.L.
Elliott, C.A.A.
Evans, A.L.
Faber, S.E.
Glaisby, A.G.T.
Grant, J.L.
Highett, C.F.
James, H.B.R.
Jenks, A.R.C.
Kane, C.R.H.
Knight, R.A.
Kunte, V.K.
Lacey, L.
Lal, B.M.
Lawson, A.B.
Leicester, H.L.
Lodge, W.J.
Mari, J.H.
Malcolm, G.J.
Maringe, T.H.J.
Mawson, H.
McHatton, A.C.
Miles, J.A.
Mills, J.C.
Mocatta, F.E.
Nicolle, A.V.
Osmand, G.
Parkinson, R.F.
Patrick, C.L.
Quirk, N.D.
Reeves-Smith, D.
Reid, H.A.
Reilly, C.O.C.
Rivas, J.M. de las
Ruck, C.G.
Schön, J.G.
Smith, A.C.
Sossidi, N.J.
Stein, J.A.
Stock, R.V.W.
Subarwal, B.L.
Tennant, J.A.
White, A.J.
Wilkinson, H.D.
Wilkinson, H.G.

1912
Allan, W.A.M.
Allen-Magil, S.W.
Baker, D.S.
Bender, O.F.C.
Boyes, F.T.
Boyes, W.R.
Bromage, J.A.R.
Brooker, S.F.
Bushby, W.E.
Campbell, W.L.
Chassereau, J.D.
Clay, A.S.
Cook, J.W.D.
Crewdson, S.C.
Daly, A.P.
David, I.J.
Dennys, R.E.G.
Desmarais, E.R.
Dew, M.T.
Desey, C.A.R.
Dewidar, M.F.
Dibley, G.A.S.
Dunn, E.O.
Eggar, J.G.
Falcon, R.R.B.
Gagnier, R.C.L.
Gjems, J.
Gotch, T.H.
Grunspan, S.
Gwynne-Griffith, G.D.M.
Hall, C.L.
Harris, L.
Harvey, H.C.
Heenan, J.N.D.
Heenan, R.E.H.
Heinig, J.E.
Jackson, C.L.H.
Lacey, C.W.
Linsell, A.A.
Lory, M.R.
Maia, O. da S.
Manes, J.A.A.
Menezes, J.A.S.
Mitchell, J.A.
Morrison, A.O.
Mounib, E.S.M.
Naish, E.P.
Newland, A.K.
Newton, B.StJ.
Peake, R.W.
Potter, J.E.B.
Prescot, C.P.
Reid, G.H.
Runge, O.J.T.
Splitter, B.
Stuart, C.S.
Sturgess, A.T.
Suckau, C.A.E.
Warde, R.H.
Wark, D.
Webb, A.G.
Weiss, A.R.
Williams, R.H.
Willox, W.A.
Wroughton, J.H.T.

1913
Bansall, J.W.
Binns, O.B.
Boyd, J.M.
Buckingham, F.
Carmichael, W.M.
Cleveland, R.G.
Collins, W.
Davies, J.D.
Down, J.T.
Edeleanu, I.
Elderton, E.F.
Fatehullah, M.
Firth, S.E.M.
Fletcher, J.H.
Foot, F.J.G.
Gill, G.E.
Groves, G.L.
Hannam, S.P.
Hoare, P.V.
Hodgson, O.
Hussaim, Q.Z.
Hutchinson, F.H.
May, E.S.
Mercer, J.A.
Milner, D.
Montagu, A.M.R.
Nanda, J.N.
Nanda, K.L.
Napier-Clavering, F.D.
Paddison, R.H.
Poole, H.W.L.
Purves, P.R.
Ramirez, E.
Richards, F.L.
Ritchie, L.A.
Roberts, F.R.
Roberts, J.S.
Robinson, E.
Saint, J.H.
Sarkaria, A. Singh
Sauerbeck, C.T.W.
Sheffield, W.R.
Singh, A.
Singh, K.
Smith, H.D.D.
Stoney, F.G.D.
Taffs, C.W.J.
Thomas, W.H.
Timbrell, E.G.
Totton, G.C.
Vigers, L.L.
Walker, A.E.
White, F.
Whitmore, C.G.
Wildy, E.L.
Willcock, M.D.
Wood, E.A.P.

1914
Arnold, C.V.
Bam, S.G.
Bartrum, E.R.
Baudry, R.G.A.
Bazeley, H.
Black, C.H.C.P.
Bolter, R.T.
Bonnaud, G.L.J.
Box, R.L.
Calvert, F.W.A.

Coxhead, H.
Darton, E.J.
Dring, S.H.
Earnshaw-Wall, E.E.
Edwards, F.A.L.
Eisenmann, G.H.
Faber, J.B.
Farrell, N.N.
Fields-Clarke, P.C.E.
Freeth, L.G.
Fryer, R.E.
Girvin, C.B.
Glen, D.C.
Goethem, H.E. van
Goñi y Germain, R.R.
Graham, M.R.
Hall, A.G.
Hatfield, M.B.
Heesem, J.M.
Hogshaw, F.H.
Key, D.P.
Khouw, K.K.
Kirkby, H.
Landray, F.G.
Loh, K.I.
Maia, R. da S.
Melinsky, M.
Montes, A.
Nicholls, H.O.
Norris, J.W.
Osmond, C.B.
Pocock, S.N.
Raj, D.L.N.
Roberts, G.W.P.
Rundlett, L.StC.
Russell, H.K.
Ryan, C.F.M.N.
Ryneveld, H.A. van
Scott, A.G.D.
Seabrooke, F.H.
Sethi, J.S.
Shilstone, F.W.
Singh, J.K.
Singh, U.
Slow, D.E.S.
Sproull, A.W.
Tapster, A.G.
Targett, E.H.
Thatcher, W.I.
Thomson, B.
Urgoiti y Somovilla, J.N.L. de
Wheater, K.R.M.
Wileman, R.F.
Willis, E.A.
Wolley, C.T.

1915
Bartrum, B.E.
Bloxam, H.P.
Bonnaud, R.C.
Bramson, M.L.
Bremner, S.A.
Comben, H.E.
Eglin, E.W.
Heath, H.D.
Hobley, F.E.
Hogan, G.W.
Howard, R.G.
Joffé, A.S.
Luscher, S.W.
Marles, H.F.
Meyer, F.E.
Nougerède, C.E.M. de la
Ower, E.
Pucknell, F.A.
Ramalho, R.V.
Sharp, F.A.
Singh, K.
Smith, A.G.
Stewart, E.H.J.
Whittmann, H.M.de
Williams, J.

1916
Calderon y Flóres, A.N.A.
Müller, K.V.
Ratner, L.

1917
Baker, W.C.G.J.
Ball, R.W.
Bird, A.F.
Bonnaud, C.A.
Martinez Carrera, A.A.
Mavani, R.B.
Richard, A.H.
Schlesinger, L.A.M.
Souza, J.F.R. de
Tonder, A.J. van

1918
Coutinho de Vilhena, A. de M
Davis, R.H.
Diepeveen, J.M.
Hillman, E.M.
Oubon, N.C.
Pinchbeck, A.S.
Poole, C.
Poznanski, M.
Stowers, A.
Watts, L.C.
Wells, L.W.
Zuberbühler, H.W.

1919
Griffith, A.G.
Griffiths, T.J.
Hopewell, G.H.
Lemos, A.A. de
Potter, R.B.McC.
Vaughan, S.
Wyatt, R.G.P.

1920
Ascanio, W.de
Butler, F.W.
Chilton, D.H.
Cramer, W.
Cronin, H.F.
Downes, E.
Goodman, R.T.W.
Harris, H.A.
Highett, R.F.
James, R.T.
Nachshen, M.
Stavridi, A.
Stern, M.

1921
Bellamy, D.A. de C.
Bound, T.
Brow, K.P.
Came, F.H.R.
Carver, M.D.
Danger, E.O.
Davies, W.W.
Duff, L.V.K.
Duvivier, J.
Evans, K.J.H.
Ferris, C.E.
Garcia, C. de la C.
Golledge, S.E.
Gowring, G.I.B.
Hamilton, W.E.
Harding, H.J.B.
Hausser, P.C.G.
Hawkins, L.E.
Heel, J.A. van
Jarvis, I.J.G.
Knight, P.E.
Leeming, J.J.
Lloyd, P.StL.
Musgrave, E.J.
Nathan, A.
Pain, J.F.
Partridge, F.A.
Penhuène, Y.J.P.M.
Pigott, F.B.
Roach, W.H.G.
Sadler, B.E.
Shaw, J.
Slight, E.L.
Vitale, F.
Welch, G.
West, H.E.

1922
Braikevitch, M.
Brazier, K.S.
Brazier, L.G.
Chaplin, C.A.
Cloke, H.F.
Crosthwaite, C.D.
Davis, R.F.
Dalgliesh, D.

Glyde, H.S.
Howes, C.F.
Hunt, F.J.A.
Hunt, H.H.
Lee, E.G.
Lewis, J.W.
MacLachlan, T.A.
Macpherson, W.A.K.
Madoc-Jones, G.W.
Marsh, C.M.
Narbeth, R.G.
Roberts, G.
Rosoff, S.
Smith, H.S.
Smith, H.StJ.
Spencer, K.T.
Taylor, W.G.
Walter, G.R.
Weekes, R.W.

1923
Bee, R.J.
Cheesman, E.R.
Cookson, E.C.
Dixon, E.J.C.
Docker, C.E.
Evans, J.T.
Finlayson, R.W.
Fulford, H.B.
Hall, G.S.
Hodges, E.E.
Hoggan, R.
Main, J.F.
Marfleet, E.H.
Moore, D.B.H.
Parry, E.L.L.
Phillips, R.T.
Piper, G.H.
Rock, L.G.B.
Sandover, J.A.M.
Schlanbusch, E.W.
Scrutton, H.
Shneerson, M.
Stewart, J.G.
Streeter, E.A.
Taffs, L.G.
Tasker, H.R.
Whiting, D.E.
Williams, G.L.

1924
Adlington, R.E.
Barrie, S.C.
Blyth, F.G.H.
Boorman, A.G.
Cochrane, R.
Coyle, D.E.
Davies, J.G.
Elven, R.S.
Embleton, J.E.
Gibbs, E.F.
Hardy, W.B.
Havers, C.G.
Hughes, G.
Iliff, E.
Körner, A.C.
Lawley, W.
Moon, C.A.
Netherton, C.H.
Saunders-Jacobs, A.B.
Scott, J.
Smith, H.J.
Thivy, E.G.
Weber, V.S.
Whitehead, J.I.

1925
Berridge, P.R.S.
Bhaduri, B.
Burke, E.
Dow, W.A.
Dyson, C.W.
Fourniss, W.H.
Fry, S.E.
Grunberg, J.
Harnack, W.
Howell, R.H.S.
Jenkins, H.G.
Morgan, H.D.
Nicholls, W.J.
Otter, J.R.H.
Pearson, H.M.
Peppiatt, C.H.
Read, R.S.
Taylor, T.F.
Terrington, J.S.
Tresham, H.A.
Wilkes, J.H.H.
Wright, H.E.
Zinovieff, L.

1926
Adler, M.
Barker, B.H.
Bradley, G.M.
Carne, J.F.
Cassidy, G.L.
Crouch, A.S.
Culshaw, L.C.
Davison, R.
d'Avray, A.M.
Fitt, R.L.
Flory, S.E.
Godfrey, D.A.
Godwin, J.S.
Jones, P.H.
Lowe, R.M.W.
Measor, E.O.
Murti, M.G.K.
Pearson, R.F.
Perera, C.B.P.
Schorstein, E.
Sharp, H.J.
Small, F.H.
Symes, E.W.C.
Tayler, E.S.P.
Taylor, H.G.P.
Vitaranaaratchy, P.
Wakley, T.G.
Wallace, J.L.
Wilson, G.M.
Woolley, G.E.W.

1927
Allum, A.C.W.
Azeemuddin, K.
Bates, P.D.
Bean, D.C.
Brewester, D.F.F.
Cantrell, W.H.
Clerke, R.W.G.
Coulson, S.E.
Goddard, A.D.
Harmer, L.C.
Hawtrey, J.H.P.
Heaton-Armstrong, R.C.
Johnson, H.R.
Lash, S.D.
Leibovitch, L.
Markwick, E.J.R.
Morum, S.W.F.
Muzumdar, B.M.
Nazareth, C.V.J.C.
Paterson, K.
Pfeil, B.B.
Rankin, W.J.
Sanger, F.J.
Squires, H.J.
Waters, H.R.B.

1928
Broomfield, R.E.
Champion, C.Ll.
Downs, R.A.
George, G.F.
Hammond, R.E.R.
Hooper, G.N.
Ittihadieh, A.
Kambhu, M.L.X.
Kumar, S.S.
Le Coultre, A.A.R.
Marshall, W.T.
Millard, F.J.
Patel, G.B.
Phillips, J.F.S.
Porter, A.R.
Savory, K.C.A.B.
Shivdasani, P.R.
Singh, Brahma
Spens, C.H.
Talintyre, E.C.

1929
Basu, S.C.
Beer, A.E.
Bingham, J.E.

Black, E.
Buchanan, C.D.
Bushell, G.E.
Clenshaw, W.C.
Combes, J.
De, K.L.
Gore, R.R.
Jenkins, R.S.
Johnstone, J.M.
Karim, F.
Kibblewhite, G.V.
Malkani, T.M.
Manthei, R.A.
Mehandru, T.R.
Palit, A.R.
Patel, M.B.
Pavry, R.
Pinto, A.J.
Pommerantz, L.
Puri, K.L.
Ramana, J.Singh
Richardson, F.J.A.
Ridgway, R.J.
Vahidy, Zahir A.
van Langenberg, W.J.A.
Wakeford, R.L.
Wijeyekoon, R.A.
Zutshi, P.N.

1930
Allnutt, A.G.
Anderson, R.E.
Barter, R.H.P.
Burns, G.V.
Claxton, E.C.
Douglas, F.S.
Draddy, F.E.
Fforde, J.E.
Gore, S.Y.
Goyal, V.P.
Green, F.L.
Griffith, F.Ll.
Hartog, N.B.
Hoare, C.F.
Humphries, J.H.
Jacobson, M.
Kenwood, T.T.
Khalid, M.
Khan, Z.
King, L.N.
Kumar, R.
Lee, T.K.
Lewis, W.H.
Lloyd, W.J.K.
Marshall, C.C.
Middleton-Stewart, D.J.
Rendle, W.A.
Ribeiro, P.X.V.C.
Skinner, J.A.
Smith, P.A.V.
Swan, G.M.
Tolhurst, J.R.
Vahidy, Zahoor A.
Wheeley, L.E.
Wood, B.C.W.

1931
Barnes, H.G.
Birkhead, J.E.
Blandford, G.F.
Brankston, A.D.
Bridger, J.E.
Brown, D.A.
Brown, J.A.
Browne, T.P.
Clarke, A.C.
Collingridge, V.H.
Davies, V.C.
Dogra, R.N.
Forrest, R.L.
Fowler, R.J.
Gomez, A.A.
Gore, V.Y.
Grunberg, S.
Harrison, J.R.
Horsfield, H.T.
Lee, W.R.
Marc, R.C.
Mehta, B.S.
New, D.H.
Nicholas, S.
Ohanessian, A.O.
Puri, C.L.
Surti, B.P.
Tarneja, R.
Thompson, J.C.V.
Tideman, C.
Underwood, A.E.
Wadsworth, C.P.
Wareham, J.A.L.
West, M.C.
Zutshi, J.N.

1932
Ballantine, K.C.
Baxter, R.L.G.
Bigg, J.
Campbell, D.H.
Cartwright, W.N.
Chatham, C.G.
Collins, A.R.
Dawson, S.E.
Gau, C.W.
German-Ribon, J.R.
Ghazi, M.S.H.
Greenhouse, W.J.
Guedes Caballero, F.
Hill, A.W.
Johnson, W.J.B.
Jones, R.G.
Khanna, W.C.
Kharegat, M.D.
Khatri, K.C.
Lankshear, W.A.W.
Martin, T.V.
Matheson, E.J.M.
Matthews, N.W.L.
Parker, T.F.
Patel, D.B.
Pinto, W.L.
Ridd, J.P.
Sahni, S.P.
Saldanha, G.B.
Sedergreen, L.N.
Singh, J.B.
Spencer, H.J.
Whittell, E.A.
Wickes, L.B.
Wingfield, G.G.
Wood, G.
Wright, M.P.

1933
Baker, A.G.
Beckwith, W.F.
Bennett, P.J.
Biggs, R.C.
Braddick, H.J.W.
Castle, F.
Clinch, F.H.
Crockett, J.H.A.
Desai, K.C.
Dodd, L.S.
Forster, F.D.B.
Gardner, S.V.
Hopkins, D.A.
Lea, C.B.
Mahy, J.H.
Man Son Hing, W.
Marwaha, R.S.D.
Nayler, J.J.
Pardoe, S.W.L.
Pavry, F.H.
Qureshi, A.H.
Sanders, F.J.
Singh, M.
Sivaprakasapillai, T.
Smith, F.J.R.
Stephen, G.D.
Tongudai, C.
Tresham, P.I.
Watson, A.D.R.

1934
Ahuja, P.R.
Booth, G.C.
Borgaonker, R.G.
Briggs, M.H.
Bright, D.J.
Castor, R.L.
Chaplin, W.L.
Coleman, L.E.L.
Coles, G.R.
Enouf, M.L.J.
Hall, E.J.W.
Hedgcock, J.H.

Hickes, J.C.
Karaso, H.
Knibbs, W.J.A.
Milne, J.E.
Moore, S.C.
Parekh, M.R.
Paterson, S.L.
Patil, G.K.
Reade, R.A.P.
Robin, M.H.
Robins, J.A.
Robinson, C.D.
Singh, Basant
Spencer, B.A.
Stewart, V.E.W.
Temple, D.
Wicks, F.S.
Wild, G.E.

1935
Adams, H.C.
Ahmed, S.W.
Allwright, E.S.
Boardman, G.
Bruce, F.E.
Cohen, S.
Cubitt, P.L.
Cuthbert, E.W.
Dudley, K.D.
Glass, W.L.
Green, F.N.
Iyer, H.I.V.
Jawa, C.P.D.
Key, J.W.
Lanham, K.
Latham, E.W.
McKenna, F.J.
Orchard, D.F.
Oyler, G.
Palmer, J.E.
Peacock, F.D.
Reatchlous, R.
Reynolds, R.E.
Robertson, L.R.
Sarpal, C.L.
Skempton, A.W.
Tanner, H.T.
Waheed, M.A.
Walshe, W.D.
Williams, S.B.W.
Young, N.H.G.

1936
Ackerley, G.E.
Ashby, R.J.
Barlow, C.B.
Baxter, J.W.
Bingham, T.G.
Croxford, I.G.
Douglas, J.F.
Fox, D.A.
Garside, D.
Harpman, G.D.
Henderson, J.I.S.
Horsfield, T.A.S.
Katinke, S.
Lee, C.R.
Leigh, J.V.
Marley, H.G.N.
Patel, A.T.
Powell, R.F.A.
Ross, C.P.C.
Tyabji, N.S.B.

1937
Allwright, H.J.
Andhare, N.M.
Burt, F.S.
Cohen, E.L.
de Waele, J.P.A.
Fox, O.J.
Gerrard, R.T.
Hartley, P.
Hicks, P.H.
Laha, S.K.
McGregor, R.R.
Marriott, G.B.
Offer, L.F.
Paskins, G.R.S.
Petri, G.
Reatchlous, A.
Thomson, I.D.
Ward, W.H.

1938
Alison, G.B.
Aston, A.C.
Bentley, J.B.
Burnett, D.H.
Glen, J.A.
Gowers, A.G.
Harris, E.T.C.
Harvey, J.A.
Harvey, J.R.McG.
Hawker, A.McN.
London, K.S.
McBretney, E.P.
Mehta, U.H.
Milverton, J.L.
Robinson, F.L.
Serota, S.
Skelt, G.J.
Smith, L.R.H.
Souter, H.A.
Sowden, J.P.
Sule, C.R.
Wild, R.M.
Williams, R.d'A.

1939
Arundell, R.
Emerton, R.F.
Flynn, C.L.
Fried, M.
Haim, S.I.
Henderson, C.McC.
Hewlett, J.P.
Hill, E.S.
Jones, J.D.
Lee, K.H.
Lester, D.R.
Lewis, E.M.
Loewy, E.I.
Manson, J.B.
Morton, M.J.
Mylvaganam, T.
Nixon, I.K.
Partridge, C.H.
Scott, W.D.
Shah, K.S.
Stelfox, G.M.
Storrar, F.M.
Walton, E.W.K.
Wint, J.McL.
Yeates, J.N.
Zubair, A.R.

1940
Bennell, B.M.U.
Constantinides, A.
Cornfield, G.M.
Cosgrove, J.T.
Dalaya, J.B.
Dyke, N.B.
Farquharson, D.G.
Fleming, A.H.S.
Griffiths, J.W.
Gwatkin, P.J.
Hallas, P.S.
Higgs, B.F.
Hoffman, G.R.
Jenkins, R.A.S.
King, J.C.
Mitchell, P.G.
Savage, H.D.
Shahaney, K.J.
Sharman, F.A.
Singh, J.
Sur, A.N.
Sutton, A.A.G.
Taylor, G.M.
Vaitialingam, N.A.
Watson, O.J.J.
Watson, W.N.G.
Williams, L.C.
Winpenny, F.

1941
Atchison, T.S.
Chacko, I.G.
Clear Hill, E.C.
Donat, J.B.
Dudley, B.R.
Duff, G.E.D.
Edwards, J.T.
Evans, C.G.

Faber, J.G.
Finlinson, J.C.H.
Gray, A.
Hannington, C.L.T.
Humphreys, H.P.
Ismail, S.M.
Jones, C.O.
Mathias, E.A.
Radbourne, S.E.
Saverymuttu, H.S.
Sethna, H.K.
Shamash, S.J.
Taylor, J.F.
Thaysen, S.C.
Turnbull, I.B.A.
Watson, C.I.
Webb, S.B.W.

1942
Agdesham, B.
Barter, H.L.L.J.
Baylis, A.L.H.
Chapman, J.G.
Clapham, D.J.
Collier, J.G.
Cox, P.A.
Elliott, A.J.
Gibbs, D.R.
Grace, L.B.
Hardcastle, B.J.
Harvey, P.M.
Humphrys, B.G.
Kraly, H.J.I.
Lindsay, D.
Lucas, G.S.
Mathew, W.L.
Ovis, S.B.
Paine, M.G.V.
Ratnatunga, D.M.
Said, Y.M.
Sinnetamby, G.S.
Thair, A.E.
Wallwork, G.
Walpole, R.H.
Webb, W.A.J.
Wilcock, E.J.

1943
Andrew, P.H.F.
Bennett, G.D.
Black, J.
Bullett, A.W.
Butcher, J.A.
Chapman, R.G.
Crowther, B.
Crystal, L.
Elam, R.J.
Fleming, J.H.
Goddard, T.A.
Goode, S.G.G.
Grover, F.
Grover, R.I.M.
Hawes, S.M.
Holder, D.W.
Isaacs, R.J.H.
James, H.B.
Judson, J.C.
Lipman, J.
Parnell, B.K.
Pickford, J.A.
Pitcher, H.F.
Reynolds, K.J.
Sandberg, A.C.E.
Sands, P.G.
Saunders, I.H.
Scott, G.T.G.
Selby, J.L.A.
Sneller, A.T.
Stainer, C.C.
Taylor, N.O.
Tucker, M.K.
Tuckwell, R.E.
Twyman, J.W.R.
Vine-Lott, K.M.
West, L.
Zienkiewicz, O.C.

1944
Ackers, P.
Andrews, P.
Bailey, E.L.
Bishop, P.W.
Brown, T.N.
Clarke, D.A.
Davies, R.M.
Diamant, H.H.
Edwards, K.W.
Farquharson, A.F.
Greaves, J.F.K.
Jenkins, L.W.
Lang, D.W.
Potts, A.J.
Sibley, F.O.
Spencer, T.A.
Thomas, J.M.
Walker, B.A.
Walters, J.A.

1945
Allen, B.L.
Antonakis, C.J.
Barber, D.G.
Bigwood, G.M.C.
Chadney, R.F.
Cope, G.H.
Doulton, J.R.
Dunster, J.A.
Elliott, R.D.
Fischer, B.H.
Flint, A.R.
Gibson, R.E.
Haase, J.
Harris, C.D.
Hill, R.G.
Holman, J.
Iweka, I.R.E.
Lee, M.A.T.
Mallett, G.P.
Mills, J.G.
Newton, P.D.
Payn, C.W.
Plowman, J.M.
Reading, E.A.V.
Spindel, J.E.
Stephens, J.H.
Thompson, P.L.

1946
Alderman, D.
Chaplin, N.J.E.
Clare, D.H.
Cole, D.R.
Crook, D.E.
Doxey, F.W.
Eathorne, J.N.
Fraser, A.J.H.
Gamse, J.D.H.
Gardner, R.W.
Godfrey, J.W.
Goldberg, V.
Goldstein, A.
Goodearl, K.A.
Gray, J.T.
Harman, A.B.
Jeffery, M.H.
Large, J.E.
Miners, J.B.
Neill, J.A.
Pegge, E.V.
Pontin, V.H.
Posselwhite, E.R.
Smallman, A.J.
Townsend, A.D.
Wilson, G.

1947
Andrews, J.A.C.
Antia, R.J.
Arnot, E.M.
Baboneau, G.C.
Barlow, J.
Cooney, E.G.
Dennington, D.
Eccleston, W.M.D.
Farish, H.G.
Ganguly, J.C.
Jenkins, W.G.
Lidstone, S.G.D.
Sandover, J.A.
Schiller, M.
Shaw, J.B.
Skinner, D.J.
Smith, B.G.
Stredwick, L.A.
Taylor, R.
Vincent, R.H.

Waller, J.A.
White, K.F.
Wideman, R.M.
Wolsey, M.G.

1948
Alexander, R.G.
Aluko, T.M.
Botsford, R.C.
Burbridge, P.A.
Cook, G.R.
Coulson, A.
Culmer, A.W.
Dorey, M.R.
Downs, R.B.
Duncanson, T.F.
Finlinson, P.G.
Gerzon, J.
Gilbert, G.D.
Greig, B.W.J.
Halstead, D.I.
Hammond, R.H.
Harley, B.V.
Helson, P.W.
Henkin, B.W.
James, G.N.F.
Jones, T.D.E.
Keith, E.A.L.
Kershaw, K.A.
Klein, R.L.
Lambert, L.C.
Layman, J.P.
McLeod, J.A.S.
Markham, W.A.
Maufe, G.
May, J.E.
Needham, F.H.
Odell, K.M.
Payne, N.J.
Powell, P.A.D.
Rai, D.
Ransom, A.E.
Redlich, W.
Rodger, J.L.
Roth, G.J.
Sadleir, N.A.
Smales, J.M.
Smeaton, D.
Smith, I.S.
Sparks, J.A.W.
Watson, R.V.
Wicks, N.
Wilson, J.F.

1949
Albany-Ward, G.F.
Browne, J.S.C.
Crawford, J..A.F.
Davies, R.
Davis, J.E.
Fells, J.N.
Fleming, J.F.
Garmirian, Miss P.
Hamley, E.W.
Hurst, M.G.
Lee, E.M.
Leighton, F.C.
Meigh, A.C.
Melvin, C.G.L.
Moller, K.
O'Neill, D.B.
Oxborrow, R.G.
Pedgrift, G.F.
Rapson, G.H.
Stewart, H.M.
Wright, D.A.

1950
Adams, M.A.E.
Bankart, P.G.
Carr, G.R.
Cumming, A.P.
Dalton, R.G.
Davies, G.N.
Edwards, P.R.
Farrall, B.S.
Foster, B.K.
Gedge, D.G.
Harris, D.J.
Hayter, M.A.
Heller, H.
Hogan, D.M.J.
Hopkins, J.K.H.
Jolly, A.G.
Martin, P.F.
Molloy, D.L.
Patrick, J.G.
Pritchard, R.A.P.
Richings, D.G.T.
Sears, L.A.
Smith, D.A.
Stephenson, J.H.
Thornton, L.D.
Townley, G.P.
Tubb, J.R.
Turner, P.M.
Walker, D.
Wex, B.P.J.
Wilson, J.W.

1951
Biram, A.
Boucherat, F.J.A.
Campbell-Little, D.J.
Chalcraft, W.H.
Cox, D.E.
Davies, W.R.
Dugdale, R.H.
Fokschanner, W.
Gilroy, J.M.
Hardy, W.D.
Hazell, M.D.
Hodgson, R.W.
Hull, M.J.
Lappin, W.B.
Lind, P.M.
Lyons, A.C.
McLean, G.
Millar, G.A.I.
North, D.W.
Parker, D.R.
Powell, T.G.M.G.
Rogers, J.M.F.
Savoie, A.P.
Smith, R.E.
Squire, D.C.
Swain, B.J.
Twelves, I.L.
Willcox, R.B.

1952
Allen, C.D.
Allen, G.P.
Allsopp, P.A.D.
Andrews, A.P.
Bailey, D.B.
Birkett, G.W.
Brook, D.G.
Collinge, V.K.
Collins, R.J.
Coombe, J.G.B.
Curson, J.D.
Darracott, J.M.
Eldridge, K.P.
Fishwick, G.
Flaxman, E.W.
Gardner, D.J.
Gear, D.
Gollan, G.A.
Hinxman, G.
Jordan, R.W.
Kafarowski, Z.
Kent, R.W.
Knill, M.W.
Last, J.D.
Maplethorp, S.C.
Martin, J.S.
Moffat, P.A.S.
Murphy, A.M.
Newman, E.C.
Page, E.G.
Polack, B.McG.
Simpson, A.
Skillman, J.M.
Smith, G.E.
Stevens, C.B.
Taylor, L.E.
Waterfield, A.W.
Wyatt, T.A.

1953
Bavister, R.B.
Broomfield, B.J.
Burne, N.J.
Carpenter, A.C.
Carpenter, D.G.

Clifford, P.A.
Collins, P.J.
Dennis, T.E.
Du Heaume, P.L.
Ellington, J.
Flint, G.R.
Grunhut, N.
Harding, E.R.
Haythorn, D.J.R.
Horn, D.T.
Hurden, D.C.
Joffe, I.W.
King, D.
Kirkor, A.
Knox, J.A.J.
Lamb, D.W.
Latter, B.V.
Light, P.
Lucas, C.J.
McKenna, B.R.
McKenna, J.M.
Marsden, J.R.
Measor, J.G.
Mendoza, A.F.M.
Morriss, C.
Neal, H.M.
Page, D.
Paige, G.A.
Powell, J.M.
Rigby, A.D.
Rothwell, M.A. deW.
Seaman, T.
Selby, J.R.
Taylor, P.
Trigg, R.T.
Weston, R.F.
Westwood, P.D.

1954
Aldridge, J.A.
Allester, A.R.
Amos, M.J.M.
Aspinall, J.S.
Bird, R.W.
Blundell, C.J.
Chase, J.T.
Clayton, J.M.
Colaco-Osorio, J.D.
Collier, P.J.
Cox, G.C.
Criticos, D.M.
Cross, P.H.C.
Duncan, M.A.G.R.E.
Finey, J.T.
Fisher, R.
Glanville, J.
Hanson, B.
Haseltine, B.A.
Hayes, H.I.
Howley, M.
Kelly, D.P.
Kirch, J.B.
Luxon, A.M.
McCann, P.D.
Nancarrow, D.R.
Newhouse, C.K.
Palmer, P.M.
Panas, G.E.V.
Peters, C.J.
Rance, D.J.
Russell, R.L.
Sankey, D.A.
Sposito, B.
Ward, J.
Weston, M.J.

1955
Abbott, I.M.
Akalewold, K.
Andrews, M.C.
Barnard, H.D.
Barnard, P.G.
Baty, M.F.
Bell, D.J.
Brown, W.T.D.
Clark, P.J.
Davies, B.L.
Deane, W.
Field, N.E.
Grantham, A.H.
Hable Selassie, S.
Hartley, A.
Hatch, B.
Hattersley, D.R.
Hemmin, I.W.
Hurst, B.L.
Kluth, D.J.
Law, R.W.S.
McDermont, J.L.
Over, B.L.W.
Owsianka, A.A.
Pearce, P.T.
Perkins, J.R.
Phipps, M.T.
Pontin, K.
Pooley, D.G.
Postlethwaite, R.W.
Quinlan, J.A.
Richmond, B.
Rotgans, J.A.
Spalding, J.A.
Taylor, E.H.
Wardle, D.G.
White, P.J.
Willett, D.C.
Wright, D.E.

1956
Aitchison, J.
Barker, J.R.
Baxter, D.A.
Benghiat, A.J.
Best, M.T.
Bishpham, R.A.
Bushell, A.J.
Canvin, R.W.
Caswell, P.G.P.
Cotterell, S.J.
Curtis, K.A.H.
Doncaster, A.A.
Ferris, R.A.
Harris, P.L.
Hill, J.C.
Hoadley, A.D.
Hussell, D.J.T.
Jones, D.P.G.
Kennedy, P.C.J.
King, G.J.W.
Kingston, E.H.D.
Lakin, D.G.
Lawrence, J.D.
Lewis, M.G.
Lewis, P.G.
McKenzie, H.S.
Mills, D.
Pain, D.J.
Pemberton, R.C.
Powell, E.R.
Robertson, J.P.
Smith, C.B.
Smith, R.C.
Smith, R.L.
Spence, R.W.R.
Sturgeon, A.J.G.
Suthers, J.B.
Toufaha, S.A.D.
Toynbee, P.M.
Turner, J.M.
Valentine, R.
Vaughan, P.R.
Wainwright, D.A.
Watson, D.M.
Williamson, D.

1957
Aquilina, C.V.
Baker, J.G.
Bell, D.C.
Butler, D.J.R.
Buxton, C.I.
Chapman, J.A.S.
Collins, P.J.
Collyer, M.L.
Cox, P.J.
Dennett, M.
Elmer, P.R.
Farrant, J.A.
Fawkes, P.E.
Godfrey, J.E.
Green, P.A.
Hardiment, P.W.
Hart, J.L.
Hoadley, P.J.
Howard, G.D.
Jolliffe, M.J.A.H.
Kulesza, R.

Leadbetter, K.E.
Lewis, T.E.
MacKenzie, D.W.J.
Modro, J.A.
Moon, R.B.
Owen, E.K.
Palmer, M.D.
Porritt, P.E.
Schwarzbard, W.
Sears, E.J.
Thomas, G.C.
Thompson, R.G.
Townson, J.M.
Vile, G.W.D.
White, R.S.
Wood, C.E.J.
Wootton, P.M.

1958
Akinde, J.I.
Al-Naib, S.K.
Aquilina, A.C.M.
Booth, J.D.
Brown, D.C.
Burdet, J.L.
Cotton, C.J.N.
Crowder, R.
Davies, Y.M.
Evans, J.S.
Finigan, A.B.
Gamble, R.G.
Gardner, D.J.
Gilson, G.E.
Godfrey, J.R.
Gray, S.R.
Gregory, P.W.
Griffin, N.L.
Harding, L.P.
Hartley, D.C.
Heath, P.
Ibbitt, M.E.
Johnson, E.M.
Khazanchi, A.C.
Lloyd, D.D.D.
Matthews, G.H.
Meller, R.E.
Melling, J.A.
Miles, J.R.
New, D.J.
Noad, W.P.B.
Nzeako, G.N.
Ogle, M.N.
Onuche, J.K.
Outhwaite, F.M.
Padmanabhan, S.
Prempridi, T.
Remmington, P.O.
Salmon, J.M.
Sandoz, D.F.
Sarjeant, B.W.D.
Sen-Gupta, B.K.
Smith, D.C.
Smith, J.E.
Snelson, C.W.
Solway, L.M.
Stebbings, M.R.R.
Tidmus, N.H.
Tonsiengsom, S.
Tuck, A.J.
Vudthithornnatirak, P.
Wright, P.E.

1959
Anstead, W.E.
Bartlet, G.A.
Bedford, I.L.
Bliss, R.H.
Brindley, C.S.
Cobham, R.C.
Corish, A.T.
Crabtree, P.J.
Curtis, B.
Dallmeyer, W.J.
Devine, J.A.
Elvy, M.R.
Faulkner, D.A.
Field, W.P.
Foster, E.
Hall, M.C.
Hallam, M.B.
Harrison, D.G.
Hue, L.E.
Hyslop, J.T.
Kapur, C.
King, E.A.
Linnell, R.H.
Loveland, R.W.H.
Nickalls, R.J.S.
Pemba, T.N.
Regan, P.E.
Roberts, W.M.
Rowe, N.D.
Rudgley, J.E.M.
Satchell, R.L.H.
Saunders, P.R.I.
Seston, M.J.
Shang, Y.S.
Sharrock, M.J.
Smith, P.
Stanton, R.J.C.
Taffs, J.D.
Tan, S.E.
Telling, R.M.
Thomas, S.M.
Vine, P.R.
Weetman, J.E.C.
Whorlow, R.G.

1960
Baird, G.R.
Barnes, N.M.L.
Benaim, R.
Bruce, C.P.
Carr, F.
Cawley, C.J.
Chikwendu, L.N.
Clare, M.J.
Cowland, D.S.
Davies, C.G.
Dix Perkin, A.J.
Evans, J.E.
Farnsworth, S.J.
Ferahian, R.H.
Griffin, P.J.
Hutty, A.R.
Loh, J.H.K.
Lorton, A.J.
Maltby, D.
Mann, P.D.
Martin, B.V.
Meiklejohn, P.
Morris, L.J.
Myers, A.P.
Newcombe, W.A.
Newman, J.B.
Nove, J.E.
Olliff, J.L.
Pattinson, D.A.
Pinfold, G.M.
Powell, A.E.
Ranawake, K.R.
Rees, C.W.J.L.
Rees, D.G.T.
Saxton, R.H.
Slingsby, R.N.
Story, B.W.
Teraszkiewicz, J.S.
Thomas, G.R.
Thompson, A.C.
Titley, D.
Topping, G.A.
Traherne, D.M.
Turner, E.D.
Vaile, R.C.
Warren, C.K.
Zelkha, J.H.S.

1961
Benfield, D.C.
Brett, M.L.A.
Brown, T.J.W.
Buckley, B.G.
Butler, H.J.R.
Cattan, L.H.
Chubb, E.A.
Cole, E.
Collier, P.W.
Connor, G.H.
Dalby, G.C.
Darling, J.G.
de Broekert, D.R.J.
English, P.H.
Felzmann, V.J.A.V.
Finney, M.R.
Franklin, R.W.D.
Goodall, J.K.

Gorb, M.J.
Grayson, M.R.
Greenaway, D.F.
Greenwood, P.R.
Hammonds, D.H.T.
Harris, G.M.
Hills, P.J.
Holmes, D.W.
Hughes, D.J.
Huntley, H.C.
James, B.T.
King, G.N.
Langdon, N.
McDonald, A.W.H.
Majumdar, P.
Manton, B.H.
Plant, M.G.
Reader, R.A.
Romer, C.M.
Sarsam, K.F.T.
Shanahan, J.M.
Smith, A.C.
Smith, J.R.
Smith, M.
Sohan, C.H.
Soubry, M.A.
Stanley, A.F.
Taylor, M.R.
Thompson, D.M.
Waylen, P.M.W.
Webb, J.F.
Wilkinson, J.E.
Woolsgrove, F.A.
Young, M.

1962
Addams, A.D.
Al-Dhahir, Z.A.R.
Arney, C.E.
Atayantz, B.
Baker, M.J.
Ballard, P.C.V.
Beckingsale, A.D.
Brown, R.G.
Carter, A.W.J.
Coatman, J.A.
Dumenil, P.D.
Ford, L.G.R.
Hancock, D.J.
Hannah, M.E.
Head, C.W.
Hill, P.R.
Hockin, D.J.
Horne, B.G.
James, D.A.V.
Lari, A.
Leadsom, B.R.
Lilley, H.A.
Lohn, M.B.
Longbottom, P.S.
Lovenbury, H.T.
Lowther, G.
Marshall, A.E.
Morgan, A.H.
Morris, G.T.
Musgrave, W.N.
Neal, F.R.
Nicholds, R.M.
Odd, N.V.M.
Oram, P.J.R.
Payne, H.R.
Potter, A.F.
Potter, R.J.N.
Putt, C.C.
Robinson, P.
Sharman, H.M.
Simons, R.A.
Smith, G.G.
Smith, N.B.
Swain, M.B.G.G.
Taurins, A.
Teather, H.D.
Temple, J.V.
Vickers, J.A.
Watts, P.C.
Wilkins, D.C.
Williams, H.L.
Williams, J.Y.
Williams, L.R.
Wong, C.S.

1963
Abraham, C.H.
Abrams, A.T.W.
Amana, E.J.
Billington, S.M.
Brewer, C.A.
Brookes, M.A.
Butler, A.T.
Cook, M.
Cox, D.B.R.
Davies, G.L.
Dean, G.
Dhanji, H.P.
Dick-Larkham, K.
Dunstan, T.
Duvivier, N.S.
Evans, J.M.
Gare, T.S.
Gibbins, D.J.
Haslett, T.G.
Hawkins, A.J.
Johnson, P.A.
Johnston, D.T.
Jones, P.R.
Knight, D.W.
Lewis, D.R.
Makinson, C.
Martel, N.J.
Matthias, C.B.
Maynard, H.C.E.
Morrison, I.M.
Mynard, P.J.
Nethercot, R.C.A.
Newell, R.G.
Peach, A.V.
Ramharry, D.
Robins, P.
Rushton, P.
Sargeant, R.H.
Saunders, J.T.
Skinner, J.L.
Smelt, R.I.
Stevens, M.G.
Sutton, M.R.
Turner, J.L.
Tyndale-Biscoe, R.N.L.
West, M.R.
Williams, M.P.A.
Withers, G.R.
Wood, P.A.
Yeomans, D.T.

1964
Allison, S.
Archer, G.O.
Atkinson, J.H.
Bailey, M.
Beynon, R.B.
Bumstead, B.R.
Burns, A.
Byrom, D.S.
Carrington, R.W.M.
Chambers, P.L.
Charles, J.A.
Chavda, S.J.
Chilton, R.K.
Coffin, M.A.
Constantine, P.P.
Coward, C.
Crews, P.D.
Dykes, B.R.
Edwards, M.R.
Flatman, A.J.
Gordon, R.W.
Griffiths, P.J.G.
Hatcher, S.J.
Heaton, D.A.
Hobbs, R.E.
Hussell, C.E.M.
Jenkins, P.C.
Jones, R.D.R.
Lam, S.C.
McGlone, P.M.A.
Martin, D.J.
Mason, I.D.
Mills, J.K.
Mitchell, R.H.J.
Morey, A.N.
Norman, A.H.G.
Reed, N.
Semple, P.J.
Shipley, N.
Skinner, R.J.
Taylor, G.H.
Taylor, I.P.

Twiname, E.
Veal, D.G.
Weatherell, R.M.
Welch, C.D.G.
Wharton, R.F.
Whitford, E.A.
Wilson, B.
Wrighton, M.E.
Youings, J.
Young, D.K.

1965
Ainsley, J.H.
Alatzas, D.Z.
Batcup, A.G.
Bourner, M.S.
Chamberlain, R.B.
Clavell, M.C.
Colgan, E.
Crossley, A.D.
Cryer, M.F.
Davison, M.J.
Devon, M.R.
Drury, P.C.
Duke, A.
Edwards, J.F.
Emami, H.A.
Flash, M.H.
Fordham, R.D.
Gardner, J.D.
Gray, M.R.
Gray, M.W.
Gray, P.R.K.
Groundsell, M.
Guess, R.A.
Harris, R.E.
Hayes, J.D.
Henderson, C.T.
Higgs, D.W.
Hight, D.W.
Hill, W.F.
Holmes, A.L.
Holmes, L.S.
Husselbury, A.
Janmohamed, B.M.
Jones, L.C.
Kamal, R.B.
Kibby, N.
Kinsey, P.J.
Knowles, N.C.
Leonard, T.P.G.
Martin, W.C.C.
Metcalf, P.R.
Norris, J.N.
Peters, J.E.
Pollard, D.C.
Purkis, G.J.
Pyrah, I.C.
Roxburgh, I.E.
Skelton, A.F.J.
Stenning, M.R.
Styles, F.G.
Sutcliffe, M.A.
Tingay, D.J.P.
Tough, J.M.
Walpole, R.B.
Wiesner, I.R.
Wilcockson, J.
Wilson, A.N.
Wilson, N.H.M.
Wright, C.C.

1966
Ahari, M.H.
Andrews, J.
Banyard, J.K.
Baron, M.
Bean, D.G.
Bentley, N.G.
Bird, C.M.
Bond, C.J.
Bowler, P.E.
Chesworth, P.M.
Cook, J.E.
Coslett, P.H.
Denny, D.M.
Griffiths, B.L.
Hall, P.W.
Hooton, T.S.
Horthy, S.
Ibbitt, R.P.
Ittihadieh, T.
Jacoby, R.G.
Jepson, M.F.R.
Johnson, M.F.
Jones, B.S.
Jones, G.M.
Joseph, A.P.
Law, B.
Lee, P.S.
Maini, Y.N.
Manley, R.E.
May, G.V.
Morrey, G.W.
Panter, A.E.
Parr, L.D.
Pratt, E.J.
Roberts, P.M.
Robertson, J.N.
Robinson, J.P.
Russell, K.G.
Rutherford, D.W.
Salter, J.B.
Sample, J.R.
Sandbrook, P.W.
Sharp, J.C.
Sharpe, B.K.
Shrubsole, J.G.
Singleton, R.D.
Smith, V.M.
Sugg, M.D.
Sullivan, C.F.
Thomas, G.R.
Upton, D.V.C.
Williams, O.P.
Williamson, D.
Wilson, A.N.

1967
Adie, E.
Ainsworth, J.G.
Alexander, P.G.
Atkins, J.P.
Barlow, B.J.F.
Bentham, P.
Bettess, P.
Beveridge, R.G.
Blunt, P.M.S.
Cagney, J.B.
Clark, M.C.
Cooper, F.
Crabbe, C.R.
Dawson, J.M.
Dean, C.D.
Dixon, S.F.
Foster, J.E.
French, N.J.
Gale, T.J.
Godfrey, P.S.
Godfrey, P.K.R.
Hallowes, C.F.A.
Harrison, C.P.
Hayes, E.J.
Hick, R.C.D.
Holmes, I.G.
Iles, D.C.
Jones, G.T.
Kerrison, P.C.
Killingbeck, M.
Lo, K. W.
Lunn, A.J.M.
Mason, P.J.
Mellors, T.W.
Mills, L.J.
Neeser, H.J.
Ottway, T.J.
Pennington, J.
Rayner, D.S.
Reilly Roe, P.J.
Robinson, D.G.
Shepherd, P.W.
Simpson, G.W.
Spencer, G.D.
Stewart, C.A.
Tetlow, J.H.
Underhill, B.J.
Usher, S.R.
Ward, J.K.
White, R.H.
White, R.L.
Wilks, P.G.
Wong, I.H.
Yell, F.D.R.

1968
Adams, M.

Adcock, B.W.
Artemis, C.C.
Attenborough, P.G.
Billington, C.J.
Birley, T.G.
Blackburn, M.O.
Bradley, P.W.
Bradley, R.S.
Bradshaw, J.B.
Brewer, R.J.
Butter, J.G.
Cattell, C.R.
Chalmers, M.L.
Claydon, J.R.
Combes, P.M.
Conyngham-Power, C.J.
Coupe, P.S.
Cresswell, R.T.
Crook, A.D.
Davies, P.
Davies, R.A.
Davies, R.L.
Edwards, D.V.
Englert, R.
Evans, M.H.
Garratt, P.
Guy, R.R.
Harper, M.P.
Heron, R.L.
Hines, P.G.
Hodkin, D.L.
Hunter, P.D.
Knapp, R.R.
Leonard, M.S.M.
Leppard, N.W.
Mamujee, F.
Martin, R.L.
May, M.P.
Moffett, D.R.
Oldfield, K.
Oldfield, R.K.
Pavry, P.J.
Phillips, C.E.
Preece, R.A.
Ramsey, M.J.
Redmayne, R.J.
Rogerson, G.H.
Roussel, B.E.
Rushbrooke, J.N.
Sik, B.
Smith, J.F.A.
Strange, R.L.
Sweeting, D.N.
Towers, D.G.
Watters, J.D.
West, M.J.

1969

Abbs, A.F.
Baker, M.J.
Barlow, R.F.
Brant, A.W.
Brownridge, J.N.
Clarke, A.W.
Coldwell, F.M.
Cork, R.S.
Cox, D.A.
Croney, P.
Crook, D.R.
Deavin, R.C.
Dews, D.A.
Dick, I.A.
Dickins, I.S.J.
Edwards, J.
Edwards, P.J.
Ferguson, C.M.
Foster, D.
Fung, H.H.
Giddings, T.R.
Gledhill, I.C.
Green, R.H.M.
Head, P.R.
Herbstritt, D.E.
Hillmann, M.F.
Hollis, A.J.
Huggard, R.C.E.
Lambert, W.
Llewellyn, C.
Mathew, D.J.
McCutcheon, D.A.
Michael, O.C.W.
Moore, G.D.
Moran, J.J.
Nilubol, P.
Noake, B.
Pattisson, J.K.C.
Pearson, D.
Pine, R.J.
Ramsay, M.J.S.
Riddell, K.J.
Rodger, D.C.
Shelley, J.S.
Shelton, P.M.
Shelton, R.C.
Squire, G.
Tawton, R.J.
Taylor, P.N.
Tomlinson, M.J.
Vareldzis, V.
Vaux, N.J.
Venables, R.K.
Wallace, G.M.
Wheeler, A.J.

1970

Allen-Rowlandson, L.M.
Anderson, S.D.
Baker, A.R.M.
Banks, C.C.
Beck, M.J.
Boyle, D.A.
Brame, S.J.
Brice, N.D.
Buttling, S.
Cope, R.
Cox, W.P.
Coyle, J.M.
Doubleday, C.F.
Frank, D.J.
Gaca, Z.Z.
Gardiner, J.L.
Geeson, P.
Gibbs, M.S.
Gissing, W.T.
Grantham, M.D.
Hamedi, N.
Hamilton, J.R.
Harding, J.E.
Hellard, R.A.
Hoddinott, T.G.
Holton, M.C.
Jenkin, A.K.
Keer, J.G.
Kelly, J.E.F.
Khen-Sen-Se-Hin-Son, K.F.
Kivlin, T.
Kyriacou, A.T.
Lewin, M.A.
Lim Tiam Giok
Loughlin, P.
Maguire, A.D.
Mahoney, J.
Megraw, B.P.A.
Napier, A.P.
Nelson, T.J.
Paluch, M.Z.J.
Powell, P.A.E.
Rudge, H.
Saunders, N.G.
Seldon, J.D.
Stephenson, P.J.
Sutcliffe, G.
Swannell, N.G.
Tait, P.C.A.
Talabi, M.A.
Taylor, M.J.
Thomas, J.K.
Thompson, P.L.
Triner, D.G.
Varcoe-Cocks, S.S.
Wan Kee Cheung, W.S.W.
Wild, J.

1971

Ackers, J.C.
Adkins, M.F.
Alder, R.P.
Amblin, G.J.
Atkins, A.M.
Blackburn, D.A.
Bloxham, J.W.
Bolat, H.
Branson, R.C.C.
Browne, R.C.
Bryan, P.A.

Chavda, S.J.
Christophides, A.
Claydon, P.L.
Crouch, R.E.A.
de Jacobi du Vallon, A.L.
Deacon, R.W.
Dent, M.J.
Dhir, V.K.
Dobson, J.G.
Harrison, M.
Haughton, D.C.
Hoddinott, M.R.
Kan, W.C.
Klement, T.J.
Kwok, W.P.S.
Leaper, D.G.
Lewis, R.M.
Little, F.R.
Lyons, J.W.
Marcel, D.J.
Mathew, H.L.
McCardle, T.
Nash, N.W.
Nassim, L.A.
Nelson, C.P.
Owen, R.H.
Packman, R.K.
Pearn, G.
Pearson, M.E.
Peckham, D.S.
Pennington, G.
Philip, J.E.
Pudney, R.J.
Quayle, D.
Quitt, E.
Rae, L.J.
Richards, G.D.J.
Robinson, M.V.C.
Sorowka, J.P.
Sorton, D.
Spicer, G.C.
Tan, P.S.
Townsley, C.H.
von Fürer Haimendorf, N.C.
Walker, D.A.
Ward, A.D.
Williams, P.M.
Yannopoulos, P.
Yates, M.J.

1972
Bardsley, D.C.
Bardsley, D.H.
Barton, M.J.
Bennett, D.W.
Brown, I.
Bunting, P.D.
Bush, K.
Butler, N.A.
Cardwell, I.P.
Chiappe, P.J.
Colbert, D.J.
Cox, G.
Crosse, C.R.
Dixon, R.A.
Evans, H.G.
Filipowicz, T.J.
Floate, P.E.
Gibson, R.J.
Goddard, R.C.
Gorf, P.K.
Gregg, C.G.
Grillo, S.Q.
Hasan, K.R.
Huggett, J.R.
Jinks, A.R.
Jofeh, C.G.H.
Jowitt, P.W.
Kemp, B.J.
Kindred, F.P.
Knowles, M.R.
Lau, K.L.
Lou Chi Tong, V.
Lupton, K.
Mardiross, E.
Martin, N.E.
Morison, A.C.
Newman, D.
Nicolls, J.C.
Novakova, V.
Osborn, S.
Pinto-Marques, C.A.
Powell, J.J.M.
Rauf, A.Q.
Rhys, D.I.
Robinson, A.
Sharp, W.G.
Smith, B.W.
Southward, D.E.
Sutcliffe, P.J.
Thomas, H.M.
Tong, M.K.
Tourville, P.J.
Walton, J.W.L.
Weeden, A.G.
Welham, T.R.
Wideson, O.A.R.E.

1973
Ainsley, S.
Armitage, R.N.
Awan, N.E.K.A.
Bhula, D.N.
Bricknell, I.M.
Buckler, R.W.
Cadei, J.J.M.C.
Cain, G.M.
Chu, H.F.
Clark, D.E.C.
Coatsworth, A.M.
Cunningham, T.M.
Davis, P.J.R.
Durrant, C.J.
Gee, C.L.
Gillett, P.B.
Guthrie, P.M.
Harris, N.T.
Hawkins, P.H.
Hooper, M.A.
Huggett, C.G.
Hunjan, T.S.
Ingham, M.R.
King, M.J.
Lathe, S.F.
Lavender, M.B.
Lawson, R.M.
Lim, B.T.
Livingston, R.I.
Lloyd, D.J.
Martensson, A.S.
McNicol, B.
Morriss, P.
Murray, S.A.
Paine, R.A.
Pidgeon, J.T.
Proffitt, D.E.
Ranjani, B.B.
Ridgers, D.F.
Robertson, C.
Rontaler, M.R.
Royall, M.D.
Shapey, K.W.
Sinclair, A.N.
Somerville, P.C.
Stopher, A.L.
Thomas, R.G.
Vafadari, K.
Wellsted, J.L.
Whyte, J.M.
Wright, B.J.

1974
Airs, P.R.
Alexandrou, G.
Astin, D.C.
Bakewell, N.J.
Bialas, D.J.
Bintliff, P.J.
Bottom, S.T.
Bubbers, G.R.
Clark, G.M.
Clarke, D.A.
Cresswell, N.P.
Cunningham, G.
Edge, M.J.
Fraser, R.A.
Ganiji, A.H.
Grant, S.C.
Haines, R.
Harrold, P.D.
Hughes, A.J.M.
Jardine, R.J.
Jennings, J.
Jones, D.M.
Jones, R.G.
King, C.R.

McCappin, W.M.
Meletiou, C.C.
Nudd, R.A.
O'Neill, W.D.
Parsons, S.B.
Pearce, A.C.
Perry, A.H.
Pike, W.M.
Rimmer, D.A.
Rotherham, S.A.
Scutt, C.M.
Sears, A.J.
Skipworth-Button, J.K.
Slota, R.E.
Spencer, M.J.
Spyrou, S.C.
Tate, G.
Taylor, A.C.
Trantas, G.
Walmsley, S.
Wherry, S.F.
Wickham, A.H.S.
Williams, B.I.
Williamson, D.J.
Wright, P.J.
Yeo, M.J.

1975
Abram, N.J.S.
Barr, J.P.
Barter, P.W.J.
Bayley, R.P.
Bellamy, M.D.
Bromley, P.
Brooks, C.J.
Calderwood, W.R.
Carrell, R.G.
Casey, R.J.
Dan, J.R.A.
Edwards, D.A.
Floyd, J.D.N.
Foster, C.N.H.
Gahir, J.S.
Gonsalves, A.T.W.A.R.
Greenwood, J.A.
Heywood, G.P.
Hill, J.B.E.
Hindle, P.E.
Hodgson, R.L.P.
Huddart, J.
Hughes, R.
Hutchins, J.M.
Johnson, A.
Kinsman, J.E.
Kwok, P.K.
Lark, R.J.
Lewis, D.B.
Littlewood, B.S.
Lowe, G.W.
Marcus, M.D.
Martin, J.A.
Missirlis, G.I.

Murrell, W.R.V.
Newton, M.A.C.
Phelps, R.S.
Pitkin, A.G.
Puaar, J.S.
Rankine, G.A.
Rogers, B.T.
Rooney, J.P.
Rowling, R.B.
Sadiq, M.K.
Sharman, D.J.
Shipley, P.W.
Spencer, M.S.
Styles, D.W.
Takel, M.E.
Teh, K.Y.
Thompson, C.F.
Tomlin, K.M.
Tomlinson, A.D.
Vickery, G.G.H.
Walker, B.A.
Warren, P.A.
Watson, P.S.
Williams, N.G.
Wilson, G.M.
Zwanziger, I.
Zwanziger, R.

1976
Abdula, A.R.
Aminpour, F.
Anson, P.C.
Basak, D.
Bayliss, J.M.
Binns, D.J.
Butcher, P.
Cannell, P.D.
Chandarana, B.G.
Clark, M.N.
Crawford, P.G.
Dapré, R.L.
Davies, A.J.
Dennison, C.K.
Dilley, P.G.
Doyle, R.J.
Ellis, I.C.
Evans, A.P.R.
Gardiner, A.W.
Gardner, I.R.
Grattidge, J.P.
Gray, M.L.
Hajipapaphotiou, P.
Hease, P.D.
Henke, J.S.
Henton, D.W.G.
Horn, S.C.
Howell, A.W.
Howley, C.M.
Hunt, R.J.
James, T.H.
Joce, W.H.
Kirkness, C.D.

Latter, W.J.
McCandless, R.J.
McMorrow, J.G.
Melbourne, J.H.
Miller, C.J.
Mills, C.R.
Morhig, G.A.
Morton, J.N.
Osman, A.H.A.
Panagopoulos, A.
Parsons, A.P.
Payne, M.K.
Pearson, M.L.
Pickard, A.M.
Pitkin, B.A.
Poullaides, M.A.
Purvis, D.
Robertson, A.M.
Romeril, P.A.
Scothern, J.C.
Short, I.
Smith, J.R.
Tonks, P.M.
Townsend, P.
Trimble, R.R.
Walpole, M.J.
Warburton, A.T.
Whitley, D.C.
Wu, M.W.

1977
Arnold, A.C.
Aspden, S.R.
Baker, S.C.
Bell, A.R.
Bell, N.C.
Blackley, N.R.
Blewitt, J.
Bowden, A.J.
Burns, D.G.
Burrows, M.J.
Cazeau, L.
Chappell, A.P.
Chen, W.P.
Clare, D.G.
Constantinou, C.
Cunliffe, D.L.
Dearing, S.C.
Fitzgerald, J.F.H.
Ford, C.J.
Goldsmith, P.A.
Gorley, J.G.
Gunns, J.M.
Hannam, I.C.
Hargreaves, J.
Hayes, G.J.
Houlden, K.P.
Huntington, I.
Jobling, A.W.
Khambalia, Y.M.
Lee, K.H.
Leeson, R.N.

Liming, D.J.
Lindon, T.W.P.
Lovell, A.H.
McNeill, S.W.
Meade, C.P.
Mohamed, S.A.
Mylvaganam, D.R.
Napier, M.A.H.
Nouromid, B.
Ockleton, J.P.
Patel, D.R.
Peall, N.M.
Reed, E.M.
Rigby, G.E.J.
Ross, P.H.
Salmon, D.C.
Scoufarides, M.
Speed, B.V.
Tobiasiewicz, R.W.
Turley, P.J.
Turzynski, J.G.
Wall, D.A.
Whelan, M.J.
White, R.J.
Willis, C.E.
Wong, K,D.
Wu, P.

1978
Acharya, C.K.P.
Al-Saraf, F.A.
Armitage, R.J.
Armstrong, W.E.
Bartlett, K.J.
Blitz, R.H.
Boon, P.J.
Brabbin, D.
Chambers, J.J.
Chan, D.G.W.
Cheng, K-S
Chin, T.H.
Chodorowski, A.R.
Church, I.H.
Church, P.
Cox, S.P.
De-Alwis, V.S.
Dick, P.S.
Dixon, A.J.
Dracott, J.E.
Esfandiari, S.
Goodyear, J.J.
Gregory, A.
Hibbert, F.W.
Howie, S.D.
Johnstone, D.I.
Jones-Gerrard, M.
Kok, J.H.
MacGilchrist, R.S.
MacKay, R.
Markland, J.R.
Martland, R.
Maswoswe, J.
Mayo, M.R.
Molloy, J.G.A.
Morgan, C.V.
Morris, R.A.
Mowat, D.J.
Newton, C.J.L.
Pang, M.K.
Raoof, M.
Russell, A.W.
Shaw, C.B.
Simm, J.D.
Smith, M.R.
Smith, M.T.
Stevens, C.E.
Tarnowski, M.
Thompson, N.A.
Vassiades, C.S.
Waiting, J.F.G.
Walker, C.P.
Whittaker, T.I.
Wright, P.I.
Young, P.H.
Yunus, F.H.

1979
Booth, J.H.
Bradley-Kidd, C.M.
Cotterell, C.C.
Cresswell, S.M.
Davenport, I.M.
Deane, P.H.
Dilipkumar, S.
Dillon, S.W.
Drozak, J.W.
Estrada Velo, J.A.
Evans, C.N.
Fairbairn, P.N.
Foley, J.
Forrest, I.M.
Geramian, A.
Gill, M.A.
Hall, A.G.B.
Harrison, J.P.
Haworth, R.G.
Hendra, M.R.
Howard, R.K.
Johnson, P.H.
Latham, P.S.
Lau, N.T.
Loh, T.S.
Lourdes-Cresswell, P.J.D.O.
McClurey, K.D.
McKie, I.D.
Mitchell, S.F.K.
Muncaster, P.J.T.
Palmer, G.L.
Poullaides, C.
Ridout, K.J.
Rutty, P.C.
Scutt, S.T.G.
Shotter, J.R.
Smith, C.J.F.
Stevens, D.T.F.
Sykes, J.E.
Tobin, M.P.
Topping, A.
Williams, A.G.
Winkler, E.I.
Wintle, R.
Wong, K.C.
Wright, D.J.M.
Yu, W.S.

1980
Abdulghani, D.K.Y.
Alabi, J.A.
Andrews, M.
Banks, E.A.
Baron, R.A.K.
Basir, A.
Bennett, G.P.
Beresford, N.G.
Bill, S.D.
Bullent, S.P.
Burgess, A.T.
Calthorpe, T.F.
Coldwell, S.J.
Cole, T.D.
Cooksey, B.D.
Crome, T.J.
Cutlack, J.G.H.
Davies, R.A.
Derby, D.J.
Dodd, A.C.
Duddy, K.H.
Ferrario, V.S.
Follett, P.R.
Gammon, A.M.
Gibbs, C.E.
Goldsmith, S.K.
Graham, K.
Heath, N.
Hood, J.F.
Howe, J.G.
Jayasinha, A.M.
Jury, J.F.
Kalsi, N.S.
Kerrigan, K.A.
Khera, D.S.
Knight, M.A.
Krysztofiak, R.J.
Lam, K.C.
Lam K.Y.
Langridge, B.R.
Lilley, D.S.
McClelland, T.C.
McKinnon, C.B.
Middleboe, S.R.
Monk, G.R.
Morison, S.M.
Mortimer, J.R.
Nash, C.J.
Naylor, G.M.

Ogilvie, R.S.
Phillips, A.
Poon, S.C.
Pullen, A.D.
Ratcliffe, D.
Reffitt, S.J.
Roche, M.J.
Tan, H.S.
Warr, J.C.
Whetstone, I.
Wheeler, M.J.
Woolford, M.C.
Wood, B.P.

1981
Ashe, D.M.J.
Bailey, P.S.
Bailey, R.C.
Bond, K.
Bowen, S.J.
Brayshaw, J.S.
Buhl Nielsen, E.J.A.
Bullock, N.P.
Burden, A.R.
Chandler, C.R.H.
Charlton, P.T.
Clarke, A.D.
Coop, M.R.
Cooper, P.M.
Davision, S.R.
Day, A.H.
Emery, A.R.
Fairs, P.J.
Flynn, M.A.
Freeman, E.R.
Germanopoulos, G.
Goldsmith, B.J.
Goring, P.G.
Gourlay, A.W.
Hirji, H.K.M.
Hope, M.J.
Huen, Y.M.
Hunt, M.S.
Iversen, I.
Johnston, J.P.
Jordan, K.M.
Julien, S.M.P.
Kemble, N.R.
Khoo, M.E.T.
Kitchin, G.T.
Leach, A.S.
Lenczner, A.E.R.
Lorans, A.K.A.
Lowe, M.G.
Mitchell, A.H.
Morgan, A.J.
Oliver, M.A.
Oliver, S.C.
Paterson, I.A.
Preston, G.N.
Prestridge, J.L.
Pryer, S.V.
Quigley, P.A.
Salah, K.W.
Simpson, I.P.
Smart, R.W.B.
Smith, P.R.
Southwood, C.W.L.
Storr, J.P.
Tranter, S.C.
Tsoukkas, A.
Tye, A.P.
Whittle, A.J.
Williams, K.A.J.
Williamson, R.J.
Wylie, G.B.
Yeung, S.K.
Zeris, C.

1982
Ahmad, M.A.H.
Al-Aqaileh, N.A.I.
Appleby, P.S.
Ashwin, B.J.
Austin, J.S.
Banasiak, M.S.
Biasi, H.
Blackburn, I.
Boxall, C.M.
Bucknall, I.K.
Burgess, J.W.
Chell, K.J.
Chifamba, E.
Daly, G.C.
Dunnett, A.R.G.
Edgell, J.C.
Fermor, S.
Fisher, A.J.
Flanagan, J.P.
Forbes, G.B.
Goh, E.L.
Gray, S.N.
Green, A.P.E.
Harris, G.P.
Hawkins, J.J.
Hodges, I.M.
Indraratna, V.B.N.
James, S.C.S.
Jesudasen, A.S.
Jones, N.R.
Leung, Y.W.
Manzoni, J.A.
McGuire, E.A.
McNicholas, M.
Melling, N.
Midha, R.E.
Nagle, J.B.
Nouri, A.
Parsloe, N.F.A.
Pelton, J.F.
Richards, S.C.
Rihani, B.S.N.S.
Rosen, A.B.
Shamma, K.
Shaw, M.J.
Tham, K.M.
Timmis, N.R.S.
Titmuss, R.J.
To, Y.
Toke-Nichols, S.R.
Truszkowski, J.K.
Urry, J.A.
Wallace, J.P.
White, J.C.M.
Wilson, T.

1983
Ball, H.W.
Balsara, M.N.
Bell, S.G.
Bell, T.G.
Bisewska, R.T.
Bolt, H.M.
Bussey, S.J.
Butler, P.I.
Cheng, Y.K.
Choo, K.H.T.
Clements, B.M.
Clifford, R.H.
Collier, R.N.
Colman, A.J.
Dalton, G.E.
Devine, R.S.
Dias, R.P.
Dova, P.
Duddles, S.M.
Duxbury, P.G.
Flanagan, N.G.
Haberlin, M.
Hale, A.
Haselden, M.G.H.
Heffernan, J.
Hicks, J.K.
Hussin, R.B.
Irani, L.R.
Johns, S.
Johnson, M.
Kellerman, A.M.
Kelsey, G.R.
King, W.R.
Lane, D.C.
Leech, I.
Lenczner, M.M.
Longstaff, A.
Loveland, A.J.
McDonnell, M.H.
Millar, M.J.
Mitchell, C.M.H.
Mornement, J.
Nagle, P.J.
Navarro, F.P.
Osikoya, O.
Purdy, A.J.
Pysden, C.M.

Razavi-Malaki, B.
Ridd, J.P.
Roberts, C.J.
Robinson, S.
Scott, C.W.T.
Simmons, M.W.
Sivashankar, M.
Smith, G.J.
Stephenson, M.R.
Stevenson, W.R.
Swan, C.
Tajbakhsh, Y.K.
Tan, A.
Tan, J.
Taylor, R.D.H.
Thomas, M.G.
Whorlow, J.R.
Younghusband, M.G.

1984
Al-Qadi, H.A.
Al-Tabbaa, B.M.B.
Amana, I.K.
Bansal, M.R.
Batoque, T.L.
Bottom, J.R.
Calvert, S.
Cattell, D.C.
Ching, E.
Chughtai, S.
Clarke, R.D.
Criticos, D.
Day, P.R.J.
De La Camp, C.H.
Diab, B.
Fricker, S.O.
Ganendra, R.
Garnett, N.A.
Handford, E.M.
Hannah, J.M.
Helsby, E.J.
Ho, C.S.Y.
Ho, K.K.S.
Ho, P.H.
Howlett, T.L.
Islam, A.S.M.
Judd, T.
Kwok, K.Y.
Langford, R.
Lawson, H.J.
Lester, R.G.J.
Lewis, J.M.J.
Lim, H.S.
Lozi, B.H.
Macleod, J.R.
Malektojar, S.
Mannall, C.M.
Martin, K.C.
McIlrath, M.J.
Nalshik, A.A.A.
Neale, M.A.
Ong, T.K.
Palmer, S.A.
Parkin, J.
Pilakoutas, K.
Poynton, J.M.S.
Price-Wooles, H.A.
Priest, A.S.
Prince-Wright, R.G.
Puller, D.J.
Quinn, K.M.
Rapley, J.
Rashid, D.A.
Rawlins, F.P.
Robinson, A.J.
Saddleton, R.S.J.
Sagar, N.J.P.
Shaw, N.
Sun, C.F.D.
Sun, P.S.M.
Tam, B.B.C.
Tan, T.C.
Thompson, S.D.
Thillainathan, N.
Warren, M.R.
Weir, J.C.D.
Wilkinson, C.C.
Wilkinson, R.J.
Williams, A.W.
Wong, J.T.F.
Woodyatt, W.D.A.
Yap, L.C.
Zadehkochek, A.

Index

Page numbers in italics indicate figures, photographs or tables. Dates indicate years spent in Department of Civil Engineering by members of staff. Square brackets denote end of service in Department, but continuation elsewhere in College. Index is basically to main text.